**Lewisham** Leisure
Library Service

Library materials must be returned on or before the
last date stamped or fines will be charged at the
current rate. Items can be renewed by telephone,
letter or personal call unless required by another
borrower. For hours of opening and charges see
notices displayed in libraries.

RAYMOND CARR

The Spanish Tragedy

THE CIVIL WAR IN PERSPECTIVE

WEIDENFELD · LONDON

First published in Weidenfeld paperback in 1993
by Weidenfeld & Nicolson,
a division of the Orion Publishing Group,
Orion House, 5 Upper St Martin's Lane,
London WC2H 9EA

A catalogue record for this book is
available from the British Library.

ISBN 0 297 81373 0

Printed in Great Britain by
Butler & Tanner Ltd,
Frome and London

Contents

Maps

Preface

This is not a narrative account of the Spanish Civil War; excellent narrative accounts exist in both English and Spanish. It is rather an analysis and a commentary. In order to make the course of events clearer, short chronological surveys have been inserted where they might make for easier comprehension. I have treated the implications of the war in international politics very briefly and concentrated on domestic developments.

I have always regarded the defeat of the Republic and the vengeance of the right after 1939 as a tragedy and I find writing on the Civil War a painful exercise, since it entails, if one is to tell what seems to one to be the truth, a severe and sometimes savage criticism of the errors of one's own side both before and after July 1936. The Republic was defeated, not only because of the failure of the democratic nations to supply it with arms, but because of the military and political failures, the factionalism, of the Popular Front. As General Rojo, the strategical brain of the Republic at war, bitterly conceded, 'In the political field General Franco triumphed'.

The book deals at some length with developments in the Nationalist zone. This reflects not political sympathy but rather that most accounts have given more emphasis to the politics and social life of the Republican zone. Yet it was the structure and ethos of Nationalist Spain which was to shape the nature of the Franco regime that lasted until its creator's death in 1975.

Rather than an extensive apparatus of footnotes I have given a bibliography which will indicate my main sources and also those works which have been published since this book was written. It is, nevertheless, a *select* bibliography. The complete bibliography of the Civil War is huge and grows more unmanageable day by day. This effusion is a result of a revolution in Spanish historiography which, in its turn, reflects an increasing rejection of the ideological premises of the Franco regime with its exaltation of the Catholic monarchs and the imperialism of the sixteenth century and its denigration of 'modern' liberalism and all its works. Hence the new concentration on the nineteenth century and the more immediate past. For it is there that we must seek the origins of contemporary Spain, not in a supposed idiosyncratic Spanish character forced by remoter historical experiences.

In the first edition of the book I lamented the fact that so many histories of the Civil War were based on the exploitation of memoirs and the press. A new generation of Spanish historians are altering this bias. The future lies in local history; above all how the Civil War affected the lives of ordinary people.

Lloyd George told Ronald Storrs that both Arabs and Jews were complaining about his activities as Governor of Jerusalem. Storrs feared the sack. 'If either side stops complaining,' said the Prime Minister, 'you'll be dismissed.' Historians rarely face dismissal – perhaps they would be better historians if they did. I cannot hope that this book will please the committed supporters of either side. I have been called a neo-fascist by the extreme left and a dangerous liberal by the hard right. Fortunately, neither force has been able to prevent the emergence and establishment of a pluralist democracy in post-Franco Spain.

Oxford, 1986   Raymond Carr

Main Governments

April 1931–October 1931   Niceto Alcalá Zamora (all shades of Republicans and Socialists)

ELECTIONS OF JUNE 1931
Left Republicans and Socialists emerge as strongest parties

October 1931–September 1933   Manuel Azaña (Left Republicans and Socialists)

ELECTION OF NOVEMBER 1933
Socialists and Left Republicans lose out to Radicals and CEDA

November 1933–October 1934   Alejandro Lerroux and Radical governments supported by CEDA

October 1934–December 1935   Radical and CEDA governments

December 1935–February 1936   Manuel Portela Vallardares 'centrist' government to preside over elections of February 1936

ELECTIONS OF FEBRUARY 1936
won by Popular Front (Republicans, Socialists and Communists)

February 1936–May 1936   Manuel Azaña (Left Republican)

May 1936–18 July 1936   Santiago Casares Quiroga (Left Republican)

July 1936–September 1936	José Giral (Left Republican)
September 1936–May 1937	Francisco Largo Caballero (Republicans, Communists and Socialists). CNT enters government in November
May 1937–March 1939	Juan Negrín. (Anti-Caballero Socialists, Communists and Republicans)

Glossary of Political Terms

Acción Popular Founded April 1931 as Acción Nacional. Changed its name to Acción Popular in April 1932. It fought the anti-Catholic legislation of the Second Republic. Its 'accidentalism' (i.e. indifference to forms of government) did not convince the left that it supported Republican legality.

ACNP (Asociación Católica Nacional de Propagandistas) A Catholic lay organization (founded 1904) dedicated to penetrating the political and intellectual élite. Leading spirit Angel Herrera (b. 1886), editor of the Catholic daily *El Debate* and promoter of Acción Popular.

Bloque Nacional A grouping of authoritarian anti-democratic monarchists founded by Calvo Sotelo in December 1934.

caciquismo The system of patronage by which local bosses (*caciques*) controlled elections under the parliamentary monarchy.

caudillo A military leader; used by Franco as 'Caudillo of Spain by the Grace of God'.

Carlists or **Traditionalists** The classic right-wing Catholic party in Spain. Rejected the 'liberal' monarchy represented by Alfonso XIII in favour of the claims of the descendants of Don Carlos (1785–1855). The majority of its activists were concentrated in Navarre where its militia (the *requetés*) was recruited. Fused with the Falange in April 1937.

CEDA (Confederación Española de Derechas Autónomas) Founded March 1933. A nation-wide confederation of Catholic right-wing parties, the core of which was Acción Popular. It had a 'left' which professed social-Catholic doctrine but was essentially a party of the conservative right committed to the corporate state.

CNT (Confederación Nacional de Trabajo) The anarcho-syndicalist trades union founded 1910. Believed in 'direct action' against employers, rejecting political action and electoral participation. The

CNT leadership deserted apoliticism to join the Popular Front government in November 1936. The CNT strength lay in Catalonia (particularly in Barcelona) in the Levante and Aragon, and appealed to the landless labourers of Andalusia.

Esquerra   The Left Republican Catalan nationalist party. Broke the power of the conservative Lliga in the 1931 elections. Its leader Macià became President of the Autonomous Government of Catalonia (the Generalidad, *q.v.*); on his death in 1933 the party was led by Luis Companys (1883–1940). Its strength lay in the Catalan petty bourgeoisie and in the *rabassaires* (vine cultivators).

ETA (Euzkadi Ta Askatasuna)   Clandestine revolutionary organization formed in 1967 by those who considered the PNV (*q.v.*) too moderate. Responsible for terrorism, including the assassination of Admiral Carrero Blanco (December 1973).

FAI (Federación Anarquista Ibérica)   Founded 1927 when the CNT was illegal. A group of activists determined to keep the CNT on a revolutionary course and true to 'the revolutionary and moral genius of Bakunin'. Largely controlled the CNT 1931–36.

Falange Española   A grouping of authoritarian nationalist parties under the leadership of José Antonio Primo de Rivera, son of the 'dictator'. After his execution (November 1936), led by Manuel Hedilla. The nearest approach to a fascist party in Spain. Grew rapidly in early months of the Civil War and in April 1937 fused by Franco with the Carlists to form the FET de las JONS — the only political 'party' in Franco Spain.

Generalidad   The autonomous government of Catalonia set up by the Statute of 1932.

Integrists   Carlist schismatics. Extreme Catholics who put the programme of the 'Social Reign of Christ the King' above dynastic fidelity.

junta   A committee whether at a village level or at a national level, e.g. the committee that governed Nationalist Spain: *Junta de Defensa Nacional.*

Lliga Regionalista   Catalan regionalist party. Founded 1901. Aimed to obtain Home Rule 'within Spain' for Catalonia. By 1931 had been outdistanced by the Esquerra (*q.v.*) as the main party of Catalanism of which it became the conservative 'businessmen's' wing.

Opus Dei   A lay brotherhood of committed Catholics, aimed at influencing university and political life. Nursery of the 'technocrats' of the 1960s. Fell from influence in 1973.

PNV (Partido Nacionalista Vasco)   The Basque Catholic Nationalist party: described by its leader José Antonio de Aguirre as a party of 'virile and integral Catholicism' with its ultimate aim full autonomy for the Basque Provinces. Accepted the lay Republic and joined the Popular Front government because that Republic granted the Basque Provinces of Vizcaya and Guipúzcoa autonomy in October 1936 as Euzkadi. Aguirre became President of Euzkadi.

Popular Front The electoral coalition of left-wing Republicans, Socialists and Communists on an advanced democratic programme formed to fight the election of February 1936.

POUM (Partido Obrero de Unificación Marxista) A revolutionary Marxist party founded September 1935 from the former Trotskyist Left Communist party of Andrés Nin and Joaquín Maurin's bloc of workers and peasants. As opposed to the CNT, the POUM held that the workers must seize *political* power.

Pronunciamiento An officers' *coup d'état*, the conventional military rebellion of Spain.

PSOE (Partido Socialista Obrero Español) The Socialist party of Spain. Founded 1879. A Marxist party that hid a reformist programme behind revolutionary rhetoric.

PSUC (Partido Socialista Unificado de Cataluña) Formed in July 1936 by the fusion of the Catalan Communist party and the Catalan branch of the PSOE. Affiliated to III International; Communist influence in the party grew steadily.

Radical party A left Republican party founded in 1908 by Alejandro Lerroux (1864–1949) journalist, mob orator and party organizer. Originally with revolutionary and anti-clerical overtones and a social policy that appealed to the Barcelona proletariat, by the 1930s a conservative party ready to cooperate with the CEDA.

Renovación Española Formed in 1933 by Alfonsine monarchists who had been expelled from Acción Popular; propagated the doctrines of counter-revolutionary authoritarianism.

requetés The Carlist para-military militia. Became an important force in the Nationalist armies.

UGT (Unión General de Trabajadores) The Socialist trades union; main strengths in Madrid, and the Asturias mining and the Basque industrial zones.

UME (Unión Militar Española) Semi-secret lodge (largely of younger officers) opposed to the Popular Front.

UMRA (Unión Militar Republicana Antifacista) Similar to the UME, but supporting Republican governments.

Main Actors

AGUIRRE, José Antonio 1904–60   Leader of the Basque Nationalist party and President of the Basque republic.

ALCALÁ ZAMORA, Niceto 1877–1949   Catholic Republican. Old-style monarchist politician converted to Republicanism 1930. Prime Minister of Provisional Government April 1931. Resigned October over anti-Catholic legislation and elected President of Second Republic. Deposed May 1936 and succeeded as President by Azaña.

ALVÁREZ DEL VAYO, Julio b.1891   Socialist, closely allied with the Communists.

ARAQUISTAIN, Luís 1886–1959   Socialist intellectual who supported Largo Caballero's 'maximalist' policies.

AZAÑA, Manuel 1880–1940   Intellectual and Left Republican. Prime Minister July 1931 to October 1933, February–May 1936. President of the Republic 1936–9.

BESTEIRO, Julian 1870–1939   Socialist, who opposed participation in bourgeois government. Against revolution in 1934; joined anti-Negrín National Council of Defence March 1931.

CALVO SOTELO, José 1893–1936   Monarchist authoritarian. Finance Minister of Primo de Rivera. Founded Bloque Nacional 1934. Murdered July 1936.

CASADO, Segismundo b.1893   Army of the centre. Engineered coup against Negrín's government.

CASARES QUIROGA, Santiago 1884–1950   Leader of the Republican Gallegan Autonomy party. Prime Minister 12 May–19 July 1936.

CIANO, Count G. 1903–44   Italian Foreign Minister.

COMORERA, Juan   Leader of the PSUC; Minister of Food in Catalan government.

COMPANYS, Luís 1883–1940   Leader of the Catalan Left Republican Nationalist party, the Esquerra. President of Catalonia.

DURRUTI, Buenaventura 1896–1936 CNT activist. Killed on Madrid front.

FAL CONDE, Manuel b. 1894 Intransigent Carlist leader.

FRAGA IRIBARNE, Manuel b. 1922 Professor of Public Law. Minister of Information and Tourism 1962–9. Author of Press Law of 1966.

FRANCO, General Francisco 1892–1975 Nationalist Generalissimo. *Caudillo* of Spain.

GIL ROBLES, José Maria b. 1898 Leader of the CEDA (*q.v.*).

GIRAL, José 1880–1962 Follower and friend of Azaña. Prime Minister 19 July–4 September 1936.

GODED, General Manuel 1882–1936 Commander in the Balearics. Nationalist general in charge of rising in Barcelona.

IBARRURI, Dolores b. 1895 Daughter and wife of miners. Through her gifts as a mass orator, she became, as *La Pasionaria*, the best-known figure in the Communist party.

IGLESIAS, Pablo 1850–1925 Socialist. 'Father' of PSOE.

JIMÉNEZ FERNÁNDEZ, Manuel 1896–1968 Member of ACNP and CEDA Minister of Agriculture 1934–5. Leader of Christian Democratic left.

LARGO CABALLERO, Francisco 1869–1946 Leading figure of UGT. Prime Minister 4 September 1936–17 May 1937.

LERROUX, Alejandro 1864–1949 Founder of Radical Republican party; in 1930s became increasingly conservative.

MARTÍNEZ BARRIO, Diego 1883–1962 Radical Republican. Prime Minister 18–19 July 1936. A Freemason.

MAURA, Miguel b. 1887 Catholic Republican. Minister of the Interior April–October 1936.

MAURÍN, Joaquín b. 1896 Marxist intellectual and leader of the POUM.

MIAJA, General José 1878–1958 Republican general in command of defence of Madrid.

MOLA, General Emilio 1887–1937 Military Governor of Pamplona and 'director' of military conspiracy in 1936. Killed in plane crash.

MONTSENY, Federica CNT/FAI militant. Minister of Health in Largo Caballero's government.

NEGRÍN, Dr Juan 1889–1956 Professor of Physiology. Socialist. Minister of Finance in Largo Caballero's government. Prime Minister May 1937–March 1939.

NIN, Andrés 1892–1937 Former Trotskyite. Leader of the POUM.

ORTEGA Y GASSET, José 1883–1955 Philosopher and essayist.

PRADERA, Victor 1873–1936 Carlist ideologue. Franco wrote preface to his collected works. Assassinated 1936.

PRIETO, Indalecio 1883–1962   Socialist. Minister of Defence May 1937 to April 1938. Opponent of Largo Caballero and later of Communists.

PRIMO DE RIVERA, José Antonio 1903–36   Founder of the Falange. Executed November 1936.

QUEIPO DE LLANO, General Gonzalo 1875–1951   Chief of Carabineros (customs guards). Nationalist general who rose in Seville.

RODEZNO, Count of 1883–1952   Navarrese Carlist who opposed Fal Conde's intransigent policies.

ROJO, General Vicente b. 1894   Republican general. Miaja's Chief of Staff and then Chief of Staff of Republican armies.

RUIZ-GIMÉNEZ, Joaquín b. 1913   Lieutenant in Nationalist Army. Minister of Education 1951–7. Oppositional left-wing Christian Democrat and founder of periodical *Cuadernos para el diálogo*.

SANJURJO, General José 1872–1936   Nationalist general, called 'Lion of the Rif'. Refused army support to the monarchy in crisis of April 1931; rose against Azaña's government August 1932. Killed in plane crash on way to lead rising against the Popular Front.

SEGUÍ, Salvador 1890–1923   'Sugar boy'. CNT leader and its finest mass orator who opposed 'useless' revolutionary violence. Assassinated 1923.

SERRANO SUÑER, Ramón b. 1901   Falangist. Franco's brother-in-law. Minister of Foreign Affairs and the Interior.

UNAMUNO, Miguel de 1864–1936   Christian philosopher and Rector of Salamanca University. Dismissed by Franco.

VARELA, General José 1891–1951   A Carlist. Nationalist general in charge of attack on Madrid.

YAGÜE, General Juan 1891–1952   Nationalist general. Falangist sympathizer.

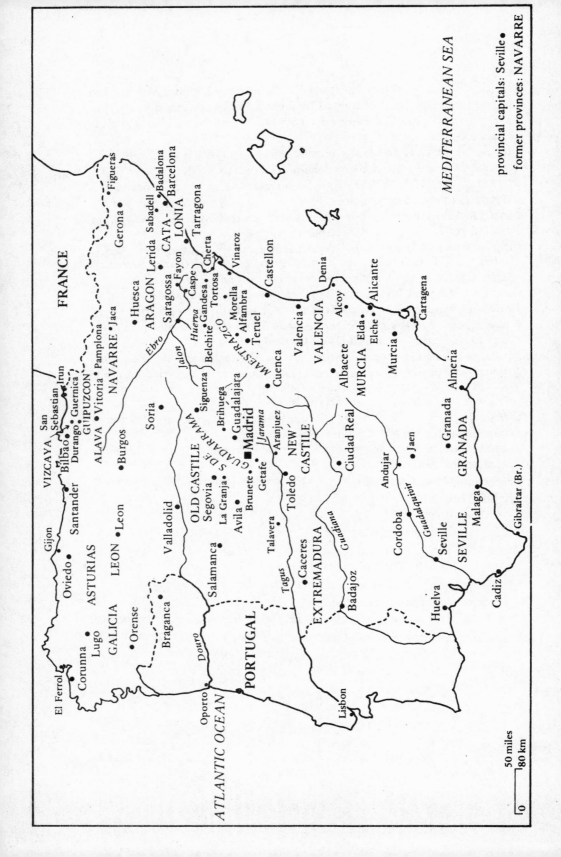

The Spain of the Ancien Régime

The Bourbon monarchy, in the person of Queen Isabella II, had been driven from Spain in the revolution of 1868 – a military rising (pronunciamiento) *of dynastic politicians out of office and Republican democrats. After an abortive experiment in constitutional monarchy came the First Republic of 1873. It quickly collapsed into near anarchy and in 1874 Alfonso XII, son of Isabella II, was restored by another military* pronunciamiento.

The Restoration monarchy was a quasi-constitutional system based on electoral manipulation with the alternation in power of a Conservative and a Liberal party. Both parties were élite groups of 'professional' politicians, parties of notables dependent, not on popular opinion expressed in democratic elections, but on the manipulation of elections by the Minister of the Interior and the local political bosses, the caciques. *The system was severely shaken by defeat by the United States and the loss of Cuba, Puerto Rico and the Philippines in the 'disaster' of 1898. This released a flood of 'regenerationist' polemics, criticizing the existing régime as artificial and demanding its renovation and democratization.*

Alfonso XIII came to the throne in 1902. His reign saw mounting political crises as the electoral machinery of the Restoration grew rusty. In 1917 a disparate collection of discontented elements constituted a real threat : conservative Catalan regionalists, whose demands were refused by Madrid ; Republicans ; workers hit by high war prices and growing in organizational strength ; and junior officers concerned for their pay and promotion prospects. Subsequently a savage class war broke out in Barcelona with serious strikes, assassinations and gang warfare.

These tensions were compounded by a colonial war in Spanish Morocco. In 1912 a Spanish army corps suffered a disastrous defeat at Anual. The king and the army and the monarchical politicians were blamed by the opposition, and the cry of 'responsibilities' was raised. The crisis of the political system was ended by a military coup d'état : *the* pronunciamiento *in September 1923 of General Primo de Rivera.*

I

In the nineteen twenties Spain was, for most Europeans, a tourist attraction where new trunk roads allowed the visitor to inspect, at a modest price, the customs of a provincial society of the old régime. In the nineteen thirties it suddenly became of absorbing political interest; when Europe seemed to be turning to the right, in Spain the traditional values of conservatism were under attack. On 14 April 1931, the monarchy fell, King Alfonso XIII left the country and a democratic Republic set about the difficult task of modernizing a traditional, semi-industrialized society. It failed in this enterprise and the tensions created by the attempt burst out, in the summer of 1936, into civil war. Expectations of a radical change on the part of the underprivileged in Spanish society had been raised but not fulfilled; that those expectations could be entertained at all was enough to release a counter-revolutionary coup.

The problems confronting the middle-class progressives who, with the socialists, dominated the new Republican government were immense. Half the national wealth came from agriculture. Whereas in England the vast majority of the population had long left the countryside for the towns, over half of the population of Spain still got its living from the soil, housed in small rural towns and villages. Yet the agrarian sector was inefficient (wheat was the main crop, with yields the lowest in western Europe), and behind a complex variety of land tenures lay great social injustices. In the north-west the peasants of Galicia struggled for a living on minute 'handkerchief' plots; the great estates of the south-west were worked by gangs of landless labourers, hired by the day. The labourers of Andalusia were the most wretched class in Europe; unemployed for months on end, they rotted in the small towns of the south. With no hope of gaining a decent living they were a reservoir of revolution and primitive millenarianism. Above these extremes of misery lay the peasants of Old Castile – conservative but hard put to scratch a living from the poor, thin soils of their scattered plots. Only on the periphery was there a moderate prosperity on the substantial farms of Catalonia, the orange-groves of Valencia and the family homesteads of the Basque country.

'Poverty,' remarks Trollope, 'to be picturesque should be rural.' Most travellers in Spain of the nineteen thirties, like Gautier a century before, were fascinated by the picturesque, noticing neither the poverty nor the injustices in the countryside. Rural society was sharply divided between rich and poor, between regions of stability and regions of unrest. Outside the regions of genuine peasant proprietorship, property was concentrated in the hands of a landowning class, and this was especially so in the *latifundia* (great estates) of La Mancha, Extremadura and Andalusia, where the owners were often absentees. Out of a total agricultural population of something over two million who worked the land, ten thousand families owned roughly half the cultivable land; 150 families owned 32% of the province of Badajoz. Spain was divided between rich proprietors (a conglomerate of upper-middle-class *arrivistes*, who had often bought their estates when the Church and common lands were sold by the Liberals in the nineteenth century, and nobles who had held their lands for centuries), 'middle' peasants who could make a decent living out of their farms, and beneath them a semi-proletariat of struggling micro-proprietors a million strong. These latter were often little better off than the million rural labourers, but it was the fate of these labourers that obsessed the reformers of the first years of the Republic; they failed to win the loyalty of the majority of the more prosperous small proprietors, sharecroppers and tenants who found the increased labourers' wages granted by the socialists in 1931–2 a heavy burden. Thus, in spite of the huge differences between rich proprietors and poor farmers, these latter did not support the Republican government *en masse* in 1936.

Besides glaring inequalities in income there was an acute regional imbalance between a relatively rich peripheral commercialized agriculture and a primitive impoverished centre: between areas of development and areas of backwardness. The vine-growers of Catalonia (the *rabassaires*) who had once supplied South America with brandy and had dominated the wine trade between 1882 and 1892, when phylloxera devastated the French vineyards, were a relatively prosperous class, though their prosperity was threatened;

phylloxera had in the end invaded Catalonia and seriously imperilled their security of tenure, based, as it was, on the life of the vine.* The orange-growers of Valencia who supplied much of Spain's foreign exchange were well-to-do by Spanish standards, though they were to suffer a setback when their markets were imperilled by the world depression.

In the eighteenth century the civil servants of the Enlightenment had puzzled over the problem of finding a basis for modernizing and reforming so 'bizarre', so monstrously diversified an agricultural system by a general law of agrarian reform. Their successors of the Second Republic still faced the same difficulties. In no country of Europe are the changes in the agricultural landscape so abrupt and violent. The traveller to Madrid from the tourist-infested beaches of the Costa del Sol – still, in the 1930s, unexploited – may pass from the intensively cultivated irrigated plots of Murcia through the great olive and wine monocultures to the bleak, desert-like wheatlands of Castile. Even Andalusia, which, to those who do not know it, may appear a homogeneous region of the great, extensively cultivated *latifundia* of absentee aristocratic landowners, includes the rich soils of the Campiña de Córdoba, revolutionized since the 1950s, with its profit-minded agricultural entrepreneurs and industrial crops and the tragically poor farms of eastern Andalusia where only seasonal emigration to France can provide a living wage. 'Every night,' wrote Costa, himself son of an Aragonese peasant farmer and whose whole life was a bitter struggle to educate himself, 'over half of Spain goes to bed hungry.' The richly varied but somewhat rebarbative Spanish regional cuisine is based on the necessity of making poor food palatable.

II

This imbalance in agriculture was paralleled by the imbalance in industrial development so characteristic of developing economies. Spain affords a classic case in Europe of a 'late-comer' to industrialization and not until the years before and during the First World War did it begin to catch up. Even then its industrial structure was weak, uncompetitive, and dependent on imports of

---

* The *rabassaire*'s contract with his landlord ran for the life of the vine. Phylloxera-resistant strains had a shorter life than the old stock.

foreign capital and technology.*

Economic development in such cases tends to concentrate increasingly in favoured areas – for instance where a skilled labour force and access to transport and credit facilities already exist – leaving the rest of the country impoverished and untouched by the wealth generated by industrial growth. Thus in Italy the north became industrialized while the south stagnated; and so it was in Spain.

Many philosophic historians have developed, since the eighteenth century, the concept of the 'two Spains' as the key to her history: the Spain of blind, rigid Catholic conservatism, inward-looking and nationalistic, in permanent conflict with the open, tolerant, forward-looking, cosmopolitan Spain of intellectuals and progressives. That this conflict existed, no one can deny: but to the economist or sociologist the 'two Spains' are the Spain of development – however slow – and the Spain of poverty and stagnation; the cities, where the workers lived in shanty-town suburbs and the wealthy built French-style mansions, stood in contrast to the rural *pueblos*, the grim, austere Castilian towns where life had stagnated for centuries and the decaying houses of a once rich nobility testified to a lost prosperity. The urban Spain of the dynamic periphery drained the villages in the decaying centre of a surplus population that could find no gainful occupation.

Thus Spain's late industrial revolution was confined largely to two regions: Catalonia and the Basque Provinces. Already in the eighteenth century Barcelona, capital of Catalonia, was the most important centre of the cotton industry outside Lancashire. By 1930, besides cotton and wool, Catalonia had developed light industry, machine-shops (the first railway engine was built in Barcelona) and shipping. The Basque metallurgical and shipping industry had grown round the iron mines near Bilbao and had been financed by the sale of ore to England. Much of this industry was controlled by relatively few members of a powerful local industrial

---

* The causes of Spain's late entry and the subsequent weakness of the industrial sector are the subject of some controversy. Some attribute it to the limited capacity for capital accumulation and the limited market provided by a 'feudal' agricultural system which could not modernize without threatening the existing structure of property; some to 'mistaken' investment, in the years after 1850, of scarce capital in railways and government stock instead of in 'productive' industry; some to the essentially ascetic, proud, conservative, unenterprising, anti-economic, etc., characteristics of a traditional Catholic society.

and banking oligarchy which had prospered exceedingly from the huge profits made during the First World War.

Both the Basque country and Catalonia saw themselves as progressive, forward-looking communities tied to a backward agrarian Castile, symbolized by the 'parasitic' capital, Madrid, where politicians and civil servants, out of touch with the economic realities of the country, controlled its destinies. These politicians – especially the Liberals – were often free traders;* the Catalan businessmen, the Basque ironmasters and shipowners, scared of British competition, were fanatic protectionists. In the Tariff Laws of 1891 and 1906 they got their way when the Conservatives erected around Spain the highest tariff barriers in Europe, barriers which protected not only the 'infant industries' of the periphery but also the high-cost wheat farmers of Castile.†

Consciousness of separate economic interests helped the development in the later nineteenth century of a demand for regional self-government for Catalonia and the Basque Provinces. There is no surer recipe for the mutation of regional tensions into full-blown nationalism than the political dependence of a prosperous region with independent cultural traditions on a capital located in a poor, backward region.

The Catalans had a separate language, a distinct popular and literary culture, the proud memory of a great medieval trading empire and a tradition of political independence dating back to the

---

* Many Restoration politicians were directors of railway companies, and on the whole the railway interest was a free-trade interest. The historian Josep Fontana has argued that it was the fall of railway shares and profits after 1860 that led many politicians to support the revolution that overthrew the government of Isabella II, held responsible for the economic recession. Railway shares *did* rise after 1868.

† This enabled Basque and Catalan protectionists to argue that protection was not a regional and sectoral demand but a *national* interest: protection by 'saving' industry provided a market for surplus Castilian wheat in the periphery and maintained high levels of employment generally. Nevertheless, in spite of the protectionist alliance of wheat growers and industrialists, the demands of Catalan industrialists were presented by anti-Catalans as a 'selfish' imposition on the Spanish consumer: cf. the reaction of the left to the campaign orchestrated by Basque and Catalan business interests in 1916 to defeat the very modest tax on the booming war profits of the 1915–19 bonanza. These war profits consolidated Spanish capitalism and the protection afforded by war fostered import substitution. When the 'artificial' protection lapsed in 1920 Catalans and Basques clamoured for higher protection to save this mushroom growth. It was Cambó who negotiated the high tariffs of 1922; when the Liberal government in 1923 threatened to lower tariffs, the Catalan business community supported the coup of Primo de Rivera.

middle ages and which had ended only in 1715, when Catalonia was 'conquered' by Philip V and incorporated into the Spanish monarchy. 'Catalanism' was a term which embraced everything from a passion for Catalan literature and history to full-blown nationalism; no party in Catalonia could neglect it. When the moderate regionalism of the Catalan business community with its demand for home rule could not find a place 'within Spain', the 'nationalist' left, ready to employ the language of separatism, increased in influence. This Catalan nationalism came to appeal less to big business than to the middle class in general. The great surprise of 1930–31 was the decline of the Conservative, regionalist Lliga, the party of the Catalan financier and businessman Cambó, and the rise of the Left Republican Esquerra (ERC). The ERC was the party of the patriarchal hero of Catalan nationalism, Macià, a retired army officer who, from his exile in France, had 'invaded' Spain in the 1920s in the forlorn hope of establishing a Catalan Republic. His lieutenant and successor was Luis Companys who had used the discontents of the *rabassaires* to bring rural recruits to urban, petty bourgeois nationalism.

It was the bogey of 'separatism' that allowed the monarchist politicians of Castile to play on 'Spanish' nationalism and to oppose any concession of home rule to Catalonia. Autonomy would lead to destruction of 'the unity of Spain created by history'. The Catalan view of Spanish history was distinct: Spain was a plural society of different peoples artificially hammered into the straitjacket of unity by Castilians – what Unamuno, the philosopher of Salamanca, called 'hollow unity, unity without content, unity for the sake of unity'. If the strident tones of Castilian nationalism were abhorrent to Catalans, the language of Catalanism was alarming to Castilians with their claim to the monopoly of Spanish patriotism. Prat de la Riba, the theoretician of Catalanism, called Spain 'a geographical expression' to denote a collection of 'nations' . . . 'Every nationality should have its state.'

Catalan discontents and the Catalan demand for self-government had dominated Spanish politics since 1900. The limited home rule granted to Catalonia was suppressed by the dictatorship of Primo de Rivera (1923–30) and the conspirators against the monarchy promised Catalonia self-government in the new Republic. But the Republic did not create, as Macià expected, a federal Spain. It made Catalonia a special case in the Statute of Autonomy (1932) by creating the Generalidad which controlled most of Catalan domestic concerns and made Catalan, with Spanish, an official language. Too much for Castilian centralists, the Statute did not satisfy the full Catalan demands; but it was enough to secure the loyalty of Catalonia to the Republic in the Civil War.

In the Basque country the national issue took a different course and a more acrid tone. The majority of big businessmen got what they wanted from Madrid and indeed dominated its financial life. Basque nationalism was not middle-class and progressive. It was in origin a Catholic, peasant nationalism, bitterly opposed by the socialists as reactionary, as a campaign against the non-Basque immigrant workers who 'defiled' the purity of the Basque race. By the thirties this racism was muted and the Basque National Party (the PNV) was becoming – at least as far as its more far-sighted leaders were concerned – a Christian Democratic party with support outside the rural areas; but it remained determined to win for the Basque Provinces an autonomy as wide as that granted to the Catalans in 1932.

III

How can one characterize the society – particularly its political life – that was erected on and in turn modified this economic basis? It was quite different from the most developed societies of northern Europe. It was, in Ortega's famous phrase, 'invertebrate'; there were gaps, discontinuities. Traditional rigidities survived beside, and weighed heavily upon, the desire for a modern, adaptive society. Catechisms, which in the fury of their opposition to any liberal idea might have been written in the sixteenth century, circulated beside apologies for modern capitalism and Marxist attacks on it.

The Spain of the thirties had been moulded by the experiences of the nineteenth century: by late industrialization and the formation under the 'Liberal experience' of 1830–75 of a loosely structured bourgeoisie; by the battle over the position and privileges of the Catholic Church.

Compared with the English aristocracy, the Spanish aristocracy, though often rich, was a feeble social force in its own right. The middle classes had bought land in the great sales of Church and national lands in the nineteenth century, and were closely connected by interest with the landed aristocracy, forming a rural bourgeoisie which provided many of the generals and politicians of the monarchy.

In the Basque country there was a 'modern' interlocking group of bankers (the banks held heavy investments in industry), shipowners and industrial entrepreneurs; there was a similar, if more dispersed, capitalist class in Catalonia. But outside the industrial and mining regions of the north and Catalonia and to a lesser extent in the Levante, there was no middle class linked, as in England, to the growth of an industrial economy. There was therefore no generalized 'bourgeois – feudal' conflict, no room for urban radicals like Cobden or Bright to mobilize the 'towns against the squires'. The class conflict, when it came, was in essence a conflict between organized urban workers together with a relatively unorganized rural proletariat, in uneasy alliance with sectors of the middle class, against an amalgam of landowners, bankers, the more important industrialists, successful civil servants, and high-ranking army officers – the 'oligarchy', the establishment of Spain.

Nineteenth-century Spaniards referred not to the 'middle class' but to the 'middle classes'. It is this amorphous sector of society that is the puzzle and problem of modern Spanish history, difficult to quantify and identify, still more difficult to analyse in its social composition and political reactions.

Conventionally it is divided into a 'traditional' middle class and a petty bourgeoisie; but these categories overlap and merge (even in the same person: a modest east Andalusian landowner might be a member of the local establishment in his *pueblo* but in the capital would be definitely middle-class). The core of the 'traditional' middle class was composed of well-to-do artisans (they were still numerous in Madrid, only beginning its industrial take-off, and in provincial towns) and modest professionals, many competing for ill-paid posts in the public sector. It included the lower ranks of the officer corps, 'the middle class in uniform'.

The struggles of the less fortunate of this class to keep up appearances (for instance the common practice of taking two jobs – a major might be a lawyer's copyist in his free time) are meticulously chronicled in the novels of Galdós. They were still struggling in the 1930s. On the whole they were natural supporters of the government that employed so many of them; on the whole they were Catholic and conservative, imitators in their modest sphere of aristocratic attitudes and without a proud, independent bourgeois culture. Nevertheless some of them (particularly the university intellectuals) were Republicans, and by 1931 many of them were disillusioned with the monarchy and voted against the king and the establishment of which he was the symbol. During the Second Republic some of them – the younger intellectuals above all – supported the social reforms of the Socialists; others drew back, fearful that the hard-won gains made in the struggle for respectability might be imperilled from below. It was this frightened, status-conscious middle class that swung to the right in the elections of November 1933 and supported the Nationalists in 1936.

The petty bourgeoisie was composed of minor officials, shopkeepers, chemists, schoolmasters and a sprinkling of non-commissioned officers. Though many shared the social mimetism and conventional attitudes of the 'traditional' middle class it was from its ranks that came the militants of nineteenth-century radicalism, the *meneurs* who orchestrated working-class democratic protest in the towns. They gathered together in a multiplicity of Republican clubs, in Masonic lodges, or in groups meeting in the back room of a chemist's shop. They were committed Republicans.

Republicanism, the most explicit challenge to the establishment, the 'oligarchy' and the political class which manipulated the Bourbon monarchy in its interests from 1875 to 1923, remained a movement of intellectuals and petty bourgeoisie. Only Lerroux, leader of the Radical Republicans, succeeded in enthusing and organizing a mass following among the Barcelona working class in the early years of the century. Republicanism had no serious social programme because it lacked a solid social base; it lived on myths and memories of the short-lived Republic of 1873. This fostered those divisions on ideological and personal grounds which weakened it as a force on the left. Republicanism, in 1931, was less a coherent left-wing political force than a conglomerate of groups. In Ortega's words, it was an 'improvisation created on the pretext of struggling against the monarchy'. These groups could rally after 1926 to defeat the monarchy, and their force was impressive and well-organized; they could not stick together to consolidate a modern, progressive Republic. Their historic agglutinate was, alas, anti-clericalism.

IV

Given the supposed 'threat' of anti-clericalism on the left, it is one of the curious features of Spanish political history that a Conservative party did not, in a Catholic country, emerge in defence of the interests of the Church. This was probably because the Liberal state after 1875 did not, once its notables had got their hands on the church lands, persecute the Church. Catholicism remained the religion of the state; bishops sat in the Senate. The Regular Orders were not harried, as in France, and retained their control of much of the secondary education; monks and nuns worked for nothing and the capital costs of the rapid expansion of the Church educational system in the later years of the nineteenth century were provided by the pious rich. An impoverished civil state simply could not compete. It was the grip of the Regular Orders over the education of the élite that alarmed liberals. There was no need, therefore, to defend a Church that was so obviously part of the Establishment, that was indeed its symbol; Republican and Socialist anti-clericalism derived its appeal precisely from this symbolic significance: the Church sanctified the system.

Extreme Catholics (the Carlists and their Integrist offshoot) wanted not a privileged position, which the Church already possessed, but a theocratic state. Carlism was a religious, rural protest movement defending historic regional liberties (the *fueros*) and challenging the urban liberals of the centralizing state. Rooted in the Basque Provinces and the mountains of Aragon and Catalonia, it sustained two major wars in defence of the rights to the throne of Don Carlos (1788–1855) and his descendants against Isabella II (1830–1904) and her heirs who represented, to Carlism, surrender to liberalism, constitutionalism and free thought. Efforts to modernize the Carlist creed, to turn it into a defence of moderate regionalism and the Catholic corporate state, with guilds replacing trades unions, failed to conceal its essential utopianism, its messianic strain or to take it out of its rural strongholds of the north. By 1930 Carlism was in decline; ill-organized, it fed on memories of its romantic past and the heroes of its lost wars. It was the Second Republic's attack on the Church which gave it a new purpose and a third chance.

Yet the existence of such extremists throughout the nineteenth century, sworn and bitter enemies of the Liberal state and constant prophets of the catastrophe it would bring, did not merely feed the flames of a virulent and often vulgar brand of anti-clericalism. It constantly drew the Church in Spain far to the right of other western Catholic churches. The Spanish Church as a whole could not accept a modern state except for the purpose of destroying all Liberal principles within it, from non-confessional education to divorce and civil burial. Liberalism was heresy, castigated as such in Father Sardá's *Liberalism is Sin* (1887). Liberal Catholicism was presented by integrists as treason, toleration as a masonic device to destroy the Church. Only a return to the sixteenth century could save Spain from materialism and loss of national purpose. This integrist strain, with its consistent exaggeration of Liberal threats to Catholic values and its catastrophist language was to poison the political atmosphere after 1900. Mass demonstrations of Catholics were matched by petty acts of anti-clerical vandalism. The poison was to work in the body of the Second Republic. The old language of a battle to the end reappeared on both sides. To anti-clerical Republicans the Regular Orders bred 'useless' monks and were responsible for every national disaster from the loss of the Philippines to the economic hardships of the artisan. To the defenders of the Orders, the attempt to limit the privileges of the Church and the Orders threatened 'our purses, our families, our very lives'.

v

No mass party of the right appeared until the Republic, when the defence of a persecuted Church rallied the support of the upper classes, a frightened middle class and a conservative peasantry. Though the Republican parties after 1926 successfully organized a mass following, the only true, durable, organized, mass party in 1931 was the Socialist party (the PSOE). But its organizational strength was of recent creation. In 1910 its leader was elected to the Cortes – the Spanish parliament – for the first time; yet in Italy, in 1900, the Socialist party had thirty-three members. This historical weakness under the parliamentary system is important. Some Socialist leaders, especially the trades unionists among them, were easily disenchanted with electoral politics from which they had derived such meagre benefits.

The weakness of the labour movement was not merely a case of late development in a weak industrial economy; it was a consequence of the division of the movement itself.

The industrial working class of Spain was concentrated in two areas: Catalonia and the industrial areas of the Cantabrian coast –

the coal mines of Asturias, the iron mines and metallurgical works of Vizcaya. Each area had its own characteristic labour organization representing the two great proletarian movements of the nineteenth century which had sprung from the split between Bakunin, the anarchist and Marx, the authoritarian Socialist.

In Barcelona and the industrial towns of Catalonia the majority of workers had been organized in the anarcho-syndicalist trades union, the CNT (founded in 1910–11); it had outposts in the neighbouring Levante and in Aragon where Saragossa was the second capital of the CNT. Spanish anarcho-syndicalism rejected political activity in 'bourgeois' politics and was committed to 'direct action' of unions against the employers and, ultimately, to the great revolutionary general strike that would destroy the bourgeois capitalist world. It was much more influenced by pure anarchist traditions than the French syndicates on which it was originally modelled. Unlike socialists in the Marxist tradition, anarcho-syndicalists did not believe in the inevitable triumph of the proletariat, least of all by legal means; to the movement's activists revolution was the spontaneous activity of the masses which might be 'sensed' by a gifted leadership. 'Nothing great has ever been achieved without violence . . . the possession of revolvers and machine-guns distinguishes the free man from the slave . . . the sins of the old and corrupt system can only be washed away in blood.' Austere and violent idealists like Durruti and the Ascaso brothers, 'social brigands' responsible for assassinations and bank robberies, were the popular heroes of anarchist activism.* 'We are not in the least afraid of ruins,' Durruti told a journalist in 1936, 'We are going to inherit the earth.'

The CNT, with its federal structure which allowed each local union great independence, and its obsessive concern with ideological debate, was never a coherent force.† It always contained

---

* Buenaventura Durruti (b. 1896), was the son of a railway worker. With Francisco Ascaso joined a CNT action group which murdered the Cardinal Archbishop of Saragossa and staged an armed robbery of the Bank of Spain in Gijón (1923). Fled to Argentina. Returned to Spain 1932.

† I once, mistakenly, reproached Federica Montseny, a CNT-FAI leader, with the CNT rejection of organization – it had neither permanent paid officers nor strike funds. She replied that the CNT 'talked of nothing else'. This was inevitable, given that anarchists were individualists believing in 'organization from below'; and yet a union, to be effective, must be organized and have some sort of bureaucracy. Since the two conditions of organization and spontaneity could not be met simultaneously, debate on their combination was at the same time obsessive and inconclusive.

at least three strains, their strength varying from time to time.

There were the 'pure' anarchists, utopians and élitists, who at times found in terrorism a moral substitute for the revolution they could not make and who at other times believed that only a long process of indoctrination could forge a working class with a revolutionary consciousness. Secondly there were the 'tough' anarcho-syndicalists who rejected élitism and saw that the workers must be organized in strong unions if they were to be an effective revolutionary force yet who were ready to risk that organization by flinging it into the streets or to weaken it by prolonged strikes which brought only defeat. Their belief in the proletarian revolution, to be attempted whenever and wherever possible, was absolute. This revolutionary optimism tended to centre on the landless labourers of the south and west and on the immigrant workers who flooded into Barcelona during the First World War – 'new proletarians' wrenched from a rural background, often illiterate, and inhabiting what Victor Serge called 'the vast world of irregulars, outcasts, paupers and criminals'. Finally, there were the 'moderate' or 'pure' syndicalists, like Salvador Seguí and Angel Pestaña, who refused to believe that revolution was just round the corner and feared that the CNT, by lurching into revolution, would waste its forces. (Seguí [b. 1890] was an indifferent housepainter and a restless autodidact with Nietzsche 'as his Bible'; he found his métier in union organization and crowd oratory. Pestaña [b. 1886], son of a wife-beating building worker, was, like Seguí, typical of the rootless background of some CNT leaders. He worked as a bricklayer, railwayman, farm labourer, watchmaker, glass worker, stage hand and minor actor, to become a journalist on the CNT paper *Solidaridad Obrera*. Union strength, they held, must be built up by successful strike action and harboured for the time when a general strike could destroy capitalist society and usher in a society based, not on the libertarian communes of anarchist doctrine but on the great unions. If the capital of the tough anarcho-syndicalists was Barcelona, the 'pure' syndicalists were strongest in towns like Sabadell, where recent immigrants did not swamp skilled native workers, and in the Levante.

It was governmental repression and the intransigence of the employers that constantly played into the hands of the extremists, often simply by putting the conspicuous moderate leaders in prison. This was the case in 1919 when the CNT might have become a powerful union under the leadership of men like Salvador Seguí, whose astonishing oratorical powers could keep, for a time, the CNT masses under his control and away from extreme courses. Instead his policies were defeated and the game lost to the wild men – the *pistoleros*, the gunmen of the 'action groups', who fought rival unions and used threats to collect dues for the CNT. Moderate leaders fought against both the revolutionary activists' indifference to the slow labours of building up organizational strength and their propensity to fall back on assassination and mindless violence. But it was difficult for the leadership to disown or control those to whom terrorism had become an interest, the way of life of 'that special class of men' as Pestaña described them 'who live on that indefinite frontier between the worlds of labour and common crime'.

The most astonishing feature of the CNT was its capacity for sudden and vast increases in membership. Socialist unionism was a slower growth. In 1914 the CNT hardly existed; yet by 1919 it numbered well over seven hundred thousand. It dominated the labour world in Catalonia in 1916–23 with a series of dramatic strikes and acts of violence. But the acts of violence were counter-productive (Seguí himself was assassinated in March 1923) and by 1924, when the CNT was suppressed, it was a shadow of its great days in 1919. The workers had wearied of 'the tyranny of our so-called redeemers'.

Clandestinity after 1924 once more favoured the grip of extremists in the CNT. Organized in the FAI (the Iberian Anarchist Federation, founded in 1927), they captured the CNT and, as a revolutionary ginger group, were determined to 'keep an anarchist soul in a syndicalist body'.

In the mining and metallurgical industry of the Basque country and in the coal-mining districts of Asturias the workers were organized in the Socialist union, the UGT. Whereas the CNT rejected politics as futile and wished to abolish the state as an instrument of tyranny and oppression, the first article of the founding statute of the Spanish Socialist party stated its aim as 'the possession of *political* power by the working class'. Meanwhile the party concentrated on getting immediate benefits for the workers, a policy of 'small gains'. Much of Largo Caballero's time as leader of the UGT was devoted to setting up burial societies, sickness insurance and cooperatives.

In spite of this comparative moderation in the world of Spanish labour, it would be a mistake to imagine that Spanish Socialists resembled their English counterparts. They may have often been moderate in practice but their rhetoric was revolutionary; 'Evolution and revolution,' argued Pablo Iglesias, the founder of the Spanish Socialist Party (the PSOE),* 'are the same thing; revolution is the acceleration of evolution.' This was playing with words. The Socialists had sometimes to live up to their rhetoric and become reluctant and inept revolutionaries, as they did in 1917. Otherwise their language would have lost all credibility and the initiative would have passed from them to the more resolute spirits of the CNT.

The labour movement was consistently weakened by division, especially that great schism between the followers of Bakunin and those of Marx. The CNT despised the Socialists as authoritarian reformists ready to compromise with bourgeois society for wage increases, as faceless bureaucrats, temporizing opportunists who directed and disciplined the party and union from Madrid. The Socialists held that the pursuit of 'small gains' increased revolutionary consciousness; the CNT that it eroded it. The Socialists dismissed the CNT militants as a collection of gun-toting utopians ready to sacrifice the material well-being of the working classes for the sake of flexing their muscles in the 'revolutionary gymnastics' of purposeless self-defeating strikes. Manuel Cortes, mayor of the Andalusian village of Mijas was a 'serious', self-educated Socialist. He regarded the CNT as irresponsible, uncultured exponents of mindless violence, 'counter-revolutionaries who were seeking to split the working class'. By 1936 the CNT had nothing which a Socialist would recognize as a practical programme.

Socialists underestimated the true force of the CNT because, like subsequent historians, they were unable to comprehend the hold of anarcho-syndicalism on the Catalan proletariat and its capacity to create a mass revolutionary unionism unique in Europe. Was it because, as Vicens Vives argues, the Catalan employers (and it must be remembered that the textile industry was dominated by family concerns, run by strong individuals rather like the 'harsh' early Victorian masters) were so resistant to 'legitimate' trades union

---

* Pablo Iglesias (1850–1925), was the son of a washerwoman. Typographer and 'Father of Spanish Socialism'. Founding member of the PSOE in 1879 with Marxists expelled from the anarchist Federation.

activity, so implacable, that socialist unionism would have accomplished nothing so that there was no alternative to revolutionary unionism? Was it a mere accident that Bakunin's disciples got to Barcelona before those of Marx? Was it rooted in the revolutionary tradition of nineteenth-century Barcelona? Or was it because the total *moral* rejection of capitalist society that stemmed from Bakunin made a special appeal to a proletariat which had never undergone a process of *embourgeoisement*, as had the working classes elsewhere in Europe?

Whatever the causes of its militancy, it was an exceptional case. The CNT had no strike funds, no permanent officials. In strikes it relied on 'solidarity' – its paper was called *Solidaridad Obrera* – the support of fellow *cenetistas* (members of the CNT). Usually, therefore, its strikes were short and therefore, to achieve their ends, violent. The CNT, when under the influence of the FAI with its rejection of all political action, dismissed as illusory and tactically mistaken all Socialist hopes of a legal advance towards Socialism; libertarian communism could only be born of revolution. It was the primitive side of the movement's revolutionary messianism that made such a powerful appeal to the illiterate landless labourers of Andalusia with their vision of 'the day' when landlords would vanish and the *pueblo* would rule itself.

The consequences of the rivalry and division of the two great labour movements were not lost on its leaders and there were attempts at union. But the differences of temperament and organization were too great to be bridged except by occasional and fragile pacts. The CNT's condition for fusion with the UGT in 1936 was 'the total suppression of capitalism and the state'; this was something that Socialists, who hoped to master the state, could not contemplate. Most Socialists believed a progressive, bourgeois democracy was a step on the road to Socialism and should be supported against reactionary 'feudal' or 'fascist' régimes. Anarcho-syndicalism was irreconcilable with any form of parliamentary democracy. In 1914 the CNT told Republican conspirators that the CNT would welcome a democratic Republic 'only in the certainty that on the following day we shall be its adversaries'. And so it was with the Republic of 1931.

Two other working-class parties must be mentioned: the Communists and the POUM. Both were relatively unimportant in 1936 but their conflicts were to have fatal consequences and precipitate the most severe political crisis of the Republic in the Civil War itself.

The POUM (The Workers' Party of Marxist Unification) was formed in September 1935. Its leader was Joaquín Maurín, the most intelligent of Spanish Marxists, whose analyses impress not merely by their Marxist rigour but also by their grasp of Spanish history. A schoolmaster in Aragon, a reader of Sorel, he had, after 1917, tried to influence the CNT in the direction of revolutionary Communism and the Third International. Disabused with Soviet Communism, he founded his own party, the Workers' and Peasants' Bloc (BOC). Setting himself up as the only true interpreter of Marx, he held that only a workers' alliance could bring about the revolution the Spanish bourgeoisie was too weak to mount. Since his party operated in Catalonia – its stronghold was Lerida – Maurín adopted a Catalan colouring. He castigated Castilian centralism as imperialism, as the domination of a backward region over a progressive periphery; the 'Spanish State' must be 'disarticulated' and the regions united in a federal Republic by the workers – once again the hesitating bourgeoisie would never do it. Other working-class parties did not realize the importance of the nationalities question: the Communists and the PSOE were 'brutally imperialist', while the CNT dismissed Catalan nationalism as 'anecdotal'.

The other main constituent of the POUM was the miniscule Left Communist Party of Andrés Nin, the genial, bespectacled 'Fanatic of the Revolution' who was, like Maurín, a Catalan. Until 1934 Nin followed a Trotskyite line (he had been a secretary of Trotsky) and was, on that account, suspect to Maurín's purer brand of Marxism. Nin parted from Trotsky, but his presence in the POUM allowed the Communists to label the party 'Trotskyite' – the most damning of all accusations – in 1936–7.

The POUM was never a large party. It never succeeded in forming a strong union of its own and in October 1934 it had no party funds to pay for the telephone calls to organize a revolution. It could, therefore, only impose itself in alliance with the stronger CNT, borrowing mass support for its own purposes. But the alliance was a difficult one. Maurín much admired the revolutionary élan of the CNT but deplored its lack of a Marxist discipline. Its failure to realize the necessity of seizing political power for the workers was, in Maurín's view, a suicidal deduction from anarchist apoliticism. For the CNT it was precisely Maurín's rigid Marxism that was repellent. It was not made easier to swallow by the airs of superiority often assumed by POUM intellectuals. Maurín could not hide his view that it was a misfortune that the largest proletariat in Spain was in the hands of revolutionary amateurs.

The Communist party is more easily dealt with. Founded in April 1921 by the Young Turks of the PSOE, its best intellectuals had left it, and with occasional murmurings and lapses it faithfully followed the changes of Soviet policy as reflected in the directives of the Third International. In 1931 it was a minute, badly led party, totally out of touch with political and social reality. It attacked the bourgeois politicians of the Second Republic and their socialist allies as 'social fascists' – worse beasts than mere reactionaries. Coming out with the exotic slogan of 'A Republic of Soviets of Workers, Soldiers and Peasants', in late 1934 it changed course in a lumbering fashion and came out for a Popular Front to support the bourgeois Republic and a workers' alliance to embrace the UGT.

On the eve of the Civil War it had perhaps thirty thousand members. It was to grow rapidly in the Civil War, especially in Catalonia where, on the eve of the Civil War, it united with the Catalan PSOE to form the PSUC (the Unified Socialist Party of Catalonia). If the Socialists thought that they would absorb the Communists they were mistaken: the PSUC should have been called, as a repentant Largo Caballero who had favoured fusion remarked, 'the United Communist Party of Catalonia'.

It was in Catalonia, therefore, that the feud between the POUM and the Communists was at its most bitter. The POUM paper *La Batalla* exposed the barbarities of the Moscow trials. The PSUC accused the POUM of Trotskyite treason. In May 1937 they were fighting each other in the streets of Barcelona.

2
The Fall of the Monarchy

The declared aim of Primo de Rivera's pronunciamiento in September 1923 was, by a short experiment in 'iron surgery', to purge Spain of 'politicians' and hand the government over to patriots 'with clean hands'.

Primo's dictatorship (1923–30) was relatively mild and at first supported by the post-war boom in commodity prices and the social consequences of an adventurous public works programme. He 'solved' the Moroccan question by defeating the Moroccan leader Abd el-Krim in 1925. However, by 1926 his popularity began to wane. The king, seeing this unpopularity, and above all that the dictator had lost the confidence of the army, withdrew his support, and the dictator resigned. Nevertheless it was Alfonso's initial support of an anti-constitutional dictatorship that fatally undermined his position as a constitutional king. Once more the cry of 'responsibilities' for the desertion of constitutional government was raised by the ostracized 'old politicians' and the growing Republican opposition.

Between the fall of Primo and the advent of the Second Republic in April 1931, the king's governments struggled to find some way to return to constitutional 'normality'. They failed. The Republicans grew in numbers and organization and in August 1930 came to a formal agreement with the Catalan left and an informal agreement with the Socialists to overthrow the monarchy, by force if necessary (the Pact of San Sebastian). A military rising (December 1930) failed, but in the municipal elections of April 1931 the monarchists were soundly defeated in the great towns. The government and the country regarded the elections as a plebiscite and the king left Spain.

I

Between September 1923 and December 1930 Spain was ruled by a
military dictator, General Miguel Primo de Rivera (b. 1870) who
came from a distinguished Andalusian military family. He tried to
found his own party – the Patriotic Union – to run a new
constitution. He failed, and it was the collapse of his dictatorship
that entailed the collapse of the monarchy. Amateur, almost
benevolent, in view of later events, as his dictatorship was, why had
it come into being at all? The epoch of rule by generals and the
accomplishment of political change by the classic officers' revolt,
the *pronunciamiento*, characteristic of the period 1830–68, had
surely passed? Spain had been in appearance a liberal constitutional
monarchy since 1875; it had enjoyed universal male suffrage since
1890. What had happened to bring about that the liberal
constitutionalism of the so-called 'Restoration system' (1875–1923)
had failed to develop into a democracy capable of both reflecting
social change and inducing it?

In the crudest terms the answer is that decisions within the
political system remained in the hands of a small political class.
Though this élite reflected *grosso modo* the interests of landlords and
the middle classes and upheld a social and economic system that
benefited them, the connection between politicians and the
'oligarchy' was not as direct as has sometimes been imagined. The
'oligarchy' itself was an amorphous body, hard put to define its
common interests. But the real point is that the political class
constituted an autonomous class with its own interests: political
survival and the profits and prestige of office.* And these could be
secured *independently* of (if not altogether insensitively to) public
opinion, even of powerful pressure groups, because politicians were
not dependent on public opinion for their seats in the Cortes but on
electoral management and the political passivity of the electors. A
prime minister had only to be given a decree of dissolution by the
king and he could be sure of a comfortable parliamentary majority.

* Many of the great politicians 1874–1923 were of humble extraction who made their way as
lawyers. It is true that their influence as politicians brought them directorships, etc., especially in
railway companies; but this is also true of all politicians in western Europe. Sánchez de Toca, a
Conservative politician, argued that the 'plutocracy governed the governors' and that the result
was an 'inversion of the functions of the governing class: instead of being agents of the national
interest they are ambassadors of business'.

The political parties regularly rotated in office and 'made' elections by management of rural constituencies. The local bosses or *caciques* (*cacique* was the word for an Amer-indian chief) distributed government patronage – jobs, tax exemptions, public expenditure for private ends – in order to produce a majority for the great elector and ultimate boss of patronage, the Minister of the Interior. To the urban worker elections were becoming a reality; to the peasant they were merely a formal kowtowing to the local 'powerful ones'. In small towns and villages those who did not toe the line suffered. 'My father,' an Andalusian shoemaker reported, 'lost his shop, his livelihood and in the end his life, due to a *cacique*. He voted for a candidate opposed to the ruling *cacique* and when the latter won he avenged himself. He got my father's licence taken away and had the shop made over to one of his own supporters.'

To its opponents, *caciquismo* – its evils often exaggerated and described in moralistic terms – became a stick to beat the political system of the monarchy. 'False' it was, always under criticism by those outside it. The Republicans, living on the memory of the short-lived first Republic of 1873, never accepted as legitimate a monarchy restored by a military rebellion in 1875; by the twentieth century they regarded the monarchy as the bulwark of a traditional, Catholic society and the main obstacle to the emergence of a modern, secular society. At the other extreme the Carlists rejected the ruling branch of the Bourbon dynasty and the parliamentary liberalism it stood for as a threat to a Catholic, 'organic' society. After 1898, when Spain lost the last remnants of its once great colonial empire – Cuba, the Philippines and Puerto Rico – after a disastrous defeat by the United States, the tide of criticism mounted. There was a cry for 'regeneration'. To regenerationists like the Aragonese polymath Joaquín Costa, the Restoration system was an oligarchy disguised as a democracy. The interests of the oligarchs prevented any serious attempt to solve fundamental economic and social problems. By 1913 a new generation of intellectuals – its most typical representative was the philosopher José Ortega y Gasset – found Spain a society condemned to stagnation by the incapacity of what he called 'the old politics' to bring Spain up to the level of western Europe.

Discredited by years of criticism as an artificial alternation of parties manipulated by the king and the politicians, weakened by the fragmentation and personal factions of those same parties and by the increasing threats, after 1900, to *caciquismo* by parties based on the mobilization of opinion,* the constitutional monarchy was shaken by a serious crisis in 1917. This weakened system now had to face the domestic consequences of an unsuccessful colonial war in Morocco (a Spanish army corps was wiped out at Anual by Rif tribesmen in 1921) and the violent labour conflicts that accompanied and followed the acceleration of economic and social change that came with the Great War of 1914–18.

By 1919 these labour conflicts in Barcelona came to open gang warfare between the CNT and the employers' unions and henchmen. Catalan businessmen turned to the army for protection against Madrid governments ready to compromise with labour, and it was the 'progressive' Catalan upper-middle classes who backed the *pronunciamiento* of Primo de Rivera in September 1923; he was the man who could deal with the CNT and restore 'social peace'. His professed purpose was to end the corruptions of the 'old politics', to purify politics by a short sharp period of 'honest' military rule. Because the political system of constitutional liberalism appeared artificial, discredited and 'exhausted', no one except the professional politicians was ready to defend it.†

Parliamentary democracy was overthrown so easily in 1923 because the king had no faith in democracy and welcomed the general's take-over bid; because the intellectuals' congenital pessimism blinded them to the possibilities of a system that they had never ceased to castigate as corrupt but which, with all its faults and evasions, had at least allowed them the freedom of the press and freedom to criticize which they soon lost and were to regain only between 1931 and 1936; because the Socialist Trades Unions soon saw the advantages of cooperating with a dictatorship which would recognize the UGT as the representative of labour and persecute the CNT out of existence.

The achievements of political systems are often buried with them; their failings live after them. So it was with the constitutional

---

* Thus in Barcelona the *caciques'* power was broken by the organization of regionalist sentiment by the Lliga (see p. 7), and by the Radical Republicans under Lerroux's leadership.

† Was the parliamentary system exhausted? I believe it was not and that the 'Liberal bloc' that came to power in the elections of April 1923 might, if not cut off by a military rising backed by the king, have laid the foundations for a more effective and democratic system. Madariaga argues that, for the first time, politics had ceased to be a 'puppet show'. But this does not affect the argument that parliamentary government was discredited in large sectors of opinion.

monarchy. Its most unfortunate legacy was a certain scepticism about politics as a proper activity for a decent man. The succession of ministerial crises after 1900 – the great novelist Galdós invented the pseudo-science of 'crisology' – fostered an obsession with the surface changes, the minutiae of political life. Politics was a game played by professionals for their own ends, not a system to solve problems. In an attenuated form these attitudes persisted to weaken the Republican enthusiasm of April 1931, once the solidarity of the fight against the monarchy dissolved into a maze of parties. Between 1931 and 1936 the Republic saw the rise and fall of eighteen cabinets. The politicians' struggle for survival began to look like a modern version of the 'old politics'. The iconography of the Republic had an old-fashioned look. Leading politicians were photographed coming from consultations in the Presidential Palace, giving reporters their versions of the collapse of the old government and the possible permutations in a new ministry. Newspaper reports of ministerial crises had an uncomfortable ring of the *ancien régime* with the President of the Republic acting as the old moderating power – the king.

Ministerial instability (and we must remember that in Spain a change of ministers meant a re-shuffle of top civil servants) reflected the absence of strong *national* parties once the 'artificial' two-party system of the Restoration was finally destroyed in 1923, leaving a vacuum. Why was there this failure to integrate interests in strong parties? It was partly the result of regionalism, particularly in its extremer forms in the Basque Provinces and Catalonia. Thus the PNV was a Catholic party – but it was cut off from its fellow Catholic parties in the rest of the country by its insistence on autonomy: Catholic parties were centralists, unsympathetic to regional demands. In Catalonia every Spanish party was duplicated by a separate Catalan party; the Catalan party might or might not make alliances with similar parties in Spain, depending on their acceptance of Catalan demands. Thus the businessmen's Catalanist party – the *Lliga* – was a modern conservative party but its relation with Spanish conservatives was often uneasy. The *Esquerra* was a left-wing Republican party with a moderate programme of social reform. It was thus similar but separate from like-minded left Republicans in Spain. Carlism, in spite of its organizational weaknesses and internal feuds, had a mass following; but its masses were concentrated in the Basque Provinces, above all in Navarre.

Regional disparities were compounded by organizational weakness and personalism. Spanish parties tended to cluster round a *caudillo* who gathered his clients round him in his *tertulia* meeting in clubs or cafés. He retained the loyalty of these 'unconditionals' by distributing governmental patronage and jobs. Spanish parties were apt to be parties of notables with little root in the countryside, artificial constructs serving only to support a class of self-interested politicians.

This vision of the selfish politician, of parties which sustained an 'unpatriotic' political class, was grossly exaggerated. But no one can understand the origins, political structure and moral tone of the Franco régime without taking into account this distrust of parties and the party system that goes back to the later years of the nineteenth century, and was reinforced by the experience of the Second Republic and by the attacks on democratic politics as 'degenerate' that had long been the common currency of the European right. To conservatives like General Franco, the party system and the selfishness of party politicians had let down the army, precipitating the military disaster in Cuba and in Morocco, and had shown themselves unable to master social unrest and strikes. Since parties are the core of parliamentary democracy, without which it cannot function, the poor performance of the party system was transformed into the doctrine that liberal democracy as such was 'unsuited' to Spain. To destroy party was Franco's aim and it remains so. In 1959, as in 1937, he thundered against 'the dismal and catastrophic achievements' of political parties in Spain where they had been 'so closely allied to the disgrace of the nation'. In this, as in so many other spheres, he was exaggerating the rhetoric and systematizing the political instincts of the minister he had served under in Morocco, General Primo de Rivera. Both saw themselves as 'iron surgeons', patriots called to cut out of Spanish life the cancer of the 'old politics'.

II

There is no need to deny the patriotic intentions of Primo de Rivera, presented though they were in an embarrassing brand of sentimental rhetoric, nor to belittle his achievements: the end of the Moroccan war, an ambitious if expensive programme of public works, his cooperation with the UGT for better conditions for the urban workers. By 1929, however, his rule, no longer bolstered by a buoyant economy, looked what it was: a mixture of old-fashioned military authoritarianism and the new-fangled corporative state run by technicians and civil servants, with little support among the old 'political' classes, whom he abused, and the army, which he tried to reform. The businessmen and landowners, who had welcomed Primo's coup as saving them from a parliamentary system which could no longer protect their interests by keeping socialists out of politics and anarchists in prison, turned against him and his mild programme of modernization 'from above'. His wage boards gave settlements too favourable to workers; his governmental agencies and marketing boards 'interfered' with private enterprise. His Minister of Finance, Calvo Sotelo, found taxation resisted by the privileged classes, 'above all the landowners'. The king's intrigues had weakened the parliamentary process between 1909 and 1923; his support of Primo in 1923 had 'legitimized' the dictatorship. In 1930 the withdrawal of royal confidence forced Primo's resignation. Already in an advanced stage of diabetes, he retired in December 1930, to die in Paris a broken man.

The dictatorship of Primo de Rivera has often been dismissed as an historical irrelevancy, a bizarre episode in Spanish history, as if it were no more than a reflection of the odd character of the dictator. Yet the dictatorship was an attempt – often ham-handed – at authoritarian government with 'fascist' overtones such as a single-party state. Hitler seems to have noted it with interest and Mussolini regarded himself as its patron. Unpopular as it became, when the democratic Republic foundered in political and social strife, many of those conservatives who had plotted against Primo came to look on his rule as a model, on his iron surgery as the only remedy for a sick society threatened by a resurgence of the proletarian forces he had cracked down on in 1923.

This was probably particularly true of the officers who had served under him: having a soldier at the top might have its drawbacks; but a general was preferable to a gang of radical civilians who hated the army. Some officers, exasperated by his Moroccan policies and his army reforms, had plotted against him, and Franco during 1925 was in contact with political malcontents among the old politicians. Yet Franco refused to commit himself. He got on badly with the dictator but he was unwilling to drag a *divided* army into a *pronunciamiento* which might fail and destroy all discipline.

If one lesson Franco learned was the necessity of preserving 'the harmony of the military family' for the army to act effectively as a political force, the other was the necessity of going the whole hog in politics. Primo de Rivera had suppressed the political institutions of Catalonia; but he had not persecuted Catalan culture out of existence. Partial suppression had fulfilled Prat de la Riba's prophecy that out of the winter of oppression would come the spring of a nationalist revival. General Franco suppressed not merely the political institutions of Catalonia, but the culture that had given them vitality.

III

The dismissed dictator had a posthumous revenge. If the king thought that by dropping the pilot of 1923–30 he could re-establish his position as a constitutional monarch – what was called a return to normality – he was sadly mistaken. Two caretaker governments failed. Many of the most important 'old politicians' could not forgive Alfonso for his desertion, in 1923, of the constitution they had manned; they demanded a constituent Cortes which should examine the 'responsibilities' for the dictatorship and reform the constitution in such a way that 'the perjured king' could not repeat the performance of 1923. The cry for responsibilities was taken up by the Republicans in order to get rid of the king altogether. From 1926 they had been gathering their forces in the Republican Alliance; in 1930 they prepared the final onslaught in a nation-wide campaign of meetings. In Catalonia the Esquerra and the other left groups committed to autonomy within a Republic swept aside all other parties; Catalans could not forgive the king for his support of a dictator who had persecuted Catalonia. The Socialists, late in the day, repented of their cooperation with the dictator and came round to cooperation with bourgeois Republicanism.

In the summer of 1930 all these groups came together and agreed to cooperate in a 'gentlemen's agreement' known as the Pact of San Sebastian; a revolutionary committee, that would become the Provisional Government of the Republic, agreed on a programme that would democratize Spain and ensure that Catalan autonomy would be a first priority of the new régime. An ill-conceived Republican military rising in December 1930 failed miserably but monarchist attempts to build up a mass party and to regain some of the ground lost in public opinion also failed.

The municipal elections of April 1931 reflected this disenchantment. They turned overwhelmingly against the king in the large cities while rural Spain voted monarchist. Republicanism and democratic radicalism had been an urban phenomenon since the 1870s. This division between a politically conscious radical urban electorate and a passive conservative rural electorate had moulded and would continue to mould the political development of Spain.*

With the results of the municipal elections came the last, the crucial desertion of the final arbiter of Spanish political life: the army. General Sanjurjo made it clear that he would not bring out the Civil Guard to save a monarchy that had lost its hold on 'opinion'. (The Civil Guard was a militarized police force under the Ministry of the Interior but commanded by a regular soldier. Sanjurjo was the most popular soldier in Spain and a hero of the Moroccan wars, much admired by Alfonso XIII.) Romanones, *cacique* of Guadalajara and archetypal 'old politician', called on Alcalá Zamora who, as chairman of the San Sebastian committee would become the Prime Minister of the Republican Provisional Government, 'bearing a white flag'. The Republic had already been declared in Barcelona and in smaller towns. To save his crown the king would have to face bloodshed with the support of only two of his cabinet. With the crowd demonstrating outside his palace, the king packed his bags and drove himself to Cartagena for Marseilles – typically enough so fast that he lost his security escort *en route*. It was all very sudden. 'The fall of the monarchy,' wrote Alfonso's polo tutor, 'gave me a greater shock than any fall from a pony.'

The Revolutionary Committee forced their way through the crowds to declare themselves the Provisional Government of the Second Republic. They themselves could scarcely believe in their victory.

IV

Régimes fall, less because of the overwhelming strength of the opposition than because those who man them suffer a loss of confidence and political nerve. They feel isolated in a sea of hostile opinion; they hesitate to use force in an effective manner and slip into haphazard repression. (The police forces of the monarchy were weak, ill-equipped and their morale, with the prospect of a change in the régime in the last months of the monarchy, very low. The

---

* Among the larger towns where the monarchists won the elections were those which were later the core of Nationalist support in July 1936: Pamplona, Burgos, Vittoria and Soria.

Director General of Security, General Mola, had to use private taxi-cabs to get his men to street disturbances.) The achievement of the Republican opposition in the late thirties was to create an atmosphere, an ambience of indifference or hostility to the monarchy that ran from the students for whom Alfonso had built a University City to officers whom he had cultivated all his life but whom he had allowed the dictator to slight. The economic crisis that was to plague the Republic, apart from a fall in the foreign exchange rate, scarcely troubled the declining years of the monarchy; the social tensions, compared with those of 1936, were manageable. The revolution of 1931 was, therefore, a political revolution. A revolution of boredom with a monarch who, in spite of a passion for motor-cars, appeared an anachronism. 'We are,' remarked Alfonso, 'out of fashion.' Cut off by his hieratic court and his pursuits (polo and shooting – he was, with George v, the best shot in Europe) from his people, he had come to symbolize the backwardness of Spain; in the parlance of the Republicans and Democrats who had exiled his grandmother in 1868 he was a 'traditional obstacle'. The monarch who had dedicated Spain to the Sacred Heart of Jesus could not be expected to lead his country into the modern world.

The only dedicated and convinced monarchists in Spain were the Court aristocracy. For others it was a conditional régime – conditional on supplying the benefits that the particular sectors of society sought from the political system. Gabriel Maura, one of the sons of the great Conservative prime minister, was the king's chosen companion in his favourite sport: pigeon-shooting. His brother, Miguel (to become on 14 April first Minister of the Interior of the Republic) believed that, once it was evident that the king could not modernize and democratize the monarchy, then the monarchy must go. The efforts of aristocratic monarchists like Gabriel Maura proved feeble and ineffective in rallying support. They watched the fall of their monarch, as one of them put it, as they might have watched a bad film.

3
The Second Republic 1931–6

Until the election of the Constituent Cortes in June 1931 the Republic was ruled by the San Sebastian coalition as the Provisional Government of the Republic. Once elected, the Cortes drew up a democratic constitution with a mild 'social' tinge. Article 26 of the Constitution attacked the privileges of the Church. This had two consequences: Alcalá Zamora resigned (October 1932) and the right set about organizing a mass party to 'revise' the religious articles of the Constitution. Its leader was Gil Robles and it was the origin of the right-wing electoral coalition of the CEDA.

With the right-wing Republicans out of government and Alcalá Zamora kicked upstairs as President of the Republic, government was in the hands of a coalition of Left Republicans and Socialists under Azaña as Prime Minister. Its most important achievement was the granting of autonomy to Catalonia, but its efforts at agrarian reform and its lay educational programme were increasingly distasteful to the right. This strengthened Gil Robles' clerical, conservative Popular Action party while monarchist activists attempted an old style military pronunciamiento *with General Sanjurjo's rising in Seville (August 1932). The government was confronted by strikes and risings by the anarcho-syndicalists and repression made it unpopular. Its failure to implement social reforms made its relations with the Socialists uneasy. Thus in the elections of November 1933 the Azaña coalition was defeated; in the new Cortes Lerroux's Radicals, now a conservative party, and Gil Robles' electoral coalition, the CEDA, held a majority.*

The 'Two Black Years' of Radical and cedista *government saw an abandonment of the progressive 'content' of Azaña's government. The left did not trust Gil Robles' professions of legalism, and when Lerroux was forced to invite the CEDA to join the government in October 1934 the miners rose in Asturias against 'fascism' and in Catalonia the Catalan nationalist left staged a feeble revolt in Barcelona in defence of their autonomy, threatened by conservative centralists. The rising and its savage repression were the watershed in the history of the Republic. The right feared a Marxist revolution, the left a right-wing dictatorship. With the Radicals discredited by corruption and scandals, the CEDA were unable to form an effective government, given the hostility of Alcalá Zamora. As the general election drew near, the old alliance of Left Republicans and Socialists came together in the Popular Front; this promised a bourgeois Republican government committed to social reform within the capitalist system. The conditions of the electoral battle were now the reverse of November 1933. The left was united and its emotional cement was amnesty for those imprisoned for their participation in the October Revolution (thus the 'apolitical' anarcho-syndicalists voted for the Popular Front); the right fought divided. Given an electoral system that favoured multi-party lists, this ensured the victory of the Popular Front in the elections of February 1936.*

I

Apart from a handful of committed aristocratic monarchists, the 'respectable classes', to use a nineteenth-century Spanish term to describe the upper and the upper-middle classes, accepted the Republic. The establishment of a middle-class Republic might offer more security for the well-to-do than an unpopular monarchy constantly under fire from the left. But this security could not last if the Republic was to accomplish what the majority of its leaders wanted to achieve: the modernization and democratization of Spanish politics and society. This was not a socialist or a revolutionary programme: a generation of intellectuals reared on the doctrine of *atraso* – that Spain was behind or 'out of phase' as the slogan now goes, in comparison with western Europe – wanted to close the gap.

If it is not impossible to transform a static, traditional society by democratic processes it is, at the very least, a difficult task. The Provisional Republican Government of April 1931 was too heterogeneous in composition to agree on anything much beyond principles of good intent.* In terms of political conviction and party history its members were a very mixed bunch. The Prime Minister was Niceto Alcalá Zamora: an old-time *cacique* and Liberal politician under the monarchy, he had announced his conversion to the Republic a year before; in his sixties, his main attributes for office were an astonishing memory and a talent for florid oratory. Miguel Maura (b. 1887), Minister of the Interior, was son of the great conservative leader Antonio Maura and another late convert to Republicanism. Like Alcalá Zamora he was a reassuring figure to Catholics. If Alcalá Zamora and Maura represented conservative Republicanism, the hero of the Republican left was Manuel Azaña (b. 1880), president of the prestigious literary club, the Ateneo, and much influenced by French radicalism. Unamuno once cattily remarked of him that he would make a revolution in order to gain an audience. He was the ablest of the new generation of Republicans and a powerful debater. His closest ally and friend was Casares Quiroga, leader of the Autonomous Republican Party of Galicia. Even more Jacobin in political style than Azaña were the two Radical Socialists. There was one Catalan. The proletarian parties were represented by three Socialists. Fernando de los Ríos was a professor at Granada University. The Minister of Labour, Largo Caballero, ex-plasterer, had left school at seven; joining the UGT in the 1890s, he was its Secretary General. His rival for influence in the Socialist movement was Indalecio Prieto (b. 1883) who, starting out as a typist, had become proprietor of the Bilbao newspaper *El Liberal*; Prieto was the leading figure in the PSOE in Bilbao, a practical statesman rather than a doctrinaire Socialist. In the middle of this political spectrum came Alejandro Lerroux and his lieutenant Diego Martínez Barrio, a prominent Freemason. Lerroux was now a 'tamed lion', no longer the fierce radical of his Barcelona days, and he was increasingly to oppose Socialist influence and policies in the government.

In spite of these divisions the Provisional Government did, however, agree that fundamental reform must not be carried through by decree in the euphoric atmosphere of April but that it must be the achievement of democratic parliamentarianism in the

---

* There are many parallels between 1848 in France and 1931 in Spain. cf. Marx's comment: 'The Provisional Government which emerged from the February barricades . . . could not be anything but a compromise between the different classes which together had overturned the July throne (i.e. the throne of Louis Philippe) but whose interests were mutually antagonistic.'

Constituent Cortes to be elected in June. Once open to debate, reforms were watered down and obstructed and the splits in the government exposed. It was only in December 1931 that the departure of the conservative Republicans Alcalá Zamora and Maura left the government in the hands of a more like-minded coalition of left-wing Republicans and Socialists. With Alcalá Zamora kicked up into the Presidency of the Republic, Manuel Azaña was the strong man and Prime Minister of the new government. Progressive bourgeois Republicans and Socialists could surely find enough common ground to carry through the reform promised in the Constitution of 1932.

Reform was made difficult by economic circumstance. There was no money for expensive government programmes and structural reforms that would pay off long after the original investment had been made. The Republic coincided with the great depression of the thirties with its dramatic contraction of world trade and business activity; it was the era of deflation and budget slashing. It has often been pointed out that the economic blizzard which froze the economies of western Europe and the United States blew less fiercely on the relatively enclosed economy of Spain; nevertheless the years from 1933 to 1936 were for Spain a period of economic stagnation at home and bad export prospects abroad. The result was persistent, if not dramatic, unemployment in the working classes and a malaise in the professional classes. The Republic could not *improve* conditions. It was less prosperous than the dictatorship. However unreliable Spanish statistics were at this time, the story they tell is unmistakable: exports down by 75% by 1934, industrial production stagnant with no new investment.

Unemployment was worst in agriculture, one of the few sectors where production increased. In 1933, of 618,947 unemployed nearly 70% were in the rural sector. It was in order to mop up this pool of idle men and to fulfil the promises of a more equitable distribution of the land held out by the Constitution that the Republic embarked on an agrarian reform. Now most historians would agree that the failure of this reform was a symbol of the failure of the Republic to tackle the deepset imbalances and injustices of Spanish society.

Agrarian reform in a democratic society which respects property rights and has not the financial resources to compensate for the expropriation of large landowners is a contradiction in terms. The legal and technical complexities of reform were exploited by a ruthless opposition in marathon debates; the government itself was divided between Socialists and bourgeois Republicans whose views on the scope of reform differed: the Republicans, many of whom came from the urban petty bourgeoisie and had no gut-feeling for the plight of the agrarian dispossessed, favoured a property-owning peasantry attached to the Republic, while the Socialists, converted to a concern for the rural worker by the growing strength of their agricultural union, favoured collective ownership. The Agrarian Law of 1932 gave the Republic the legal instrument to tackle the agrarian question; but it did not provide the cash or the determination. Starved of money – its budget was less than half the expenditure on the Civil Guard – the Institute of Agrarian Reform handed over to peasant settlers an area the size of one huge estate. The Agrarian Law was typical of the Republic's reforms in that it was mild in practice but threatening in principle. 'It seriously threatened the strongest economic class in Spain . . . and awakened the hopes of the impoverished peasantry.'*

The failure of agrarian reform was crucial to the fate of the Republic. The Socialist Federation of Agricultural Workers had so grown in strength in the years 1930–33 – it constituted nearly half the membership of the UGT – that the Socialist leaders could not be indifferent to demands for redistribution of land. The failure of the Republic to deal with the agrarian problem therefore disabused leaders like Largo Caballero of the possibilities of socialist progress within a bourgeois democracy.

Nevertheless, we must not underestimate the achievements of the first years of the Republic. Rural wages were forced up dramatically, not always to the liking of modest farmers. The bargaining position of Socialist trades unions in wage disputes was vastly strengthened in the system of mixed committees of employers and

---

* This is the verdict of Edward Malefakis, whose *Agrarian Reform and Peasant Revolution in Spain* (1970) is central to the understanding of the history of the Second Republic. The law of 1932 confiscated grandees' land without compensation; other uncultivated land and farms over a certain size were expropriated (with compensation) to be distributed to peasant colonists. Perhaps the main weakness of the law was that, though it was aimed at breaking up the great absenteeists' *latifundia*, it threatened a large number of small proprietors and probably turned them as a class against the Republic. Nevertheless, complex as the law was and unintended as were some of its consequences, it did make available for redistribution enormous tracts of land at a price the state should have been able to pay. But the Azaña government was unwilling to foot the bill. Azaña himself, as a typical urban intellectual, seems to have had no real interest in agrarian questions; they are hardly treated at all in his collected works.

workers in which the workers were consistently supported by the Ministry of Labour.* Azaña's personal contribution had been a military reform aimed at reducing the size of the officer corps by allowing officers to retire on full pay and modernizing the army – a measure which Ortega y Gasset qualified as 'marvellous, incredible, fabulous and legendary' but which was carried out with Azaña's characteristic political acerbity. (Why, he was asked, did he rub salt into the wounds he inflicted on his enemies? 'Because it amuses me,' he replied). Moreover, his reforms failed in their main purpose: the depoliticization of the army. An effort, the mark of a Republic of intellectuals, was made to wipe out the backlog of neglect in the primary education of a population, nearly half of whom had been left illiterate by monarchist politicians and where secondary education was still largely in the hands of the Church. Even so it lacked the funds to replace the Church schools it dismantled.

Only by a drastic increase in direct taxation could the early Republican governments have found the resources to carry out the promises of the Constitution of 1932. This they failed to do, because even the Azaña government lacked the necessary confidence to force through a drastic redistribution of income. (Income Tax ran from 1% to 4% on incomes over 100,000 pesetas.) It was therefore obliged to leave economic and social power in society much where it had found it in April 1931. Prieto, as Minister of Finance in the Provisional Government, did not discipline the Banks; it was rather that the Banks disciplined him. When the Azaña government pressed for the creation of a Bank of Agricultural Credit to help the newly settled peasantry, the private banks sabotaged the project. Azaña's cabinet was alarmed at the level of unemployment; but it could neither tax the wealthy to provide the money for unemployment benefits nor compel the employers to contribute. Even Socialists like Prieto feared the immediate results of a violent disruption of capitalist society. Once in government, like the British Labour party in 1929, they found themselves in charge of the capitalist economy they had damned for years. As Malcolm Muggeridge wrote of Ramsay MacDonald's Labour cabinet, they were 'like prohibitionists unexpectedly made responsible for the

---

* The CNT was committed to 'direct action' against employers and therefore opposed to any arbitration or compromise solution to wage disputes. The result was that the wage boards favoured the UGT unions and the CNT regarded its self-imposed splendid isolation as 'persecution'.

management of a derelict brewery'. Azaña's Republicans believed that capitalism could not and should not be destroyed; it must be made 'humane' by appropriate legislation.

This moderation and a budgetary orthodoxy as rigid as Snowden's in the British National Government, did not prevent the 'respectable classes' thinking that their privileged position was threatened by a continuation of reformist policies, which they professed to see as a case of creeping socialism. Azaña time and time again dismissed this as an alarmist propaganda device. As the Socialists had a majority neither in the Cortes nor in the government, there could be no Socialist take-over bid. 'What are called Socialist policies – in the revolutionary and class sense of the word – are nothing more than the most elementary demands of social justice which no Republican party can refuse to implement. . . . What is all this talk of socialist policies and the handing over of the Republic to the Socialists? When will this fantasy end?' Fantasy or no, talk of a socialist threat worked. (The 'Jacobin' image of the Republic in these years was less the creation of Socialists like Largo Caballero and Prieto than of the Radical Socialists, a relatively small non-Marxist party, much given to emotional outbursts against the church and the 'feudal' establishment. Azaña himself was not averse to oratorical Jacobinism though his style was more restrained.)

Yet, at the same time as they proclaimed the dangers of socialism, the right sensed the weakness of the government, its 'village notion of political economy' which stopped short of any serious attack and left them in command of the economy. As with the mild legislation of Léon Blum in France in the days of the French Popular Front, the modest measures of the Azaña coalition were perceived as a threat; but they were only a threat, not a resolute attack on conservative interests.

Nor did the right see threats solely in social and economic terms. Many non-Catalan conservatives – and in particular army officers – were outraged by one of the most significant of the Republic's achievements: the grant of regional self-government to Catalonia. Conservatives regarded the Autonomy Statute which set up the Generalidad and gave Catalonia control over most of its domestic concerns as a 'destruction of Spanish unity', as a sop to separatists.

The resentment of conservatives – and one is apt to forget that Spain had been ruled in the conservative interest since 1876 and that the web of interests so created was still strong – concentrated on what was a symbolic issue. The attack on the privileged position of the Catholic Church.

This attack was understandable, given the enormous emotional significance of the Church as a pillar of the *ancien régime*, but it was a godsend to those looking for a suitably decent stick with which to beat the Republic. To left-wing Republicans, to the Socialists and progressives in general, the Church, through its large share in secondary – even technical – education symbolized all that was 'backward' in Spanish society. Anti-clericalism was part of the Spanish progressive tradition or, as Prieto put it more crudely, 'its only intellectual baggage'. The creation of a lay state and secular education was the historic mission of Republicanism; as *El Socialista*, the PSOE daily put it, 'an elementary aspiration of democracy'. With the benefits of hindsight we can see (especially since the Vatican would have gone a long way to come to terms with the new government) that the attack on the Church was a mistaken priority. Article 26 of the new Constitution and the subsequent legislation separated Church and State, expelled the Jesuits and clipped the Regular Orders' control over education. It must be admitted that, however conciliatory the Vatican may have been, Catholic influence over education was the one thing it would not surrender and this was, at the same time, the one thing that the left Republicans were determined to destroy.

In May 1931 the Provisional Government did nothing to stop a savage outburst of what Ortega called 'Mediterranean fetishism' – the church-burning which had been a standard performance of Spanish extreme radicalism. It started in Madrid as a protest against a monarchist meeting. Only Miguel Maura, Minister of the Interior, demanded that the Civil Guard should be used; the rest of the government, fearful of its popularity should there be casualties, did nothing. For this act of political cowardice Azaña must take the blame. 'All the convents of Madrid,' he told the cabinet, 'are not worth the life of a single republican.' Maura clearly believed that Azaña's political conduct was based on his undisguised physical cowardice. According to Maura the church-burnings were 'the sectarian manifestation of a handful of bogus Ateneo intellectuals and the diversion of a crowd of layabouts who were given absolute impunity'. The Ateneo was a sort of middle-class Athenaeum, of which Azaña was a leading spirit.

The defence of a 'persecuted Church' provided the rallying cry of the right. Gil Robles, who was to make his political career as the leader of this Catholic reaction, called the Republican legislation not merely an injustice but an error. 'The religious problem from that moment (the passing of Article 26) was converted into a battle-cry, sharpening to the point of paroxysm the combat between the two Spains.'

It is characteristic of the Second Republic that the right both gained the propaganda value of 'persecution' and yet avoided its consequences; the legislation against the schools of Regular Orders was evaded by subterfuge – the formation of limited companies which ran schools staffed by monks and nuns in civilian clothing while the rachitic finances of the state could not provide alternatives. But with the legalization of divorce, the creation of secular cemeteries and the removal of the crucifix from schools, it seemed to traditionalists that Spain was to be given over to the excesses of materialism and free love. It was not that the faithful were driven into the catacombs. They suffered, rather, a host of minor persecutions at the hands of some of the new Republican municipalities: fines for the ringing of church bells, prohibition of religious processions; the removal of religious sculptures on the façades of churches; the civil burial of those who had not, in their wills, specified a religious burial.

II

Joaquín Chapaprieta* a monarchical liberal converted to a conservative brand of Republicanism, believed that the municipal elections of 1931 and the subsequent installation of the Republic had been a triumph for the left, not because of its strength in the country, but because the conservative forces, disillusioned with the monarchy, had voted against it. He believed that these forces must be rallied in a respectable, centrist Conservative party if the Republic were to survive as a bourgeois institution.

This centrist party of moderate men, in spite of the efforts of Miguel Maura and the Byzantine intrigues of Alcalá Zamora as President, failed to emerge. The discontents of the conservative classes first took the classic form of military rebellion – General Sanjurjo, involuntary military midwife of the Republic in April and

_____

* Joaquín Chapaprieta (b. 1871), was a landowner and lawyer from the Levante. He was a Finance Minister and briefly Prime Minister in 1935–6.

now the standard-bearer of 'the forces of order', staged a *pronunciamiento* in August 1932. It was a fiasco. The main vehicle of conservative protest was Acción Popular (founded in December 1932 it was at first called Acción Nacional) later to be the core of a confederation of rightist parties, the CEDA (Confederación de Derechas Autónomas).

Acción Popular was inspired by a Catholic pressure group, the National Catholic Association of Propagandists (ACNP), whose leading spirit was Angel Herrera, editor of its paper *El Debate*. ACNP had aimed at capturing the political and intellectual élite of Spain; it now abandoned its instinctual élitism and set about creating a mass party of the Catholic right. Herrera chose as its leader Gil Robles, a young lawyer from a Carlist background with great debating gifts and formidable organizational drive.

The immediate aim of Acción Popular and of the CEDA was the defence of the Catholic Church against the onslaught of the secularizing left. Its ultimate aim was the implanting in Spain of a Catholic corporate state. The problem arose over means. It professed the doctrine of 'accidentalism' (i.e. that forms of government were immaterial provided Catholic interests were respected) and the old Catholic tactic of accepting and exploiting the 'lesser evil'. Thus without openly acknowledging the Republic it could operate as a legal political party within it.

The nature and fate of the CEDA is one of the keys to the fall of the Second Republic. What was it? Was Gil Robles a 'fascist' out to destroy democracy, or was he ready to accept its processes provided he was allowed to use them? As the election speeches of November 1933 prove, Gil Robles' 'accidentalism' was not far removed from the position of those Socialists who argued that democracy was acceptable provided it was a socialist democracy. To his opponents 'accidentalism' was a sham and, as long as his party was financed by rich monarchists, he kept his party together by studied ambiguities and by outbursts against decadent democracies. 'We must impose our will with all the force of our rightness, and with other forces if this is insufficient. The cowardice of the Right has allowed those who come from the cesspools of iniquity to take control of the destinies of the fatherland.'

At the time and since, it has been argued that these outbursts made clear Robles' intention to destroy the Republic by *violent* means. He resisted the pressures of the monarchists in the party: he refused to support Sanjurjo's military coup and the activists were expelled from Acción Popular. That in the last resort he envisaged this possibility is as true of him as it is true of the Socialists who followed Largo Caballero. 'The right,' he later confessed, 'had no other means of gaining power than by using the established régime (i.e. the Republic), introducing themselves into it and *making it their own*.' Was this not to use democracy in order to modify it out of existence? 'Deep down,' the Socialist Prieto argued, 'Gil Robles wanted a dictatorship'; his verbal concessions to the right of his party – and it can be argued that the duty of a party leader is to keep his party together at all costs – merely confirmed this suspicion.

Just as the Socialists were divided, so was the CEDA. Even after the monarchist activists had been expelled it embraced monarchists and genuine Christian Democrats like Jiménez Fernández, who, as CEDA Minister of Agriculture in 1934–5 tried to implement his ideal of a property-owning peasantry and the social policies of Leo XIII and Pius XI. But the social programme of the CEDA remained a dead letter in a party weighed down by the Conservatives on its right. It became more and more a party of the frightened upper and middle classes and in the end Gil Robles gave party funds to the conspirators of July 1936.

If the Republic of Azaña had become hateful to Conservatives, it had not won the benevolence, let alone the alliance of the extreme left.

The return to legal trades union activity had seen one of those sudden and dramatic surges of membership so characteristic of anarcho-syndicalism; by the summer of 1931 the CNT had grown from a few thousand to claim to be, with a membership of seven hundred thousand, larger than the UGT. And it was dominated by the extreme anarcho-syndicalists of the FAI, determined to use this new strength for immediate revolution; they believed that the Republic could be pushed aside by a determined strike. Buencasa, an activist leader, confessed that the CNT committed itself in the early years of the Republic 'to the most absurd enterprises'. In January 1932 the CNT staged a full-scale rising in the industrial zone of the Llobregat valley in Catalonia; then an even more senseless revolutionary strike – with 37 killed – in Barcelona.

These 'absurd enterprises' split the CNT. The moderate syndicalists, with their belief in a revolution imposed by well-organized, powerful unions, regarded the FAI strikes as premature, risking the whole future of the syndicalist movement. Angel Pestaña, who had become one of the best journalists in the CNT and editor of its daily paper *Solidaridad Obrera*, rejected the extremism of the FAI 'bully boys' and, driven out of the CNT, formed his own opposition syndicates. With the 'moderates' outside the CNT, the FAI controlled the weakened union; to the FAI, parliamentary democracy was a farce, the Cortes a 'brothel'. 'Our revolution is made, not on the benches of Parliament, but in the street.'

The Azaña government repressed the revolutionary strikes with massive imprisonments; to the CNT it became, therefore, 'a government of hangmen', indistinguishable from the worst of monarchical governments.

What the government did not foresee was the rural revolt which began in the winter of 1931. Civil Guards were murdered in an Extremaduran village; Civil Guards, in turn, shot down peasants. Cabinet ministers were howled down with cries of 'Assassin!'

It is easy to exaggerate – as the right did for propaganda purposes – the extent of these disorders or their effects on the electorate; Spain was, in general, peaceful compared with Germany on the eve of Hitler's rise to power; a swing to the right was to be expected. But the hopes of April had vanished. The most depressing feature of the new Republic was its apparent political kinship with the old parliamentary monarchy. Civil governors (as the representatives of the central government in the provinces the key figures in the Spanish administrative structure) were, according to the Minister of the Interior, second-rate hangers-on of politicians. The Republic seemed to have its own version of *caciquismo*: *enchufismo* – the 'plugging oneself in' to jobs under the new régime.

By 1933 the Republic of Azaña was in the Spanish phrase 'worn out', under fire from both right and left, its glamour clouded by sterile political debates and petty crises. Moreover, its political base – the alliance of Socialists and Left Republicans – was in peril. Julian Besteiro (1870–1939), a respected professor of philosophy and, with Prieto, Largo Caballero's rival for the leadership of the Socialist movement, had always opposed his party's 'opportunist' collaboration with bourgeois Republicans in government; Besteiro was a non-revolutionary but dogmatic Marxist whose aim was the peaceful capture of the Republican state by the working-class organizations. Collaboration, he argued, had brought no rewards.

Article 46 of the Constitution promised social security, unemployment pay, workers' participation and profit-sharing; but nothing had been done. When the Socialist Congress voted for the abolition of the Civil Guard, the Socialists in government voted to raise its pay.

By the summer of 1933 Largo Caballero himself, the apostle of collaboration, was beginning to have private doubts about its benefits and the effects on his following of his sitting in a government that suppressed strikes and shot down workers. 'Today,' (August 1933) 'I am convinced that to accomplish socialist aims in a bourgeois democracy is impossible.'

It was Joaquín Maurín of the BOC who elaborated the most damning analysis of the course of the Republic from the point of view of the Marxist left. It had given itself a petty bourgeois constitution in a country where the petty bourgeoisie was weak and incapable of carrying through a fundamental reform of the country. It was 'not enough that the king should go away'; the monarchy was merely a form of government that presided over a 'limited company' of class interests. The form had gone but the company was still in business.

One of the prospective directors of the new company was Alejandro Lerroux: his Radical Republican party had increasingly become a party of the 'respectable classes' capitalizing, in its propaganda, on the 'capture' of Azaña's Republicans by their Socialist allies; the old anti-clerical orator now defended the rights of the Catholic voter.

While the right was gathering its forces, the elections of November 1933 caught the 'Azaña coalition' of Socialists and Left Republicans in disintegration and disarray; they fought as separate parties and this was to invite disaster with an electoral system that gave great advantages to broadly-based coalitions. On top of this the CNT organized a massive campaign of abstention. 'Don't Vote' was a slogan that robbed the left of the working-class vote in much of Catalonia.

The elections came at the worst possible time. A sharp fall in agricultural prices alienated large and small landowners alike; 1933 was the worst year of the slump. The CEDA and the Radicals, though neither party had a clear majority in the Cortes, were triumphant over the weakened and divided Republican-Socialist coalition.

The election had been characterized by oratorical violence and what is most significant is that the loyalty of both the CEDA and the left-wing Socialists to the democratic process appeared conditional. Both accepted the Republic as a form of government – though Gil Robles avoided an open declaration of Republican loyalty he had no intention of restoring Alfonso XIII. What concerned them both was the *content* of the Republic. If the electorate voted for the wrong content, then the electorate must be by-passed by what both called 'other means'. 'The Republic,' thundered Largo Caballero on his election tours, 'must be a Socialist, not a bourgeois Republic. We may delay but we don't hide that we are going to have a social revolution ... we will have to expropriate the bourgeoisie by violence. On the 19th [November] we vote, but don't forget that circumstances may demand more energy, more decision than merely registering a vote. The triumph of reaction [i.e. the victory of the right at the polls] must be avoided, first in the ballot-box and then in the streets. We mustn't stop the fight until the red flag of the Socialist revolution waves over the official buildings of the Republic.' Gil Robles was making similar threatening noises. Since Gil Robles' party gained a striking victory in the elections his threats did not materialize. Largo Caballero and his party lost. Their threats became, in October 1934, a reality.

III

The first prime minister of what the left were to call the 'Two Black Years' of right-wing governments was Lerroux. The former 'Emperor' of Barcelona working-class radicalism had achieved the goal of every ambitious politician under the old monarchy. 'I will not die,' he remarked, 'without leading a government.' But he could not lead a government without the parliamentary support of Gil Robles and the CEDA. The Republic was in the hands of the conservative classes.

While they despised Lerroux's Radicals as Johnny-come-lately 'saviours' of the middle classes, the left regarded Gil Robles as a fascist. Thus, while they could scarcely reject the claims of the Radical Republicans to form a government, they announced that the entry of Gil Robles' party – the largest party elected to the Cortes – into the cabinet would 'deform' the Republic, i.e. that he and his party would use their parliamentary influence to pass legislation which threatened the legislation of 1931-2. Just as the right could not tolerate that half of Spain should want to establish through their votes a modern society, so the left could not tolerate the idea that the conservative classes should be able to reverse, through the ballot-box, the 'content' that they, the left, had given the Republic.

Gil Robles had broken with the violent courses of his rich monarchist supporters once the failure of Sanjurjo's rising had exposed the futility of conspiracy. He now announced his readiness to act as a parliamentary party, though he could not bring his party to an overt declaration of loyalty to Republican institutions. The left used Gil Robles' ambiguities and his anti-democratic outbursts in his campaign speeches to deny the sincerity of his conversion to legalism, and they had some grounds for these fears when he pressed for an amnesty for General Sanjurjo, the rebel of 1932, and Calvo Sotelo, the leader of the revolutionary right. They had always regarded Gil Robles' 'accidentalism' as a mere tactical device, adopted because the right was too weak to overthrow the Republic by force. They now regarded his 'legalism' as a 'Trojan horse' tactic, a device to infiltrate Republican institutions in order to destroy them and replace them by an authoritarian, Catholic, corporate state. They claimed he supported Lerroux in the Cortes, not because he had any faith in parliamentary institutions, but because, without an overall majority, he had no alternative. He had not achieved the full power he so insistently demanded in the election campaign. He would now achieve it by stages.

Gil Robles had declared himself an anti-Marxist; that socialism must be defeated at all costs. His followers talked of purging the fatherland of judaizing Freemasons. To Socialists, 'an anti-Marxist front is a fascist front'. It was a simplification, understandable in terms of socialist fears. Socialism had been brutally crushed in Germany by Hitler and in Austria by Dolfuss, a Catholic authoritarian whose social ideas were not unlike those of Gil Robles. Was Spain next on the list? Was Gil Robles a 'Spanish Dolfuss'? When he had declared in the election campaign that 'Democracy is not an end but a means to the conquest of the new state,' would that new state include Socialists?

With the fate of Socialism in Europe in view, the minds of militant socialists (especially among the Socialist Youth) became dominated by slogans with revolutionary overtones: 'Either Socialism or fascism'; 'We must prepare to assault power'; 'It is necessary to adopt whatever means are necessary for the total implantation of Socialism'. Moderates like Professor Besteiro fought against this language and this mood. Besteiro, stern critic of Largo Caballero's 'collaborationism' in the past, was even more appalled by this new lurch into revolutionary infantilism. 'It is more revolutionary to oppose collective madness than to allow oneself to be dragged along by it.' Largo Caballero and his supporters were mad; but they were gaining ground. In January 1934 Besteiro and his allies lost all control of the PSOE and the UGT to Largo Caballero, intoxicated by his new image as 'the Spanish Lenin'. By February the party and union executives were committed to armed revolution.

Yet the Socialists were ill prepared for such a venture. It was one thing to use the language of Lenin; another to act as Lenin acted. Moreover, their relations with the more militant CNT and the Communists were unsatisfactory. Indeed it has been argued that their talk of revolution was a mere threat to force President Alcalá Zamora to call back the Azaña coalition to power. Thus when the revolution came in protest against the entry of the three CEDA ministers in October 1934, it was not a national revolution but was confined to two areas: Asturias and Catalonia. Only in Asturias did the CNT, the UGT and the Communists come together in a workers' alliance and therefore feel strong enough to rise. In Barcelona the Catalan nationalists, fearing an attack by the right on their newly won autonomy and radicalized by the emergence of an ultra-nationalist fascistoid wing, rose half-heartedly in Barcelona without the support of the CNT. The Spanish Left Republicans were opposed to revolution; but they could neither stop it nor could they, had it been successful, have disowned it. It can be argued that Azaña did not set his face as firmly against revolution in 1934 as Gil Robles had done in 1932.

The 'Red Days' of the October Revolution of 1934 when, for a fortnight, the mining districts of Asturias were controlled by workers' committees of the Socialist Republic and the 'Red army' militia with its famous dynamiters, were a watershed in the history of the Republic. They created with the slogan 'Unite Proletarian Brothers' a solidarity amongst the proletarian parties – Socialists, anarcho-syndicalists and Communists – which, if it never came to formal union, never quite lost its emotional force. With its brutal repression by native troops and Foreign Legionaries brought over from the Spanish Moroccan Protectorate, the Asturias rising reached the dimensions of a civil war with four thousand casualties and a great deal of physical destruction caused by the miners' attempt to take Oviedo.

When it was over, the nation was morally divided between those who favoured repression and those who did not. Surrender of the vanquished did not reassure the victors, or discourage the defeated. 'We have been beaten only for the time being. . . . Our surrender is simply a halt on the road where we correct our mistakes, preparing for the next battle which must end in final victory of the exploited.' Asturias divided Europe as well as Spain: the charges of atrocities committed by both sides exercised the consciences of right and left, and were taken up in the European press. Like the October Revolution itself, this was a prelude to the greater resonances and divisions of July 1936. More immediately important, it divided the Socialist movement around the contrasting personalities of Prieto, a journalist, witty and with contacts among bourgeois politicians, and Largo Caballero, a trades union leader who had been a plasterer and who had taught himself to read at the age of twenty. Prieto now rejected revolution – it had failed because the workers were not strong enough – for a working relationship with left-wing bourgeois Republicans; Largo Caballero blamed the Republicans for failure and drew away from them towards a proletarian alliance such as that forged in Asturias.

IV

The year after the Asturian revolution saw the failure of Gil Robles' famous tactic – the assumption of complete power when the Radicals proved too weak to govern. They did, indeed, discredit themselves with a series of financial scandals; but President Alcalá Zamora refused to hand over the government to Gil Robles whose Republican loyalty he mistrusted.* Instead, he formed a weak centrist government (which he hoped, in the old-fashioned style, would be able to favour the electoral fortunes of his own Catholic Republican right) and called a general election for February 1936.

While the Asturian rebellion had terrified the right with the spectre of a Soviet Spain, the repression provided Azaña with

* In the Lerroux government of May 1935–September 1936 Gil Robles became Minister of War and had four other members of his party in government. This was the nearest he came to the 'power' he so insistently claimed.

emotional support for the re-creation of the Socialist-Left Republican coalition. As the Popular Front, it fought the elections of February 1936 and won an unexpected triumph over the CEDA; but this 'triumph' hid the fact that nearly half of Spain voted against the Popular Front.

It has been argued that the polarization of Spanish political life into two antagonistic blocs was the consequence of an electoral system, the mechanics of which crushed the centre. An analysis of the figures does reveal a 'hidden' centre vote; the system of lists meant that two mammoth electoral coalitions – each composed of various parties – confronted each other; no small party stood a chance alone and must seek allies either to the right or to the left. The change from 1933 was that the left coalition was well organized while that of the right – of which CEDA was the core – was weak, put together at the last moment as a result of deals which inhibited a clear programme. Even if the polarization was a consequence of an inept law, the campaign itself was bitter and tended to create in the minds of Spaniards the notion of two blocs. The Popular Front hammered home the threat of fascism and the Republic in danger. Largo Caballero announced that his party would accept the electoral victory of the Popular Front and work within it; but if the right won, 'we must of necessity move to civil war. And don't let the right have any illusions and say that this is an idle threat. This is a warning. We don't say things for the sake of saying them. Remember October' [26 January]. Gil Robles' posters blared out from every wall 'Against the Revolution and its accomplices [The Socialists and their left Republican electoral allies]. Vote for Spain.' The language of the right was, as it had long been, full of military metaphor and exaggeration: the left wanted a *reparto* (sharing out) not merely of property but also of women. 'The hosts are drawn up against each other'; on the one side God, Spain and order; on the other revolution. 'For God and Country; to conquer or to die.'

The right was defeated; but it did not accept its defeat, arguing that it was the consequence of illicit pressure and the ruthless use of a parliamentary majority by the Popular Front to increase its strength by giving disputed elections to its own supporters. Chapaprieta, who in the last months of the Two Black Years had struggled to patch together some sort of centre-conservative government, was appalled at the victory of the left. It meant 'the end of bourgeois Spain and its civilization'. By March 1936 he was advising President Alcalá Zamora to call on a general to form a government to save civilization.

V

What was the balance of the Two Black Years, what was their political and social significance? It was not a period of resolute reaction. Socialists were jailed, their clubs closed, but the movement remained legal. The Catalan Statute was suspended, not repealed. Left-wing mayors and town councils were sacked; some union branches were closed down. But, it can be argued, this was the kind of harassment to which the right had been subjected by Azaña – a harassment that was always counter-productive in that it encouraged outraged protest against the violation of democratic principle by the government without being firm and harsh enough to make protest, as such, impossible. Only after the left had risen against the conservative Republic in October 1934 did repression become fierce. Even then it was conspicuously less comprehensive than the extreme right demanded (and they demanded no less than the complete political liquidation of the left). If, in December 1935, Gil Robles was playing with the idea of a counter-revolutionary coup, relying on generals like Franco, it all came to nothing. To the right he lacked counter-revolutionary guts; to the reformers in his party he was a prisoner of the landlords and ex-monarchists.

Rather than a counter-revolutionary episode the Two Black Years seemed a return to the political style of the monarchy, a period of weak coalition governments interspersed with old-fashioned cabinet crises which brought out to the full Alcalá Zamora's talent for intrigue in the formation of governments (it was the President who 'called' a politician to form a ministry) and his political and personal prejudices. The President disliked Lerroux – he could not swallow a hostile speech of the tame lion at a political banquet – and distrusted Gil Robles, preferring to both colourless politicians.* The newspapers preferred to discuss the minutiae of personal politics rather than policies. The Republic did not look

---

* Alcalá Zamora's political ambition was respectable enough: to bring the Republic back to 'centre' – away from the extremes of socialism and the right. This utopian ambition finally led him to appoint a political friend, Portela Vallardes, as Prime Minister with a decree of dissolution to engineer from the Ministry of the Interior an electoral victory for the centre. Portela Vallardes was reputed to be a master of the ancient science of 'electoral geography'; but his Byzantine deals were disastrous, e.g. in Alicante.

'serious'; it seemed to be returning to the political mores of the discredited monarchy.

Under the protection of conservative governments those who had been 'punished' in the first years of the Republic recovered their privileges and took their revenge. In the countryside large landowners drove down rural wages and evicted tenants. It was the attempt of Catalan landowners to evict the *rabassaires* that sparked off the October cabinet crisis and the entry of CEDA into the government. Jiménez Fernández, CEDA Minister of Agriculture and one of the few genuine believers in the social mission of the Catholic Church, hoped to alleviate the lot of tenant farmers; but his bill was sabotaged by the right of his own party.

Gil Robles later called the Two Black Years 'sterile'; unproductive because the 'suicidal egoism' of the rich defeated what constructive social policy the more moderate members of the CEDA may have wished to implement. Given the budgetary deficit, such a constructive policy – apart from the prevailing political climate – would have been impossible. Chapaprieta as Finance Minister in 1935 and later, for a period, as Prime Minister, sought to balance the budget by drastic cuts in government spending – the pre-Keynesian orthodox recipe in times of depression – and a mild taxation of the rich. But the rich of the CEDA defeated his proposed death duties. 'The comfortably-off classes in Spain (*las clases acomodadas*)', he complained, 'fell into the grave sin of egoism for which they paid a terrible price.' For if the comfortably-off classes had it all their own way in the Two Black Years, the classes who had suffered took their revenge after their representatives had triumphed in the elections of February 1936.

4
The Popular Front in Power

The Popular Front pact put the Left Republicans in government on a programme of democratic reforms. The Socialists remained outside the government, divided between Prieto, who clung to the 'bourgeois' alliance, and Largo Caballero, who was moving rapidly towards a 'maximalist' position which implied a pure workers' government. The left and the right in the Cortes combined to dismiss Alcalá Zamora as President of the Republic, a post in which Azaña succeeded him; Azaña was replaced by his friend Casares Quiroga, a weaker politician.

The pressure of the Caballero Socialists, Communists and the anarcho-syndicalists, and the rising discontent of the landless labourers, created what the right considered a collapse of public order (church-burnings, strikes, etc.). Gil Robles' 'tactic' of legalism lost its appeal and the right turned increasingly to the authoritarian conservative Calvo Sotelo, and to the army which he hailed as the saviour of Spain. Military conspiracy in this period was organized round the UME (the Spanish Military Union) which, however, had weak links with civilian conspirators, the most active of whom were the Alfonsine monarchists, much influenced by the more belligerent Carlists, and the Falange.

Though the military rising had been planned some time before, the murder of Calvo Sotelo (13 July 1936) made revolt inevitable. The military conspirators could take up the nineteenth-century self-appointed mission of the army: to save the Spanish nation from bad government and to restore public order.

I

A vigorous Leftist-Socialist government, consolidating the old Azaña coalition, might have survived an attempt at violent overthrow *manu militari*. The increasing tensions of the spring and summer of 1936 sprang from the refusal of the Socialists to join the Popular Front government and from the reaction of the right to its own electoral failure.

The left-wing Socialists moved towards a 'maximalist' policy which rejected cooperation with bourgeois governments of Left Republicans under first Azaña and then his successor and political ally, Casares Quiroga, as prime minister. The maximalists' strategy implied continued pressure on that government for radical social reforms leading to the installation of a resolutely Socialist government. The extreme right moved towards aiming at a violent overthrow of the Popular Front government powerless, in their view, to resist a drift to the left under pressure from the left Socialists and to control 'the streets'. The legalist centre was eroded; the extremes clashed head on. The 'politics of civility', the solution of conflict by compromise, became an impossibility as the electoral spring turned into the violent summer. For those who prefer resolutely realist fiction to history, this decline into violence is described in Gironella's novel *The Cypresses believe in God*.

The leader of this maximalist trend among Socialists was Largo Caballero, the vastly experienced leader of the Socialist trades union, the UGT. He had joined the Popular Front with reluctance. It was an 'alliance with no future'. Its aims were too modest. 'The Republic that the Republicans have in mind,' ran the Popular Front pact, 'is not a Republic inspired by social and economic class considerations but by a system of democratic freedom.' Liberal reformism no longer satisfied Largo Caballero; he had seen its limitations as Minister of Labour in the Republican governments of 1931–3. In January he had defined the Popular Front as a 'circumstantial alliance'; the task of the Socialist movement was to go beyond this and to establish Marxist Socialism. 'Our aim is the conquest of political power. By what means? Those we are able to use ... by acting with the Left Republicans we are giving up absolutely nothing of our ideology and action.' His followers talked of the 'dictatorship of the proletariat'; in June he invited the Republicans to withdraw from government and 'leave things to the working class'. His language was violent enough to scare any respectable bourgeois: 'I want a Republic without a class war; but for this it is necessary that one class disappears.' His enemies in the party accused him of wanting to forge a united proletarian party in order to create the capital of a new Socialist Republic in Madrid, with himself as its *caudillo*.

In this drive for proletarian unity he was supported by the Communist party, whose membership had grown fivefold in three months. 'We shall follow the path of completing the bourgeois democratic revolution,' *Mundo Obrero*, the Communist daily, declared on 18 February, 'until it brings us to a situation in which the proletariat and the peasantry themselves assume the responsibility of making the people of Spain as happy and free as the Soviet people, through the victorious achievement of Socialism, through the dictatorship of the proletariat.' There was constant talk of Spain's 'undergoing the same historical process as Russia in 1917 . . . a brief transitory phase and then the Soviets'. *Mundo Obrero* had not quite absorbed the new tactic of the Comintern: an alliance with bourgeois progressives against fascism.

This process of 'bolshevization' was bitterly contested by Largo Caballero's rival for the leadership of the Socialist movement, Indalecio Prieto, whose power base was the executive committee of the Socialist party, not the UGT. Prieto believed that the Socialist party should join the government, not seek to discredit it in order to prepare for a workers' take-over. Largo Caballero's playing with revolution he termed infantilism; if bourgeois democrats were discredited by the action of Socialists in the streets, then only the fascists would benefit. Thus throughout the spring and early summer of 1936 the Socialist movement was split from top to bottom. To Prieto and his followers, as to Besteiro and his small group, Largo Caballero was 'a cold bureaucrat who is playing the part of a mad fanatic'. To Largo Caballero Prieto was a reformist, contaminated by his contacts with the bourgeoisie, 'never a Socialist . . . envious, full of arrogance . . . believing he was superior to everyone'. This personal feud was the unedifying surface manifestation of a deep political division which was to grow with time until, finally, Prieto became an architect of the fall of Largo Caballero in May 1937.

The generals justified their rising in July on the grounds that they were thwarting a highly organized Communist plot to create a 'red' Spain. This was a propaganda invention. However, it covered fears that the 'bolshevization' of Spain by the maximalists was a distinct possibility – a possibility reflected in Largo Caballero's attempts to come to some sort of understanding with the CNT and his acceptance of negotiations for a common front with the Communists. The Communists, seeing the possibilities of exploiting Largo Caballero's genuine enthusiasm for proletarian unity, built up his role as the 'Spanish Lenin'. (The alliance with the CNT did not materialize and a fierce conflict between the UGT and CNT broke out over a building strike in June 1936. The UGT was still 'reformist' enough to accept a negotiated wage settlement; the CNT wanted a revolutionary confrontation.) Azaña's ministers backed Prieto's moderation; Prieto himself would have been ready to form a government that would have renewed the Azaña coalition; but Largo Caballero vetoed any collaboration with the bourgeois left.

'All the militants,' wrote a sympathetic observer in May, 'both anarchists and socialists, believe that only an armed insurrection can give decisive victory to the workers.' But there was no plan, no timetable, for such an insurrection. Largo Caballero was obsessed by the fear that the CNT – weakened by the secession of Pestañas's opposition syndicates and still dominated by the FAI – might outdistance him on the left and seize a revolutionary initiative; he had threatened a dictatorship of the proletariat for months, but he had no plans in July. He went to London for an international conference.* Those who believed in a proletarian take-over probably hoped that a counter-revolutionary coup of the right would clear the air and end in a workers' government of defence – a consistent illusion of the revolutionary left since 1917 and which Prieto denounced as a criminal folly. The result of leaving the bourgeois Republic undefended would be neither a workers' government, nor a successful *pronunciamiento*, but a bloody civil war.

That was precisely what happened. For, while the left were making revolutionary noises, the right were planning counter-revolution. All that was in doubt was the precise timing of that counter-revolution and the scale of the support that it might win.

II

Just as moderation and faith in parliamentary government was at a

---

* Those familiar with the history of Spanish socialism should not be surprised at Largo Caballero's combination of verbal violence and reformism in practice, of the rhetoric of revolution and the politics of compromise. It was standard behaviour, and gave the PSOE a far more revolutionary colouring than its deeds warranted.

discount on the extreme left, so it had suffered a severe blow on the extreme right. Whatever the ultimate designs hidden behind his famous 'Trojan horse' tactic, Gil Robles had always struggled with his own violent men; but in spite of a huge propaganda build-up, he had failed to win his much publicized electoral victory in February. To reactionaries and activists who had supported him as the best bet against 'Marxism', he was now expendable and his former emphasis on legalism irrelevant.

The most outspoken and enthusiastic proponents of counter-revolution were two psychologically and historically incompatible elements: the Falange and the Carlists.

The Falange, founded in October 1933, was a collection of authoritarian nationalist groupings, formed round the vivid personality of José Antonio Primo de Rivera who had entered politics to redeem the reputation of his father, the 'dictator' of 1923–30. A rhetorical patriot, his aim was to win over the working classes to the *patria* and to turn intellectuals – some of his odder ideas derived from Ortega y Gasset – against parliamentary democracy which he regarded as anti-Spanish. Spain was being torn apart by the class struggle – a legacy of 'foreign' liberalism envenomed by another importation: Marxism. For liberal capitalism the more radical Falangists had only scorn. José Antonio quoted Marx's strictures of bourgeois capitalism with its permanent injustice and its periodic crises of over-production. The old organic artisan society had been turned by 'financial capitalism' into a dehumanized agglomeration of alienated men; the citizen was reduced 'to a number on an electoral register or to a number in the queue at the factory gates'. The class struggle and the farce of inorganic democracy must be brought to an end by a revolution which would reconcile the classes in some new form of nationalist capitalism with a social conscience, engineered by a strong state which would 'reconcile the destiny of man and the destiny of the Patria'. Falangists saw in a 'revival of Empire' – vague and unreal as this might be in 1936 – the possibility of uniting all classes in a 'national enterprise' which would raise Spain from the ranks of the second-class powers, an expansionist nationalism that brought them close to the new order of Fascist Italy and Germany. This programme made little impression on unionized workers and its most explicit appeal was to the middle classes 'crushed' by 'the huge, immense, uncontrolled advance of big capital'; to the artisan put out of business by cheap factory products; to the shopkeeper undercut by the multiple store. The artisan might not produce cheap goods; but he worked with dignity and had no international connections.

The Falange was a mixture of poetry and gang warfare against socialists. 'We do not beg for crumbs; our place is in the open air watching our weapons with the stars shining above us.' The key word of this heady rhetoric was austerity. Its similarities with Italian Fascism were obvious; but so were its purely Spanish roots. Although José Antonio was moved to passion by the hard lot of the rural poor, Falangism was an urban movement which appealed, above all, to university students who disliked the grip of the governmental left on student unions.

It was, as far as numbers went, scarcely a threat (there were twenty thousand members). It failed to return a single member to the Cortes in 1936; its press was bankrupt; its leaders were arrested in March 1936; and its organization was torn by local feuds. Its street terrorism and battles with the Socialist Youth and the CNT contributed to an atmosphere of violence – thus Falangist militia attacked the building workers gathered outside the sites in the June strike and they, in turn, were shot up by CNT militants. But they did not constitute a serious threat to the government. Their relations with the rich monarchists, who at one time had seen in the Falange an instrument for the violent overthrow of the Republic, were strained; and contacts with the army were confused. José Antonio realized that without an army rising 'his' revolution could not succeed; but at the same time he feared that the Falangist revolution would be absorbed and tamed by conservative generals. On 4 May 1936 he acknowledged that 'without your force – soldiers – it will be titanically difficult for us to conquer in the fight.' Even so, on 29 June he tried to make terms with Mola which would save his militia from absorption into the army.

Because of its later prominence in the Nationalist state the Falange has been often given a prominent rôle in 1936. The monarchist right was a much more serious threat.

The monarchists shared with the Falange an increasing penchant for counter-revolutionary violence. They were divided between the rich, aristocratic Alfonsists and the more popular Carlists who rejected the claims of Alfonso XIII because his dynasty had 'betrayed' tradition and presided over a parliamentary system. They now drew together, especially as the ageing Carlist pretender had no direct heirs. Tortuous negotiations for a reconciliation of the Alfonsist and Carlist dynasties failed. But it was the more militant Traditionalists, as most Carlists now called themselves, who tended to influence towards violence the Renovación Española, founded in February 1933 in order to rally the monarchist right. The origins of Renovación lay in a group of right-wing intellectuals of whom the best known was Ramón de Maeztu, formerly the prophet of Europeanization and now a believer in a Jewish-Masonic plot against the true essence of Spain.

Both the Alfonsists and the Traditionalists were represented in the Cortes by small parties. But the Alfonsists were losing all faith in constitutionalism and the Traditionalists had never accepted the Republic *in foro interno*. As a permanent minority the monarchists had no other parliamentary rôle but that of a vociferous opposition in 1931–3 and as carping critics of the 'legalism' of the CEDA in the Two Black Years. With twenty-seven representatives in the Cortes of 1936 they saw no means of imposing their ideals except by violence.

As the classic anti-liberal party of Spain the Carlists had for a century opposed the 'mechanistic' parliamentary monarchy – 'the government of half plus one' run by Freemasons – and supported the extreme claims of the Church as the dominant power in an 'organic' state. Utopian idealists, who sought to present some modernized version of medieval society, they had a long tradition of guerrilla warfare. Before the October Revolution of 1934 they had been drilling *requetés* in the mountains of Navarre (they had obtained arms from Mussolini in 1934 and sent officers to Italy for training). After the October rising of the left in 1934 they made no attempt to conceal their determination to overthrow the 'immoral' Republic by force: '*Requetés!* Let us not forget the red of our beret, the blood we must offer for the cause.'

The militancy and passionate faith of the Carlists was not weakened by their often Byzantine internal squabbles. These centred round the new young leader of the Traditionalist Communion – Manuel Fal Conde. A dour, obstinate politician but a superb organizer (he restructured the old loose Carlist local organizations into something resembling a modern party which could expand outside the traditional strongholds in the north and east), he had no time for those Carlists who were willing to sacrifice principle and the true dynasty in order to win political friends. He made negotiations with the Alfonsists difficult and ultimately sabotaged them; his insistence on the acceptance of the full Carlist programme by the military conspirators came near to wrecking the rising of 18 July. The Conde de Rodezno, leader of Navarrese Carlism, an older man and a more accommodating politician, close to his fellow aristocrats in the Alfonsist movement, saw that Fal Conde's plan of a purely Carlist rising was a dream: the Carlists could not go it alone. For him the content of Carlism was more important than the person who represented it. It was the cautious Rodezno, not Fal Conde the militant defender of Carlist principle, who would commit Navarre to the military rising.

Navarre, the bastion of militant Carlism and scene of its past glories, was the only region of Spain where there was to be a mass rising in support of the Nationalists. Whereas the Basque Provinces of Vizcaya and Guipúzcoa supported the Popular Front government because it promised Basque home rule, their neighbours the Navarrese never forgave the Catholic Basques their 'treason' against Catholic unity. Although Basque by race they were passionate defenders of Spain, and within Spain of the local liberties of Navarre – the *fueros*. Their hatred of 'dissolvent' Basque nationalism was fierce and unremitting, a war of kith and kin, passionate and bitter. Those Basques who sacrificed Catholic Spain for the prospect of autonomy were denounced as the allies of 'Jews, Masons and Communists'. 'You must impose unity on them,' Victor Pradera, the Carlist ideologue, told Franco. 'Unity above all.'

Strident 'Castilian' nationalism was characteristic of the tone within the conservative right. It was increasingly set by Calvo Sotelo, former Finance Minister under Primo de Rivera. Much respected in rich monarchist circles, involved in Sanjurjo's 1932 coup, he had returned from his French exile in 1933 and his formidable powers as a parliamentary debater gave the Alfonsists the leader they had been looking for. In December 1934 he became leader of the Nationalist Bloc (*Bloque Nacional*). The aim of the Bloc was to weld together all those who 'rejected Parliament based on inorganic universal suffrage' in order to 'conquer the state'. Its core was composed of the Alfonsist monarchists of Renovación Española whence its funds came; the Traditionalists were not very enthusiastic joiners, and the Falange and CEDA remained outside. Rather than creating a great conservative parliamentary coalition, it merely injected life into 'the drawing-room conspirators', as Alfonso XIII called his supporters, and made the political atmosphere more heated.

Calvo Sotelo disowned old-fashioned conservatism – his model here was the French authoritarian right – and admired Roosevelt's New Deal. The nationalist state should direct a mixed economy limiting the excesses of 'financial capitalism' both in the interests of social justice and to cream off its 'improper' profits for the benefit of the *patria*. Labour could look after itself; it was the duty of the state to protect the consumer. Like José Antonio, Sotelo made a strong appeal to a frightened middle class crushed between the unions and the 'big cartels'. Such a new state must be 'an integrating State, above classes, a State which administers social justice as it administers civil and criminal justice and which bans from its territory every appeal to force in economic conflicts'. It must limit profits, plan industry, destroy trades unions. 'Faced with a State ready to realize social justice by force,' ran the Manifesto of the Bloc 'the trade unionist State is a crime.'

As a radical counter-revolutionary, Calvo Sotelo detested Gil Robles' 'milk-and-water' legalism as heartily as the Falangists. The CEDA leader had failed to implement a counter-revolution 'from above', i.e. when in power after October 1934; he now deserted legalism too late and too half-heartedly to save his credit with the activists on the right. Thus he lost his Youth Party to the more resolute Falange.* As for the Carlists, the October Revolution, for Calvo Sotelo, meant 'that the possibility of parliamentary dialogue in Spain had disappeared'. There was only one way out. His rejection of democratic procedures was absolute; democracy was 'the supreme inanity'. The civil state was a corpse consumed by worms; it could not be revivified by elections. Only a new state, 'authoritarian, integral and corporative' could save Spain. He openly appealed to the army to instal such a régime in order to save Spain from Marxism and disintegration.

As so often in its history, the Spanish right had entered an era of

---

* It seems to me that Gil Robles, at this time as before, was running two policies, one legalist and one subversive, simultaneously. If he could have engineered (possibly with the support of Prieto and Azaña) a 'centrist' government he would have supported it; since the attitude of Largo Caballero made such a government impossible and as the drift to the left continued, he was ready to support a military rising and supplied it with funds in June.

paranoid politics, embracing a Manichean vision of absolute evil and absolute good. Some vast international conspiracy was threatening the essential values of society. Spain was threatened by Marxists and Masons – the old bogey of the right – supported by international communism in whose activities General Franco had long been interested. When absolute evil confronts absolute good no compromise is possible: things must be fought out to a finish. Nor were their fears calmed by the style of the more extreme left with its reference to the beauties of the Soviet system and the relevance of the Russian model to Spain. The left, too, had its share of paranoia. Since 1934 it had seen the world as divided between fascism and democratic Socialism, Gil Robles as an agent of the Vatican, Calvo Sotelo the agent of international capitalism, and José Antonio in the pay of Mussolini (as indeed he was). In the early summer of 1936 it seemed as if the leaders of the extreme right and the extreme left were determined to show that half of the population of Spain could not live in peace with the other half.

What, one might ask, had the Republican experience meant to the 'respectable classes'? It meant the sudden entry of uncultured barbarians into regions of power hitherto inhabited by their superiors, the consequence of a vast and perilous process of mass politicization. The evidence of this process was visible in the glaring posters on every wall-space in Spain, audible on the wireless which was now available in all but the poorest villages and was also reflected in poetry. Many of the gifted poets of the 'generation of 1927' deserted aestheticism and the ivory tower of art for art's sake; (cf. Alberti's statement that from 1931 his life and work were at the 'service of the Spanish Revolution'; or García Lorca's 'We must leave lilies and jump into the mud up to our waists.') Elections were no longer gladiatorial contests between professional politicians but appeals to an electorate for their votes. Majorities were no longer created by the Minister for the Interior and his cronies – as President Alcalá Zamora had discovered to his cost in February – but were the work of organized mass parties. Politics were 'real' and the result of an election now conditioned the lives of millions.

III

We can best understand this phenomenon at local level. A study of a small Aragonese town has shown how violent, sudden and apparently thorough was this process of mass politicization. The town had been a relatively stable society of smallish proprietors and labourers, historically dominated by the *pudientes* (the 'powerful ones') who possessed enough land to enable them to set the tone of town life. Suddenly, after April 1931, the tensions between rich and less rich were dramatized and publicized; and they corresponded with the division between Catholic and anti-Catholic. Party organisers came from the city; there were mass meetings. The municipal council became the focal point for the new political rivalries. Personal relations, in the old style, became impossible. Catholics turned religious fiestas into political demonstrations; the left soaped the church steps so that the devout would slip up. Socialist control of labour exchanges destroyed old relationships in agriculture. Even women, excluded from public life in traditional Spain, began to take part in politics.

Yet the difficulties and contradictions of the Republic did not lie in mass politicization as such. What the Republic failed to do was to satisfy the masses it had politicized. Given the gradualist approach of its governments, this disappointment of expectations and the resultant tensions were inevitable. The social structure remained as it was and it was the persistence of this *ancien régime* in rural Spain that set off, in the spring of 1936, a revolution in the countryside by an exasperated rural proletariat. Sixty thousand Extremaduran *yunteros* (so called because they possessed only their team of oxen) invaded the great estates; elsewhere the Institute of Agricultural Reform was 'settling' peasants who had seized land illegally. It can be argued that, but for the outbreak of the Civil War, agrarian reform would have become a reality as the consequence of a revolution from below that the government could not have contained. This rural unrest, more than any other factor, terrified the traditional middle classes and the small farmers, who were forced to employ workers they could ill afford to pay.

When rural unrest was combined with the increasing militancy of the urban workers, culminating in a builders' strike in Madrid in the summer, the ideologues of the left sensed a pre-revolutionary atmosphere, the makings of a Spanish 1917. Luis Araquistain, one of Largo Caballero's intellectual props, argued that backward societies like Russia (in 1917) and Spain (in 1936) are open to sudden gusts of revolution. 'History, like biology, is full of leaps.' What Araquistain and the believers in 'bolshevization' forgot was that, while in Russia the forces of conservatism were, in 1917, enfeebled by war, in Spain the conservative tissue of society was rooted, living and strong. This was a point constantly stressed by Besteiro, a Marxist but a moderate, who saw that the 'bolshevization' of a traditional society would entail a dictatorship either of the left to enforce bolshevization or of the right to resist it – the latter supported by the army. It was conservative Spain which was to call a halt to the process by which the majority of Spaniards were being drawn into political life. Its core was hard, unyielding and militant. While English conservatives, with some notable exceptions, are pragmatic and yielding to pressure in order to survive by concession, the true Spanish conservatives were harsh dogmatists whose recipe for survival was resistance à l'outrance. Social conflict could not be mediated; conflicts involved ultimate values, not negotiable interests. This was the contribution of the conservative-Catholic vision of modern Spanish history as a process of degeneration, of the destruction of Spanish values by a liberalism that was the child of Protestant individualism and of the eighteenth-century Enlightenment.

General Francisco Franco,* though coming from a relatively humble Galician family, had made his way into this conservative class by a successful military career – he was in 1926 the youngest general in the army – and marriage. Though better informed and more intelligent than most of its members, he shared its prejudices, its marked distaste for the consequences of the mobilization of the masses by political parties. He subscribed to the monarchist counter-revolutionary magazine *Acción Española* and his instinctive dislike for 'politicians' was given an intellectual structure by the general attack on liberal democracy, so characteristic of the European right in the 1930s. It is curious to reflect that the Caudillo's consistent opponent in later years, Salvador de Madariaga, wrote in 1936, a criticism of 'orthodox' western democracy – 'a statistical or numerical democracy' based on

---

* Born in 1892 in El Ferrol (his father was a naval civil servant) Franco entered the Military Academy of Toledo in 1907. From 1912 to 1927 (when he became Commandant of the Military Academy of Saragossa, closed by the Republic) he served mostly in Morocco with great distinction, both in the native *Regulares* and in the Foreign Legion which he commanded. He married in 1923 and was a divisional general at the age of forty-one. In October 1934 he directed operations from Madrid against the Asturian miners and in May 1935 Gil Robles appointed him Chief of the General Staff. After the Popular Front victory he was 'relegated' to the relatively unimportant post of Military Governor of the Canary Islands. For an analysis of his political views, see below, p. 179.

universal suffrage – as incapable of facing up to the problems of the thirties and fighting off the twin totalitarianisms of the epoch. 'True liberty' could only be preserved in 'unanimous organic democracy' where only 'active' citizens participated in politics and where the class struggle would be eliminated in a state with neither trades unions nor employers' organizations. 'Excessive individualism' must not threaten the unity of the state. These were the views of a man who wished to save the liberal heritage. But it was from Madariaga's book that Franco culled his political slogan – 'organic democracy'.

Though they shared a hatred of liberal democracy, there was little in common between the political personalities of Hitler and Mussolini and that of Franco. Mussolini was a socialist until he saw the possibilities of a mass anti-socialist movement based on violence; if the working classes would not carry him to power, then the enemies of the working class would do just as well: 'I am a reactionary and revolutionary according to circumstance.' Franco was not a political opportunist, though capable of skilful political manoeuvring; he was a man of principle, a conservative cast in a rigid authoritarian mould.

Nevertheless he and his fellow conspirators fulfilled the same historical mission representing, more or less, the same economic and social forces as Mussolini in the 1920s and Hitler in the 1930s. Let us look at the Italian case. In 1920 'reds' had occupied factories and labourers had seized lands. Within the liberal state – and a weak liberal state at that – Italian conservatives could not create mass parties to capture the levers of power and government in order to resist 'bolshevization'; they therefore turned to the only instrument that could give them a semblance of mass support for reaction: the fascists whose techniques were based on violence and intimidation.

Although such parallels are dangerous, the situation in Spain in the summer of 1936 was similar. The right had failed to build up a mass party to defend its interests against 'bolshevization'. Calvo Sotelo's party was a group of aristocratic monarchists and the distressed upper middle class that could muster only 27 deputies in the Cortes of 1936. Gil Robles had likewise failed and he saw his followers desert him for more resolute counter-revolutionaries.

The difference between the rise of Fascism and the rise of the Nationalist state was that the right in Spain appealed, not to private armies and mass parties, but to the traditional instrument of political change in Spain: the army. Calvo Sotelo saw the necessity of this appeal immediately; Gil Robles, though he might play with the idea of forming a loyal opposition in a 'moderate' republic, in the end came to the same conclusion.

If the *direct* appeal to the army cut Spanish reaction off from Fascism, even more so did its attachment to Catholic values and the defence of the privileged position of the Catholic Church. (Thus the Corporate state did not appear to Spanish conservatives merely as the creation of Mussolini; it had a respectable history in Catholic social and political thought as the only alternative to 'inorganic' democracy.) Hence the influence of the French right-wing movement 'Action Française' because it avoided the 'paganism' of the Nazis. What united Fascism and Spanish reaction was a certain mimetism in political paraphernalia – uniforms, salutes, youth organizations, the women's section of the Falange – and in economic institutions and policies. Above all they derived their central ideas from a common source – the commonplaces of nineteenth-century anti-democratic and anti-Liberal thought. But there was a difference. Only the Falange believed in the desirability of a mass party. Army politicians like Franco distrusted the Falange; their chosen technique was not the manipulation of political passion but the quick, clean, officer coup. Their model was neither Hitler nor Mussolini but Primo de Rivera, the 'iron surgeon' of 1923.

5
The Conspiracy and the Rising

Prepared throughout the spring and early summer, in the later stages largely by the 'Director', General Mola, at Pamplona, the rising began in Spanish Morocco on 17 July 1936. It spread to Spanish garrisons; on the 18th to Valladolid and Seville; on the 19th, when a state of war was declared by the conspirators throughout Spain, to Saragossa, Pamplona, Burgos, Segovia, Avila, Cárceres, Zamora, León, Valencia and Salamanca; on 20 July to Galicia; on 21 July Colonel Aranda revolted in Oviedo; on 24 July Granada was taken over. Toledo remained in the hands of the Republic but Colonel Moscardó shut himself in the Alcazar with a thousand assorted Civil Guards and civilians (20 July).

On the same day that General Mola's forces started from Pamplona on their march to Madrid, General Franco landed in Morocco and took over command of the African Army (19 July) which began its air lift to the mainland on 1 August. Italian aeroplanes arrived in Morocco on 24 July and were followed by twenty Junkers transports and six Heinkel fighters from Germany. On 3 August the Army of Africa began its advance, via Extremadura, towards Madrid.

The Republican government's first reaction was to seek a compromise with the conspirators; this failed with Martínez Barrio's government on 19 July. His successor, the Republican Giral, armed the working-class militias and other para-military organizations.

Where the security forces (the Civil Guards and Assault Guards) sided with the Republic and in those towns where the proletarian forces were strong and were not deceived (as in Oviedo and Saragossa) nor left without arms (as in Seville), the rising was defeated. Thus the government held the two great cities: Barcelona and Madrid. After a fortnight's indecision the rising in Valencia failed (2 August) and with it the whole of the Levante was saved for the Republic. While Navarre was Nationalist (the word was coined on 7 August by the insurgents) the Basque Provinces of Vizcaya and Guipúzcoa defended the Republic as the best guarantee for their autonomy, formally granted in October.

I

All those who were planning the overthrow of the Popular Front government knew there was not the remotest chance of success without the support of the final arbiter of Spanish political life – the army. Those officers willing to act did not think exclusively in terms of class interest: their minds were dominated by their conception of the traditional rôle of the army and their concern for its preservation as an institution. No other officer corps in Europe had intervened so consistently and dramatically in politics; none had so clear a concept of its political rôle or had evolved so clear a political theory to justify a century of military intervention. It was the duty of the army to save the nation and the state from politicians who 'betrayed Spain' by their policies or who failed to keep public order, allowing government to 'slide into the gutter'. The officer corps was the true repository of the national will when it was frustrated by the sectional interests and private feuds of party politicians. It had created the unity of the nation now destroyed by those politicians' concessions to 'separatists' and 'communists'. The army must now rise against the government to save the nation whose real will was to be discerned in the officers' mess, not in the ballot-box.

Who were these officers, and why had they decided that the time had come to stake their careers on a risky military take-over? Regular officers, for the most part, were neither aristocrats nor gentlemen with private incomes. Constancia de la Mora, who married the chief of the Republican air force and became a Communist and a power in the Popular Front press service, was a granddaughter of the great, self-made Conservative prime minister Maura; but after a generation the Mauras considered themselves aristocrats. 'In our family,' she wrote, 'generals and lesser army officers were openly despised.' Most career officers, like General Franco himself, came from a modest middle-class background, and their life was a struggle to keep up appearances on meagre pay and allowances in provincial garrisons. Many of them sought postings to the large cities where they could take off their uniforms at lunch time and earn extra money in some form of business – a process which brought them into close contact with middle-class political reactions. As family men, they had no desire to risk their careers in a military rebellion; nor did most of them join the quasi-secret societies organized in support of the Popular Front government or to plot its overthrow. 'They lived outside the great political and social problems of the world and Spain,' wrote one of them (Segismundo Casado, who later, in the agony of the Republic at war, led the last *pronunciamiento* in Spanish history), 'they only wanted to better their conditions and receive from people the consideration they believed they deserved.' Like many middle-class Spaniards, they felt that they were not receiving due consideration from the government of the Popular Front. They had resented Azaña's army reforms of 1932, less because they were wrong in themselves in their efforts to modernize an archaic military structure, than because of the vindictive spirit with which they conceived those reforms to be inspired. The more conservative officers now resented the 'political' promotion of 'sincere' Republican officers, regardless of merit. Nothing irritates professional soldiers (except for those promoted) more than 'interference' by politicians in the military hierarchy.

General Franco was above all a professional, a soldier's soldier with a brilliant reputation made in the hard-fought Moroccan campaigns of the twenties. Immensely 'correct', he resented every slight on the army; he particularly objected to the mass political promotions made by the Azaña government between 22 and 28 February 1936. On 23 June, the very verge of rebellion, he wrote to Casares Quiroga, the Prime Minister, from his remote post in the Canary Islands, protesting against the promotion of 'inferior' officers; the army should be treated with 'consideration, fairness and justice'. General Mola had served in Africa and written a book criticizing the military reforms of the Republic and complaining of the contempt of politicians who put the officers 'in pyjamas'. He now refurbished the traditional political theory of the officer corps. Discipline (i.e. obedience to the constituted civil authorities) must not be confused with lack of dignity (*carencia de dignidad*). 'Indiscipline is justified,' he had written in 1933, 'when the abuses of power (i.e. the actions of the legal government) constitute an insult and a shame, or when they lead the nation to ruin.' In 1936 he thought the hour had come for indiscipline.

It was not against the Republic as a political régime that Mola and his fellow officers were conspiring. Though many officers had monarchist sympathies and a sense of guilt for their 'desertion' of the king in 1931, they were not plotting to restore Alfonso to his throne. Their *pronunciamiento* would be a rising against the 'content' of the Republic when in the hands of the Left Republicans and their Socialist allies.

The organization of the military conspiracy proved a difficult business, not least because the army itself was divided in a concealed civil war between those who accepted the Republic loyally and those who, like Mola, believed that the politicians were bent on destroying the army 'morally' if not physically. On 10 February 1936 General Franco, alarmed lest 'the masses should overwhelm us' after the victory of the Popular Front, was ready with the Prime Minister's cooperation to declare a state of war which would have made the army, by a recognized legal process, the effective ruler of Spain. But he was not prepared for the army to 'save Spain' by a military coup which would split the army. Much as he admired aspects of Primo de Rivera's rule he never forgot the dictator's fatal blunder in ruining what was called the 'harmony of the military family'. It must not be threatened, as it was by General Sanjurjo's premature rising in 1932. 'The army,' he stated, 'lacks the moral unity to accomplish the task.'

The impetus of the conspiracy came from a minority of junior officers, the only group in the army with any sympathy with the Falangists. 'The children are good,' wrote a conspirator, 'the commanders bad.' This accounts for the 'blindness' of the government and the President of the Republic, Azaña. They were constantly reassured by recently promoted high-ranking generals that the insistent warnings of Socialists of imminent military rebellion represented alarmism or a ploy to push the government into arming the workers' militias. They were more concerned to avoid provoking the 'neutral' officers than in building up a force against a military coup. Relatively sure of the loyalty of senior officers, the government completely underestimated the conspiratorial effectiveness of a dedicated minority of younger officers. It was Azaña who remarked with the wisdom of hindsight that 'Generals *under sixty* are a national danger'.

There was some ground for what with hindsight appears to have been irresponsible optimism. The conspirators' plans, serious after April, were nevertheless constantly modified, and the grand design often appeared to the conspirators themselves as a collection of overlapping plots destined to failure through lack of effective coordination between the junta of generals in Madrid and General Mola, who was organizing his conspiracy at Pamplona. The general plan was clear: a military take-over and declaration of a state of war in garrisons where the rebels were strong enough; where success was doubtful, troops should be confined to barracks until relieved. Since Madrid, as the seat of the government and where there was a strong union organization, was the most doubtful city in all Spain, the rebels were to march on it in the hopes that it would fall 'in a few days'. The capture of the capital would mean the final triumph of the insurgents.

The plan was a pure military operation and would put Spain under the control of juntas (local committees) dominated by officers. Cooperation with civilian elements was therefore imperfect. General Mola, who was in charge of the final organization, was on bad terms with the Falangists. The Falangists regarded generals as old-fashioned reactionaries; to most soldiers the Falange was a weird collection of youthful enthusiasts. Nor could Mola come to a satisfactory arrangement with the Carlists; he welcomed their commitment as a stiffener for his own doubtful conscripts, but he mistrusted their political ambition to implant a traditional monarchy. As late as 7 July he was writing to the Carlist leader, Fal Conde, 'You must understand that everything is paralysed by your attitude'; in desperation he twice contemplated suicide. As a man who had made his career under Primo de Rivera he wanted, at least for a period, an authoritarian, modernizing, military dictatorship. This vision of traditional military 'iron surgery' was shared, in spite of his sympathies with the Carlists, by General Sanjurjo, the recognized chief of the conspirators. He wanted a 'purely apolitical' government of soldiers. 'It is necessary that the activities of political parties cease so that the country can calm down. . . . Restructure the country destroying the present liberal parliamentary system.'

General Franco himself – a key figure given his tremendous prestige in the army – exasperated activists by his caution; more than anyone else he realized that a military coup might meet with widespread resistance in the cities, and therefore escalate rapidly into full-scale civil war. Above all he was concerned, as in February, with the 'moral unity of the army'.

Placed in virtual exile by a suspicious government as governor of the Canary Islands, his hesitations earned him from the activists the title 'Miss Canary Islands 1936'. He committed himself finally to a rising only late, and demanded in return the command of the only effective military force: The African Army.

To both civil and military conspirators the inability of the Popular Front government to keep order was the justification for rebellion; it was a symbol of some general, societal collapse, a surrender of 'essential' Spain to Marxists and Masons whose models were the materialist society of the Soviet Union or the permissive, anti-Catholic countries of the West. How 'serious' this breakdown of public order was can never be settled. From its very beginnings the Republic had been plagued with violent strikes, CNT rebellions, and outbreaks of rural desperation.* In July the CNT and the UGT had organized a joint strike of the building industry in Madrid which degenerated into violence; peasants occupying land were clashing with the Civil Guard in Extremadura and Andalusia; in Yeste, near Alicante, when six peasants were arrested for cutting down trees on a large estate, their neighbours fell on the Civil Guard with pitchforks and clubs. Eighteen peasants were killed. For those conservatives who remembered the enforced social peace of the dictatorship this was chaos; to the left it was an expression of the frustration of the disinherited after two years of reactionary government, a frustration that must be met, not by repression but by rapid legalization of land invasions. Maurín, as always, pointed to the class contradictions that bedevilled the Republic: the government of a well-intentioned bourgeoisie was presiding over a revolutionary situation.

Enthusiastic and, it must be said, naive supporters of the Popular Front like the American Ambassador Claude Bowers, maintained Spain was peaceful and that 'disorder' was a propaganda creation of the right to discredit the Popular Front government and justify its forceful overthrow; he drove over Andalusia without seeing a sign of revolutionary peasants and workers. On the other hand the right-wing press in Spain and all over the world repeated a lurid story of

* Number of days lost by strikes: 1926 – 235; 1927 – 1,311,891; 1928 – 771,293; 1929 – 313,961; 1930 – 3,745,366; 1931 – 3,843, 260; 1932 – 3,589,743; 1933 – 14,440,629; 1934 – 11,115,358. For those with longer memories Spain had seen worse strike waves and a rural jacquerie from 1917 to 1923.

church-burnings and assassinations under the Popular Front. Gil Robles catalogued them in the Cortes: 160 churches destroyed; 269 people killed; 43 newspaper offices sacked; 146 bomb explosions. The right was intoxicated or convinced by its own propaganda, its consistent exploitation of the disorder and violence for which it was itself, in part, responsible. That this disorder had reached an intolerable pitch, that 'government was in the gutter' and at the mercy of the streets, was, to the right, a central justification for military rebellion. And so it has remained ever since for Franco's apologists: the rebellion was a defensive coup to save authority in a disintegrating society.

The government's failure to enforce public order, it is important to realize, was not an invention of the counter-revolutionary right, however ruthlessly they exploited the situation. The ministry was losing control of its own agents in the provinces: the mayors and Civil Governors. Thus a neglected factor in accounting for the state of mind of the army in the summer of 1936 is the tension between Republican Civil Governors and their military counterparts. Many officers wanted to act severely against left-wing demonstrations that got out of hand; the Civil Governors, conscious of their dependence on the political support of the left, usually held back the Civil Guard. One of Franco's generals told me he found this situation 'agonizing'; it clearly weighed on Franco's own mind.

Nor was it only potential rebels who found Casares Quiroga's verbal threats against disturbers of the social peace empty tokens. The conservative Miguel Maura, a founding father of the Republic, published on 18 and 19 June an appeal for a 'national dictatorship' as the only solution for 'unbearable indiscipline' which 'the government is powerless to control',* since it was the tool of the extreme revolutionary sector of the working class. Prieto (himself stoned by a *Caballerista* at a meeting) came out against 'mindless bloodletting' after the culminating act of violence: the murder of Calvo Sotelo.

* Maura's articles have been considered as almost indistinguishable from Mola's programme. This is mistaken. Maura wanted a *civil* dictatorship 'extending from right-wing Socialists to the conservative middle classes'. It was the issue of public order and the incapacity of the government to resist the revolutionary left that drove Gil Robles from 'legalism' to support of the conspirators. 'No solution other than a military solution could be envisaged and the CEDA was ready to give it all support. I cooperated with advice, with moral support, with secret orders for collaboration, and with financial support in not insignificant amounts taken from the electoral funds of the party.' This statement in February 1942 is much toned down in his memoirs, written in the late sixties.

On 13 July, at three o'clock in the morning, Calvo Sotelo was shot in the neck by a gunman as he sat in the front seat of a government car between two government security policemen, after having been taken from his house by a Civil Guard captain. To the right, order had collapsed when their leader was murdered in the company of government agents. If the army was to act at all as the saviour of public order, it must act now or never.

But the murder of Calvo Sotelo was neither the signal nor the direct cause of a military take-over; already, on 9 July, arrangements had been made to fly General Franco from the Canary Islands to Tetuan where he would take over command of the Army of Africa. Shaving off his moustache and buckling on his general's sash he set off in an English aeroplane guided by Michelin road maps. In the north Mola had finally by-passed Fal Conde's disastrous intransigence and come to an agreement with Rodezno's Navarrese which committed them to join the rebellion. He sent the key telegram for the rising on the 18th.

As with most military conspiracies, plans leaked out and, to forestall preventive action by the government, officers committed to the conspiracy rose on 17 July in the Melilla garrison in Morocco. The atmosphere in Melilla had been tense for months. Officers known for their right-wing sympathies had been insulted in cafés and in the streets and were convinced that the workers' parties were smuggling arms across the frontier in preparation for a 'red' rising. The high command was either ignorant of the conspiracy or frightened of fostering it by punishment. On 12 July, at a banquet on manoeuvres, the conspirators felt their strength and shouted out 'coffee!' to the waiters (CAFÉ in Spanish = Comrades, Arriba Falange Española). On 17 July the committed officers took over the town; the Foreign Legion and the Moroccan Regulares obeyed without questioning; as for the other troops, 'we knew nothing about anything' wrote one of them 'and merely obeyed the orders we were given'.* The workers' resistance was soon conquered and loyal officers were arrested, later to be tried and shot.

The Moroccan rising was the signal for the army in metropolitan

---

* As in the Peninsular garrisons many troops on one year's service were on leave. There was a striking contrast in attitude between the regular units (i.e. the Legion and the Regulares) and the conscripts. José Llordes, a conscript whose testimony I quote above, cried when he learned of the shooting of his commanding officer. Llordes states that the sergeants of non-African units were loyal to the government.

Spain to resume its traditional rôle in politics. By declaring a state of war in each garrison, the army was to take over Spain.

II

By Monday 20 July it was clear to the by now exhausted journalists, who had spent two nights sitting up in the cafés round the Ministry of the Interior hoping for hard news, that the generals had lost the supreme advantage of surprise and failed in their optimum programme: the declaration of a state of war by garrisons throughout Spain. What the continuous government wireless programmes concealed – throughout the war wireless played its first major role in armed conflict – was that the rising could not be dismissed, as it had been by the prime minister on 18 July, as 'an absurd conspiracy' without prospects of success in Spain itself. Wireless bulletins on the 19th from cities that had fallen to the rebels told another story; the rising had been successful in nearly a third of Spanish territory and civil war between what the Nationalists were to call 'red Spain' and the Spain in the hands of the army must be the result.

According to the left, it was the government's refusal to hand over arms to the para-military forces of the unions that allowed the military conspirators their initial success. 'A government that refuses to arm the workers,' thundered Largo Caballero, 'is a fascist government.' It was a government, not of fascists, but of civilian legalists, appalled at the consequences of an armed struggle and willing to do anything to avoid it.

Casares Quiroga went to pieces under the pressures. 'His ministry is a madhouse and the maddest inmate is the prime minister. He is neither eating nor sleeping. He shouts and screams as if possessed. . . . He will hear nothing of arming the people and threatens to shoot anyone who takes it upon himself to do so.' Martínez Barrio,* prime minister after Casares' panic resignation, hoped to form a government that would pull the generals back from revolt; he spent the evening of the 18th and the night of the 19th telephoning every important garrison. This was not time wasted, nor was it treasonable; it probably saved Malaga and Valencia for the government. But Martínez Barrio's government of middle-of-the-

---

* Diego Martínez Barrio (b. 1883) was a former follower and minister of Lerroux. He formed his own left-wing Radical party, disgusted by Lerroux's move to the right and cooperation with Gil Robles.

road Republicans was doomed. By midnight on 19 July, the workers' militias had taken over the railway stations, the communications system and the streets. Armed patrols in motor cars – that symbol of the early days – were racing through the streets. Martínez Barrio threw in the sponge; his successor, Giral, had no alternative but to arm the workers.

The generals had always feared failure in the two greatest cities of Spain: Madrid and Barcelona. Indeed, their plan was based, as we have seen, on a march on Madrid from the garrisons that had declared against the government.

Nearly a quarter of the officers on active service were stationed in Madrid and it proved impossible for the conspirators to 'organize' them all. Most of the higher officers were loyal, as were the security forces *in toto*. For two days the hard core of conspirators hesitated against such odds and then General Fanjul, in charge of the Madrid conspiracy, shut himself up in the austere Montaña barracks, whose commander had declared himself in a state of rebellion by refusing to obey a government order to hand over the rifle locks stored in the barracks to the unions. The defenders themselves were divided and could not hope to stand up to the Assault Guards – the élite armed riot police of the Republic – and two field guns. On 20 July a huge crowd stormed the barracks and, enraged by firing after white flags had been flown by those who wished to surrender against the will of the resisters, murdered the officers, throwing them from the windows 'like rag dolls'. In the other Madrid barracks around the city, the conspirators were likewise divided and when they acted, did so in a confused and incoherent manner. Madrid was saved for the Republic; and it had been saved by the divisions in the army, the loyalty of the majority of the higher officers and the Assault Guards. The 'armed people' added enthusiasm; but it was only later that the press converted them into the main architects of victory.

In Barcelona President Companys' autonomous government of the Generalidad and the workers' organizations knew the rebels' plan: to march from the peripheral barracks to the city centre. Companys could count on the loyalty of the Republican Assault Guards and his own security forces. The CNT was the most militant workers' movement in Europe and could be relied on to fight. At dawn on 19 July, after a vote, the officers led their troops down the long straight streets towards the centre, harassed by Assault Guards and sniped at by the CNT from the side streets or from behind hastily improvised barricades. Later in the day, with the rebels under heavy fire in the central squares, the Civil Guard came out for the Republic. This was decisive. General Goded, who had arrived late in the day by hydroplane to take command of the insurgents, was captured and after much pressure announced his defeat on the wireless, releasing 'from their obligations all who have followed me'. The last rebel stronghold, the Atarazanas barracks, without food for thirty hours, was stormed by the CNT. This episode – the FAI leader Francisco Ascaso was killed in the attack – helped the CNT to claim the main rôle in the defeat of the insurgents; yet the decisive event was the intervention of the Civil Guard, and its commander became a hero of Malraux's fictional version of the early days of the war.

The myth of a CNT 'victory' persisted; it was clearly in the interests of the CNT and it fitted in with the image of a popular rising against a military coup. That this rising took place amid great enthusiasm is indubitable; but it is another matter to claim that it was *militarily* decisive. Rather afterwards did a massive burning of churches, the smell of smoke mixing with that of putrefying horses, reveal the presence and strength of the proletarian revolution.

Failure in Barcelona meant failure in the whole of Catalonia; garrison commanders waited for news by their telephones, and when Goded's surrender came over the wireless gave up the game for lost. Failure in Barcelona was due in part to the hesitations and doubts of the officers themselves – the conspiracy had been organized by a captain, and the commander of the IV Division remained loyal to the government – and their reluctance to abandon the concept of a purely military coup in the old style. As a young Catalan Falangist activist complained, soldiers thought of the civilian right 'as an additional chorus, never as a force'. He claimed that a para-military force of three thousand might have been mobilized; yet only two-hundred-odd assorted Falangists and *requetés* came out on the streets with the military.

In Seville, the third great city of Spain and a city with a strong, if divided, labour movement, the audacity of one man, General Queipo de Llano, gave an unexpected victory to the rebels. He started by assuring the civilian authorities of his loyalty – he had, after all, been a Republican conspirator in 1931. Early on the Sunday morning he rounded up doubtful officers at pistol point; then, quite alone, he confronted the commander of the garrison. 'I have come to tell you that the time has come to decide whether you support your comrades in arms or the government that is leading Spain to ruin.' When he announced his loyalty to the government Queipo de Llano threatened to shoot him, bundled him and his officers into an office and tore out the telephone wires. 'Gentlemen,' said the commander, 'I wish you to notice I am submitting only to force.' Queipo de Llano seized the radio station, giving out bulletins that persuaded lukewarm officers and civilians of his success; he then terrorized the centre of Seville by producing his handful of troops over and over again like a stage army. Once in control he proceeded to 'clean up' the working-class quarters. Convinced by wireless of the success in Seville, the garrisons rose in Cadiz and Cordoba.

The western Andalusian rising was an astonishing success, a tribute to one man's audacity and the power of a wireless station in a confused situation. Queipo de Llano, the former Republican conspirator, finished his career as a marquis in Nationalist Spain.

Elsewhere the pattern was similar if less dramatic. The second core of the Nationalist rising was Mola's organization in Castile, Aragon and León: the garrisons of Burgos, Pamplona, Valladolid and Saragossa. Once secured, they were to march on Madrid. By the 19th the main garrisons had been secured for the rebels. Except in the barracks where commanding officers sided with the rebels, the conspirators arrested or shot their superiors or handed them over to be executed – this was the fate of General Campins at Granada – and by declaring a state of war took over the civil government.

The myth soon gained currency that it was the government's failure to arm the proletarian militia that allowed the rebellion to succeed and, conversely, that it did not succeed where the armed resistance of popular forces was possible. But the critical factor, in many towns, was the attitude of the Assault Guards and the Civil Guard, who were well trained but whose loyalty to the government was suspect in spite of (or perhaps because of) massive changes in the higher commands. Where the security forces were loyal the government generally held; where they joined the rebels – as the Civil Guard did in western Andalusia – the government was lost. Two towns in Extremadura illustrate this. In Badajoz the security forces supported the government and kept the town loyal; in Caceres they sided with the rebels.

There was little that the apparently strong working-class parties and unions could do once a town was seized. Galicia was soon in the hands of the rebels in spite of strong, well-organized working-class movements in Corunna and Vigo. The strike proved a useless weapon once the rebels were in command; strikers were quite simply shot in Valladolid and Seville. Saragossa was the second capital of the CNT; the leaders of thirty thousand organized workers were deceived by the feigned loyalty of the officers and lost a vital day. Colonel Aranda mastered Oviedo, capital of 'red Asturias' by a similar stratagem. He then got rid of the workers' militia by sending them off to León to 'save' that town for the government. In towns where working-class support was *over-whelming* and enthusiastic – Valencia, Malaga – the officers hesitated and lost; elsewhere, as in conservative Avila, a colonel and fifty men could decide the day. Casualties were often surprisingly light. When two hundred troops tried to storm the civil government offices at Malaga, there was shooting and roof-sniping for several hours but apparently only one casualty.

Only in one area of Spain was there a popular reaction in support of the rebels similar to the working-class enthusiasm that came to the defence of the government in the great cities of Madrid and Barcelona; and that was in Carlist Navarre, around Pamplona. 'On the evening of 18 July, lorries hired by the mayors began to arrive from the villages far and near, crammed full with young and old of Navarre who responded to the call with indescribable enthusiasm. Each lorry, as it circled the main square of Pamplona, received an ovation from the crowds which, at the sound of the bugles, appeared at balconies hung with flags. . . . Music and applause.'

III

After two confused weeks the generals' rising divided Spain into two zones: 'red' and 'white'. Spaniards only gradually realized that they were cut off from each other as telephones, railway trains, letters and road traffic stopped at the frontiers of the zones. The failure of the rising in Barcelona, Valencia, Alicante and Malaga secured Catalonia and the Levante for the government; the centre stood with Madrid while Old Castile fell to the rebels. The northern coastal provinces, the Basque Provinces and Asturias, remained with the government; Galicia, which was left politically, fell to the insurgents in a matter of days. Santander and its province presented an opposite case. It had voted for the right throughout the Republic; both the monarchists and the Falangists were strong locally. But Mola's preparations had gone awry. The garrison was apathetic and a major loyal to the government saved the day.

The two zones did not correspond neatly either with previous political loyalty or with social class, and without the concept of 'geographical loyalty' the Civil War is incomprehensible. Those caught in either zone had to conform, escape, or risk imprisonment or shooting. Thus the bullfighters' union in Madrid supported the government; but in Vitoria the bulls were killed in honour of General Franco's wife. While the two greatest Spanish actresses took opposite sides, those theatre companies caught on tour in the rebel zone had no alternative but to earn a living by performing propagandist plays and classical drama in Nationalist cities.

Although class division was thus cut across by the accidents of war and conquest, nevertheless a division emerged, where free choice was possible. In spite of Falangist propaganda for a national, classless revolution, the unionized workers supported the Popular Front; the rich, the aristocrats and *upper*-middle classes of the old pre-1931 political and economic establishment sought protection with the Nationalists. Thus many senior civil servants and almost all diplomats defected from the legal government; the directors of the Bank of Spain who represented private shareholders vanished from Madrid.

It was the allegiance of the middle class proper – amorphous and ill-defined, including the 'traditional' middle class that fed the professions, the civil service and the army – that was in doubt. It was partly for this reason that the Communists were to expend such effort in reassuring them that the Popular Front was a respectable, moderate, democratic concern, determined to protect the property of the 'little' man. If the Communist assertion that the Republic represented *merely* a bourgeois revolution against feudalism had been true, then bourgeois loyalty would have been secured for the Popular Front. But the Republican experience in the spring and summer of 1936, in words if not in deeds, went beyond this. The allegiance of the middle classes was therefore selective. The Spanish middle class as a whole had not suffered, as had the German bourgeoisie after 1919, a dramatic deterioration in their living standards and a blow to their national pride that turned them towards Nazism. Yet the milder depression and the increasing threat of 'proletarianization' was not without its effects. Many small-time traders and professionals, historically a bulwark of Republican radicalism, saw in the strong government promised by the Nationalists a security against descent in the social scale. The 'sufferings of the middle class' had long been a standard theme. These sufferings were now seen not, as in the past, as inflicted on the modest man by his indifferent superiors, but as a price paid for working-class advances. Gerald Brenan noted 'the look of triumph on the faces of the workmen' in the streets of Malaga; this was a painful affront to traditional middle-class values, as was the cheaply produced pornography which seemed in some way to be connected with the advance of democracy.

In general, older middle-class professionals and intellectuals often sympathized with the Nationalists, driven by distaste for the proletarian style of the Popular Front: the vogue for Soviet films and literature was uncomfortably un-Spanish. The younger intellectuals, in so far as they had not been influenced by Falangism, sided with the Republic with enthusiasm – for instance, the poets Alberti and Hernández. The more prominent, older established writers had lost faith in the Republic by 1936. Others, like Antonio Machado, a schoolmaster in a poor province and the purest poetic talent in Spain, stayed with the Republic till he crossed the border in 1939 to die, broken, in France.

But the tepid and doubtful sympathy of the older generation did little to diminish the hostility of the Nationalists to intellectuals as such: they were abused in Nationalist propaganda as a 'dissolvent' element, as representatives of 'anti-Spain' influenced by the pernicious currents of a Europe in democratic decline.

The Nationalists were indeed correct in emphasizing the European inspiration of the younger generation of intellectuals, a generation which had made intellectuals a force in Spanish life as never before or since. In Ortega's words, they had restored Spanish culture to 'the place in Europe it had lost for centuries' and there is a sense in which, for a short time, intellectuals replaced the old political élite which had vanished in the twenties. Azaña was deeply influenced by French radical thought. Negrín, later Prime Minister of the Republic, is a typical representative of the middle generation of Spanish intellectuals loyal to the Republic. He had studied physiology in Germany and was a representative 'of the first

European generation' in Spain; he became a Socialist because he considered the party the most 'European' party.

If the middle classes were divided, neither did the mass of the peasantry act as a bloc, driven by economic hardship to support the declared enemies of the 'powerful ones'. The small farmers of Valencia and Alicante, relatively prosperous, were to show little enthusiasm for the social experiments of the Popular Front government in whose territory they remained till the end. The peasants of the Castilian heartland joined the Nationalists and provided, with Navarre and Galicia, the bulk of its army. This peasant basis of the Nationalist army was to be of great significance. To a certain extent it made the war a war of the countryside against the great cities, of the rural, conservative heartland against the 'progressive' periphery (except for the greatest Castilian city, Madrid). It was the Nationalists who spoke of the Castilian and Navarrese peasant as the 'moral reserve' of the nation.

As in the case of the middle classes in general, the allegiance of the peasantry was selective. In the civil wars of Mexico, Russia, China and Vietnam the allegiance of the peasantry was clear; but, as Professor Malefakis points out, this was not the case in Spain. 'In Spain . . . the Civil War was also to a very significant degree a fratricidal conflict of peasant against peasant'. The sons of the Catalan *rabassaire* fought against the families of the Castilian small farmer. As for the day labourers of the south-west, their allegiance was not in doubt. They murdered (or witnessed the murder by FAI militants) their landlords; but they quickly fell under the military dominance of the Nationalists and their revolutionary potential was therefore neutralized.

While no one can deny the class nature of the Civil War, all attempts to break down allegiances *solely* in terms of class, professional interest, status or age neglect the fact that men act by temperament as well as by interest; that in the same social situation different men perceive their interests differently; that class interests may be overlaid by religious affinities or regional interest. Where the mass of the middle class supported the Popular Front as it did in Catalonia, that allegiance was given as much out of nationalist enthusiasm as in support of a bourgeois revolution: the Popular Front would support the hard-won Catalan autonomy now effective in the Generalidad, an autonomy which the Nationalists would destroy. Only the businessmen of the *Lliga* put their class interest above the defence of Catalonia. In contrast, conservative, pious Basque peasants fought for the Republic because it was the guarantor of Basque autonomy.

The assertion that all *Africanista* officers were enthusiastic rebels, not least because their promotion was blocked by Azaña's legislation, is an oversimplification.* *Africanistas* were among the most enthusiastic and dedicated conspirators; yet many, like General Riquelme and Colonel Jurado, fought for the Republic; so did Lieutenant-Colonel Romero Bassart – his African services for which he was promoted did not prevent him becoming the political ally of the CNT in Malaga. Moscardó, the hero of the Alcazar, had seen his promotion blocked by Azaña's legislation; but so had Major Pérez Farras who went with the first CNT columns to the Aragon front. Colonels Aranda and Asensio had seen men promoted above their heads: Aranda saved Oviedo for the Nationalists, Asensio became Largo Caballero's military *éminence grise*.

The ultimate tragedy of a civil war is that it is often a war of brother against brother. The Pérez Salas family had five brothers in the army. Four served the Republic in important commands; the fifth joined the rising and became a lieutenant-general in Franco's army. As it turned out, he made a wise choice: his brother Joaquín was shot by the victors in 1939 and another went into permanent exile.

One simple fact must be stated over and over again; if *all* officers had joined the rising it might well have been successful in a matter of days. As we have seen, in Madrid the officer corps was deeply divided and its divisions doomed the conspiracy of the younger activists to failure.

Though it would be fashionable exaggeration to speak of a generational conflict, on *both* sides the tensions of the summer of 1936 revealed the pull of youth movements on older statesmen. The Revolution of October 1934 had been, according to the Socialist intellectual Araquistain, 'the work of younger proletarians'; it was the Socialist Youth (amalgamated with the Communist Youth) that encouraged Largo Caballero's move to the left, and which after July

---

* *Africanistas* were officers who had served in the Moroccan campaigns; they were the army's most professional and war-hardened officers and formed a group interest against 'sedentary' officers who were regarded by the *Africanistas* as little better than civil servants. Nevertheless the division can be exaggerated.

1936 became a dominant force in the loyal towns. It was the younger generation of CNT leaders who organized the great Madrid building strike of June 1936.

The generation gap was apparent on the other side of the barricades. Young Falangists hid their pistols from their parents in hollowed-out books; Gil Robles was under constant pressure from his own youth movement, attracted by the wilder spirits of the Falange to which it ultimately deserted. Among the Carlists the abrasive leader of the Carlist Youth, Fal Conde, outdistanced in his harsh militancy the older, more accommodating Conde de Rodezno. It was the younger officers who were the most militant conspirators; in Pamplona it was Captain Barrera who organized the garrison conspiracy, later to be taken over by General Mola. In the key rising in Morocco the older, senior officers were loyal to the government; it was an affair of majors and captains organized by a colonel. 'In the military sphere, as in the civil,' wrote José Maria Fontana, a Catalan Falangist, 'the bulk of the [Nationalist] movement was *cosa de gente joven* – a young people's affair.' If these young enthusiasts imagined they were making a world safe for the under-forties, they were sadly mistaken.

IV

I have chosen four biographies to illustrate how the acceleration of political change after 1931 and the process of mass politicization changed men's lives and determined their choices in July 1936.

Manuel Cortes was born in 1905 (the rainless year that reduced the poor to starvation) in the Andalusian hill *pueblo* of Mijas. In this remote area – the road was frightful and there was no telephone – its two thousand inhabitants made a living out of the esparto grass of the surrounding hills, the produce of vineyards, and from smuggling tobacco. There were smallholders, tenant farmers, sharecroppers and eight hundred day labourers working on the surrounding estates. Since childhood Cortes saw little but poverty, backbreaking work and the oppression of the local *cacique* and his cronies. Before 1923 elections were 'a form of terror' and under the dictatorship of Primo even mild political satire was stamped on and the village ruled by an irascible retired major.

Thus up to 1930 the *pueblo* had no real experience of politics. Suddenly, with the fall of Primo de Rivera, politics burst in. Cortes set about organizing a branch of the Landworkers' Federation

(FTT) affiliated to the UGT. It grew rapidly. The landless labourers joined *en masse*; the tenant farmers, sharecroppers and smallholders needed some persuasion to see that their interests were not in conflict with the hopes of the landless. The enemies of both were the 'powerful ones' of the village *camarilla* who had monopolized both political power and land. Suddenly, in April 1931 with the declaration of the Republic, the powerful ones were stripped of their political power. Cortes, the self-educated, socialist village barber, became first town councillor and then mayor of Mijas.

Economic power remained unaltered; it was still in the hands of the powerful. 'A lot was done about education and very little about the land.' The unions doubled the wages of the day labourers but agrarian reform stayed in the government offices at Malaga; smallholders were often too frightened to join the union or form a cooperative to challenge the landowners. In the 'Two Black Years' the landowners had it their own way. After the Popular Front victory they fought a bitter rearguard action; they simply refused to employ labour even if it meant tearing up their own vines. 'Let the Republic find you work, let the Republic feed you.' 'The landlords are attempting to stage a boycott in order to crush the labourers. . . . That's the way the bourgeoisie is here, intransigent. For them a Socialist is the very devil himself. They could never understand that they were driving the masses towards violent solutions far more extreme than any the Socialist party, for my part, would have advocated. But that's how they are, reactionary, traditionalist, frightened of any change – and with a terrible fear of the proletariat.' But now the proletariat was losing its fear of them. On May Day 1936 the local rich escaped lynching only through Cortes' influence and astuteness as mayor.

Manuel Cortes hated violence and despised the gun-toters of the CNT. But he equally believed that the Republic had been weak. 'The Republicans were always thinking about legality. Look at the business of claims I've described. That sort of legality and paperwork existed in everything.' To Cortes, even after the Popular Front victory in February 1936, the revolution remained in the hands of a new brand of Republican bureaucrats without the strength to make a clean sweep of 'everything that was old'. 1931–6 was a disillusioning experience for an overworked mayor, without funds to pay unemployment benefits and in constant battle with recalcitrant employers on the one side and extremists who lacked 'seriousness' on the other. But even if the Republic had been a disappointment there could be no doubt where his loyalties lay in July 1936. He had seen oppression all his life. He now fought for the Republic against the 'powerful ones'.

Manuel Hedilla was born three years before Manuel Cortes in a village of the northern province of Santander; his father was a civil servant whose death left his mother a hard-up widow working to keep her family 'respectable'. Educated in Catholic schools in Bilbao, he was apprenticed in the shipyards. Uninterested in politics, his whole effort was concentrated on earning enough money to support his mother. As a ship's engineer he could do this but the post-war shipping slump left him unemployed. He was saved by the ambitious public works programme of Primo de Rivera, becoming a transport contractor on the new tourist road in Cuenca. Primo de Rivera's fall put him out of a job once more and he came to Madrid to set himself up as a garage and lorry proprietor; once more he failed, a victim of the depression. All his early life, therefore, had been one long and lonely struggle to gain a decent, middle-class competence. The highest wage he earned before 1936 was six hundred pesetas a month, on which he supported a wife and two sons.

From Madrid Hedilla came back to his native province to become an engineer in a Catholic dairy farmers' cooperative and under the influence of a Capuchin monk he joined the Traditionalists. He soon joined the Falange and set about organizing a National syndicalist union. It was an uphill task. The Falange had no funds and was fighting the powerful UGT unions and their closed shop policy: recruitment in taverns brought in only marginal workers. Hedilla changed his job once more (he considered his employers 'red' because they were only feeble supporters of his struggle with the UGT) and became a supervisor in a glass factory. By the spring of 1936 his small band of enthusiasts was persecuted, its meetings broken up by the unions or prohibited by the civil governor. José Antonio had warned in November 1935 that the coming struggle might be 'more dramatic' than a mere electoral contest. The Santander Falange managed to get fifty rifles from a sympathetic officer.

Hedilla was a walking contradiction. His whole ambition had been to become an independent entrepreneur; his failure to do so, combined with an intense sympathy for the working class and a hatred of the UGT for 'politicizing' the struggle for better conditions, turned him into a radical Falangist. This was the only position that combined an attack on liberal capitalism with a rejection of the Marxism which his Catholic background made unacceptable. Hedilla fought the attempt of conservative Falangist sympathizers to set up an employers' union; he was a strong supporter of José Antonio's radical line. 'The Falange wants to dismantle the capitalist system so that its benefits may go to the producers.' As a National Councillor he helped draw up a report on unemployment. 'The principal cause of unemployment is the principle of liberal individualism that informs the present economic system . . . the profit motive.' Banks, usury, absentee landlords, multiple stores must vanish once the economy had been re-organized 'organically'. In the end, as we shall see, Hedilla failed to impose his populist radicalism on the Nationalist state; his conservative enemies won out in April 1937.

The two Manuels, Cortes and Hedilla, could not have been more of a contrast: one a self-educated free thinker, the other a Catholic schoolboy; one with a passionate belief in education, the other believing that higher education had already gone too far and that the liberal professions should be 'dignified' by restricting university entrance. One was a Marxist who had no time for the CNT and its contempt for 'serious' politics, the other had a sneaking sympathy with anarchist direct action. Yet they shared characteristics common to the best spirits on each side. They were austere men. Hedilla neither smoked nor drank, and possessed only one suit. They both believed they should serve their cause for no reward. They were both patient organizers and persistent propagandists by example and persuasion: Cortes in his barber's shop trying to persuade smallholders to combine with landless workers; Hedilla in taverns struggling to convert socialists to the true unionism.

Hedilla and Cortes came from modest backgrounds. Juan Ansaldo was an aristocratic air force officer, a friend of Primo de Rivera's family, at home on golf courses, bathing beaches and at 'La Peña', the White's of Madrid. He was a passionate monarchist, a pious Catholic and a brave and determined conspirator whose aeroplane was constantly used to carry messages and persons in repeated plots. From the day the Republic came into being he was convinced that it must be overthrown by force. And for Ansaldo there was only one force that could accomplish this: the army.

He was an active supporter of Sanjurjo's abortive coup in August 1932 and on its failure immediately set about with his monarchist friends 'to put in train a new national rising'. Again it must be a military rising ordered 'from above' by generals who could immediately take over the administration by declaring a state of war. Civilians could only be 'auxiliary elements capable only of secondary missions'. He was an active member of Renovación Española, to him a mere 'camouflage for the preparation of a military plot'. He was 'maddened' by generals like Franco who hid their intentions and would not act; he despised Gil Robles and the 'legal' right as 'monarchists of weddings and baptisms' unwilling, as they were, to risk life and fortune for the cause.

For a time he joined the Falange, because it appeared the only instrument of the violence he sought; he insisted on reprisals in the gang warfare of the militia. The 'intellectuals' of the movement could tolerate neither his monarchism nor his violence; he could not bear José Antonio's distaste for political murder and his leader's 'court of *littérateurs* and poets'. He was expelled from a movement which he had come to consider weak in numbers and purpose.

He found in Calvo Sotelo's National Bloc a more congenial home: it was, to him, a 'cover-up for and stimulus to the military coup'. He organized its militia, took a sporting pleasure in eluding the police and sending up balloons with monarchist slogans. He soon found himself at odds with most of the Bloc's leaders who could not 'abandon their political mentality', i.e. put their trust in Ansaldo's guerrillas. No one lived up to his expectations: above all Franco, whom he came to hate with his refrain 'the time has not yet come'. When the time came Ansaldo botched it. He was sent to Portugal to fly out General Sanjurjo to become the Head of State of Nationalist Spain, the Monck who would restore the monarchy. On a poor airfield he crashed and Sanjurjo was killed. The 'Franquito' he despised, and the Falangists whom he had come to see as 'foreign' fascists, triumphed.

It is impossible to understand the history of the Republic without remembering that throughout its life men like Ansaldo and his rich monarchist friends, meeting in smart restaurants and drinking 'select wines', had no other aim but to destroy it. After every failure they began again, collecting funds, approaching officers, talking in the bars of Biarritz and St Jean de Luz of the 'day'. Ansaldo, it is true, was extreme in his persistent plotting. Other rightists at times believed they might defeat the revolution by legal means: Gil Robles or even Lerroux might save Spain. But, like Ansaldo, they never abandoned 'the way of force', if legalism – as it did with Gil Robles' failure to win a crushing victory in February 1936 – yielded no dividends. The activists were let down time and time again. But even failure had its uses. To defend itself the Republic closed down newspapers, arrested politicians and prohibited meetings. 'All this accentuated the discrepancy between its [the Republican government's] theoretical democratic base and its authoritarian actions.' The attempt to repress the activist right and the revolutionary left discredited the Republic as a democratic régime; but repression failed to stamp out conspiracy and the persistence of violence discredited the Republic and 'proved' that it could not maintain 'order'.

Cortes, Hedilla and Ansaldo were conscious and committed militants. Pepe S.* was a militant *malgré lui*. 'The revolution is like a hurricane,' wrote the Mexican novelist Azuela, 'if you're in it you're not a man . . . you're a leaf, a dead leaf, blown by the wind.' So it was with Pepe S.

The father of Pepe S. was a retired provincial doctor, a Catalan by origin, who was an enthusiastic follower of Lerroux. In the last years of the dictatorship the son came to Madrid University to study law and found himself 'shouting slogans' in the streets with his fellow students. 'I was not politically minded but, like most students of my generation, I looked on Primo de Rivera as a shameful ruler. He was bankrupting the country and throwing our best intellectuals, like Unamuno, out of their jobs. Though my father had always opposed Catalan nationalism – he thought Macià† a lunatic and we never spoke Catalan at home – my cousins were in the *Esquerra* and hated Primo. So I was glad to see the back of Primo and King Alfonso. A Republic must be better than they had been.'

In 1932 Pepe S.'s father was hit by the depression because most of his income in retirement came from a small farm let out to an insolvent tenant. The son was forced to work in a bookshop at the 'humiliating' job of delivering books to customers. He could not

* A pseudonym: the person concerned was interviewed in 1950 and may still be alive.

† Macià was the founder of *Estat Català* which in the twenties proposed self-determination for a Catalan state in an Iberian Federation. He later became the first President of the Generalidad.

earn enough money, by changing jobs, to marry his sweetheart whom he had been courting for three years. He could not bring himself to join any party. He was 'muddled'; he was 'frightened'. His father, by this time, had moved with his leader to the right.

In June 1936, depressed and out of a job, he went to stay with his sweetheart's family in Saragossa. There the rising of 18 July caught him. After a month's hesitation whether he should try to get back to his own home near Barcelona or stay in Nationalist Spain, he volunteered for the Nationalist army and served throughout the war without distinction in an office job. Yet by family tradition – his father and grandfather were Republicans – economic status and nationality he should have fought on the other side.

He failed to get a commission; 'perhaps because I was not enthusiastic enough or perhaps because all my own family were for the Popular Front.' (Even so, his cousin was imprisoned in Lerida by the Popular Front.) In 1950 he was an embittered minor civil servant, the fate of many a 'geographical loyalist'.

v

What were the resources of each zone now that Spain was divided into two camps? Old Castile, León, Galicia, Navarre, Alava and within a few months a great part of western Andalusia and Extremadura were in insurgent hands. New Castile centred on Madrid, Murcia, nearly all the Mediterranean coast with its two great cities of Barcelona and Valencia remained with the government. There were thirteen million Spaniards in the Republican zone; eleven million with the insurgents.

At first sight the balance of economic forces seemed overwhelmingly favourable to the government. Prieto, in a broadcast speech in early August, insisted that, in terms of material resources, the insurgents were condemned to failure. With the gold reserves of the Bank of Spain the government could not lose. This exaggeration highlighted the fact that the financial centres – though not the financiers – remained loyal to the Popular Front. Prieto was right in emphasizing that the great industrial areas, the mixed industry of Catalonia, the heavy industry and iron of the Basque country, the coal of the Asturias and the arms industry of Vizcaya were in government hands.

Madrid was not merely the financial capital of Spain. The apparatus of administration, such as it was after July, was still centred there – the maps to plan campaigns, the statistics with which to plan the economy. The insurgents held the agrarian core of Spain: the wheat lands of Castile, the home of a conservative peasantry and three great semi-industrial cities: Saragossa, Seville and Cordoba. It was not apparent that the problem of feeding the great cities of 'red' Spain by a government that was to hold only 30% of Spain's cereal and meat producers would become a major problem by 1938. Nor was it immediately apparent that the problem of obtaining foreign exchange for the purchase of arms would be crucial for both sides. The government held the great industrial areas of Spain: but these industries – particularly in Catalonia – demanded raw materials that in turn demanded foreign exchange. The two great agricultural exports – oranges and olive oil – were produced in government territory; so was the iron of the north. But much of Andalusia would be lost, as was the iron ore of Vizcaya in the summer of 1937. In July 1936 these difficulties and losses could not be foreseen; Prieto's optimism seemed justified. The government had the means to win the war and those who had risen in arms against it 'were inevitably, inexorably fated to be conquered'.

Nor was the military balance as unfavourable to the government as was supposed by the foreign press, with its talk of an 'army rebellion'. A majority of *senior* officers were loyal to the government. What was soon to be called a 'revolt of generals' included only one general in command of an organic division (Miguel Cabanellas, at Saragossa, a soldier with a Republican past) and four divisional generals out of twenty-one; 70% of the brigadier-generals were loyal, as were a majority of the colonels. Their loyalty, as we shall see, was sometimes tepid if not treasonable. The strength of the Nationalist army was to lie in the fact that it captured the allegiance of the majority of younger officers – a cadre which the Republic could not improvise – and enough experienced senior officers to command them. 'The army' as a unit did not desert the government. If roughly half of the military resources of Spain in terms of troops and somewhat less than half of the officers remained with the government, more than half of the equipment, artillery and arms factories and almost all of the air force did so. Since the military balance was equal in the peninsula itself, the decisive factor must be the élite corps, the Army of Africa whose 24,000 men followed their officers and went over completely to the insurgents under its commander, General Franco. (After the first week of the war the balance of forces was *approximately* as follows: army, loyal to the Republic 55,000; siding with the Insurgents, 62,000; air force 3,200 to 2,200; Civil Guards and Assault Guards 40,500 to 27,000.) The African Army tipped the balance numerically as well as qualitatively.

But the Army of Africa was in Africa, and the bulk of the navy and the great Mediterranean base of Cartagena was in government hands. In the army the rank and file followed their officers in spite of Mola's fears that working-class conscripts might prove unreliable. In the navy the sailors mutinied and often murdered their officers in a class war and set up ratings' committees to run the ships. Three cruisers and a battleship, because they were based in rebel Galicia, went over to the insurgents; but the rest of the fleet, the modern destroyer and submarine flotilla remained loyal. The government thus had the means to command the Mediterranean. However inefficient the revolutionized Republican navy may have been, apart from a risky convoy on 5 August, Franco could not send the bulk of his troops by sea until the Republican fleet sailed north in September. He sent them by air. It was the failure of the Republican air force to shoot down the few lumbering Junkers transports that allowed the Army of Africa into Spain. It was the Army of Africa that was, in the early decisive months, to hold the military balance in the peninsula and it was the greatest misfortune, or blunder, that the Republic did not or could not use its superior resources to prevent it from ever reaching Spain.

6
The Summer Revolution

Giral's government in Madrid was a purely bourgeois Republican concern; as such, it was weak in face of the proletarian parties and the unions. In Barcelona the power of the CNT was irresistible and it was accepted by Companys, president of the Catalan Generalidad, as a 'parallel government' in the Anti-Fascist Militia Committee.

With the orthodox government paralysed, the workers and the unions turned their mass reaction to the rising of 18 July into a 'spontaneous revolution' in July and August. This revolution took the general name of 'collectivization' (i.e. a variety of forms of shop floor or union control). Local government was taken over by ad hoc *committees. The most unacceptable feature of the revolution was indiscriminate terrorism.*

Central government control over this spontaneous revolution for an efficient war effort was demanded by the Communists, who were gaining in strength. Since they were a political party with weak union backing, this new power could only be exercised in an 'orthodox' central government; such a strong government was desired by the bourgeois Republicans who disliked social revolution; the Communists could also hope for support from moderate Socialists like Prieto, the rival of the trades union boss, Largo Caballero.

The first solution to the problems of spontaneous revolution and a step towards the recovery of the powers of the central government was the incorporation of the revolutionary forces into government under Largo Caballero (4 September 1936) in the hope that this would 'tame' the revolution and enable a rational planning of scarce resources in the war effort. Giral's left Republican government was replaced by a ministry that included the Socialists, the Communists and the UGT as well as the Left Republicans. On 4 November, with Franco's forces on the outskirts of Madrid, the CNT entered the government. Anarcho-syndicalists thus deserted their tradition of revolutionary apoliticism and non-cooperation with bourgeois governments and sat in the same cabinet as their rivals and enemies : the UGT and the Communists.

I

'To organize the apocalypse.' Thus André Malraux, the French novelist who served as a volunteer pilot for the Republic, defined the task of Professor Giral's government of Left Republicans which had come to power after the confusions of 19 July. The enthusiasm of the early, heroic days was described by Gustav Regler, the German Communist, as 'a spirit of intoxication'; it was imprinted on the mind of Europe by photographs of clenched fists in mass rallies, of militiamen drilling and manning improvised barricades. How could this enthusiasm be transposed into a war government and an efficient military machine? For as Regler concluded, 'hot-blooded unreason . . . could never lead to the construction of an orderly state on any earlier pattern.'

An orderly state that could organize a regular army was becoming an imperious necessity. As Franco's Army of Africa closed in on Madrid in October, and as Mola advanced in the Basque country, the deficiencies of the militia system, expression of proletarian voluntarism, became increasingly apparent. It is against the advance of the Nationalist forces that we must consider the Republican efforts to organize the apocalypse.

The mass reaction which helped to defeat the generals' rising in Madrid and Barcelona weakened if it did not destroy the conventional structures of command in the Republican zone. 'The whole state apparatus,' wrote Dolores Ibarruri, the Communists' leading mass orator known as *La Pasionaria*, 'was destroyed and state power lay in the streets.' At the same time the rôle of the workers in resisting the generals became a claim to power and a proof of the efficacy of proletarian voluntarism where tepid legalism had failed. 'Spain is the UGT and the CNT' ran the slogan. For two months this was a fact.

Confronted by the union take-over, the regular government in

Barcelona (the Generalidad set up under the Statute of Autonomy) simply caved in. In the first days of the revolution the CNT leaders, fresh from the barricades, arrived in the office of Companys, President of the Generalidad, unshaven and with rifles. 'You have beaten the fascists and all is in your power' he told them. If the CNT did not need him he would resign but perhaps, he added, 'with my party comrades my name and my prestige I can be useful to you'. Since the CNT's principles forbade it entering any government – let alone a bourgeois government – this appeal of Companys gave rise to a dual system of 'parallel governments'. Effective power in Barcelona lay not with the 'legal' government of the Generalidad, but in the Central Anti-Fascist Militia Committee – a committee the CNT could join without loss of ideological face.

How are we to explain Companys' attitude? Had he, as his enemies declared, merely lost his political nerve? Was it that, given the CNT control of the streets of Barcelona, he had no alternative? 'We must either go with them (the CNT) or behind them, for in the long run they must dictate the law.' Was it that he sincerely believed that the historic mission of his party, the Esquerra, was to domesticate 'the blind and destructive revolution' of the CNT, to use its force to convert Catalonia into a respectable social democratic state? 'I have said and I say again that the time has come that political power should pass to the working classes.' Or was his strategy more machiavellian? The mindless revolution of the CNT would exhaust itself, leaving the field to the Esquerra? In July, however, the CNT was in the saddle. But, as Maurin hammered home, its seat was precarious. It should have swallowed its principles and seized *political* power for the workers: the opportunity to do so would not recur.

In Madrid the take-over was less drastic and public. Giral's government was largely replaced by the unions and proletarian parties; its messages were monitored by the UGT, already in complete control of transport, the wireless system and telephones. Only by shooting the workers could the government have recovered control; and this Azaña and his ministers were unwilling to contemplate.

In small towns and villages all over Republican Spain the surrender was repeated; a committee of the Popular Front, weighted often in favour of the locally dominant political forces, replaced or controlled the mayor and municipality and thus severed the connection with the state apparatus.* The conventional authority of civil governors and mayors disappeared. 'The workers and militiamen's committees,' wrote a French journalist from Malaga in early August, 'hold all power here. The Civil Governor is a mere rubber stamp. He is a pale Girondin trembling before Jacobins beside whom ours were small children.' At the entrances of villages men in armbands sat with shotguns to defend their newly won independence; their colleagues on the committees taxed the town, requisitioned food and confiscated the land and factories of the 'factious', their militia replacing the Civil Guard as the guardians of public order. Picturesque as this revolution was in its re-enactment of the local juntas set up in the early days of the War of Independence of 1808 to resist the French invaders, it pushed the war effort into the background. Borkenau, who was repeatedly halted by village guards on his journalist's visits to the front remarked, 'all the villages and towns which we passed through, though passionately guarding their own territory, have not sent a single man to the front.'

The least attractive side of the collapse of central government authority and the dominance of the proletarian committees was the revolutionary terror. This was rarely a mass vengeance by the dispossessed; it was more often the work of the 'uncontrollables': trigger-happy, semi-organized groups of militiamen who shot 'fascists' in cemeteries or on lonely roads. Manuel Cortes, as mayor of Mijas, struggled to save rightists who had not actively supported the rebels from the clutches of the extremists on the town committee and visiting squads of FAI militants; he was labelled as a fascist for his pains.† Estimates of victims vary wildly from twenty thousand to a hundred thousand.

How are we to account for this terror? There was an atavistic reversion to the priest murders and anti-clerical violence of the 1830s – even down to the traditional stories of poisoned sweets given to children by nuns. The murder of 6,832 priests in the

---

* The Committees varied in origin, composition and function; some were the electoral committees of the Popular Front, chaired by the mayor; some were elected by the unions, some self-appointed.

† So were many moderate leftists in the Levante. Denia, now a tourist centre, then a small port, was terrorized by 'El Zaragozano', whose gang was alleged to come from neighbouring *pueblos*; the mayor and a sergeant of the Caribineers saved what lives they could. The mayor was shot as a 'red' in 1939. Denia was a town of 10,000 inhabitants of whom 40 were shot between August and November 1936.

Republican zone was politically meaningless; like the massive church-burning, it was a symbolic act performed amid general indifference by a small minority. Franz Borkenau, who visited Spain in August 1936, was surprised by 'the absence of pathological excitement among the masses'. He imagined that a Catalan church-burning would be 'an act of almost demoniac excitement of the mob, and it proved to be an administrative business'.

In part terror is the concomitant of all revolutions; they release, as the FAI leader Federica Montseny noted, 'a brutish appetite, a thirst for extermination, a lust for blood inconceivable in honest men before'. The rumour-laden atmosphere of all civil wars always sets off retaliatory killings. The September massacres of the French Revolution had their parallel in the massacres of the Carlist wars of the 1830s when stories of Carlist atrocities in the countryside set off street killings in the towns. In the first three months air raids, in particular, unleashed terror: after a raid on Alicante in which three people were killed, 'the masses' assaulted the provincial prison and 49 prisoners were shot.

The government early recognized the harm done by meaningless revolutionary violence: the *paseos* when victims were bundled into cars by 'patrols' and shot by the roadside or in cemeteries. In particular the government was embarrassed by the massacre of the prisoners of the Model Prison of Madrid committed against its wishes and under its nose. (This was a clear example of a retaliatory reaction; it was vengeance exacted on the news of the massacre of Republicans in the bull-ring of Badajoz.) Ministers saved whom they could by private deals, not by public action. There were nasty features: rackets in protection money, plain robbery and private vengeance. The CNT leaders themselves came out strongly – if late – against patrols of their own uncontrollables. 'For the sole fact of being wealthy capitalists or simply lower-middle-class people,' wrote one of them, 'hundreds of men who have nothing to do with fascism or the military revolt have been shot. Many of these have been murdered after having been forced to hand over large sums of money – money which has not gone to the support of the revolution or the war, but simply to satisfy the greed of individuals much worse than the capitalists whom they murdered in so vile and cowardly a fashion.' Throughout the summer Civil Governors and local authorities repeatedly attempted to control self-appointed execu-tioners, particularly in the Levante. Their efforts were not always successful. In November the Committee of Public Order in Alcoy, a Levante textile town where the CNT was strong, resigned *in toto* 'given our impotence to suppress and avoid such lamentable happenings (the murder of three townsmen)'.

By early 1937, with the functioning of Popular Tribunals, the wave of indiscriminate killings had become a trickle.* It was soon to be replaced by a colder terror: the destruction of political 'unreliables' on one's own side.

Atrocity stories are the 'pornography of revolution'. The Nationalists made of these indiscriminate killings a main emotional element in the defence of their cause, and their propaganda agencies spread accounts of these atrocities throughout the European Catholic and right-wing press. The British stationed in Gibraltar were Nationalist sympathizers to a man and talked obsessively of the 'brutal massacres' perpetrated by the reds. If, as by British naval officers, the war was seen 'from a purely class angle' then there was something profoundly disturbing about what seemed the systematic physical elimination of one's own class. The British navy accomplished a difficult task policing the Mediterranean, but the sympathy of the officers was never in doubt. They could not stomach a government whose supporters on the lower deck had flung the carcases of their officers overboard.

II

The unions used the power they had seized to carry through 'a proletarian revolution more profound than the Russian Revolution itself . . . the last revolutionary Iliad of the West'. The nature and scope of this revolution is the subject of some controversy. To those who believed the war would be won by discipline and centralization it was at best an irritating nuisance, at worst total disaster; only by its elimination by force could the war be won and the Republic become a government respectable enough to qualify for military aid from the western democracies. Others saw in the revolution of July and August an expression of the spontaneous creativity of the masses once liberated from the control of their social superiors; and, consequently, that its defeat at the hands of the forces hostile to

* The Tribunals were set up on 29 August. They were composed of 14 jurymen elected by the political parties and three judicial assessors. The moderate press made much of the crowded courtrooms, the sweating jurymen without coats, etc.; of Tribunals which were reminiscent of 'the worst excesses of the French Revolution'.

social change from below would mean the alienation of mass support and the end of any prospect of winning the war. As the anarchist Berneri put it, 'the only dilemma is this: either victory over Franco through revolutionary war, or defeat';* or as Largo Caballero's newspaper *Claridad* declared in August, 'the War and the Revolution are the same thing'.

The key concept of this revolution was collectivization – control of the means of production by workers. In the early days collectivization assumed a multiplicity of forms. 'Collectivized' factories were controlled by a workers' committee responsible to a general assembly of all the workers in a factory; 'socialized' factories were controlled by the unions; 'intervened' industries by a workers' committee and government agencies. Collectivization was both a practical necessity – the owners and technical staff had often just deserted or been 'eliminated' – and, for the proletarian parties, a doctrinal imperative. Doctrine, however, differed. Whereas the Socialists and Communists believed in 'nationalization' or 'municipalization' i.e. control from above, the CNT held to their view that workers' control meant control from below, from the factory floor. As the Saragossa conference had put it just before the war broke out, power must be 'diluted' the higher up one went. The PSUC of Catalonia – that is the Communists and Socialists – wished to leave much of small industry in private hands; only factories employing more than 250 men should be collectivized. The CNT wanted to collectivize and group together all enterprises with more than fifty employees.

Like the terror, collectivization was most intense in the areas where the CNT was powerful; elsewhere it was usually less complete and less radical – it scarcely touched the north outside Asturias. In Talavera the notice on shops 'In this firm one works collectively' merely meant that the owners paid, in agreement with the UGT, a proportion of the profits to the workers and the militia funds. In rural Aragon and industrial Catalonia, the libertarian communism of anarchist dreams sometimes became a reality. The

---

* The most able defence of Berneri's viewpoint is to be found in N. Chomsky, *American Power and the New Mandarins*. Chomsky accuses liberal historians, rightly, of neglecting the significance of the 'spontaneous' revolution. His thesis, nevertheless, demands that it was the workers who 'put down the insurrection' in Barcelona and Madrid on 19–20 July and that the revolution had no 'revolutionary vanguard'. The first proposition is as great an exaggeration of the rôle of the UGT and CNT as the second is a gross underestimation. No CNT leader would have liked to admit that the Barcelona proletariat lacked a revolutionary vanguard.

workers, under the guidance of their unions, seized factories and estates and controlled them with workers' committees. In factories 'the egoism of centuries' according to the CNT press, had been ended; on the agrarian collectives the brutal force of landowners and estate managers had been 'replaced by social love'; sometimes money 'that turns men into wolves' was 'abolished'; coffee, alcohol and prostitution frowned on; the local café closed as a 'frivolous institution'; 'capitalist' modes of thought and action overnight replaced by the *religiosité prolétarienne* of anarchist militants.

Collectivization, to its supporters both during the war and since, was a social experiment justified by the satisfaction it gave the workers and the loyalty it created. To its critics it was a system forced on workers and peasants by the union leaders. Above all, these critics maintained and still maintain, it was a calamity for war production and responsible for the alienation of middle-class support.

How 'efficient' was collectivization in meeting the vital industrial demands of a government at war? Since collectivization was most intense in Catalonia it might seem that here is a test case. Unfortunately the evidence is far from clear. Catalan industrial production declined throughout the war.* Yet, given the rapidly increasing difficulties of obtaining raw materials – coal and raw cotton for instance – and foreign exchange, this was to be expected. Moreover the switch of the economy to a war basis (workers making lipstick-cases were turned over to the production of cartridges) inevitably meant a decline in the sectors which had to make sacrifices of scarce resources to war industry: thus chemicals and metallurgy performed fairly well.

In Catalonia it was left to the Generalidad and its agencies to find some mechanism of coordination, some compromise between the new social order of workers' control, which it had no alternative but to accept in the early days, and a rational distribution of scarce resources.

This task had to be approached with caution. The Generalidad Decree which, by regulating collectivization, recognized the workers' take-over, came only on 24 October. It collectivized, without compensation, all factories employing over a hundred workers and those where the owners had fled; those employing

* Production, according to Bricall's figures, with January 1936 as 100 had sunk to 64 by August 1936, recovered to 70 by January 1937, and in 1938 sank steadily from 60 to 33.

between fifty and a hundred could be collectivized on the vote of two-thirds of the work force. This left an 'artisan' private sector, the clientèle of the Left Republican and Catalan nationalist parties. Each factory was to set up a works committee to control its activities. Coordination was to be achieved by the Economic Council (on which all parties were represented and with the workers' parties and unions predominating) and, under it, by Councils of Industry which should coordinate each branch of industry. The Economic Council had a representative on each factory committee. In November the Generalidad set up an Industrial Credit Corporation to which collectivized concerns were to pay 50% of their profits; these would be used to finance new investment and to support concerns in deficit.

These decrees recognized that 'the victory of the people (on 19 July) was equivalent to the death of capitalism'. But this did not mean that profits were to be redistributed to the workers (they disposed freely of only 15% of profits); that would merely mean setting up a new race of proprietors. The economy as a whole was to be regulated in order to suppress 'the economic contradictions of capitalism' and to return profits to the community as a whole. And that community was Catalonia, not Spain.

How did the new system, ambitious on paper and celebrated in December by the 'Day of the New Economy', work out in practice? The answer is that it did not. The overall control of the Economic Council was feeble; the CNT, represented as it was on the Council, nevertheless aimed at control by the unions, not by the Council. Unions acted as if the Council did not exist, pressing wage demands 'as if in a capitalist system'. There was a good deal of inter-union feuding. The result was that collectivized factories acted each according to its immediate interests (for instance, the factory committees often refused to authorize payments other than for wages). Above all, the Industrial Credit Corporation (Caixa de Crèdit Industrial), on paper the dynamo of the whole system, never functioned; there were few profits for it to collect and what profits there were often went to union funds. There were endless complications with foreign or part-foreign owned firms. Thus the 'new economy', so carefully planned on paper, never got under way before its enemies moved in to destroy it. Those enemies could point to 'depressed morale' and plead the necessity of establishing pre-war work patterns. (The first demand of the POUM was for a thirty-six hour week: hardly a bright start for war production.) By July 1937 the Catalan economy was controlled and regulated by the agencies of the Generalidad and the central government. The CNT utopia of a 'planned economy without state intervention' had been replaced, according to those who still believed in it, by an incompetent and wasteful bureaucracy controlled by the enemies of the revolution.

Where collectives were willingly accepted, when they concerned factories where conflicts between labour and management had been fierce, the workers found a new sense of security – an important gain, given the continuing high level of unemployment and the sharp inflation which eroded the new wage increases. Less successful was the collectivization of small enterprises – barbers, tailors, garage proprietors. If not forcibly amalgamated in a collective (as happened with Barcelona dairy shops) their owners were forced by unions to take on superfluous hands when business was bad: this was one way the unions could penalize the petty bourgeoisie and deal with unemployment. Nor were peasant farmers as eager to join collectives as were tenant farmers and landless labourers. Force was sometimes used. Koltsov, the Soviet journalist and prejudiced witness, gave a dramatic account of collectivization in rural Aragon pushed through at gunpoint by Durruti, CNT hero of the barricades, and his militia.

Unlike the Communists who sought the alliance of the rural and urban small bourgeoisie, the CNT believed *all* ownership of the means of production to be evil. 'We do not consent to the existence of small farms ... private property in land *always* creates a bourgeois mentality.' True, the CNT/FAI tried persuasion as well as force: the grocer who spent a whole day selling a few cabbages would, under the new dispensation, have time to read books; the agrarian collective would release the peasant family from grinding labour and give an opportunity for its sons to be educated and for the father to be shaved twice a week. *Solidaridad Obrera* (4 February 1937), when the CNT collectives were coming under fire, fell back on the standard criticism of the most entrepreneurially minded capitalists who held that the Catalan economy was weakened by the excessive dispersion of industry in small plants, a *minifundio* of enterprises. These artisan-like workshops and retail traders should be concentrated in collectives. 'The system of production in small units is inefficient.'

Around Valencia CNT enthusiasts succeeded in disrupting rather than revolutionizing the small-scale orange production – a valuable source of the Republic's scarce foreign exchange. CNT militia scoured the countryside 'founding' unions. 'We succeeded in rousing the villages from their slumber. All the villages *which we control with an iron will* follow the norms and directions of the CNT.' At Burriana 'we burned all the useless archives (i.e. the land registers which contained the titles of the 'old' proprietors to their property) of the Town Hall'; if the small peasant got no more land then 'all this bloodletting will have been worthless'. At Foyos the land registers – 'these scribblings which related unemotionally and with the perfect stupidity of officialdom the immense tragedy of the Spanish peasantry' – were ceremonially burnt. Yet symbolic incendiarism did not solve the central problem of Valencian rice and orange growers or earn their enthusiastic cooperation. They could not buy fertilizers from abroad and Covent Garden returned a consignment of oranges stamped 'Popular Executive Committee' as an unknown brand. A sophisticated export economy could not be revolutionized overnight.

Any judgement on collectivization as a whole, in the agrarian sector – the largest sector of the economy even in Republican Spain in the summer of 1936 – is impossible because of the diversity of local forms it assumed. (In the Levante a small *pueblo* might have three collectives [one controlled by the CNT, one by the UGT, one by the Left Republicans]. Each would be run on different lines with different results. In all there were 220 collectives in the province of Alicante.) In loyal Castile collectivization was frequently a mere change of nomenclature to cover the old system of production, with labourers working for wages but with the UGT committee replacing the expropriated landlord, and around Jaen it seems to have been successful. In the CNT collective at Castro in Andalusia visited by Borkenau, money had been duly abolished but the day labourers' conditions had not improved merely because they received their 'wages' in chits with which they could buy food from the committee store.* 'Their hatred of the upper class was far less economic than moral. They did not want to get the good living of

---

* cf. the conditions at Mijas, as described by Manuel Cortes. The committee took over expropriated estates and distributed the produce, with food as wages. 'But there wasn't any fundamental change for the tenant as sharecropper.' The beneficiaries of the village revolution were the underemployed day labourers.

those they had expropriated, but to get rid of their luxuries (including coffee-drinking) which to them seemed so many vices. Their conception of the new order which was to be brought about was thoroughly "ascetic".' To leave the self-contained moneyless world of the collectivized village and to go into the local town for purchases, the villagers around Alcora had to exchange their labour chits for cash, with the committee keeping an eye on too frequent visits to the cinema. Given the shortage of consumer goods, to preach asceticism was perhaps, as so often in Spanish history, to make a virtue of necessity.

The defenders of agrarian collectivization use two arguments. Firstly that it satisfied the dignity of a downtrodden sector of the population. This it undoubtedly did in the early months; but as the war went on the countryside got less enthusiastic about collectivization and more resentful of food levies for the towns and the militia, paid for at official prices below the market value when they were paid for at all. The second defence is that collectivization did not affect production and sometimes increased it. This, it is argued, means that collectivization could not have been 'forced' on the peasantry or hated by them;* its success, in war-time conditions, writes Chomsky, was 'amazing'. What this argument tends to neglect is that, whereas a radical change in organization may quickly lower industrial production, it is almost impossible to conceive that agricultural production could be either raised or lowered significantly within one season by any such change. What went wrong with the Republican agricultural sector, and caused near starvation in cities, was less any drastic decline in production than a breakdown in marketing mechanism. Food did not get to the towns.

Whatever its effects on morale, there can be little doubt that collectivization fragmented the economy at the very time when planning of scarce resources was a war-time necessity. Each collective committee competed for supplies 'in a more materialistic way than any bourgeois'. Horacio Prieto, secretary of the CNT, hit out at the 'atavistic property mentality' of the new syndicalism; the leading CNT economist condemned the 'lack of social spirit . . . the pronounced egocentric zeal' of collectives which considered their

* Thus defenders of collectivization point out that the Communists had to halt their campaign against the agrarian collectives in order to secure the cooperation of peasant labour for the harvest of 1937.

resources as their 'exclusive property'. In Prieto's view the economic failure of the collectives was 'notorious'.

To the latter-day defenders of collectivization and enthusiasts for the grandeur of a great social experiment, economic failure was, when not irrelevant, explicable. No bold experiment in communal control of economic life had a fair chance when impoverished and constrained by the shortages of war. More than that, it could not succeed because the social revolution which must support it was incomplete. The CNT had not 'made' the necessary national revolution; it had gone off at half-cock, affecting only certain areas and certain sectors of the economy. How could collectivization work when embedded in an incompletely revolutionized society? Manuel Cortes saw the problem: 'What's the good of doing these things in one or two places? To have any meaning it must be done on a national scale.'

The Communists exploited the contradictions of this incomplete CNT revolution. Capitalism – if roughly treated – had survived. The middle class had survived. The allegiance of this class must be secured for the war against Fascism. 'Its aid,' as the Communist Socialist Youth of the Levante put it in October, 'is invaluable'; Spain was experiencing, not a socialist but a 'bourgeois democratic revolution'. In such a revolution collectivization was 'absurd'.

The CNT made heroic efforts to make the collectivist experiment less of an absurdity in a war economy by seeking to set up some coordinating mechanism; but they could not agree among themselves, let alone impose their ideas of coordinating councils on others. The war economy was in the end coordinated, not by the CNT and its allies, but by the Republican state manned by their enemies. By 1938 the revolution of July was beginning to look like an uncomfortable memory. By March of that year the Prime Minister could speak as if collectivization had never taken place. 'The concept of private property,' declared Negrín, 'has not been modified as far as I know.'

The 'perfect economic and social system' of the collectivist experiment had to face not merely the shortages of war but the determined hostility of the Communists and their allies. Uribe, the Communist Minister of Agriculture, was determined to win for the Republic at war the allegiance of peasant proprietors – the one class which, on the whole, had little to gain from collectivization. 'We say that the property of the small farmer is sacred and that those who attack or attempt to attack that property must be regarded as enemies of the régime.' Uribe's decree of October 1936 condemned compulsory collectivization of small properties and by legalizing the seizure and collectivization of the land of *Nationalist* sympathizers, implicitly made illegal collectives on any other land so that the decree could later be used to dismantle them. The Communist solution to the agrarian problem was the retention of individual proprietorship with the proprietors organized in cooperatives. This was an organizational and ideological affront to the CNT. In the Levante, to the indignation of the CNT, the Communists set up a new union to protect small proprietors.

The Communist party mounted campaign after campaign against those 'who want to collectivize right, left and centre' as a 'sport'; they protested time and time again against the collectivization of small enterprises; they defended butchers (who left the CNT rather than be collectivized by them) and became the champions of the small barber shop. To bring all the barbers of Alicante and Denia into one establishment, they argued, was 'silly'.

For their defenders, therefore, collectives failed not through any egocentric zeal, incompetence or vice of organization, but simply because, once their initial resources were exhausted, they were denied credit by their enemies who managed the banking system and controlled foreign exchange and foreign trade. Juan Fábregas, CNT delegate on the Economic Council of Catalonia, was confronted with blank refusals in Madrid. 'It was sufficient that the new war industry in Catalonia was controlled by the workers of the CNT for the Madrid government to refuse any unconditional aid. Only in exchange for government control would they give financial assistance.' Negrín told the journalist Louis Fischer that the collectivized factories of Catalonia had spent all their cash reserves on wages and were now running to him, as Minister of Finance, for money. 'We will take advantage of their plight,' he added, 'to gain control of the factories.' In other words the collectives were to be starved into surrender by the political enemies of the CNT.

No conclusions on the viability of libertarian communism can be drawn from the troubled life of collectives; they lasted long enough to leave in the minds of the idealistic anti-communist left the tantalizing remembrance of the ideal society that, for a few brief months, seemed on the way to becoming a reality.

III

Where it occurred – and it is important to remember that in many areas of the Republican zone life went on as usual – the 'spontaneous' revolution of July provided sympathetic foreign observers with the exhilarating vision, as the English poet W.H.Auden put it, of the working classes doing what their 'betters' denied their capacity to do. Kaminski was reminded of the *'tableaux de la Révolution Française'*; the ubiquity of men in dungarees, 'one of the original creations of the Spanish revolution', was a symbol of a 'Bohemian and chaotic revolution', the absence of hats 'a sign of a general proletarianization'. In Barcelona it was as if the working-class districts had invaded and taken over the bourgeois quarters: the Ritz was a canteen labelled 'Gastronomic Hotel No.1 UGT-FOSIG [the waiters' union] CNT', serving meals on the presentation of chits. Militiamen were rushing about the city in requisitioned Hispano-Suizas. The CNT-FAI headquarters were installed in the offices of the great financier and conservative Catalanist politician, Cambó. Like all revolutions, the July revolution affected the status of women – now the legal equals of men in Catalonia. The women's prison was 'abolished' by the CNT; free unions blessed revolution as 'the great aphrodisiac'. The symbols of bourgeois respectability – hats and ties – disappeared in spite of the protests of the CNT hatters' and tie-makers' union. The symbols of bourgeois beliefs, the churches, convents and monasteries, 'dens of obscurantism', had for the most part been burnt, pillaged or converted into barracks and regimental stores. Modes of behaviour that reflected class distinctions – tipping, for example – vanished.

Behind the symbolic defiance of bourgeois values legislation had changed the bourgeois concept of property; the reduction of rents by 50%, the prohibition of eviction had made much urban property valueless and expropriated a class of small rentiers. Traditional notions had been shaken by the legalization of abortion in Catalonia. Yet elements in the CNT had their own brand of respectability. Brothels were closed (they soon opened again) – 'an anarchist should merit kisses, not buy them'. Dance halls, 'as the antechambers of prostitution', were frowned on.

George Orwell was one of the many to whom revolutionary Barcelona gave the feeling of having suddenly emerged into an era of equality and freedom. Human beings were trying to behave as human beings. 'It was the first time I had ever been in a town where the working class was in the saddle. Practically every building of any size had been seized by the workers and draped with red flags or the red and black flag of the Anarchists . . . almost every church had been gutted and its images burnt. Waiters and shop walkers looked you in the face and treated you as an equal. . . . There were no private motor-cars. . . . The revolutionary posters were everywhere. . . . Down the Ramblas, the wide central artery of the town where crowds of people streamed constantly to and fro, the loud speakers were bellowing revolutionary songs all day and far into the night. . . . In outward appearance it was a town in which the wealthy classs had practically ceased to exist.'

It is significant that the extremes of revolutionary euphoria which so impressed foreign sympathizers were largely confined to Barcelona, the Catalan towns and Durruti's fief in Aragon, and that they lasted only a few months. The general feeling of a workers' take-over in the first days was emphasized by the fact that the first reaction of the unions to the rebellion was the declaration of a general strike: the workers, therefore, were free to parade in the streets. Already in September Borkenau found Barcelona quiet and empty – 'the revolutionary fever is withering away'. Valencia remained 'a petty bourgeois town'; Madrid itself did not impress visitors who had seen Barcelona as a revolutionary capital. 'Cafés are full, in Madrid as in Barcelona, but here they are filled by a different type of people, journalists, state employees, all sorts of intelligentsia; the working-class element is still in a minority.' The visual indices of revolution were absent; churches were closed, not burned down; workers with rifles parading in the street were 'quite exceptional'. Begging had disappeared in Barcelona; it was visible in Valencia; in Madrid it was obtrusive.

This contrast between a 'serious' Madrid, preoccupied by the advance of Franco's army and Barcelona, where the CNT was talking of a revolutionary take-over once Saragossa had fallen but where no serious military effort to take it was evident, depressed more perceptive minds. Barcelona seemed a city of endless talk of the revolution or of crushing the revolution, and behind the excitements of the revolutionary façade these observers sensed a city divided against itself politically, and an unpleasant atmosphere of party feuding.

T.C.Worsley, a naive British observer early in 1937, was

appalled at the sectarian bitterness of Barcelona; instead of enthusiasm for a Popular Front he found an atmosphere of mutual abuse – largely, for the reasons which we shall see, between the Communists on the one hand and the CNT and other extreme left groups on the other – with the Communists specializing in an acrid mixture of contempt for the intellectual level of anarchist rhetoric and fear of its possible consequences. 'Barcelona,' Worsley writes, 'just because of its distance from the war itself, seemed to have this curiously embittering effect on people. Everyone seemed to be ready, at the slightest provocation, to start a malicious, ugly little row.' By January these rows were public property; by May 1937 they had degenerated into street fighting.

The security for the spontaneous revolution, where it had taken place and above all in Catalonia, was the workers' militia. The militia had vastly expanded after 18 July – like the pullulation of committees and the seizure of estates, this represented the completion of a process begun in February 1936 when the unions began forming para-military forces. Once the militia were detached from their anchorage in the syndicates and merged in a regular army, the revolutionary conquests of July would be defenceless. Hence the resistance of the CNT to 'militarization' of the militia and its conversion into a disciplined, regular 'Popular Army' dependent not on parties and unions but on the central government. The CNT wanted its own army to preserve its own revolution. From a revolutionary point of view the central failure of the CNT was its incapacity to create in the first month an efficient revolutionary army; this doomed to failure its consistent obstruction of any efforts to create a conventional army based on conscription, which it considered 'reactionary'. 'Militiamen Yes; Soldiers No.'

IV

It is a strange paradox that the Communists, cast in Nationalist propaganda as the architects of a 'red' Spain, were most concerned to dismantle the revolutionary conquests of July and August, restore orthodox governmental controls and militarize the militia; in short, to restore the power of the central government of Madrid and to create a regular army under its control.

Their motives were mixed. The Spanish party was subject to Soviet direction. Stalin's search for an effective alliance via Popular

Fronts with the western democracies against Germany meant that the Popular Front in Spain must be presented as a bourgeois-worker alliance in defence of democracy against Fascism; a 'red' Spain would scare well-meaning and cooperative liberals in France and Britain whom the Communists hoped to bring into Popular Fronts. Soviet officials and advisers, who soon came to play an important rôle in Spain, instinctively distrusted revolutionary enthusiasm and believed in discipline. Stalin's treason trials were at this very moment eliminating the last traces of revolutionary spontaneity in Russia. Rudolf Rocker, the anarchist, believed that the success of the spontaneous libertarian revolution in Spain would prove to 'the Russian autocrats . . . that the much-vaunted "necessity of a dictatorship" is nothing more than one vast fraud which has led to the dictatorship of Stalin.'

A most powerful motive for the Communist apostolate of moderation and the bourgeois alliance was, however, rooted in the Spanish situation. The Spanish party was small, though growing fast; as its failure to create a large body of affiliated syndicates revealed, it had little mass working-class support. Its growing influence could *only* be exercised effectively in a 'normal' government which had dismantled the competing syndicalist parallel committees and police, either by directly participating in such a government itself or by influencing parties that did so participate. Its most likely allies were the white collar workers and the middle classes, dismayed at the threats of collectivization that hung over small enterprises.

Hence the Communists insisted that the revolution must be postponed and the bourgeois alliance – that is, the presence of the middle-class groups in the Popular Front governments – must be maintained at all costs. The need for bourgeois 'respectability' was reinforced by the vain hopes of effective military aid from the western democracies – France and Great Britain. This was recognized by the CNT leader Peiró in a broadcast speech in October 1936. 'From now on, those comrades who talk of implanting a perfect economic and social system are comrades who forget that capitalism has international ramifications and that our triumph depends on the warmth and sympathy that reaches us from outside.'

The Communist party's restraint of workers' take-overs (they defended Giral's pure Republican government against the criticism of the proletarian left), must have seemed strange to those who knew the history of the 1917 October revolution in Russia; a startling departure from Lenin's 'April thesis' that had demanded the destruction of bourgeois government and its replacement by a workers' government. But now the party's theorists declared that 'objective historical conditions do not permit a proletarian revolution'. The alliance of bourgeois democrats must be won by a resolute protection of their interests against the attacks of the extreme left. Time and time again Communist orators openly defended the 'small man' and ordered government. 'The Revolution that is taking place,' repeated Dolores Ibarruri, 'is a bourgeois democratic revolution.' There were signs that this radical revisionism of August, after the revolutionary noises of March, was a difficult pill for some of the younger spirits of the party to swallow. It was gilded by a new slogan: the democracy that the Communists were defending was 'a democracy with a profound social content'. Thus the Jacobins silenced the murmurings of the *enragés*. For, like the Jacobins in the French Revolution, the fact that their ultimate revolutionary credentials were impeccable allowed Communists to oppose *immediate* social revolution and pose as temporary social conservatives.

This 'conservative' alliance of the Communist party, the moderate Socialists and bourgeois Republicans was fundamental to the politics of the Civil War. 'El Campesino,' the unlettered Communist road contractor who became a commander in the Republican army, came to regard the consequent subservience of Republican politicians to Communist policies as *the* disaster of the war. 'How many Spanish politicians and military men were there who did not welcome the Communist agents with open arms and did not refuse to play their game? At least I was a convinced Communist and my attitude had some logic to it; but what logic was there in the attitude adopted by the others? Without the lack of understanding and the complicity that were almost general, would it have been possible, in the course of a few months, for a party as weak numerically as the Communist party to penetrate – and nearly dominate – the whole governmental apparatus?'

In their struggle for power and influence the Communists were helped by three factors: their control of Soviet arms supplies; the weakness and divisions of both their prospective allies and their enemies alike; the iron discipline of their own party.

As the party backed by the Soviet Union the Communists enjoyed a political and military leverage denied to liberal Republicans and Socialists who looked in vain to the western democracies for arms. It was the arms supplies of the Soviet Union which kept the Republican armies in the field. Guadalajara, the first resounding victory of the Republic, was claimed by the party as 'our victory' – the victory of Soviet tanks and of disciplined Communist units in a battle planned by Russian technicians. On 8 November, a critical day in the defence of Madrid, the Communist-organized International Brigades took up their position on the front while the Monumental cinema was showing *The Battleship Potemkin*.

It was the weakness of the bourgeois Republican parties, their lack of self-confidence, their political and social isolation after the July days, that made them respond to Communist advances. They were, Largo Caballero complained to Stalin, 'doing very little to assert their own political personality.'

Nor could the Communists have got far without the persistent divisions of the Socialists. The party played on the antagonism between the Prieto and Largo Caballero followers, manoeuvring between them to their mutual destruction. 'We managed,' wrote Jesús Hernández, a member of the Spanish Politburo and a minister, 'to derive the utmost benefit from their suicidal antagonisms' – the recurrent political vice of the Spanish left.

With politicians cast in this mould, the iron discipline, the unquestioning loyalty to the party, was an immense advantage; a discipline, a loyalty all-embracing and exclusive, 'accepted with a fanaticism which, at the same time,' wrote the Italian Communist Ettore Vanni, who worked in Valencia as a journalist, 'dehumanized us and constituted our strength'. The CNT could simply not compete in this league: it was attached to personalities and ideologies, not to a party. An ideology is open to different interpretations; a party instruction is not.

In its wider sense Communist discipline appealed to the professional classes: regular officers admired the organizational ability and singleness of purpose that created the Communist Fifth Regiment, the best military unit of the early days, and the apparent sacrifice of that regiment to the higher purpose of creating a regular army. To become a Communist was, by a curious paradox, to become respectable and to be protected by a powerful apparatus. Thus General Pozas, a professional much concerned with his military reputation, became a party member. So did José Bergamín, a Catholic intellectual and a particularly valued recruit, who was to repay party flattery by a defence of the party line.

Right-wing Socialists like Prieto, and bourgeois Republicans, supported a return to administrative normality and military orthodoxy pushed by the Communists at every meeting. The Communists would have remained relatively powerless without the support of the Left Republicans and Prieto's followers. These allies did not have to be Communist dupes; they were simply conventional politicians appalled at the chaos of competing authorities, the dissolution of customary forms of central control and the military failures of the militia system. Like the Communists themselves, they distrusted revolutionary enthusiasm as a receipt for victory in what was rapidly becoming a 'regular' war. To the enthusiasts of the CNT, if the revolution was sacrificed to the war then the war would be lost; to the Communists the revolution must be postponed until Fascism was defeated.

V

How, given the strength of the unions and the enthusiasm of the masses, was governmental concentration and the purposeful articulation of the anti-fascist forces to be achieved? Clearly the task was beyond Professor Giral's pure Republican ministry. All it did, by issuing decrees that no one obeyed outside Madrid was, by its bare existence, to maintain the principle of a central government. This was not unimportant; the Republic, if it was to gain sympathy in Europe, must present itself as the elected, legal government of Spain attacked by 'fascist rebels'. But Giral's government neither represented nor controlled the proletarian parties. The followers of Largo Caballero in the UGT dismissed it as inefficient, incompetent, a 'farce' and 'reactionary'. They wished to replace it with a workers' government. Prieto believed that only a Republican-Socialist government could present a respectable face to the outside world and, at the same time, get the workers behind it. To supporters of order, discipline and international respectability, the government, as Azaña put it, must either repress the revolution or adopt it. Since it could not repress it – since it probably lacked the means and, if it had had them, could not risk a civil war within the civil war – it attempted to 'adopt' the revolution.

The Prime Minister chosen for this task and to lead the coalition of bourgeois Republicans and proletarian parties was the 'Spanish Lenin' of Communist propaganda, Largo Caballero. To Prieto he was 'an imbecile' but he alone had enough prestige with workers' organizations to bring them to heel; he had achieved immense popularity by his regular visits to the militia holding Mola's advance in the Guadarrama mountains.

With Franco's armies advancing on Madrid Largo Caballero formed his ministry on 4 September. It included not merely the Socialists, Catalans and Left Republicans of the old Azaña coalition, but two Communists and a fellow traveller. For the first time representatives of the Communist party sat with bourgeois ministers in the same Cabinet. To observers of nineteenth-century popular revolutions in Spain, the formation of Largo Caballero's government repeated a traditional pattern. Time and time again Madrid governments, confronted with provincial revolutions and parallel governments 'took the revolution into government', as the phrase went, to recover political control.

The final step which brought all the forces of the revolution into government was the entry of the CNT into the Generalidad government in September and into the Madrid cabinet on 4 November.

The proletarian parties now had a voice in the governments of Spain and Catalonia. The price they must pay for a share of political power was the abandonment of the institutional creations of the spontaneous revolution: a politicized militia, an independent police force, and committee rule. In Barcelona, the shift towards ordered government was immediately apparent in an offensive against the parallel government of the Anti-Fascist Militia Committee and, above all, against the police functions of the militia patrols.

The decision of the CNT leaders to enter the Popular Front government in Madrid was the most momentous decision in the history of Spanish anarcho-syndicalism. It was a decision that denied the whole tradition of the movement. Federica Montseny, a minister of the new Cabinet, was a daughter of anarchists to whom the 'words *government* and *authority* signified the negation of every possibility of freedom for men. . . . What inhibitions, what anguish I had personally to overcome in order to accept that post.'

Why, then, did she and her colleagues act as they did? The simple answer is that they had no alternative in practice and their theory could not embrace the circumstances in which they found themselves. The anarcho-syndicalists, always afflicted with a peculiar brand of revolutionary optimism, had assumed that they would be the only power on the morrow of victory of the revolution. The revolution that anarcho-syndicalists had planned as their own work was handed to them in July suddenly as a reaction to a right-wing coup against a bourgeois-democratic government. 'The generals started,' wrote Federica Montseny, 'the revolution we all wanted but none of us expected.'

Their revolutionary instincts had, indeed, led them to seize effective power wherever they were the predominant force as the CNT-FAI had done in Barcelona. But they had avoided a clash with their apolitical, anti-bourgeois principles by avoiding entry into a *government* and setting up the Anti-Fascist Militia *Committee*, a step which the POUM castigated as a semantic nicety which concealed a criminal reluctance to seize political power for the working classes. Powerful in Barcelona and elsewhere in Catalonia, they were clearly not a predominant force in the Republic as a whole; if they sought to force through 'their' revolution they would not merely fail, but would, by a dictatorship, outrage libertarian principles as such and weaken the war effort against 'fascism' which, if it triumphed, would destroy both liberal democracy and the CNT alike. Anarcho-syndicalism had not developed, because it never contemplated, the political strategy of a wartime alliance of bourgeois democrats and workers' organizations against a counter-revolutionary right.

Joining the government was, therefore, a defensive act inevitable once the leaders had rejected a revolutionary dictatorship. Conscious of the growing power of their political rivals in the Popular Front government and the consequent fragility of the revolutionary conquests before the attacks of their political enemies in the ministries, the CNT leadership joined a government led by a Socialist and in which bourgeois parties were represented. This they did, in order, as Federica Montseny who became a minister in the new government told me, 'that we should not be without influence in the direction of Spanish public life'. *Fragua Social*, the CNT newspaper in Valencia, had been warning for months that 'under a cloak of democracy' their political enemies – the Communists and the Socialists – had been using the machinery of government which they controlled to reverse the revolutionary conquests; 'under the cloak of democracy' Republican mayors were taking land from the peasants and restoring 'petty feudalism'. By September it drew the inevitable conclusion. The CNT must enter the government 'to prevent trickery and impose radicalism. . . . If this be called indirect participation in politics we must not flinch from the demands of historic destiny so that the revolution may completely fulfil its aims.' The movement tried to avoid this strange interpretation of its historic destiny by somehow or other avoiding the dirty word 'government' but at the same time securing for the unions decisive power: it proposed 'auxiliary committees' to watch over ministers and then a National Council of Defence (5 UGT; 5 CNT; 4 Republicans). Horacio Prieto dismissed all this as a refusal to face unpleasant facts; with its power outside government ebbing away, the CNT must shed its principles and enter a government.

Entry into the government on 4 November opened a gap between the CNT leadership and the CNT militants that was never bridged. The militarization of the militia, the destruction of committee rule was, to the militants, a suicidal concession of a nerveless leadership in return for the doubtful protective benefits of collaboration.

What had the CNT gained in return, not merely for a sacrifice of principle but for participation in the process of the dismantling of the power base of the CNT – the committee system and the militia? Four unimportant ministries. The leaders had seen, in Federica Montseny's words, the weaknesses of revolutionary 'egoism', and that a dictatorship of its enemies would be the result of 'the constructive incapacity of the proletariat'. But instead of fighting the enemies of the revolution, the leadership had compromised with them.

The rank and file of the CNT did not share this pessimistic collaborationism; they were not yet disenchanted with their revolution. If it was surrounded by enemies the last thing the movement should do was to preside over, in government, the dismantling of the militia system.

'One cannot be in the streets and in the government,' Federica Montseny confessed. When the collaborationist tactics of the leadership reduced rather than enhanced the power of the CNT then the militants claimed that the true place of the movement, if threatened, *was* in the streets. 'We have died for the democrats too many times.' When the new government fled before Franco's advance from Madrid to Valencia – a move which the CNT ministers had failed to prevent, an early indication of their relative impotence in government – it narrowly escaped being shot up *en route* by a CNT column.

VI

Largo Caballero's government sought to achieve the stabilization of the revolution by legalizing it and, where possible, cautiously dismantling it. Militia committees were replaced by non-elected municipal councils nominated by the party bureaucracies and by government-appointed mayors. Collectivization slowed down and was codified in the General Decree of Collectivization of October. The new Communist Minister of Agriculture stopped any extension of agrarian collectivization. The police were neutralized, professionalized and cut off from any allegiance to political parties; they became a public force, not congeries of private armies. The 'uncontrollables' were brought under control. The process of turning the militia into a Popular Army with pay and regular officers was begun.

Largo Caballero strove, after his fashion, to organize the revolution as he became increasingly aware of the necessity for respectability if his government was ever to get arms from France and Britain; but he was not the man to destroy the revolutionary conquests of the syndicates themselves. He changed from overalls to a lounge suit and an Anthony Eden hat, but he remained a trades union leader. He would not condemn those whom the Communist party accused of revolutionary infantilism. As President Azaña insisted, the dilemma of July persisted. The government could neither destroy the revolution nor adopt it. The result was continued administrative confusion. Nor were the CNT ministers in a stronger position. 'They neither contained nor encouraged [the social revolution]. . . . Their presence in the government was anodyne.' Quite soon the Communists were criticizing Largo as 'a burnt-out trades union boss'. They drew even closer to his old enemies in the Socialist party and the Republican groups. His cabinet was disintegrating and his control over the factions increasingly asserted by what his opponents called his 'dictatorship'.

VII

It was not only the competing claims of parties and unions that fragmented power and weakened the central government. It is important to realize that unified government control was never established throughout the whole Republican zone. The instinctive federalism of Spain, which can only be suppressed by an 'iron surgeon', reasserted itself in July 1936 as it had in the early days of the War of Independence against Napoleon's invasion (1808). 'At the present moment,' said Martínez Barrio in January 1937, 'Spain is a federal Republic.'

Catalonia and the two loyal Basque Provinces, now called Euzkadi, both had Statutes of Autonomy. Under Companys in Barcelona, and Aguirre, leader of the Basque Catholic Nationalist Party (PNV), they were rather independent cantons than integral parts of the Republic at war. Companys himself declared that, as a result of the generals' rising, Spain had become in all but name a federal state; that the position of Catalonia as a separate unit in that state was 'an irreversible reality'. It only remained to recognize this reality *de jure*. More resolute nationalists went further. Batista y Roca, later to be a leading figure in the Catalan exile movement, told the press, 'We should recognize the fact that today (August 1936) Catalonia lives and fights as an independent people.' The Statute of 1932 had been turned by the collapse of the 'Spanish state' into an 'historical souvenir'; from this collapse must come 'the reunion of all the Catalan-speaking countries: Catalonia, the Balearic Islands, Valencia and the Catalan [speaking] zone of Aragon.' This was pan-Catalan imperialism with a vengeance. It appeared to the politicians of Madrid as an 'exploitation of the crisis of democratic Spain', a typical expression of Catalan political selfishness.

Friction developed between Madrid and Barcelona. Azaña accused Companys of 'acting against the government ... moving towards a *de facto* separatist régime', or 'playing at politics' instead of fighting a war. The Generalidad 'robbed' the central government of all the services it could lay hands on with 'the miserable pretext' that seizure was necessary in order to stop them falling into the hands of the FAI. The Generalidad quickly seized the Catalan assets of the Bank of Spain and issued its own banknotes; it pursued its own strategies with its own army. After eight months Companys had organized 'no useful armed force' and after a year the Aragon front stood where it stood after the advances of July. Later, Prieto believed that the Generalidad's conduct of its war industry was lamentable; Catalans, he maintained, would not work overtime in war factories when the Republic was desperately short of aeroplanes.

Needless to say, these verdicts of Azaña and Prieto, both hostile to Catalan claims, were not accepted by Catalan Republicans at the time, nor have they been since. Companys, executed by Franco after the war, was presented – and not only in Nationalist propaganda – as a weak, vacillating and selfish political operator ready to make any compromise with the proletarian parties in order to stay in power and enjoy its fruits in the form of cars and official banquets. In fact he had not the security forces to tame the revolution. What Madrid governments saw was the way the CNT reinforced the separatist leanings of Catalan nationalism; Companys' claims to govern Catalonia with little regard for the rest of Spain were supported by the CNT because, though he sought to control its excesses, he was willing to allow the Generalidad to preside over a collectivist revolution. The events of 19 July in Barcelona had created a tacit alliance between Catalanism and anarcho-syndicalism against the central government to which both became increasingly obnoxious. Thus once the central government recovered its control of Barcelona in May 1937 it must destroy the strength of the CNT and Catalanism alike.

What Azaña called 'frivolous provincialism' was not confined to the two autonomous governments of Catalonia and Euzkadi. Santander had its own council, even its own representative in London. Asturias was controlled by the CNT-UGT Council – later to become 'the Sovereign Council of Asturias'.* But the most striking example of revolutionary cantonalism was the Council of Aragon.

The Council of Aragon is interesting for two reasons. It was the one independent power base of the CNT-FAI and its performance and dissolution gave rise to a controversy that still remains unsolved. This controversy illustrates the great difficulties surrounding the history of the Civil War; we so often have two conflicting testimonies. The Communists regarded the Council as a

---

* Valencia is a special case of 'double power' and cantonalism. In the early days authority was divided between Martinez Barrio's Provincial Junta, an agency of the Madrid government, and a Popular Executive Committee on which the proletarian parties were dominant. The army remained in barracks. Martinez Barrio tried to dissolve the Executive Committee (23 July) but failed, and after the militia had attacked the barracks the Executive Committee became a real power. Valencia, therefore, had a similar local power structure to Barcelona and was equally independent of Madrid. This independence vanished when the central government fled to Valencia in November; Barcelona was not brought under the control of the central government until May 1937 and its independence ended when the government moved to Barcelona in November 1937.

monstrosity and ultimately destroyed it; the CNT-FAI regarded it as the supreme social achievement of the twentieth century. Both described its origins and evolution according to their party prejudices.

When Durruti's columns entered eastern Aragon they set up an enclave of libertarian Communism – organized in agricultural collectives – according to the Communists at gun point, according to the CNT with the enthusiastic support of landless labourers, tenant farmers and peasants. The CNT had, in its national *Pleno* of 15 September, come out for a National Council of Defence, a confederation of regional defence councils that would represent the maximum concession to war-time centralization compatible with anarchist principles. In fact the only regional council on the CNT pattern in existence was that of Aragon, at first entirely a CNT affair. In November it was, unwillingly, recognized by the central government, in return for the CNT concession that the Council should be composed of all parties in the Popular Front. The capital of the Council was at Caspe, and its president Joaquín Ascaso, brother of the FAI hero killed in the assault on the Atarazanas barracks.

Was Aragon under the Council the utopia described by its president? 'Speculation and usury were suppressed; an infinity of new roads constructed with the disinterested aid of the militia; telephone lines were extended; the construction of a branch line, projected but forgotten for sixteen years, was begun; the municipalities assumed their true sovereign functions; the Aragonese collectives, in spite of their shortcomings, were the marvel of the Revolution.'

Or was the Council of Aragon the corrupt tyranny described by the man who dissolved it *manu militari*, the Communist commander Lister: a collectivist nightmare, where peasants were robbed while the CNT leaders stored hams for the black market and 'ministers' lolled back in confiscated cars?

It is pointless for the historian to try to steer some middle course between anarchist and Communist testimonies; they diverge too wildly. Again, for similar reasons, it is exceedingly difficult to judge the efficacy of the Catalan war effort. Was Catalonia, as Azaña maintained, 'the great drag (*remora*) on our military action'? Or did the Generalidad succeed, where the central government would have failed, in absorbing and later 'organizing' the revolution of the

CNT-FAI? Azaña's testimony is suspect as the testimony of a defeated and embittered man conscious of a failure to assert his authority; and much of Prieto's writing is an attempt to shift the blame for the ultimate downfall of the Republic on to his political enemies.

Nevertheless there can be little doubt that the competing power centres that emerged in the summer of 1936 put great difficulties in the way of a unified economy and an efficient war effort. 'Revolutionary cantonalism' in the economic sphere was reflected in the multiplicity of local paper notes. Towns, provinces and factories issued their own notes designed to overcome a shortage of small change which made shopping a tiresome and tiring occupation. Even more serious was the failure to achieve a united military command, a single general staff – the *mando único* of the Communist slogan, immune and insulated from the pressures of political parties. This failure led General Rojo (who had to bear the military consequences of political fragmentation) to a verdict that must stand. 'In the political field, General Franco triumphed.'

7
The Counter-Revolution

Concentration of power for an effective war effort was achieved with relative ease in Nationalist Spain. With the political groupings of the right either in disarray or relatively weak, the power of the army was uncontested in the Burgos junta. Fresh from the relief of the Alcazar of Toledo, General Franco was elevated by his fellow generals to supreme command of the armed forces (21 September) and nominated as Head of the Spanish State and of Government (29 September). He was assisted by a technical junta, a purely advisory body, which replaced the generals' junta.

While neither the Vatican nor the Spanish hierarchy formally recognized the Franco régime, the blessing of the Catholic Church was not in doubt.

I

Nationalist Spain presented a contrasting picture to the political mosaic of the Popular Front. There were frictions, overlapping agencies, the persistence of traditional bureaucratic techniques, the chaos of competing political tribes – Falangists, Carlists, Alfonsine monarchists, the remnants of the CEDA, even conservative, right-wing Republicans – and no formal government at all until 23 July. But from the outset political control was firmly in the hands of the generals. The declaration of a state of war gave the generals the legal basis for their local authority; political activity and union action was simply forbidden. Once Franco had become Head of State his authority was never seriously challenged: he was the indisputable *caudillo* and with him the army became the backbone of the new state.

It is curious to reflect that this imposition of military rule was a product of failure. There can be little doubt that had the army conspirators succeeded in their rapid military take-over bid, then the political parties sympathetic to the rising would have staked their claims and demanded their rewards. When Queipo de Llano revolted in Seville he declared that the army had taken over the direction of the country 'as a safeguard for the nation' and was 'ready to hand it over, when order and tranquillity is restored, to civil elements'. But after a year of war, a different message was heard over Radio Seville. 'I state that the army must hold power for a long period, which could well be a quarter of a century.' It was the necessities of war leadership that pushed the civilians aside; and this margination was all the more easy because the civilian leaders of the right had vanished: Calvo Sotelo had been murdered, José Antonio Primo de Rivera was executed on 20 November 1936 by the Popular Front in Alicante, and Gil Robles went into exile.

The original authority in the rebel zone was the junta of generals set up by Mola in Burgos, capital of the Nationalist embryo state; its chairman was Cabanellas who had rebelled with success in Saragossa. He was sixty-four – he wore a long white beard – and a Republican. Mola, in command of the Northern Army, was an intelligent man with defined political views; but he was junior to Franco. From his capital of Seville 'the radio general' Queipo de Llano was organizing a private fief based on the agrarian exports of Andalusia; but his rapid successes meant that his zone became militarily less important and he was too eccentric to be a national figurehead. (He had been a Republican conspirator in 1930. He followed a familiar conservative trajectory, in his case turned into a personal issue by the 'sacking' of his relation, President Alcalá Zamora.) Soldiers realized quickly, as difficult supply problems emerged, that there must be a single commander-in-chief. General Kindelán, chief of the air force, set about organizing the appointment of Franco as generalissimo by his peers.

Franco's claims were outstanding: a soldier's soldier with a well-earned reputation for bravery and competent staff work, he was in command of the best Nationalist army. Even if some enthusiastic conspirators had cursed his caution, there was no one of comparable rank to match him. After Sanjurjo's death Mola, organizer of the rebellion and known as the 'Director', was his only conceivable rival. Mola recognized his outstanding claims. On 21 September the leading generals elected him Commander-in-Chief.

Franco's elevation to the command of the Nationalist armies was uncontested and inevitable; but as a condition of acceptance he insisted on supreme political power as a *sine qua non*. This was unexpected and met with some opposition, particularly from Cabanellas who saw that he would be relegated to obscurity. The opposition collapsed. Franco had established himself in the nationalist press as prospective *caudillo*. The liberation of the Alcazar of Toledo (see below, p. 153) made his claims irresistible and when the news of the relief came through he had been acclaimed by the crowd in Caceres on the night of 27 September. On 29 September his close supporters engineered his declaration as 'Head of the Government of the Spanish State'. The Generals' Junta of Defence was dissolved and the Technical Junta of the state replaced it. It was, as its name implies, an advisory body and its secretary was Franco's brother, Nicolás. Cabanellas' son, a bitter opponent, called these manoeuvrings 'the eighteenth *Brumaire* of Francisco Franco'.

The prime movers of Franco's elevation to supreme military command were the small group of Alfonsine monarchists – the one political grouping in the Nationalist camp without a pretence of mass support and therefore committed to seek power by personal influence. They had no alternative but to accept his terms to rule what was called, simply, on the postage stamps of Burgos, 'the Spanish State'. But few of his monarchist supporters could have believed that the *caudillo* would postpone for decades a clear commitment to his monarchist successor. They thought of him as a Spanish General Monck about to restore the Bourbons on the morrow of victory, not as the lifelong and absolute ruler of the Spanish state.

The decree appointing Franco as 'Head of Government of the Spanish State' gave him absolute powers: 'all the powers of the New State'. He was President-King and Prime Minister in one person. As time would show, the only process that could limit these powers was a process of 'autolimitation' – the voluntary surrender of total power by the *caudillo* himself. The powers won in a war-time emergency were never surrendered in principle, and in practice very slowly. No one had doubted Franco's competence as a soldier; what came as a 'revelation' – to use the Spanish phrase – was his expertise in political manoeuvre and his nerve, his tenacity as a

politician. Like most short men he was strong-willed to the point of
obstinacy, conscious of his dignity and jealous of his power –
interviews and cabinet meetings were a great trial to his more
nervous ministers. Though not a humourless man, he had the
capacity to make others sense his power. Though bourgeois in his
tastes, a family man, and austere in his private life – he drank little
and neither smoked nor permitted others to smoke in his presence –
his Court was formal, dignified, surrounded by a modest version of
royal panoply, far removed from the vulgar familiarities and
eccentric hours of Berchtesgarten. He did not harangue his
interlocutors, impress them or flatter them as did Hitler or
Mussolini. As others had in the presence of Louis xiv, they simply
lost their nerve; protests, criticisms faded in his presence. His
supporters praised his pragmatism, his refusal to commit himself
irrevocably to a given policy as his outstanding political gift. This
might be put in another less flattering form: he had an unerring
instinct for political survival, and the force, in the shape of army and
police, to secure it.

II

Compared with revolutionary effervescence in Republican Spain,
life in Burgos and the Nationalist zone appeared 'normal'. Military
rule was uncontested. In the barracks atmosphere of Burgos and
Salamanca where Franco set up his headquarters in the Bishop's
Palace, civilian politicians were at a discount. The prevailing style
was military: whereas a uniform was the insignia of reaction in
Madrid it was the passport to privilege in Burgos. Ordered
government was a psychological necessity for the Nationalists.
Unamuno, doyen of Spanish letters, had been dismissed as rector of
Salamanca University for a brave and bitter personal attack on the
much wounded hero, General Millán Astray, on the occasion of a
speech that was an outrageous and brutal outburst of crude
militarism. Yet Unamuno had asserted 'it is absolutely necessary
that order be restored'; and this, he concluded, could only be done
by soldiers who could discipline themselves and knew how to
impose discipline on others.

　　Discipline and order were buttressed by terror: the ruthless
elimination of 'Masons' – a definition of the enemy which revealed
the nature of the war as a continuation of the nineteenth-century
struggle between anti-clerical liberals and Catholic conservatives –

and working-class leaders. Some of the early exploits of local Falangists and commanders who captured Republican towns were 'uncontrolled'; later executions were in the main ordered by the military authorities. The 'old shirt' Falangists complained that they were turned into executioners. This was not the rôle in the National Revolution that the followers of José Antonio had imagined for themselves; Hedilla, who represented the radical tradition in its efforts to 'redeem' the working class, began to criticize the lack of imagination in the higher command and the prominence, on the Nationalist side, of the representatives of a Catholic bourgeoisie out to revenge itself on a working class that had scared it stiff in October 1934 and between February and July 1936.

The most notorious execution of all was that of García Lorca, then at the height of his international reputation as a poet. A timid man by nature, he had fled from Madrid to his native Granada on the eve of the war. His connection with left-wing intellectuals was common knowledge, as were his anti-Nationalist views on Spanish history – he regarded the conquest of Granada by the Catholic kings in 1492 as a cultural disaster – while his homosexual sympathies were anathema to the adherents to the cult of virility, so essential a part of the Nationalist ethos. One of his assassins boasted, 'I fired two bullets into his arse for being a queer.' Once he came under suspicion he took refuge in the house of a Falangist poet whence he was taken by a right-wing *cedista* and executed on the hillside outside Granada on the order of the Civil Governor, a Falangist. García Lorca was thus the victim of the collective revenge and the obscure fears of a bourgeoisie which he himself had called the worst in Spain, cowed in March 1936 by demonstrations, church-burnings and sacking of the premises of right-wing organizations. The Nationalists soon realized that, as in the case of the bombing of Guernica (see below, p. 186), they had committed an egregious error that was soon exploited by Republican sympathizers to prove the brutality and 'lack of civilization' of the rebels. The Falangists blamed the CEDA, 'elements possessed of a provincial and not easily definable rancour and who were, needless to say, anti-Falangist'; officially his death was presented as the consequence of left-wing feuds, confusion and later as a private homosexual revenge.

It does not help to excuse Republican executions as the work of hot-blooded militants who had suffered repression while those of

the Nationalists are condemned as cold-blooded murders perpetrated by an upper class defending its threatened privileges. It is
of little consequence to the condemned man whether he is the
victim of a popular tribunal or shot on the orders of a general. In a
sense the Nationalists were bound to commit more atrocities than
the Republicans because they advanced into former Republican
territory. It was in newly captured towns like Badajoz and Toledo
that victorious troops shot in cold blood, and that the 'Black
Squads' wiped out Republican town councillors, labour leaders and
'Masons'.*

The Republicans, since they captured back no significant
position of Nationalist territory, were never confronted with the
problem of mass 'cleaning up' by terror in newly conquered
territory. Their problem was the Fifth Column in the rearguard –
the word was invented in the Civil War. In territory that might fall
to Franco the temptation to establish one's loyalty to the Nationalist
cause by sabotage and spying was strong. A cynic observed aerial
reconnaissance on the Madrid front was rare because spies were two
a penny. There were extensive spy networks in Madrid and
Barcelona – as late as the battle of the Ebro government tanks were
halted by oil laced with iron filings. The result was a spy mania
which bolstered up intelligence agencies and justified their
practices – secret executions and private prisons, the notorious
chekas of Nationalist and anti-Communist propaganda.

On both sides blood created a hatred that was to outlast the war
by a whole generation. Atrocity stories brought by refugees from
the Republican zone were the common gossip of Nationalist Spain,
possibly as a surrogate for political discussion, certainly as a weapon
for the creation of emotional solidarity. They were fed into the
Nationalist press and propaganda machines by the flood of refugees
from the Republican zone who filled the hotels and boarding-
houses of Burgos and Salamanca. A refugee could establish his
political *bona fides* by lurid tales of suffering at the hands of bestial
'reds'. And refugees from Catalonia had indeed witnessed horrors
even if these did not extend to walls made of children's bodies. If

* The total number of Nationalist executions is still a matter of controversy and guess-work (e.g.
some authorities multiply the number of Republican executions in a recaptured town by ten on
the strength of an *ex abrupto* statement of that chronic exaggerator, Queipo de Llano). Thomas
estimates the number of executions at 50,000 on each side; Jackson estimates that 200,000 people
were executed during the war itself and 200,000 more died in prison or were shot between 1939
and 1943.

nuns had not been raped, priests had been slaughtered.

The establishment in Nationalist Spain was a small concern; scarcely a single member of it had not lost a relation in the violence of July. Ramón Serrano Suñer, Franco's brother-in-law, had seen his political allies murdered in gaol and his brothers 'taken for a ride' by militiamen. For him democracy had become not merely unsuitable to Spain, but hateful; he was to be one of the chief architects of the new Spanish state.

To most native Catholics Nationalist terror was justified by the militant traditions of the Spanish Church and by the sins of the executed. For most professing Catholics outside the Basque country, the choice was clear even if there was no *formal* blessing by the Vatican, worried about the fate of Catholics in 'red' Spain. The Republicans burnt churches and massacred priests. 'The working class,' wrote the POUM leader Andrés Nin, describing the situation in Barcelona, 'has solved the religious question in a straightforward manner; it has not left a single church standing.'

From the early days of the war, priests appeared on balconies with generals and blessed flags, and the bells of Burgos Cathedral had rung out for the National Junta of Defence. Navarre, the most Catholic province in Spain, had in the first three months of the war provided with the *requetés* forty thousand of the finest volunteer soldiers on either side. 'As they marched they sang religious and patriotic songs. Their breasts were covered with religious badges and medals. Many of them had rosary beads and crucifixes hanging round their necks. At six o'clock in the morning I used to find them praying devoutly in the churches.' It was less an army than the 'Church militant on the march'. 'Spain is divided,' wrote a visiting Irish journalist, whose views were characteristic of right-wing Catholicism, 'between the men who fight for Christianity and the men who fight against it.'

Once the rising of 18 July had failed as a military take-over and become a fratricidal war, the blessing of the Church became all important. It turned a civil war into a crusade, the rising of 18 July into a legitimate rebellion to save Christian civilization. On 30 September the Bishop of Salamanca issued a pastoral, 'The Two Cities'. 'On the soil of Spain a bloody conflict is being waged between two conceptions of life, two forces preparing for universal conflict in every country of the earth. . . . Communists and Anarchists are sons of Cain, fratricides, assassins of those who cultivate virtue. . . . It [the war] takes the external form of a civil war, but in reality it is a Crusade.' In November, Cardinal Gomá saw the war as a punishment for 'laicism'. 'Jews and masons poisoned the national soul with absurd doctrines, with mongol tales converted into political systems in sinister societies manipulated by international Jewry.'

There were those on the Nationalist side who mistrusted what appeared to be a revival of clericalism: the Falangists respected the Church as part of Great Spain but they did not like political priests, and the German ambassador observed with distaste that priests were welcome members of the generalissimo's household. But these doubts were stifled in the atmosphere of the crusade. The generals in July knew what they were against; as one of the conspirators observed, the ideology of the counter-revolution 'defined itself in negatives' – against 'Communism' and against 'anti-Spain'.

The defence of the Church – by no means emphasized in the declaration of July 1936 – became the most emotionally charged positive element in Nationalist thinking. Nothing contributed more to the unity of Nationalist Spain; no such simple emotion welded together the warring factions in the Republican zone. Politically and ideologically Nationalist Spain was becoming a monolithic structure.

8
The Organization of War

Whereas the Nationalist armies soon organized their 'columns' into regular units, the militia system of the Popular Front persisted, often with calamitous military consequences, until the organization of the Popular Army got under way in October. The 'militarization of the militia' was resisted by the CNT militants and the incorporation of militia units into a regular army was a slow process.

Both sides were short of arms and both appealed to foreign allies. The Republicans first appealed to France; after an initial supply of aeroplanes and munitions the French government stopped all supplies in early August. Soviet aid took the form of tanks and aeroplanes (October) and the Comintern organized International Brigades which first went into action in November. The Nationalists appealed to Germany which sent transport planes (28–29 July) and fighters (6 August) and to Italy. Italian planes landed in Spanish Morocco on 30 July. These aeroplane deliveries helped Franco to transport his African Army to mainland Spain – a decisive factor, since it gave the Nationalists a seasoned army corps and made Franco the most important general on the Nationalist side.

The Non-Intervention Committee was set up on French and British initiatives in September. Its professed aim was to prevent the escalation of the Spanish war into a European conflict by cutting off arms supplies to both sides. This it failed to do since Germany and Italy continued to send troops (the Italian Volunteer Force and the Condor Legion) and supplies, while Soviet supplies supported the Republican war effort.

I

Victory in war – and it was soon evident that the war would be a long affair – goes to the side with a disciplined army well supplied with arms. In the improvisation of an army the Nationalists possessed psychological advantages: they had seasoned generals and enthusiastic younger officers and the whole ethos of Burgos and Salamanca was military. Military values and a concept of Castilian honour and discipline were at the core of the Nationalist collective mind. The labour leaders of the Republic suspected armies as such and officers in particular. They showed none of Trotsky's realization that a revolutionary army must make the best use it can of the reservoir of capacity in the old officer corps. They could justify their suspicions; there were frequent desertions after a period of feigned loyalty. Captain Reparaz of the Civil Guard hated the Popular Front as 'beasts'; his brother officers loyal to the government were 'traitors to the cause of Spain . . . incapable of spiritual grandeur', worthy only of being shot. He concealed his feelings, played along with the Popular Front authorities at Jaen, comparing his 'tortures' to those of a Calderonian hero. As soon as he could escape to the Nationalist line at Cordoba he did, taking his men with him. There were many like him.

The mistake of the Popular Front government was to see a potential Captain Reparaz in every officer in the Republican zone.

As we have seen, taking the armed forces as a whole, almost half of the officer corps and above all the experienced senior officers, remained loyal to their oaths. The task of building a new model army must, to a great extent, be entrusted to these men; but they were subject to a political purge run by a military cabinet. Its chairman, Diáz Tendero, was a highly politicized officer who had organized the quasi-secret UMRA to unite officers with Republican sympathies; 'it is an error,' he reported, 'to believe that officers who do not feel in the depths of their souls the emotion of the historical moment can serve the régime.' Any past contact with a right-wing politician, however slight, evidence of subscription to a right-wing paper or any exhibition of religious conviction meant classification as 'indifferent' or 'factious'. Diáz was a fanatic; nevertheless there was some basis for his axiom that there was no alternative to a 'revolutionary' army when the government could not count on the 'secure loyalty of the armed forces'. Obviously many officers who sympathized with their Nationalist brother officers were caught out in the Republican zone. Some escaped. Some remained behind to become fifth columnists and, as

Nationalist agents, to emerge from hiding and take over power in the last chaotic days of the Republic. Of the 7,300 officers in the Republican zone, only 3,500 were classified as loyal.

Units loyal to the Republic, in the early days, were often swamped and swept aside by the 'spontaneous' creations of proletarian voluntarism, fed on the epic of the Montaña Barracks and the barricades of Barcelona. 'We are actors,' wrote a CNT militant, 'in a great drama.' The actors were the militia men and women. Pictures of these men in overalls, the uniform of the militia, were flashed across the screens of Europe. They were a powerful image of a people in arms. Later it became evident that most of these photographs of the militia in action were carefully posed behind the lines; it was only in the Second World War that photographers braved the front line with modern telephoto lenses.

The militia columns were formed haphazardly by those with enough political pull to get rifles or lorries – usually the Socialists, the CNT and the UGT – and enough force of personality to command respect. 'El Campesino', who had joined in the storming of the Montaña Barracks, describes the origins of 'his' column. 'I rounded up some twenty men and we went to the mountain pass of Somosierra . . . it was my first command: twenty-nine men, two lorries, rifles and one machine-gun. . . . Thus we set out, not even in uniform, with our single machine-gun, to stop General Mola's regular soldiers.'

Columns varied bewilderingly in size, equipment, political allegiance and nomenclature. Some were largely composed of regular soldiers under 'popular' officers; others of civilians in dungarees. Their competing demands made the organization of supply and the control of units in battle a nightmare for the staff officers who tried to work out the logistics of a campaign. Militia commanders besieged the War Office, desperately short of arms, bullying the War Minister himself with chits for rifles signed by political leaders. Azaña, with a characteristically bitter historical allusion, remarked that every local commander demanded guns and aeroplanes for 'his' district just as the old politicians used to demand bridges, roads and schools for their constituencies. 'My authority,' complained the Minister, 'ends here at the office door. I can stand it no longer.' General Asensio, the under-secretary, found it hopeless to try to enforce 'elementary truths which are valid in all armies at all times'. The militia had suffered all the defects of a volunteer force; on the Madrid front in the early days units left the line at will to visit their families.*

In the field such troops broke under fire, panicked at flanking movements and disobeyed orders to resist. Martín Blazquez, a Republican regular soldier, denied them 'real grit'; on the Huesca front a British volunteer found among the CNT militia a 'hopelessly slipshod, unscientific way of fighting'; 'sheer inefficiency and incompetence all along the line'. At Talavera, a critical battle that opened the way to Madrid, Borkenau found 'not the slightest trace of a unified command in this motley crowd'.

These are the judgements of a disabused soldier after the event and of a critical journalist. Even more damning are the reports of commanders we can now read in the archives. In October the chief of staff of the Republican forces in Andalusia reported to the Ministry of War that the Nationalists had occupied the village of Alcalá la Real without resistance: 'everyone fled . . . the morale of the militias is terrible . . . they obey nobody . . . if the enemy appears they simply run away.' These collapses were not the result so much of individual cowardice as of the lack of coordination and confidence in sector commanders that can *only* be achieved by discipline.

Bitter criticisms of the militia system were made by the political opponents of those parties – the CNT and the POUM – which believed in 'revolutionary discipline' or 'organized indiscipline'. For anarchists a salute was an indignity, uniforms a symbol of slavery. Commands would be obeyed if given by elected officers and if they were reasonable; obedience was not a reflex action but the response of trust in a popular leader like Durruti or the end process in a long discussion on the philosophy of power. 'If we don't discuss this kind of thing we might as well be fascists.' George Orwell, who served in the POUM militia on the Aragon front, remained a consistent defender of the militia system and discipline through discussion. Its failures, he held, were failures of training and equipment: in the trenches he found no maps, no electric torches,

* cf. the behaviour of Durruti's CNT column. Durruti himself was only persuaded with difficulty to leave the Aragon front (though he appreciated the need to send reinforcements from his column to Madrid). On his death (20 November 1936) on the Madrid front, the majority of his column refused orders to remain in Madrid and returned to the CNT fief in Aragon. Durruti had soon realized the necessity for discipline and refused permits to visit 'sick' families in Barcelona. CNT columns included a number of semi-criminals and their activities were attributed to Durruti himself before he brought these elements under control.

no tin hats, one grenade between five men, rifles that went off by themselves or jammed. There were nights when the lines could be stormed 'by twenty girl guides armed with battledores. . . . Any public school OTC is far more like a modern army.' Yet for him the human experience outweighed all else – cold, dirt, lice and incompetence. 'No titles, no badges, no heel-clicking, no saluting . . . a sort of temporary model of the classless society . . . one had been in a community where hope was more normal than apathy or cynicism, where the word "comrade" stood for comradeship and not, as in most countries, for humbug.'

It soon became apparent that a disciplined army must be created. Initial enthusiasts for the militia like War Minister Largo Caballero and the CNT leaders had seen its shortcomings in war. Federica Montseny had been against the creation of a conscript Popular Army. But by October she had changed her mind: 'because of your incapacity, your lack of understanding we have had to recognize the need, at this moment, of a Popular Army that will end the error of the militias, who attack when it suits them'. Another CNT/FAI leader García Oliver came out against revolutionary camaraderie which abolished the distinction between officers and men; enlisted men should become 'cogwheels in our military machine'. By October 1936 the painful process of building up a regular conscript army which would combine the 'revolutionary discipline' of the militia with the minimum demands of war was under way. In December a government decree refused pay to non-regular units. The most notorious of the CNT units, the Iron Column, mutinied; but, after a long debate, it submitted.

The process of militarization was slow and not completed until the summer of 1937. Conscription was introduced and the new Mixed Brigades of the Popular Army consisted of conscripts and militiamen commanded by officers appointed from above. The organizational innovation was the departure from the column structure where each column was of differing size, heterogeneously armed and 'loyal' to a particular party rather than to the military command. *Theoretically* the Mixed Brigades were uniform in size and equipment and they were complete combat units of infantry, artillery, engineers and auxiliary services. They could therefore be more easily transferred to new divisions and fronts.

All this represented an immense effort on the part of the military bureaucracy. The fetish for numbering the new Brigades (Arabic for the Spanish units, Roman for the International Brigades) was symbolic of the true purpose of the reorganization: to cut units off from their dependence on political parties. In Barcelona each barracks had been taken over by a political committee; its name indicated the affiliation. The PSUC were quartered in Carlos Marx and Vorochilof (*sic*); the CNT, more wide-ranging in its range of historical reference, in Miguel Servet, Ferrer (the martyr of 1909), Fermín Salvochea (the anarchist lay saint), Spartacus and Bakunin. The names of the early columns likewise celebrated the heroes of each party; the new numbered Brigades were anonymous units in a regular army. Needless to say, the change in nomenclature was often superficial and did not cut the umbilical cord which bound a unit to its patron party. The Communist fifth regiment was Communist-led; the CNT battalions, though they lost their picturesque titles, remained CNT-dominated. Indeed, the CNT accepted conscription and the militarization of its columns only on condition that a conscript could choose the unit to which he was to be attached. The CNT could never completely overcome its instinctive anti-military bias, its philosophic objections to a military hierarchy – Cipriano Mera, the best of the CNT commanders, complained of the effects of 'excessive friendship' between officers and men. This put it at a disadvantage in its struggle with the Communists: the Communists *believed* in discipline. They did not suspect the new Popular Army: they penetrated it.

The Popular Army wore uniform and received pay – ten pesetas a day – which was higher than that of the Nationalist forces. The individual units no longer elected their own officers. The new corps of commissars was appointed from above; its task was less to watch over the political reliability of officers than to handle relations with the parties. They were intended as an instrument to combine political awareness with military discipline – a combination rarely achieved. The Communists, as proponents of the new discipline, dominated the corps: the best commissars backed up their officers and enthused their men; the worst made party propaganda or were little better than agents jockeying for scarce supplies.

The new army had a new ethos. Saluting was enforced and the officers of Tagüeña's brigade got their uniforms from the best military tailors of Madrid. When a minister visited his troops he received them with the 'full honours' of the old army after carefully consulting the pre-war regulations.

Given its *point de départ* the Popular Army was a remarkable creation and it was the creation of regular officers who remained loyal to the Republic and the enthusiasts of the Communist party. By the spring of 1937 it consisted, on paper, of ten army corps and 209 Mixed Brigades and 451 batteries.* But it was weakened by shortages of arms and remained, in the words of its chief of staff, 'the skeleton of an army . . . more artificial than real . . . the basis for what we hoped would be our army'. George Orwell, consistent in his belief that freedom and decency could be combined with military discipline, maintained the Popular Army was no more effective than the militia it replaced – a view untenable when the great battle offensives of 1937 and 1938 are examined, operations inconceivable with a heterogeneous assemblage of militia columns varying from fifty to a thousand men.

Republican officers like Lister, a former quarryman, or Modesto, an ex-carpenter – whose rapid rise illustrates the extraordinary military social mobility of the Republican zone – made remarkable commanders of large units; both were Communists – though Lister's high spirits made him suspect; both had been trained in the Soviet Union and used Russian advisers including Malinovsky, the future Marshal and Defence Minister of the Soviet Union. Tagüeña, another Communist (who joined the party, as did so many of the more conscientious officers, because they felt that the Communists were the only group who faced up to the military problems of the war) was a science student and at the age of twenty-five in command of an army corps of thirty thousand. These men at the top were, as the Republican press put it, 'a revelation'. A middle range of officers were less easily improvised. It was the *junior* officers who flocked to the Nationalists and the gap on the Republican side was filled by the promotion of sergeants. Training was imperfect and improvised, often pushed through in the lulls between or on the eve of battles, rather than in the schools set up by the Republic. Ludwig Renn, the German Communist novelist and ex-soldier of the 1914–18 war, set up a school for company commanders only to find that 'the understanding of a written order was beyond them'; his elementary handbook of modern tactics was never printed. The tactical failures of the great Republican

* Theoretically a Mixed Brigade consisted of 132 officers, 9 doctors, 233 sergeants and 3,169 soldiers equipped with 2,413 rifles, 100 automatic rifles, 98 mortars, 36 machine-guns and 11 guns. Needless to say this strength occurred on paper more often than in the field.

offensives are nearly all explicable by a breakdown in the lower levels of command – what a Russian adviser called 'the absolute absence of proper communication and the consequent haphazard coordination of troops'. Units got confused and the impetus of advance was lost after one or two days.

The Popular Army never completely overcame the weaknesses of the militia system: the primacy of politics over war. Inexplicable collapses continued to occur, and because the army had not been depoliticized the explanation of these collapses became the source of bitter accusations and counter-accusations, of rumour and counter-rumour. The death in battle of an outstanding commander was seen as the work of his political enemies; Durruti was probably killed by a stray Nationalist bullet on the Madrid front; but stories soon circulated attributing his death to Communists or to members of his own column who resented his new emphasis on discipline. Similar stories later surrounded the deaths of the International Brigade commander General Luckacs and the German Communist Hans Beimler. Each party turned these deaths into a party demonstration or a piece of party propaganda: Durruti's funeral in Barcelona was a mass parade of the strength of the CNT; Hans Beimler was said to have died with *Rot Front* on his lips and an unpublished article on the theme 'to conquer Hitler in Spain is to conquer him in Germany' in his pocket.

As a fighting force the Popular Army remained inferior to the Nationalist army and it never felt the firm hand of a single command. The independence of the various fronts and army groups was never absorbed in the *mando único*, the central command.

It is, however, a mistake to imagine that, apart from Franco's all-important African Army, the generals found a ready-made army to hand in July. 'At the beginning of the conflict,' wrote the German Ambassador to Franco, General Faupel, 'the essential military offices (General Staff, War Ministry, Military Geographic Unit with all maps) were in red Spain, as were numerous depots and arsenals *and the majority of the officer corps*. Some of the officers were murdered, and some cast into prison. Some are still in hiding in red territory, and others are in the ranks of the reds, so that, aside from the troops in Morocco, Franco did not have a single usable military unit available but only the wreck of an army.' The Nationalist forces, in the early months, like the Republican armies, were organized in columns and shared many of their weaknesses both in equipment, command and organization; this was evident when the two 'armies' came into contact in the ding-dong actions in the mountain passes to the north of Madrid. Thus Doval's column of Gil Robles' youth movement, stiffened by Civil Guards, panicked on 30 July; total disaster was averted only because Mangada's militiamen failed to press their attack. The Nationalists, too, needed junior officers and, like their enemy, promoted sergeants *en masse*; but they were infinitely stronger in this respect than the armies of the Popular Front. There can be no doubt that, in purely military terms, this relative abundance of combat officers was an initial advantage their opponents could never match.

If both sides had had only the forces they could command in metropolitan Spain a stalemate might have developed. It was the African Army that tipped the balance. By November there were 34,000 troops from Africa in Spain. The Foreign Legion was composed of Spanish long-service volunteers with a sprinkling of foreigners; largely the creation of Franco himself, it was fiercely disciplined, dominated by its peculiar *esprit de corps* expressed in its cry 'Long Live Death'. The Regulares were native troops, officered by Spaniards, and ruthless fighters. They were experts at using cover and in night fighting – in the trench warfare round Madrid they wore down the nerves of the Republicans by their capacity to keep up desultory sniping (their ability to see in darkness was notorious) and with their blood-curdling cries throughout the night. Juan Beigbeder, Franco's High Commissioner in Morocco, saw the importance of the Protectorate as a reservoir of manpower. He was a fine Arabic scholar, a romantic admirer of Arab civilization. He set up cultural institutes, financed pilgrimages to Mecca and a Morocco House in Cairo, and gave a thousand sacrificial sheep to 'our brothers' in the struggle against a godless Republic. He even discreetly subsidized Moroccan nationalist groups and then set them about each other's ears. This imaginative policy secured for Franco a steady supply of hardened men – one in ten of his combat forces.

For the novelist Francisco Umbral the war was 'above all the presence of the Moors and the Regulares' visiting the whore-houses of his provincial home. But it proved hard to incorporate these Muslims in a Christian crusade and their presence in Spain was a godsend to the propaganda machine of the Popular Front.

It was behind the shield of the African Army that Franco built up the Nationalist army through careful officer training – at its peak one thousand cadets a month – in which he was aided by German instructors.* In the San Roque Academy the training of sergeants – a crucial element in any army – was particularly thorough. Both armies came to depend on conscription; Franco called up only those he could train and by the end of the war he had built up an army of 879,000 men commanded by experienced generals and trained junior officers.

II

The critical factor was not the raising of armies but finding arms for them. The Spanish war industry was divided – at first it was largely in the Republican zone – and in any case incapable of supplying large armies. Arms had to come from abroad.

Both sides appealed to potential allies and their agents scoured the private international arms market. France, in the first month, supplied the Republican armies with small arms and ninety planes. With the planes came the novelist and adventurer André Malraux who formed a squadron of mercenaries; he knew nothing about air combat and his squadron was criticized as an expensive encumbrance. Since most of the air force was loyal to the government in the early days, the Republic held superiority in the air. This was not to last long; French aid petered out early in August. Already the Nationalists were in touch with Italy and Germany.

Just as there was a determination to prove that the Spanish right was 'fascist', so there was an early determination by the left to prove that the generals revolted, secure in a *previous* promise of German and Italian aid in the form of arms, particularly aeroplanes, and that such aid was part of a 'Nazi conspiracy'. A fascist conspiracy would be effective propaganda in democracies fearing the advance of Fascism, and early in the war the Communists sponsored a book called *The Nazi Conspiracy in Spain*.

In the case of Italy there had been negotiations in 1934 which had led to Italian arms and officer training for the Carlist *requetés*; but by 1936 these negotiations had petered out. José Antonio received funds from June 1935 onwards at the rate of fifty thousand pesetas a

* The officers were called provisional subalterns and the sergeants provisional sergeants; 'provisional subaltern, certain corpse' ran the joke. Over 20,000 provisional subalterns were trained; after 1939, as an old comrades' association, they were to become the most zealous supporters of Franco.

month – almost the sole financial prop of his Falange, once monarchist supporters had dropped off. But Mussolini knew nothing about the generals' conspiracy, and Franco's agent, Bolín, arrived without contacts in Rome, demanding an interview with Mussolini from the doorkeeper of the Palazzo Venezia. The Duce's military advisers and the king were against involvement in Spain and it may be that the news of French aid tipped the balance of Mussolini's mind towards intervention. Though he would present his aid to Franco as part of an ideological crusade (or, as his critics put it, an expensive personal gesture) it was based on the calculation that the rebels would win in a matter of weeks and that he would thus gain on the cheap (for aeroplanes provided in return for ready cash) an ally in the Mediterranean against France. Twelve Savoia bombers left on 30 July, three of which crashed in French North Africa.

Only when it was apparent that Franco would not win in a matter of weeks did Mussolini commit over forty thousand ground troops; they would, the Duce thought, speed up a final victory. Franco, however, did not relish the prospect of an Italian triumph; 'when all is said and done, Italian troops have been sent here without asking my authorization. . . . The usefulness of these troops is greatly reduced by the requirement that they always be used together.' This attitude towards an independent triumph by Italian troops was to have serious results in the battle of Guadalajara (see below, p. 162).

German aid was the consequence of a personal decision of Hitler and again it was based on a calculation that the war would be won by the rebels in a few weeks and that it would be a good bargain to have a friendly power on the southern frontier of France at the cost of a few aeroplanes.

In the case of Germany there was no official contact whatsoever with the generals' conspiracy, nor any close and *organized* connection with the activist right.* The rising caught the German Foreign Office, the Gestapo and Canaris' *Abwehr* (secret service)

---

* The extent of the connection seems to have been as follows. José Antonio had visited Germany as a fairly low-level guest of the Nazi party; Sanjurjo had visited Germany and had contact with the arms industry, civil aviation circles and the army; Gil Robles' government had negotiated with Germany for police cooperation and arms and he had visited Germany where, like Sanjurjo, he was not regarded as a very important guest; Admiral Canaris knew Spain well from the time of the twenties. Kuhlenthal, the German military attaché in Madrid until 1934–5, knew Spanish officers and had struck up friendships with Spanish officers in Morocco.

completely by surprise. Hitler himself had shown little interest whatever in Spain before July 1936, though he soon evolved characteristic global explanations for the course of Spanish history.

How should Franco approach Germany? At first he tried Kuhlenthal, a former military attaché in Madrid, an 'official channel' (22 July). But this was not to be the decisive approach. On 21 July Franco received in Tetuan, 'serene' in spite of the mainland failures, Johannes Bernhardt, member of the small group of Germans in the AO (the Nazi party organization for Germans living in foreign countries) and a merchant who had extensive contacts with Spanish officers in Morocco. With Bernhardt came the possibility of going over the head of 'official channels' (which Mola was using at the same time) direct to Hitler. Bernhardt flew to Berlin in a confiscated Lufthansa aeroplane, taking with him the aged head of the AO in Morocco. The approach was therefore via the AO and party channels and over the heads of Foreign Office officials who scouted any idea of helping a rebel. Hess arranged an interview with Hitler after a performance of *Siegfried* at Bayreuth on 25 July. Franco's demands were modest. After three hours Hitler had taken the decision to send twenty Junkers transport aeroplanes to Franco, for he saw that the African Army must get to Spain if the rebels were to win quickly. It was his own decision, first to aid Franco rather than Mola, and secondly to aid him with transport planes. It was Hitler's decision, therefore, that made Franco the most important general of the rebellion and underwrote his claims to leadership. In deep secrecy and with great speed the twenty Junkers transport aeroplanes were sent to Spain. Franco therefore knew on 28 July (before the arrival of Italian planes on 30 July) that he was 'master of the straits'. 'We dominate the situation,' he told Mola on 29 July.

Why had Hitler taken this momentous decision to aid rebels against a government in a country about which he knew little and had cared less? He was quite aware of the diplomatic complications of 'official' aid to rebels, hence his insistence on complete secrecy. It was only later that Germany developed important economic bonds with Spain, and Goering's famous statement, at the Nuremberg trials, that Spain was a testing-ground for his new air force did not bear on the decision on the night of 25 July. Hitler's motive was strategical: if the Republic held out then the Franco-Soviet bloc would retain an ally; if the generals won, as he believed they would in a matter of weeks, then France would lose an ally. Hitler knew that France had already responded favourably to a request for military aid when approached by the Republic, and may have believed that the Soviet Union would do likewise. No doubt, as he told Ribbentrop, he wanted to stop the spread of Communism as a 'question of principle'; but it was a pragmatic short-term decision, a personal decision taken over the head and against the inclination of the Foreign Office; a triumph of the AO and a degradation of 'official' channels.

It is easy to see how the myth of a previous promise of support from the Fascist powers arose. It was very soon clear that Italy and Germany were sending equipment to Spain in spite of elaborate – even ludicrous – efforts by Germany to keep the operation secret. Journalists like Tabouis in France therefore argued that there must have been some previous commitment, some understanding without which the conspirators would not have risked a rising – she made much, for instance, of Sanjurjo's visit to Germany. *Post hoc, ergo propter hoc.* Thirty years later Modesto could still insist that the officers in the UME (the semi-secret organization, rival of the UMRA, that united officers willing to conspire against the Republic) were 'an appendix of Nazism in Europe' and that there was an explicit promise of aid.

By August, Junkers 52s and Savoia bombers were helping Franco air-lift the African Army to Spain; German Heinkel 51 fighters with their pilots arrived in Cadiz on 6 August. Thus by September the rebels had regained control of the air. By this time Hitler and Mussolini realized that their short-term hopes had gone awry. Their new ally would be an expensive attachment. Once they had recognized Franco in November their supplies became regular; though they might curse his 'slowness' and bombard him with advice to which he paid scant attention, even threaten withdrawal, they could not afford to let Franco lose the war. Goering sent the Condor Legion (kept at a strength of a hundred planes, it first went into action on 16 November), tanks, guns (especially 8.8 cm anti-aircraft batteries) and superb signalling equipment, together with technicians and instructors. Tank commanders and pilots shuttled in and out of Spain. The supply of war material cost Germany about £32 million.

Quite early Hitler left the main burden to Mussolini. At their maximum there were some 47,000 Italian ground troops; more important was the supply of aeroplanes (perhaps 700), light tanks and artillery. In the battle for Santander (August 1937) 80 out of 250 guns were under Italian control, apart from Italian guns in Spanish units. Mussolini's aid in material cost perhaps £80 million. Unlike German aid it was generously given by Mussolini, and presented as help to a fellow fighter in the anti-Bolshevik crusade; 'delicate, disinterested and noble' in the words of Serrano Suñer, the most pro-Italian of Franco's circle.

The Republic had no such accommodating allies in the West. French arms supplies ceased. Blum, under pressure from the conservative British government, 'his soul torn' as he put it, gave in to the arguments of cabinet colleagues who feared the effect of arms supplies to the Republic on French opinion, deeply divided on the Spanish issue. However, before the cabinet panicked and decided to suspend any supplies to Spain, Pierre Cot had organized the dispatch of Dewotine-371 fighters and Potez 540 bombers. These were the most modern planes in the French air force and they were flown by French pilots, who were paraded in triumph down the Ramblas of Barcelona in two Rolls-Royce cars and were paid 50,000 francs a month. After Blum's fall the Pyrenean frontier was closed so that arms from other countries could not reach Spain by land.

Effective aid, after initial hesitations, came from the Soviet Union. It took two forms: the supply of arms and military advisers, and the organization via the Comintern of the International Brigades.

Russian tanks arrived in late October and immediately went into action outside Madrid in a battle which distressed the Soviet military advisers. Throughout the war the Russian tanks were superior to the Panzers Mks I and II (the Mk IIIs came later) and the Italian Ansaldos, so that the capture of Russian tanks by Nationalists was a major objective.

The Spanish war revealed clearly, for the first time, the importance of air superiority, particularly in support of ground operations. Heavy air strikes were a decisive factor in the Nationalist breakthrough on the Aragon front in 1938 (see below, p. 203). The Republic had lost its initial superiority by October 1936; Soviet supplies began to come through on 12 October. Russian fighters came as an unpleasant surprise to Nationalist pilots who could not get the measure of them; they put an end to unescorted bombing raids by lumbering Junkers 52s. By December Russian planes had once more given the Republicans superiority in the air.

Thus by the end of 1936 Soviet military aid had given the Republic the edge in equipment and armament.

But this was not to last. Soviet supplies remained the chief prop though they arrived rather to stave off defeat than to underwrite victory. When the French frontier was closed, supply by sea had to face the risk of attack by Italian submarines. Thus superiority in the air (which was such an important factor in the Jarama-Guadalajara battles when the mercenary pilot, Tinker, who fought for the Republic, talks of an effortless air superiority) was lost in mid-1937, though local superiority could be achieved in the centre while Franco's main forces were in the north. But in 1938 the French frontier was open again: the considerable supply of arms put the Republic on its feet once more. Republican hopes rose, only to fall as Germany and Italy stepped up their aid. Prodded by Chamberlain, France closed its frontiers again in June: this was a near fatal blow. Stalin was preoccupied by the threat to his eastern frontier posed by the Japanese invasion of China and turning his mind towards some sort of accommodation with Germany. After the battle of the Ebro, Soviet supplies ceased, but they had given the Republic an initial advantage, largely dissipated by the failure to improvise an efficient army, and saved it in moments of crisis.

The Soviet Union did not merely send arms; it organized a supply of men. The International Brigades, like the militia, played a great role in the imagination of the left. The Brigades were not technically sent by the Soviet Union; they were organized by the Comintern agencies in Paris. British volunteers, arriving on cheap weekend tickets, were sent to broken-down hotels in the working-class districts. In the early days the volunteers left the Gare d'Austerlitz in the 'Red Train', sent off by banner-waving enthusiasts; later elaborate cloak-and-dagger precautions were taken to elude the French police and get the volunteers over the Pyrenees by night.

The hard core of the Brigades were the political refugees who had seen Fascists stamp out the left in their own countries: men like the German Communist Gustav Regler and the Italian Liberal Pacciardi; Polish miners working in Belgium; Czech, Hungarian and Yugoslav militants; workers' leaders from all over Europe who had sought refuge in the Soviet Union and now hoped – in vain – for an independent rôle in western Europe. To the International Brigades came the politically conscious intellectuals of the left –

John Cornford the poet and Ralph Fox who had proposed to write a novel on Dimitrov, the Communist hero of the Reichstag Fire Trial, both committed Communists.*

The publicity given to the presence of intellectuals obscured the fact that most volunteers were ordinary workers, together with a core of committed Communist militants, hardened in the class struggle. The French contingent (fifteen thousand strong) was composed largely of factory workers recruited by the CGT, the dominant trades union, and the Brigades were under the control of the French Communist, André Marty. Communist control and the Comintern's role as a recruiting agency was carefully hidden; all brigaders were described on their papers simply as 'anti-fascists'.

The English contingent was less politically homogeneous, less proletarian. Motives were mixed: idealism, unemployment, and sheer boredom with a depressed and depressing Britain. 'I happened to be in Ostend at the time,' wrote one volunteer, 'and was bored to desperation.' Most, however, felt, however dimly, that they were fighting against Fascism. Jason Gurney, a convivial sculptor and habitué of King's Road pubs, who believed that Mosley was a serious threat in England, felt that 'by fighting against Fascism in Spain we would be fighting against it in our own country, and every other.' Intellectuals found a sense of purpose lacking in a Britain that could offer neither purpose nor the prospect of employment. The public-school rebel Esmond Romilly, who left a vivid account of his experiences in the International Brigade, had sold silk stockings and advertising-space in a film magazine, and proposed to set up a night-club. He left for Spain with £9 in his pocket. Recruitment to the Brigades is understandable when we remember the psychological and material effects of the depression, and the sense of despair it left in the working classes.

Once in Spain, idealism underwent a severe test. The Brigades were controlled by humourless Communists, more inclined to hunt out political dissidents than to provide for the creature comforts of the men. When Gurney's battalion arrived at the front 'bread was scarce and always stale ... at no time was any attempt made to consider the welfare of the men. Owing to the absence of washing facilities for either person or clothing, the entire battalion became

* Cornford first joined the POUM militia on the Aragon front; he later joined the British contingent of the XII International Brigade; he was killed on the Cordoba front in December 1936.

infested with body lice.' Pep-talks, propaganda and visits from Professor Haldane, Cartier-Bresson, Hemingway, Clement Attlee and Errol Flynn did little to satisfy the standard grouses of soldiers. What disgruntled brigaders did not always realize was that Spanish soldiers were accustomed to low living-standards and they were often merely sharing the lives of the nation they had come to save. Leadership was often incompetent, self-righteous and vindictive. Political witch-hunts undermined morale. 'We had reached the position where individuals suddenly disappeared from circulation and it was unwise to ask about their whereabouts. . . . Fear and suspicion tempered the whole life in Albacete.' Desertions became a standard subject of conversation. But without passports and with no help from their embassies, the discontented and disillusioned ('they told me this was a revolution, but it's nothing but a f – war') soldiered on.

Like the militia, at first the Brigades went into battle after a few days' barrack-training at the base camp of Albacete; some battalions went into battle without rifle practice. Nor were they initially the disciplined body they became, but 'little soviets, discussing each order before they obey it or don't obey it'. Not surprisingly some of their early actions were disastrous, with officers wandering about looking for troops and transport. Only fierce discipline turned a polyglot force – it used an invented Franco-Spanish *lingua franca* – into units that could be flung into difficult actions. Even so, executions did not cure indiscipline and could undermine enthusiasm, exacerbating factional feuds between the different nationalities and their commanders.*

By mid-1937 recruitment had fallen off and it became increasingly difficult to ferry the recruits to Spain. The Brigades suffered heavy casualties at Brunete and morale was low. Increasingly the gaps were filled by Spanish conscripts. The Republican government had never liked the military and financial autonomy of the Brigades. Prieto, as Minister of Defence,

---

* For example, when Dumont took over the XIV Brigade he replaced many officers by his old companions of the XI Brigade. His fierce executions were partly intended to restore discipline 'among drunks and desperadoes' partly, it was alleged, to get rid of awkward enemies. Even so discipline was bad, and in the La Granja offensive (May 1937) the troops refused to extinguish their lorry lights, thus helping to spoil what was intended as a surprise attack. The heavy losses in the action and the execution of deserters and malingerers seems to have broken the spirit of the XIV Brigade and caused a split between the French, who supported Dumont, and the Slavs who supported the Polish general, Walter, in command of the operation.

distrusted them as a communist *imperium in imperio*. In September 1937 he put them under the control of his ministry.

Nationalist propaganda made a great deal of Russian arms and the International Brigades. Although perhaps fifty thousand men, at least a quarter of them Frenchmen, served in the Brigades, their maximum strength at any one time was probably twenty thousand. After December 1936 there were always more Italians and Germans in Spain than International Brigaders. By September 1938 only twelve thousand international volunteers were left and Negrín decided to send them home in order to satisfy the consistent objections of the Non-Intervention Committee. To the brigaders, who had left ten thousand dead in Spain, it seemed a shabby end to what many had conceived of as a great crusade.

On the Nationalist side there was no Comintern to organize an international volunteer force. The German combatants were not volunteers, nor did they feel committed in the same sense as did the best spirits in the International Brigades. Galland, the German air ace, though he shared the common 'anti-bolshevik' feelings of his class, felt not for Spain but for the greatness of the new German air force. Whereas the Internationals were seen off at stations with demonstrations and greeted as heroes in Spain, the German pilots were slipped in secretly and, it was hoped, unobserved. The German newspapers – and to a lesser extent the Italian press – gave little publicity to aid to Spain. Brecht's play on the rise of the Nazis presents such a curious picture of the Spanish venture because it is based on no hard information from the German press.

Apart from a division of regulars, the Italian ground troops were initially more genuine volunteers. They were members of the Black Shirt Fascist Militia and may be likened to English territorials. They had volunteered for service abroad and the early arrivals included veteran fascists; later they were afforced by 'volunteers' who were indistinguishable from conscripts. Franco was less eager to welcome the troops than Mussolini was to send them; throughout the war he insisted on the primacy of guns and aeroplanes. Nor did he want the Italian troops as autonomous units, but he gave in to Mussolini's insistence on a separate force which was organized as the Corps of Volunteer Troops (CTV). They were poorly trained and poorly equipped by European standards – some units were still using Austrian pre-World War artillery – though better equipped than many Spanish units. After an early success at

Malaga, against the worst trained and worst equipped forces of the Republic, their ambitious motorized offensive at Guadalajara failed against the best tank units of the Popular Army. Their later performances improved, but as the war went on the ranks were increasingly filled by Spaniards. By the last great battle of the war, the Ebro, the CTV formed only four divisions out of 22, and of these three were mixed. It was Mussolini who insisted on the retention of ground troops, against the advice of their commander, Berti, and when even Ciano developed cold feet as the war dragged on. The Duce wanted an Italian triumph. Italian help was generous and the Italians made fewer claims than the Germans; but Franco wearied somewhat of their claims to glory and their strategical nostrums for an early victory. To the end, the all-important contribution of the Italians was in artillery and aircraft.

With no recruiting organization to enlist and ship foreigners who sympathized with Franco, volunteers came as individuals, often wandering from Burgos to Salamanca, finding it hard to get attached to a Nationalist unit. Most were convinced Catholics – individuals like Gabriel Herbert, who volunteered as a nurse in a hospital near the front in Huesca. There was a handful of Rumanian fascists, a substantial number of Portuguese anti-Communists, a sprinkling of White Russians and members of the Croix de Feu who formed the Jeanne d'Arc *bandera* in the Foreign Legion. The only organized – if that is the word – contingent was General O'Duffy's Irish Brigade. Whatever fighting qualities it may have had were ruined by its commander's political ambitions and his propensity for hard liquor; the Brigade was shipped home having had little opportunity to fight in the Crusade.*

There were a few British upper-class volunteers. Peter Kemp had been at school with Esmond Romilly, who fought on the other side; a right-wing conservative, he came down from Cambridge with a poor degree and no firm prospects in life. He came to Spain with his Cambridge OTC certificate and joined first the Carlist *requetés* and then the Foreign Legion (where there were only three other Englishmen). He arrived 'wrapped in a naive, romantic day-dream,

* Noel Fitzpatrick had volunteered for the Foreign Legion and to his regret was posted to the Irish Brigade; he was a British regular officer whose eccentricities proved too much for his commanding officers. Fitzpatrick thus describes his state of mind when he volunteered for Spain: 'At the time this war broke out, I had a motor business of my own in London. But then I discovered that my secretary, whom I rather fancied, was sleeping with my manager, and I reckoned they were both having a good laugh at me. So I packed up and came out here.'

featuring myself as a modern (Cid) campeador'; but he had a hard war (including the horror of shooting a British prisoner of war from the International Brigades) and was badly wounded.

The extent of the rôle of foreign military advisers is hard to gauge; it was in the interest of both sides at the time to conceal their presence and activities. Both sides had to use foreign pilots and tank drivers until Spaniards had been trained. If the Nationalists had more foreigners fighting for them – the Condor Legion and the Italian ground troops – the Republicans, less confident in their own competence, leaned more heavily on the advice of foreign 'technicians' attached to the divisional and army staffs. The Russian military mission was numerous and discreet, equipped with false names; the degree to which its original head, Berzin, and his successor Gorev helped operational planning remains obscure; like so many Russians who served in Spain, they became suspect and were purged. Malinovsky, then a colonel and attached to Lister, claimed a major rôle in the planning of the battle of Brunete; his memoirs show him to be capable of gross untruths in the interests of the party line and perhaps for that reason he survived to become a Marshal of the Soviet Union and die a natural death. What gave the Russian advisers their leverage was their control of Soviet tanks and aeroplanes: thus Pavlov's tanks decided the battle of Guadalajara; the 'adviser', called in Spain General 'Douglas', by refusing to supply the air cover of his 'planes, helped to stymie an offensive planned by Largo Caballero and his chief of staff in Extremadura.

The nature and amount of arms aid and the presence of foreign technical advisers was a closely guarded secret on both sides. Journalists ran into German-speaking men in Nationalist uniform in the hotel lounges of Seville and Salamanca, into Russians in the bar of Gaylord's hotel in Madrid, but censorship kept reports out of the foreign press. This silence was necessary because in September 1936 the Non-Intervention Committee started its interminable meetings in London under the benign chairmanship of Lord Plymouth. Inspired by a desire to stop intervention in Spain that might lead to a general European war, it sought to enforce a voluntary series of unilateral declarations against arms supply to either side in Spain.

Its architects were the Socialist premier of France, Blum, whose sympathies were with the Popular Front, and the British Conservative cabinet. Blum had at first been ready to supply the

Republic with arms; divisions in his own cabinet and an outburst of indignation in the rightist press made him change his mind. To save the Popular Front in Spain would destroy the slender chances of Blum's own Popular Front government in France. 'We would have had a Franco coup in France. . . . Spain could not have been saved but France would have gone Fascist.' Blum now apparently shared the belief of his Foreign Minister that the effective stoppage of German and Italian aid would favour the Republicans. The British government was anxious to avoid a general war and any complications with Germany and, above all, Italy, and it made it clear to France that she could expect no help if armed support of the Republic brought on a contest with Germany.* The result of non-intervention was to deny the legal government of Spain the right to purchase arms abroad.

Those powers determined on intervention – Italy, Germany, Portugal and Russia – were not deterred by the activities of the Committee. While it is true that the Italians and Germans were brutally cynical in their intention of making the machinery of non-intervention 'platonic' and ineffective when applied to their own volunteers and arms deliveries, it is also true that they believed other powers were intervening as well as themselves. One of the calamitous results of Blum's early offer of aeroplanes, given his subsequent withdrawal, was that this offer convinced Italy at an early stage that France *was* intervening. Later there could be no possible doubts about Russian direct intervention, and the Axis powers' refusal to accept the Russian disclaimer that the Soviet government had no control over the aid furnished by 'proletarian organizations whose seat happened to be in Moscow' is comprehensible.

Britain and France stuck to non-intervention even when there was early and ample evidence of its failure. For Eden, the British Foreign Secretary, a leaky dam was, in his own words, better than no dam at all. Whereas Germany and Italy saw some utility in maintaining the façade of non-intervention, provided it did not stop them pouring arms into Spain, the Soviet Union regarded it with

---

* The French government had suspended any government-to-government aid on 25 July and all deliveries on 8 August. The decision to try non-intervention was taken on 2 August after the arrival of Italian 'planes. Pierre Cot and Auriol argued that France must now openly help the Republic, Delbos, the Foreign Minister, the opposite case, 'so as not to give a pretext to those who might be tempted to supply arms to the rebels'.

increasing irritation. It was the only great power which insisted that, once non-intervention failed to stop German and Italian supplies, then the legal right of the Spanish government to obtain arms must be respected; otherwise 'non-intervention' was equivalent to intervention *against* the Republican government.*

Maisky, the Russian Ambassador to England and the Soviet representative on the Non-Intervention Committee, was determined to extract every ounce of political capital out of the 'farce of non-intervention'. Whereas Plymouth tried to keep debates cool, private and technical, Maisky made them political and public, through calculated press leaks. He held the proceedings of the Committee in contempt – 'diplomatic spaghetti . . . words, words, words' – using the weary sessions to attack Fascism and to make the Soviet Union appear as the only world power ready to defend democracy.

Neither side got all the modern weapons it wanted, when it wanted them; both sides were supplied with enough arms to keep the war going. Foreign arms and foreign 'technicians' notwithstanding, the war remained a pauper's war. Long stretches of front were held by a few troops with antiquated and worn-out weapons. At the Jarama battle the International Brigades' machine-guns were described by one who used them as 'a job lot of junk' and at the last great battle on the Ebro the Moroccans captured rifles of eight different makes and six calibres in the same unit. The Foreign Legion was one of the best-equipped units on the Nationalist side; yet until the Aragon offensive of 1938 it was equipped with old machine-guns whose firing-pins broke time and time again. A few new aeroplanes from Italy, a warm jersey or good goggles from English friends, a battery of anti-aircraft guns or a cargo of wheat from Russia, were the cause of great rejoicing. At the Ebro the Nationalist guns were so worn out that they could scarcely find their targets, while the Republican batteries were using shells made in Barcelona the night before and brought in lorries to the front.

It was vastly different from the war of 1939. A concentration of two hundred tanks was achieved with difficulty for a major battle; the Germans conquered France with 2,500. Air forces remained modest. No Spanish fighters were equipped with radio, which gave

---

* Mexico was the only other major power that attacked non-intervention and upheld the Republic's right to buy arms; unfortunately for the Republic, Mexico had no considerable armament industry and found it difficult to buy arms from other countries to send to Spain.

dog-fights a 1914–18 flavour. Heavy aerial bombardment against ground troops produced collapses of morale – the Spanish pilots claim to have invented dive-bombing – but there was little strategic bombing. Both sides bombed civilian populations – the Nationalists more consistently. Madrid was raided after October 1936, Barcelona and the Mediterranean ports in 1938. These were the first air raids since the relatively minor German raids in the 1914–18 war and in Barcelona the raiders met with neither effective anti-aircraft fire nor fighters. The effects of the raids were therefore observed with interest in a Europe where many felt a greater war was coming. There were no mass panics, and heavy casualties from high explosives could be avoided by adequate shelters – a lesson that was drummed into the British government by those who, like the scientist J.B.S.Haldane, considered its air-raid precautions entirely inadequate.

This paucity of arms and the length of the front dictated the strategy of the war. With over two thousand kilometres of thinly held front either side could stage a breakthrough. It was impossible to hold a line three times the length of the 1914–18 front with a third of the men against tank attacks and heavy aerial bombardment. 'If either of the two opponents succeeds in forming a strong combat unit,' wrote Faupel, the German Ambassador, 'he can break through the enemy's front and thus bring about a turn of events that will decide the war.' Success, in such a breakthrough, would depend on capacity to 'follow through'; successful counter-action on capacity to bring up reserves to stop the gap. The Nationalist superiority lay in its consistent satisfaction of these two conditions.

9
The War: July 1936–March 1937

The first aim of the Nationalists was to take Madrid. After a relatively easy march through Extremadura, General Franco's army, after relieving the Alcazar of Toledo (27 September) arrived outside Madrid and planned an attack on 7 November. The government left Madrid for Valencia (5–6 November) but the capital did not fall. This meant that the war would be a long one.

In the north, General Mola took Irun and San Sebastian, thus sealing off the Republican zone from the French frontier. Further west Colonel Aranda saved Oviedo for the Nationalists; the Republican forces failed to retake the city which was partially relieved on 17 October. Catalan forces failed to take Mallorca which became an important base for Italian operations and in Aragon the CNT columns stuck within sight of Saragossa.

In February the Nationalists attempted to cut round Madrid on the south but were stopped at the hard-fought Jarema battle (February). After taking Malaga (7–8 February) the Italian CTV attacked at Guadalajara in March. The attack was held. This victory, together with the successful resistance of Madrid, proved that the Republican army was a serious fighting force on the defensive.

I

In their plans the conspirators foresaw that the rising in Madrid would have to be helped by columns from Burgos and Saragossa; but Fanjul and his officers were defeated and dead before any Nationalist troops could reach the capital. The principal object of Nationalist strategy, the obsessive concern of General Franco, now became, and remained until the late spring of 1937, the capture of

Madrid by direct assault. The African Army, ferried to Andalusia, would advance via Extremadura to take the city from the south-west; Mola's army and the Navarrese *requetés* would cross the Guadarrama mountains to attack from the north-east. The plan failed. This failure was the central strategical fact of the war. It committed Franco to the conquest (the 'liberation') of the whole government zone and the destruction of the Republican army. First attacked, the capital was the last major city to fall.

In the summer of 1936 there were no fronts; the war was a war of columns on both sides, for neither had mounted a centralized war effort and the initiative lay with column commanders. The Nationalist columns were organized and from the outset had a recognizable hierarchy of command; but they included a high proportion of civilian volunteers who were trained on the march.

Mola's column, with twelve old aeroplanes and short of ammunition, set out for the capital which he hoped to capture in

Nationalist advances, August to October 1936

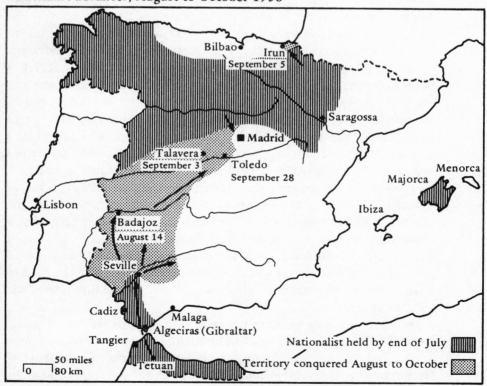

seventy-two hours; but he was held in the mountain passes north-east of Madrid. Here the government militia and regular units proved effective. Mola turned aside from Madrid and sent the bulk of his forces to cut off the Basque country from France.

Had Mola's offensive not been held in the mountains then he would have arrived as a conquering hero. As it was, the southern thrust of Franco's well-trained troops now became all-important in the battle for Madrid, and its transport to mainland Spain the decisive act of the war. The small Nationalist air force, later helped by German and Italian planes, compensated for the lack of a Nationalist navy. By October, in the first air-lift of history, twenty-three thousand seasoned Moroccan troops had arrived in Seville. The remaining thirteen thousand troops came by sea. It was the air-lift that was decisive and for its success Italian and German aid was essential. The Nationalists, Hitler remarked, should have erected a memorial to the Junkers 52s.

Once in Spain and after 'pacifying' the provinces of Cadiz and Seville, the Foreign Legion and Moroccan native troops set out for Madrid in a column of only three thousand; reinforced on the march, they cut through the militia 'like a knife through butter'. Everywhere militia columns fought along the roads and fled when outflanked and subjected to artillery – and later aerial – bombardment; individually brave, collectively they fled in bus and lorry or were shot to pieces in the open country beside the roads. Merida fell on 8 August after an advance of two hundred kilometres in one week, and north of Merida the Army of Africa joined Mola's forces; this meant that supplies could reach both Nationalist armies across the Portuguese frontier. Serious resistance came at Badajoz. Cut off with no retreat, the government forces inflicted heavy casualities on Yagüe's column; he gave no quarter and the 'massacre of Badajoz' became for the European Left an atrocity, a mass murder by barbarous and bloodthirsty 'Moors'. On 3 September the militia abandoned Talavera in buses 'like a crowd after a football match'. It was a key defensive position on the road to Madrid. By 22 September Franco was at the Toledo junction of the road to Madrid.

Here he took a decision much criticized by armchair strategists. Instead of pressing on to Madrid he turned south to Toledo. There Civil Guards of the surrounding district and a handful of Nationalist civilians, two thousand in all, under the command of an obscure colonel, Moscardó, specialist in gymnastics, had taken refuge in the Alcazar, an enormous fortress of Charles v's time which dominated Toledo and which was used as a cadet school. Just as the barricades of Barcelona and the Montaña Barracks became a symbol of the defence of the Republic by the workers, so the resistance of the Alcazar became the symbol of Nationalist will to victory.* With the castle in ruins it appeared every day that the Alcazar would fall; its siege became a tourist attraction, much visited by journalists from Madrid. It did not fall because of the determination of the defenders and because the militia – collectively rather than individually – could not match this determination. 'I looked for this heroism at Toledo,' was Louis Fischer's harsh judgement of the militiamen, 'but I never found it.' There was much wild firing but all attacks failed in spite of mines and heavy bombardment. On 27 September General Varela's troops relieved the Alcazar after a siege which had lasted seventy days.

In civil wars symbols count. The 'heroes of the epic of the Alcazar' could not be left to be massacred; it was necessary, Franco told General Kindelán, 'to convince the enemy that we will do what we say we will do'. Franco could have taken no other decision than he did, even if by relieving the Alcazar he lost the chance of a stroke in Madrid.† Only by taking into account the enormous machinery of propaganda devoted to the siege by both sides can we understand Franco's gnomic utterance as he climbed into the ruined fortress: 'Now we have won the war.' Indeed he had other grounds for optimism: since it had left Seville on 7 August the Army of Africa had conquered twenty-five thousand square miles of 'red' Spain without serious casualties.

II

In the first days of November Madrid appeared in dire peril; the entry into battle of the first Soviet tanks on 29 October, in an offensive on which the Madrid government set great hopes, had been a failure. Franco and Mola were making formal arrangements

* Rebuilt, the Alcazar still remains a major monument. Colonel Moscardó's command post and the underground rooms in which the garrison set up a hospital and flour mill have been carefully preserved.

† Critics of General Franco have maintained that he wanted an 'easy success' to consolidate his leadership (he became Head of State on the morrow of his entry into Toledo) realizing that Madrid would be a hard nut to crack and might even resist successfully.

for taking over the public services and for policing the city. The Nationalist press was full of the forthcoming triumphal entry; the politicians thinking about office space for their parties; the military bands – a particular feature of Carlist enthusiasm – practising for the victory parade; the Falange had seven hundred banners prepared; San Sebastian ran out of electric bulbs for the forthcoming illuminations; a huge altar was built in Navarre for transference to the Puerta del Sol in Madrid where no Mass had been celebrated since 18 July; José María Pemán had written a victory speech and the authorities of Pamplona were debating the propriety of boys and girls mixing in the victory parade.

In the face of this confidence the Republican government itself seemed to make no serious effort at defence. Without leadership the citizens themselves seemed passive; they had been lulled into a false sense of security by the government's announcement of the ambitious 29 October offensive against the advancing African Army that would 'save' Madrid.*

Franco chose to direct his main attack through the undulating ground of the Casa del Campo and across the barrier of the river Manzanares. This would lead him through broad streets and middle-class quarters to the centre of the city; a feint attack was to be made on the working-class suburbs to the south of the main attack. The attack – in essence a repetition of the frontal attacks which had worked against militia all the way to Madrid – was planned by General Varela, a bold commander, for 7 November. It soon became plain that Varela's troops would have a hard struggle. His army had reached what Clausewitz called the culminating point of advance, the moment of maximum weakness when the force of the punch is lost; he had arrived, with a relatively small army that had been fighting on the march for a month, to assault a city of a million inhabitants. The Republican press spoke of 'fascist hordes' to describe a force of twelve thousand men, of whom nine thousand, in six columns, were to be used in the attacks supported by fifteen armoured cars and thirty tankettes. Varela had in front of him in the Madrid sector, forces, disorganized it is true, of about twenty-three

* The Communists and their Soviet advisers blamed the failure on Largo Caballero who had announced the offensive publicly on 28 October. In fact the militia – largely Communist – failed to keep up with the tanks; it was the first large-scale Republican offensive. A subsequent attack on 5–6 November was equally disappointing. In these actions the Nationalists used 'Molotov cocktails' (bottles filled with petrol and tied to a grenade) for the first time.

thousand men. A crushing superiority, if it could be mobilized, to meet an attack across difficult country.

At the same time the Republican resistance had stiffened and was better equipped; the later stages of the advance had become anything but a walk-over and it had taken as long to get from Talavera to Toledo as to get from Seville to Talavera – a mere five kilometres a day. Soviet heavy tanks – they completely outclassed the rebels' small Italian tanks – and Soviet experts had already arrived. On 4 November with Russian fighters – faster than the Italian and German planes – the bombing attacks which had demoralized the militia were no longer so easy.

More important than increased material aid was a new spirit in the organization of the defence. On 6 November the few journalists who had stayed in Madrid found ministries with their doors unlocked but inexplicably empty except for caretakers and porters; the government had secretly fled to Valencia. The pessimistic

Battle for Madrid, November 1936 to February 1937

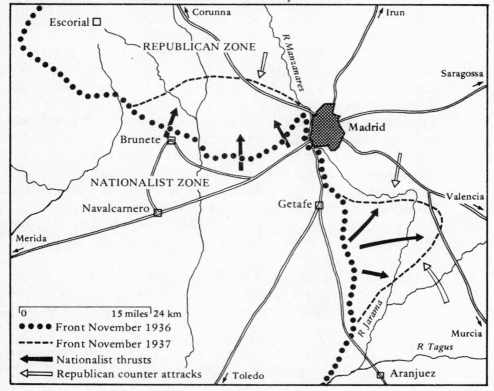

politicians – Prieto, for instance – believed Madrid would fall in three days; but at least the disappearance of the government brought about a remedy for the curse of competing agencies. The defence of Madrid was left in the hands of a single authority – the junta headed by General Miaja. It is a reminder of the chaos of evacuation that the secret instructions of Miaja were addressed on the envelope to the Commander of the Army of the Centre, General Pozas, and *vice versa*. Miaja was not a brilliant commander but he was popular with troops; he became, in Prieto's words, 'the centre of a collective passion' and the object of adulation in a Communist-orchestrated propaganda drive. His chief of staff, Colonel Vicente Rojo, was one of the ablest officers in the army; he immediately set about bringing some formal order into the mosaic of militia columns and regular army units flung back in disorder on Madrid, putting the newly trained Brigades in line. Studious, reserved, an efficient organizer infuriated by meddling politicians – an egotistical élite he called them – Rojo was helped in planning the defence by the capture of Franco's battle orders on the eve of the main attack; he knew he could withdraw troops from the feint in the south to meet the true onslaught farther north.

The battle for Madrid started as a series of frontal attacks by trained troops on the rapidly organized army of the Republic. The critical days were 8 and 9 November. On the 8th it was clear that, in spite of sudden collapses of morale opening gaps in the defence which were stopped up with enormous difficulty, the Republicans would put up a respectable resistance; it was on the night of that day that the first of the International Brigades went into the line. Nevertheless it was the remaining units of the old army and security forces and the hastily improvised Spanish units, the new 'Mixed Brigades' commanded by professional officers who were loyal to the Republic, which 'saved' Madrid; already on the 9th a Mixed Brigade made a counter-attack which threw the Nationalist command off balance.

The rôle of the International Brigades was exaggerated by the Communists who built up their commander, General Kléber, as the saviour of Madrid, an exercise not to the liking of Rojo and Miaja;*

---

* Rojo went as far as to complain, on 26 November, that the press build-up of Kléber threatened a revival of the evils of military *caudillismo*. Kléber was removed from his command in February and appeared again only in the attack on Belchite (see below, p. 193). He returned to the Soviet Union and was purged.

the Communist propaganda machine would have agreed with General Franco that 'the shock troops of international Communism . . . bore the brunt of the fighting in Spain'. On 8 November they were hardly trained shock troops. The first Brigade (the XI) had been formed in Albacete only on 22 October; it had a motley supply of arms from 1896 rifles to modern machine-guns. On 13 November the second Brigade (XII) failed as disastrously as any improvised Spanish unit in an attack on a strong position south of Madrid; supplies failed to arrive and its general spent the whole night looking for his command posts. To Luigi Longo, later secretary of the Italian Communist party, it underlined 'the frightful organizational deficiencies of our improvised Brigade'.

On 15 November both sides attacked at the same point on the front. It was a terrible day. Among others, Durruti's CNT column broke and let the rebel troops into the University city; the situation was saved by the XI International Brigade.

By the 17th it was evident that Madrid would not fall. The attack bogged down in the ruined buildings of the University city. On 23 November Franco met his officers at Leganés: they decided to end the frontal attacks on Madrid. December and January saw the failure of the Nationalist attempts to cut through the flanks and isolate the city. In these battles the International Brigades fought well and suffered heavy casualties; it was these actions that made obscure place-names like Boadilla del Monte and the Corunna Road familiar to the reading public of western Europe; it was these hard-fought battles, with much heavier casualities than in the November defence of the approaches to the city, that proved that the Republican army was a match, on the defensive, for the Nationalist columns. The battle of the Corruna Road (3 January 1937) was a particularly hard-fought battle in which the Republican front nearly gave way; the situation was redressed by a counter-attack, made in a thick fog, on 11 January. By mid-January both sides were exhausted. The front settled down, in the winter rains, to a battle of positions and trenches. For those engaged in it the main personal concern was to get hold of a decent pair of shoes that would keep out the mud. Desertions, on both sides, were common and became increasingly problematic.

The successful defence of Madrid after the early calamities brought new heart to Republican sympathizers in Europe just as the sufferings of the civilian population under the November bombing outraged them.* The 'epic of Madrid' with its famous slogans 'Madrid the tomb of Fascism' and 'They shall not pass' was orchestrated by the Communist party – hence the emphasis on the rôle of the International Brigades. It was presented to the European left as a defence of civilization against barbarism. 'Here in Madrid,' the Madrid wireless station repeated, 'is the universal frontier that separates liberty and slavery. It is here in Madrid that two incompatible civilizations undertake their great struggle. This is Madrid. It is fighting for humanity . . . with the mantle of its blood it shelters all human beings.' The symbolism was to hand in the ruins of the University City where, it was reported, Moorish troops trod on microscope slides and lit their fires with index cards in an attempt to cook virus-infected laboratory rabbits.

At the same time Cornford, the Cambridge poet volunteer in the XI Brigade, was reading a collection of the Everyman Library found in the Philosophy building. Yet victory in Madrid was not a triumph of spirit over matter, of what Zugazagoita, the editor of *El Socialista*, called the 'collective madness of the people' over the cold calculations of army officers. Throughout the battles of Madrid the government had more men and material than the Nationalists.

III

If the Communist boast that Madrid would be the 'grave of Fascism' looked like becoming a reality, elsewhere the war was going badly for the Republic. In the south Republican forces, after retaking Albacete, failed to retake Cordoba and to stop Queipo de Llano's rapid conquest of western Andalusia. In the north, the Republic was losing ground as Mola, thwarted in the passes above Madrid, turned back to the Basque country.

Aguirre, leader of the PNV, had no time for the terrorism and anti-clericalism of the CNT; his relationship with the Socialists had been one of acute rivalry. Before the organization of the Basque government in October, resistance in the north was, therefore, weakened by struggles between the Basque Nationalists (the PNV)

---

* The bombing of Madrid, by later standards, was insignificant. The worst raids in November killed 244 civilians. Photographs of the coffins of sixty children killed in a raid were a powerful propaganda weapon. Those who believed aerial bombing would destroy morale were disappointed; it clearly strengthened determination to resist; but, as later bombings of Barcelona proved, heavier bombing of a city where the will to resist is *not* present, has the contrary effect.

and the other forces of the Popular Front. Mola's troops, now better equipped, took Irun on 5 September – an important victory as it cut the Basque country off from France – and the summer resort of San Sebastian a week later. Once the Basque government was organized and dominated by the Nationalists it became clear that the conduct of the war in 'their' provinces would be an independent concern; relations between the Basque government and the central government were often strained.

Like the northern front, the Catalan zone became an independent theatre of operations. From the military point of view Catalan autonomy was a disappointment; an attack on Mallorca proved a disastrous failure. The CNT militia seemed more interested in revolutionizing the peasants of Aragon than in advancing towards Saragossa. Durruti's column stuck at Pinar del Ebro whence it could see the lights of 'the pearl of anarchism' where, it was alleged, thirty thousand militants were waiting to rise. Thus the Aragon front became a military backwater and Largo Caballero wrote bitterly to Companys, President of the Generalidad, on 27 December that with forty thousand militiamen against ten thousand Nationalists he had done nothing. The Communists blamed the revolutionary infantilism of the CNT; the excuse given by the CNT was that its units were starved of arms by its political opponents in the central government. The real answer seems to be that militia could fight well only on the defensive and in cities; they could not mount an offensive, even against thinly held lines. Thus towns like Huesca, from the military point of view a seemingly easy target, survived without serious attacks.

If Madrid filled the newspapers in November, it was Oviedo, together with the Alcazar of Toledo, that made the headlines in the early weeks of the war; it was to Oviedo, with Toledo the symbol of the Nationalist will to resist, that Franco sent some of his best Africa units. Colonel Aranda had 'risen' in the city on 20 July and was resisting the attacks of thirty thousand Asturian miners and militiamen. On 17 October the Nationalists opened a narrow corridor from Galicia but the attacks continued until the summer of 1937. They sometimes held down as many Republican troops as the Nationalists had committed to Madrid; casualties were as heavy. And the lesson was clear; it was the air superiority of the Nationalists that compensated for a startling inferiority in ground troops.

IV

By Christmas it was clear that Franco could take Madrid neither by pressing an increasingly costly frontal attack, nor by limited – and equally costly – flanking moves to the north-west. The only course was to attempt the encirclement of the capital. By striking south-west in February Franco hoped to reach the road to Valencia at Arganda; if successful, the attack would have isolated Madrid from supplies and surrender might have followed. The second offensive was largely entrusted to the Italians and developed along the road from Saragossa to Madrid. It is a tribute to the increased fighting skill of the Republican armies that the two major flank attempts at encirclement were defeated.

General Orgaz broke the front with troops who had not rested for months and reached Arganda on 7 February 1937, at the very moment when the Republican Army of the Centre was planning an offensive in the same area. The two offensives met head on. The determination and skill of the Moroccan troops, particularly their use of cover, exploiting the smallest fold in the ground in the olive groves, earned the praise of an enemy – the Soviet journalist Koltsov.

By 9 February the government troops outnumbered the National-ists and after nine days the front settled down in dreary rain. The Jarama was the first real battle of the war and it was bitterly fought – total casualties were around sixteen thousand. 'I had finally grown up into the reality of war,' wrote Jason Gurney, 'only when I stood amongst that ghastly collection of dead and irretrievably mutilated men.'

Two features are particularly illuminating. Brave in defence, the Republican units failed in their counter-offensive. Nor were Republican chances improved by the tiresome 'demarcation' disputes between General Miaja, in command at Madrid, and General Pozas, commander of the Army of the Centre. The battle took place near the junction of their jurisdictions, with the main battle in Pozas' command. Miaja refused to send troops to the Jarama front in spite of the orders of the government – his chairmanship of the Junta of Defence enabled him to pose as an independent power. Once the government caved in and created him commander of the whole zone, he changed his tune. 'Madrid will be saved on the Jarama'; he rushed up troops and embarked on a counter-attack, abandoning the favourite strategic *idée fixe* of his chief of staff, Rojo, for an offensive towards Brunete.

The brunt of the defence and some of the more costly counter-offensives had often fallen on the International Brigades; these were now probably at the height of their battle efficiency – trained by combat but still relatively enthusiastic soldiers. Commanders pushed troops hard and the British contingent lost nearly half its number on Suicide Hill in one afternoon. 'It was murder,' wrote an English volunteer in the Nationalist army of a Republican attack across open country. 'The poor creatures fell in heaps.'* General Gal pushed the Americans of the Lincoln Battalion into an attack in impossible conditions. Ernest Hemingway could not forgive him for almost destroying the XV Brigade 'in one single, idiotic, stupidly conceived and insanely executed attack'. Shot on his return to Russia 'he should have been shot at the time. He was a Hungarian and he hated newspapermen.' Hemingway's military judgements were always distorted by his attachment to certain units whose officers he happened to drink with or admire as 'men'.

v

If the Jarama battle proved that the newly organized Republican units could hold their ground against a violent attack, it was during this battle that Malaga fell to Italian troops (7 February) without any serious resistance.

This defeat expressed the weaknesses of the Republic in transition from militias and committees to a regular army and control by a government of the political parties. Franz Borkenau, a disillusioned Marxist of great intelligence, observed the effects of this transition crisis at first hand. The Civil Governor of Malaga 'sat alone in his office; nobody seemed to bother about him'. He was still confronted by the claims of committees and militia commanders, the self-proclaimed victors of 18 July. The result of these squabbles and conflicts of jurisdiction was impotence. 'No one commands in Malaga.' By early 1937 there was neither the impetus of popular revolution nor the strength of organized government.

While the official administration was powerless, the welter of

---

* A Glasgow Brigader wrote a song to the tune of 'The Red River Valley':
>There's a valley in Spain called Jarama
>It's a place that we all know too well
>For 'tis there that we wasted our manhood
>And most of our old age as well.

improvised committees had lost the authority they had seized in July. Thus the repeated government decrees enforcing the militarization of the militia were simply ignored. The population of the town was apathetic and cowed by aerial bombardment. The Republican navy skulked in Cartagena. The political parties of the Valencia government were more concerned with keeping 'their' troops at hand for inter-party rivalries than to send them to the front, and maintained that there were enough equipped troops to resist an attack over difficult country and that any arms sent had been swallowed up by the political parties. As a result of the struggle *within* Malaga no preparations were made to resist the Italian troops and tanks advancing towards it. 'I do not make fortifications. I sow the revolution,' a 'captain' (possibly Colonel Romero Bassart, the *Africanista* friend of the CNT) told Azaña. 'If the rebels enter Malaga the revolution will swallow them up.' It did not. On 7–8 February the government authorities, the troops, and many of the townspeople simply left the town without any resistance and fled along the coast road to Almería. This vast, quasi-military exodus stretched for seventy miles, bombed from the air and shelled from the sea; fit in the front, sick and aged at the rear, they arrived at Almería starving, having pillaged every house en route.* Their panic was not unjustified: the Nationalist purge in Malaga was ferocious.

VI

If Malaga was a disaster for the Republic, the battle of Guadalajara in March 1937 appeared as its first spectacular triumph. Intended to drive through to Madrid from the north-east, the offensive was largely an Italian affair. Had it been combined with the Jarama offensive it is hard to see how the Republic could have put enough troops in the field to avoid defeat. As it was, the two operations were independent. This was largely a consequence of Franco's grudging attitude to the Italian troops. He regarded the CTV's commanders' requests to mount an independent operation as 'an imposition'. He approved the Italian plan for an attack on Guadalajara only with great reluctance and showed enthusiasm for it only after the Jarama battle had reached a stalemate.

General Roatta, in command of the Italian offensive, believed

---

* Rafael Alberti wrote one of the best-known poems of the war on the fate of these pathetic refugees: '*Retornos frente a los litorales españoles.*'

that the easy conquest of Malaga could be repeated in a motorized *Blitzkrieg* which would break through to Guadalajara before the Republic could rush up reserves. His troops consisted of one regular army division and three divisions of volunteers. According to Cantalupo, the Italian Ambassador, the volunteers included 'the most romantic of the Italian fascist militia'; but many of the CTV were reluctant soldiers; none had seen combat and they were ill-prepared for it, some still wearing the tropical clothes handed out for a supposed expedition to Ethiopia. Thirty-five thousand troops, fully motorized with two thousand lorries, attacked on 8 March along the road from Saragossa to Madrid; on their right were fifteen thousand Nationalist troops. The ten thousand Republican troops broke on 9 March.

But the front was narrow and the weather broke with sleet and biting winds on the eve of the attack; off the road, the Italian tanks and lorries sank hopelessly in the mud. Once Madrid could rush up reinforcements the attack was held. On 11 March the Republican general staff began planning a counter-offensive, and on 18 March the Republicans broke the Blackshirt and Littorio divisions, taking the town of Brihuega. While Nationalist planes were grounded by the appalling weather 'we [the Republican air force] had nothing to do but watch the progress of the battle'. The Italians were mercilessly bombed as they were strung out along the road; later the Russians who witnessed the battle were to hold it up as a model of how not to mount an offensive on a narrow front. Perhaps it was not surprising that Roatta's logistical coordination was imperfect. He had to plan his offensive with the aid of Michelin road maps.

In the first days the battle had been touch and go. Ludwig Renn describes in his memoirs how the XI International Brigade was rallied on the edge of collapse. The later stages proved that not only the International Brigades but the Spanish Mixed Brigades, now organized in four army corps, were capable of sustained fighting. André Malraux's *L'Espoir* concludes with a description of the battle; for him it represented the triumph of discipline. The Apocalypse had been organized.

The initial facile 'Malaga' optimism of Roatta and the reluctance of Franco to cooperate with the Italians must be held responsible for the Guadalajara débâcle. If Franco did not want a defeat he certainly did not want to aid an Italian triumph. A major Italian victory as the final act of the Civil War would have left him compromised internationally and would have weakened his claim to rule 'liberated' Spain as the victorious leader of a patriotic, national crusade. The Nationalists were not unduly depressed by a defeat which national pride attributed to Italian hubris; it was even rumoured that Franco's officers held a dinner in Salamanca to celebrate the occasion.

For the Left in Europe, Guadalajara was both a massive emotional experience and a political and diplomatic triumph. Arthur Koestler, disguised as a reporter for the *News Chronicle*, had been sent to Spain by the Communist party to find evidence for a 'fascist' plot and German and Italian intervention. Guadalajara now provided irrefutable proof, in the shape of prisoners and captured material, of Italian intervention.* The war, reported the French Consul in Madrid, was losing its character as a war of classes and becoming a war of independence against foreign invaders – a view that was to be consistently maintained for foreign consumption.

With the characteristic optimism of March, Herbert Mathews, the *New York Times* correspondent, wrote 'that the defeat was decisive, that the stream of history had been deflected into new channels, that a change had taken place not only in the war, but in the world'. For Hemingway Guadalajara was destined to 'take its place in military history with the other decisive battles of the world'. Yet it was not a great victory either in terms of prisoners and equipment taken or territory recaptured after the initial advance. It was a moral as much as a military triumph.

The world, with the Republican White Paper and its photographs to hand, did learn of the extent of Italian intervention but it did not change. Eden, who in January 1937 had made the so-called 'gentlemen's agreement' with Italy, now criticized the readiness of his Prime Minister, Neville Chamberlain, to shut his eyes to the deceit of the Italians. Non-intervention was proving a very 'leaky dam', but Chamberlain was unwilling to risk the displeasure of the fascist power in order to patch it up. Mussolini and Hitler both saw that they must step up their aid. They were prepared to keep Chamberlain happy by discussing the withdrawal of volunteers. 'A

---

* Propaganda soon distorted the history of the battle. Italian volunteers of the XII Brigade had fought their countrymen in the CTV for the Ibarra Palace; the action received much publicity but in the sour comment of Salas Larrazabal, the Nationalist historian of the Popular Army, it 'was no more than a local conflict without greater significance'.

withdrawal is out of the question at present,' wrote the Head of the political division of the German Foreign Office. 'The Italians are therefore only interested in gaining time and do not wish to start a real discussion, if possible, until the defeat at Guadalajara has been made good.' It looked to the German Ambassador in Salamanca as if, given Franco's 'slowness', this might take some time.

10
The Crisis of Government

In the spring of 1937, in both the Nationalist and the Republican zones, there was a reorganization and concentration of governmental authority.

On the Republican side the Communists and the moderate Socialists with their left Republican allies staged a cabinet coup against Largo Caballero. Long in germination, the crisis was sparked off by a bitter struggle in Barcelona between the POUM and CNT activists on one side and the Communist-dominated PSUC on the other. On 17 May Largo Caballero, who resisted Communist demands for strong action against the POUM as 'traitors', was replaced as Prime Minister by Negrín. This represented not merely a 'concentration' of government but precipitated a more determined campaign against the 'spontaneous' revolution. The main victims were the CNT and the Caballeristas.

On the other side, concentration of government meant the subordination of the political life of Nationalist Spain to General Franco. Taking advantage of the splits in the Carlist movement and the Falange, he 'unified' them 'from above' in what was to become known as 'the Movement' under his control (18 April 1937). The losers were the independent-minded Carlists and the radical Falangists.

I

On 7 April General Franco announced that the Falange and the Carlist *requetés* had been amalgamated in a single party under his leadership. On 16 May Largo Caballero was forced to resign as Prime Minister and War Minister. These were the outward signs of a crisis of government in both zones. But the bitterness of the divisions in Barcelona, and in Valencia, where the Republican central government had taken refuge, and the relative ease with which differences were papered over in Salamanca, reveal the growing political strength of the Nationalists and the enduring political weaknesses of the Republic. There was a similar process of governmental concentration and political consolidation on both sides; but whereas on the Nationalist side it was the consequence of a dust-up among the political clans, on the Republican side 'concentration' under the government of Dr Negrín came after a minor civil war in Barcelona costing, perhaps, five hundred lives. On the Republican side concentration left a legacy of bitterness and continued feuding; in Burgos and Salamanca rumbling discontent among displaced persons.

The fall of Largo Caballero was in part a consequence of his own intractable political personality. Stubborn and morose, he struggled for hours with a war cabinet of eighteen. His enemies accused him of hiding his ignorance behind the advice of his 'military friends', of avoiding facing up to crises by his old peace-time habit of going to sleep regularly at nine o'clock; of aiming, in his twin capacity of Prime Minister and War Minister, at 'personal dictatorship'.

More profoundly, the cabinet crisis of May represented the conflict between those who could not sacrifice the conquests of the revolution and those to whom the war could not be won without such a sacrifice; between those who believed that the élan of the workers was the basic condition of victory and those who believed that the broad coalition of the Popular Front must be maintained in a war of 'democracy against fascism'; between those to whom the power of the syndicates was an aim in itself and those to whom political parties represented the proper instruments of communication and control; between trades union bosses and party leaders. Above all, it was a triumph for the Communist campaign for 'discipline' and the re-establishment of central government control over what the party secretary called 'a plethora of committees'. Already on 18 December the Central Committee had included in the conditions of victory 'full authority to the government . . . iron discipline in the rearguard' and the organization of the economy for one end only: 'to win the war'.

In the Spanish political spectrum, therefore, the Communist party was a conservative party and in this lies the secret of its success in recruiting an extensive middle-class clientèle. This was particularly evident in Catalonia. The middle classes were scared to death by the revolutionary terrorism of the CNT in July and August. Where could they find protection? Not in their own party, the Esquerra of Companys, which seemed incapable of standing up to the CNT. They therefore turned to the Communists. The PSUC came out as the defenders of the legitimate profits of the small man: to seize those profits would be to 'decapitalize' 50% of the Catalan economy.

The same process was at work in the market gardens and orange groves of the Valencian *huerta*; the orange growers, harassed by the CNT and bitterly resentful at the prices paid them by the joint CNT-UGT marketing organizations, approved of the Communist party's outright defence of private property and the free market. The Valencia party headquarters showed, besides a huge picture of Stalin, two posters: 'Respect the property of the small peasant' and 'Respect the property of the small industrialist'. Manual workers remained in their old unions – the CNT and the UGT – but the Valencian petty bourgeoisie certainly approved of, and sometimes formed, Communist unions. It is one of the ironies of history that these frightened property owners were later classed by the Franco régime as dangerous 'reds'.

Strengthened by its bourgeois allies it was the Communist party that led the offensive against Largo Caballero, who was reluctant to preside over the liquidation of the revolution of July and whose allies in the cabinet were its architects – the CNT ministers. By the spring of 1937 the 'old man' was the most powerful, the most persistent obstacle to the ambitions and growth of the Communist party. Its relations with the Prime Minister became increasingly ragged. He opposed the party's two main thrusts: the creation of a united Socialist and Communist party and the acceptance of Soviet advisers' and party control of the army, its operations and its personnel.

The first he opposed as a Socialist aware of the history and traditions of his party. He had been an advocate of fusion in March because he believed that the Socialists would 'absorb' the smaller Communist party. With the mushroom growth of the Communists – they now claimed 387,000 members – fusion now threatened to absorb the Socialists. It would mean the infiltration of the PSOE by ruthless Communist organizers who had already 'stolen' the

Socialist Youth from Largo's followers, won over favourite advisers like his Foreign Minister, Alvarez del Vayo, and turned the UGT in Catalonia into a Communist union.

The second he resisted as Minister of War, jealous of outsiders' interference in his department. He waged a protracted one-man war of independence, 'defending national sovereignty', as he claimed, against the pretensions of Soviet advisers – especially Ambassador Rosenberg who pestered him daily about the promotion of 'reliable' officers and the relegation of those of the Minister's 'military friends' who were cantankerous in their rejection of the Russian advisers' advice.

The Communist offensive began by probing the 'responsibilities' – a tremendous word in Spanish politics given the cry for responsibilities raised against Alfonso XIII – for the fall of Malaga. José Díaz, the party secretary, thundered against incompetence and treason in high places. 'Either the government takes the necessary measures to win the war or it ceases to be the government.' The party had always supported and still supported Largo Caballero and the government. But, he added, there was a higher loyalty to the people. This exhibition of political piety was a clear warning to the Spanish Lenin; either he must toe the line or he must go. The Communist ministers then proceeded to an attack on General Asensio, Largo Caballero's favourite military adviser, as responsible for the fall of Malaga. Asensio was pilloried as an idle *bon viveur*, as a homosexual or, alternatively, as a lecher to be found in brothels at the time of military disasters. When the Soviet Ambassador demanded Asensio's dismissal Largo Caballero shouted, 'Get out! Get out! Spaniards are poor and desperately need help from abroad, but we are too proud to let a foreign ambassador impose his will on the head of the government.'

Then came Largo's attack on the appointment of Communist commissars by Alvárez del Vayo without War Office consent; the Prime Minister called del Vayo a traitor and dismissed all commissars whose appointment he had not sanctioned. The party replied by open defiance. 'Commissars, stay at your posts' was the slogan. In late March, at a meeting of the Spanish Politburo in which 'advisers' like Togliatti outnumbered Spaniards and, apparently after a shouting match in which Marty called Jesús Hernández 'a piece of shit', it was finally decided that Largo Caballero must go. The last campaign was the blocking of Largo's favourite strategic plan: an offensive in Extremadura that would cut the Nationalist zone in half. Largo Caballero struck out in public against his enemies: the campaign against him was the work of fascist agents; 'intrigues and passions are coiled around our feet like reptiles'.

These dissensions and squabbles in government were, alas, only too evident to any intelligent newspaper reader. They pointed to a central weakness. In war democracy rarely functions normally. The Cortes met infrequently and exercised no effective control over the executive. Responsible government ceased and until May 1937 the Republic at war enjoyed only a surrogate for democratic politics: party conflict. And without responsible government and the strength this gives, party conflict was debilitating.

II

The catalyst of the May crisis, when his enemies moved in to the kill of Largo Caballero, were the May 'troubles' in Barcelona; this minor civil war gave the Communists their opportunity to oust the Prime Minister.

In the eyes of the Communist party and in much of the subsequent literature, the Barcelona troubles were the work of the revolutionary Marxist party, the POUM. It was not, as the Communists maintained, a Trotskyite party in the sense that it was under Trotsky's direct influence though it was now led by Trotsky's former secretary Andrés Nin.* Trotsky had, in fact, disowned the party; but its revolutionism, its hatred of Stalinism was as resolute as Trotsky's and its press exposed the iniquities of Stalinism in the Moscow treason trials.† Its characteristic feature was its rejection of the Popular Front, presented by the Communists as an anti-fascist, anti-feudal, war coalition of bourgeois and workers. To the POUM the Popular Front was a 'sham', a betrayal of the cause of the workers.

---

* Andrés Nin (b. 1892 – assassinated 1937) was the genial, bespectacled 'fanatic of revolution'. Son of a small farmer. Joined CNT but like Maurín an 'outsider' in it. Formed Left Communist party following Trotskyite line.

† A great deal has been made, by anti-Communists, of the falsity of the Trotskyite label when applied to the POUM. While Andrés Nin had broken with Trotsky and therefore was technically not a Trotskyite, his ideas were still 'Trotskyite' with one important difference. In 1934 Trotsky had wanted Nin's Left Communists to join the PSOE and form its revolutionary wing. Nin reinforced the supposition that he was a Trotskyist by appealing to the Generalidad government to grant Trotsky political asylum in November 1936.

As we have seen, the POUM differed from the CNT in its Leninist belief in the necessity of a workers' state and *government*, where the CNT believed in no government at all outside the unions or the libertarian commune.* According to the POUM analysis, the CNT had committed a profound error in rejecting political power as such; it had then compounded its error by finally accepting power in Largo Caballero's bourgeois coalition government. 'Our comrades of the working class did not know what attitude to adopt to power. Rather than urge the working class to seize it for themselves, they preferred to regard it as a simple question of collaboration.'

Apart from a few members in Madrid – where the Communists complained that they had seized the best houses and hotels as party offices – the strength of the POUM lay in Lerida and Barcelona where its daily, *La Batalla*, was edited. Its enemy was the PSUC.

Once the PSUC unleashed its offensive, against both the POUM and the revolutionary conquests of July – the collectives, the committee structure, the militia and the police 'patrols' – the POUM appealed to the CNT to wake up to the dangers surrounding it. The POUM was merely first on the list; the next blow would fall on the CNT.

Militant revolutionaries though they were, the POUM alone would have been powerless to mount a defensive revolutionary *journée*, had this been their intention. The real power in the streets belonged to the CNT. Yet the CNT leadership seemed deaf to the POUM warnings of the advance of the counter-revolution. The bickerings of the PSUC and the POUM seemed to anarchists a private intra-Marxist feud. In December 1936 they gave in to the PSUC campaign and did not oppose the exclusion of the POUM from the Catalan government. Thus, in their resistance to the PSUC, the POUM could count on sympathy only among the discontented and disoriented rank and file activists of the CNT, convinced that their leaders had sold out the movement in their zeal to collaborate with the forces of the Popular Front in the Generalidad government. Strong in the Libertarian Youth movement, these activists set up a separate organization called the Friends of Durruti.

If the CNT leaders thought that, by entering the Catalan

* For the formation and political strategy of POUM see above, p. 18.

government, they could save the revolutionary conquests of July and halt the Communist suppression of all evidence of the 'spontaneous revolution' they were sadly mistaken. The secretary general, Vazquez, regretted any lapse into 'the old mentality where everything can be arranged by bombs and rifles'; yet he was alarmed at the erosion of the political influence of the CNT. The regularization of government, above all the reorganization and strengthening of the security forces responsible for public order, was seen by the CNT militants as a surrender to their enemies – the Communists and bourgeois radicals. 'We have made too many concessions; it is time to turn the tap off' ran an editorial in *Solidaridad Obrera* on 8 April. But the leadership remained uneasy and on the defensive.

In the Spring of 1937 the factional feuds of the PSUC and POUM could no longer be concealed. The POUM leaders knew perfectly well what was happening in the Moscow trials; that Robespierre's technique of lumping all opponents under one label as traitors, a technique employed by Stalin against 'Trotskyite' traitors, was now being employed in Catalonia by the PSUC against its enemies. *La Batalla* opposed all the measures proposed by the PSUC to halt the revolution and to restore normal governmental control in Barcelona. The PSUC's drive to restore 'counter-revolutionary' free trade in food was denounced as a measure to favour the rich; the CNT and POUM press denounced Comorera, leader of the PSUC and Minister of Food, as personally responsible for the bread queues and the brutal police tactics used in breaking them up. The CNT Youth organization distributed stickers denouncing the minister as an inept traitor. The PSUC 'militarization' of the militia and the repression of militia patrols in favour of 'normal' police were seen by militants as measures to deprive the workers of their only political weapons. *La Batalla* denounced them. 'The only guarantee of the working class is its own army. And the army of the working class can be none other than . . . the militia'.

Late in March the Communists seem to have decided that the '*poumiste canaille*' must be destroyed.

In late April two political murders brought tension to boiling point. On 1 May *La Batalla* issued what looked like a declaration of war. 'All workers [must enforce] absolute control by the working class.' On 3 May Rodríguez Salas, the PSUC police commissioner, seized the ground floor of the central telephone exchange; CNT control of the building had long been resented by political enemies whose calls were tapped. This action set off confused street fighting between the POUM and its allies among militant anarchists on the one side, and the forces of public order on the other.

This revolution of desperation was not a planned rising but, in Orwell's words, a 'dust-up' between the government police and the militants which developed into a spasmodic, incoherent revolution of barricades. 'The devilish racket of firing went on and on. But so far as I could see, and from all I heard, the fighting was defensive on both sides. People simply remained in their buildings or behind their barricades and blazed away at the people opposite.' It is at least arguable that, if the Catalan government had immediately removed both Rodríguez Salas and the Catalan councillor for public order, this would have satisfied the militants and they would have left the streets. It did not. The police authorities remained and the fighting went on.

The CNT leaders in Valencia, where political nerves had been on edge for weeks, were dismayed. They sought to negotiate a truce with their own militants and proposed a provisional government in Barcelona which should attempt first to negotiate a cease fire, and then to impose terms on the militants. This would avoid the danger of the central government taking over from the Catalan government by using the argument that the Generalidad could no longer control the streets of Barcelona.

This element now came to dominate the confused situation, an element which explains the failure of the CNT proposals. Prieto and his followers and the Communists in Valencia had long resented the quasi-independence of Catalonia and the power of the CNT which the Generalidad seemed impotent to break. They now saw an opportunity of ending both once and for all. The Communists and their temporary allies – above all Prieto – demanded that the Catalan Statute be suspended and that Assault Guards be sent to Barcelona. Largo Caballero and the CNT ministers were outvoted after a long struggle with the hard liners. But by the time the Assault Guards reached Barcelona the hard core CNT militants, without the support of their leaders and short of food, lost heart and left the barricades on 7 May. The POUM could not fight on alone, even had it wished to do so.

The POUM, soon to be condemned to clandestinity, persisted in its advocacy of the seizure of power by a Revolutionary Workers

Front. But as its historian, the former *poumista* Victor Alba, confesses, they must have known in their hearts that there was not the slightest chance of success. On 19 July the CNT, had the leadership been *à la hauteur de sa tâche*, might have seized power in Barcelona. Such an opportunity was not to come again. It certainly was not present in May 1937. The reaction of the extremist elements to the PSUC offensive forced the POUM leadership to live up to its analysis. It was the moment of truth; the POUM leadership had to mount its workers' take-over when the forces of the revolution were scattered and uncoordinated. 'Our party joined the movement [the 'Friends of Durruti'] even though we knew it was condemned to failure.'

The CNT leadership had likewise been caught out when it found itself making constant wireless appeals for moderation while Communists were tearing up CNT membership cards and seizing CNT offices. The leaders could not, Secretary General Vazquez explained in a circular, 'face up to the definitive battle' and 'go over to the offensive' as the local militants wanted. 'Even supposing, which is supposing a great deal, the organization [of the CNT] conquered everybody in Catalonia. What would we do with victory?' Local triumph would be a disaster for the 'anti-fascist struggle'. The fronts would collapse; foreign powers would intervene – their battleships were anchored outside the port – to impose a mediated peace. 'We perfectly understood the tragedy of our comrades who saw themselves corralled and provoked.' But to fight on would have brought down the full power of the central government against the CNT. It was the old problem, the insoluble dilemma of anarchism after July 1936. The CNT could not make a *Spanish* revolution except through an anarchist dictatorship which was a nonsense theoretically – here the CNT parted from the POUM – and a practical impossibility. No one in the CNT had contemplated a situation in which the revolution would come as a reaction to a military coup and therefore coincide with a civil war – a war against 'fascists'. 'We must not forget,' Vazquez concluded, 'that if the war is lost the revolution and all the proletarian conquests are lost.'

As a consequence of the May events both the revolutionary forces in Barcelona and Catalan independence of the central government were destroyed; it was as if one could not survive without the other. The central government took over control of public order and sent

General Pozas to command 'the army of Catalonia'. The powers 'robbed' by Companys and the councillors of the Generalidad passed back to Valencia. Azaña, the man who had pushed the Catalan Autonomy Statute through the Cortes, was delighted. The Catalan politicians had shown little respect for the President of Spain, leaving him unprotected in the Presidential Palace whence he sent panic-stricken teletype messages to Prieto. Now for the first time the Republican flag was flown all over Barcelona, replacing that of the Generalidad and the CNT.

III

It was now that the Communists saw the opportunity to destroy Largo Caballero, with whom their relation was now one of undisguised hostility. On 13 May the Communist ministers demanded the abandonment of the Prime Minister's Extremadura offensive, suppression of the POUM and the trial for treason of its leaders. The 'old man' would not tolerate the repression of a workers' party and the Communists refused to yield.

The Communist offensive would not have succeeded in forcing the Prime Minister's resignation without allies in the Cabinet. The Left Republican ministers had never liked Largo Caballero; Prieto detested him, and his friends in the PSOE executive now determined that Largo must go. President Azaña was deeply offended that Largo Caballero, whom he found 'cold and inconsiderate', had made no effort to get him out of Barcelona to safety in the May crisis; and his constitutional position as heir to the king in a cabinet crisis now, at last, gave him, for the first time since July 1936, a taste of power and an opportunity for revenge. He offered to keep Largo on if he would give up the Ministry of War. Obstinate to the last, the 'old man' refused. Without the support of his cabinet (except for the CNT ministers who had no alternative but to support him as the last symbol of the revolutionary conquests, their sole bulwark against a Communist offensive) he was forced to resign. Azaña appointed Dr Juan Negrín, a former professor of physiology and Finance Minister, acceptable alike to Socialists, Communists and Republicans. The new government was presented as the 'government of victory'. Prieto was revenged and Azaña felt a certain sense of achievement.

Were Communist policies, as opposed to the methods by which they sought to implement them, correct? Probably yes. Concentration of power, strong government, was an absolute necessity as it had been in Russia during its civil war. Largo Caballero was a bad War Minister. The POUM's refusal to accept the Popular Front was an absurdity. It would have shorn the anti-fascist front of half its proletarian and all its middle-class support; worse still, it would have deprived the Republic of Soviet arms.

It was the Communist *methods*, the tone of Communist propaganda which stank. The creation and maintenance of the Popular Front, the determination to secure the loyalty of the middle classes, the insistence that, in order to attract international support, the war must be presented as a defence of democracy were, in Communist jargon, 'objectively correct'. What was ruinous was their determination to use the Popular Front for the ends of their own party and the Soviet Union. The elimination of the POUM became a Communist obsession; it was labelled 'Trotskyite' and accused of mounting a planned rising in collaboration with fascist *agents provocateurs*. It is true that Franco claimed credit for provoking the troubles; nevertheless, with sixty rifles at their headquarters, the POUM were scarcely in a position to risk armed revolt.

To non-Communists the vendetta against the POUM looked like compulsory homework, heresy hunting carried out at the behest of Soviet advisers. The blackest stain was the assassination of the leader of the POUM, Andrés Nin, by the Communist secret police, outrageously camouflaged as the work of German agents. This blatant lie was soon exposed and the vendetta backfired. The Communists wanted the POUM leadership condemned as fascist *agents provocateurs* and traitors. At the trial, in October 1937, their forged evidence failed to convince. Defended by Largo Caballero and Federica Montseny the POUM leaders were convicted of the crime of rebellion against the constituted government.

Nothing is more distasteful than to read the accounts written by intelligent Communists – Ludwig Renn, Koltsov and Longhi – of the May events and their consequences. Their verbal violence against the POUM is astonishing: 'beasts of prey that must be destroyed'. Yet such was the power of the Communist voice on the left in the late thirties that it was the Communist version that was accepted as the 'official' version. George Orwell's attempt to salvage the truth, by a defence of the POUM, from a sea of 'the most appalling lies' met with no response on the English left. The *New*

Statesman would not print his articles; Gollancz refused to publish his classic *Homage to Catalonia*. When it was published by Secker and Warburg it sold 'damn all'.

IV

The elimination of Largo Caballero and the appointment of Negrín was a Republican response to the need for a strong united government at all costs. The corresponding need – and it was far less a necessity – on the Nationalist side was satisfied by the creation of the Unified Party on 18 April 1937.

Political differences and party squabbles symbolized in the early days by a multiplicity of uniforms, existed in the Nationalist zone; party struggles, in the sense that they prevailed in Madrid, Barcelona and Valencia did not. The largest pre-existing political group in Nationalist Spain was the right-wing electoral grouping CEDA created by Gil Robles. This simply disintegrated since it was dependent on a parliamentary life which did not exist, and Gil Robles' concessions to legalism made him the political *bête noire* of the hard right and Falangists. 'He,' declared José Antonio, 'is responsible for everything.' In February 1937, from Portugal, he ordered his own party Acción Popular, the core of CEDA, to end its political activities. The old upper-class monarchist grouping supported by Alfonso XIII was never a mass party; the king himself had once referred to it as a collection of drawing-room conspirators. In March its political expression, Renovación Española, followed Gil Robles' example and dissolved itself. But this group was to have considerable influence in high government circles precisely because it was not a mass party and could not, therefore, rival those groupings in Nationalist Spain that did claim mass support.

The two mass popular forces that remained were, therefore, the Carlists and the Falange. Both had political philosophies and ambitions distinct from the neutral authoritarianism of the generals, all of whom (oddly enough with the exception of that most strident prophet of the New Order, Queipo de Llano) had loyally served the non-party 'national' dictatorship of Primo de Rivera. The Carlists wanted the restoration of the monarchy; the regent for the future king was Don Javier Bourbon Parma whose Saint's Day was celebrated with solemn masses, processions and parades of *requetés* in Navarre; the Falangists declared for a national revolution which would make them, in the phrase of Hedilla, 'the sole foundation of the new state'.

On 18 July the Falange was a small party of enthusiasts and adventurers. Its organization, never strong, had been broken by arrests after February 1936. Thus its mushroom growth – so great was the rush of dubious recruits that the clothiers of Pamplona were forbidden to sell blue cloth for party uniforms without party permission – involved it in serious difficulties; there was no structure in which to incorporate the new converts. Its leader José Antonio was in prison; he was executed by the Popular Front authorities in Alicante on 20 November, becoming the 'absent one' in Falangist ceremonial. The party was degenerating into a conglomeration of warring clans with the provincial delegates as chieftains. More than this, the 'new shirts' who flooded the party did not share the ideas of a radical transformation of Spanish society that haunted 'old shirts' like Manuel Hedilla, the provisional leader of the movement.

Hedilla sought to make his leadership effective; not from ambition – he was a man of simple tastes and an abiding dislike for the flashy quasi-military elegance affected by some of his rivals. He feared a divided movement might not be able to resist the orthodox conservatism of the Salamanca GHQ and the consequences for the Falange of the creation of a united party now being talked of among Franco's political intimates. Hedilla had already seen the fate of the Falangists of Andalusia where the movement had been subordinated and emasculated by Queipo de Llano. The generals wanted to 'depoliticize' the Falange by absorbing its 'first line' militia into the regular army. Hedilla made it clear, in an interview with Farinacci, the Italian Fascist, that it was the Falange that must depoliticize the army. Its militias – a strange echo of the CNT – must be the safeguard of the Nationalist revolution, and the army return to its normal functions. He had no time for the old right. It was the old right that was purging the rearguard and blaming the Falange for their atrocities. Peasants and workers must be won over, as José Antonio had argued, not shot. 'I prefer repentant Marxists to rightists corrupted by politics and *caciquismo*.' Every day Hedilla saw the determination of the Salamanca GHQ to discredit the Falange, to whittle down its independence and destroy its 'revolutionary' programme, to close down its syndicates and censor its press into banalities.

In his resistance to the dangers of a right-wing restoration he found a sympathetic hearing with the German Ambassador Faupel, a left-wing Nazi. In March his Italian colleague reported the Germans were prepared to organize a pro-Falangist coup against Franco. When rumours reached Franco he summoned Faupel and warned him; three days later, after consultation with the Nazi party representative and the Italians, the German Ambassador came to the conclusion that 'in spite of all their inclinations towards the Falange' they must support Franco at all costs.

The generalissimo had already brought the Carlists to heel and here he was helped by the divisions of the Carlist party. The national leader, Fal Conde, strident and obdurate as ever, was determined to preserve Carlism as an independent force loyal to the true dynasty; he was at odds with the Navarrese Carlists who followed Rodezno, a more accommodating figure with strong contacts with those Alfonsine politicians who were pushing the idea of a unified party which might compromise on Don Juan, Alfonso's son, as a candidate for the throne. On 8 December Fal Conde had published, without consulting Salamanca, a seemingly innocent decree setting up a Royal Carlist Military Academy.* The 'Royal' appellation, if accepted, would commit Franco to a Restoration backed by an independent militia. Franco distrusted Fal Conde; he was told to leave the country in forty-eight hours and the new leader, Rodezno, was more malleable, if not cynical, by Carlist standards. To show Faupel his ruthlessness with political dissidents the Caudillo told him he would have had Fal Conde shot but for the effect on Carlist morale at the front.

The restiveness in the ranks of the Carlists and the Falange and the abortive attempts in the early spring to bring about some real unity of action between them were an affront to Franco's deepest political convictions. These can be summed up in two concepts: order and unity. Sociologists who scrupulously analyse the class structure of officer corps frequently miss – and being model-makers themselves the omission is odd – that the officer himself has a model of civil society formed by years of habituation to military hierarchy. The officers order; the troops obey. In political life dissension is what mutiny is in an army. For Franco, the great evil of 'inorganic democracy' (a parliamentary system based on universal suffrage) was the subordination of national interest to party interest. Now the squabbles of the political clans in Nationalist Spain, their failure to form a national front, threatened to transfer to the new state the party factions of the old.

The fundamental conviction of Franco was – and remained – that parties had destroyed the remnants of Spanish greatness and their disappearance was a condition of its revival. Years later he was still repeating that parties were 'an abomination'. The conclusion of the victor of the Civil War was, therefore, to be that Spain must not be allowed the expensive and degrading luxury of party politics. 'In the sacred name of Spain and in the name of all who have died through the centuries for a great, united and world-wide Spain . . . I ask one thing of you: Unity.' This unity he now imposed from above by the creation of a single party.

At the end of January 1937 his brother-in-law, Ramón Serrano Suñer, had escaped to Salamanca. A lawyer, politician and student of the history of the greatness of Castile, he was alarmed at the improvised nature of Nationalist government – by now a group of secretaries and a technical junta dependent directly on Franco. It had no structure, no ideological basis. It rested on a 'state of pure force' that could not be prolonged. The new state must not resemble the old democratic state which had ruined Spain; the model seemed to be a one-party authoritarian state where the party could act as a link between the ruler (for Serrano Suñer saw that nothing other than Franco's rule was possible or desirable) and the ruled. The party would transmit orders and reflect opinion.

Franco himself was turning over in his mind the possibility of a united party at a moment when the faction fights in the Falange reached the level of scandal. Hedilla's provisional leadership was contested by Aznar, leader of the Falangist militia, who thought Hedilla too 'artisan', too politically unsophisticated for the post of leader; and by ambitious local chieftains (Dávila of Seville, Garcerán of Salamanca) with good contacts in the army. Probably alarmed at the prospects of unification engineered by his enemies in the movement, Hedilla summoned a National Council of the Falange at Salamanca for 25 April. The Falangist clans converged on Salamanca and on 16 April, 'the longest and blackest day in the history of the Falange', open warfare broke out between the gangs. Hedilla's opponents mounted an office *coup d'état* against him and installed themselves as a triumvirate. In the evening Sancho Dávila's gunmen shot Hedilla's personal guard in an hotel. The Civil Guard arrested all concerned. On 18 April Hedilla tried to defeat his opponents by calling the National Council; it elected him leader. But the victor of ugly feuds was neither Hedilla nor his rivals but the generalissimo. On 19 April the Falange ceased to exist as a separate party; it was absorbed in the new single party under Franco.

The Carlists were less of a problem. Their divisions allowed Franco to by-pass the intransigent National leadership and impose his terms on Rodezno, who then persuaded his Navarrese followers to accept unification since the new Unified party would enshrine 'the essence of tradition' even if it left the restoration of the true monarchy for some future, unspecified date.

The Decree of Unification was the outcome of Franco's meditations on the undesirability of a pluralistic society in Spain and Serrano Suñer's Castilian version of totalitarianism. Both saw that the Falange and Carlism shared with each other and with them the desire for total rejection of the parliamentary system, referred to in official terminology as 'inorganic democracy'; that the Falange shared, even exaggerated, their own imperial vision; that both Carlists and Falangists professed to criticize the grosser evils of capitalist society and were prepared to use the term 'national revolution' to describe this disinclination towards the end products of *laissez-faire* liberalism. They were recognized in the Decree as 'the two authentic exponents of the spirit of the national rising initiated by our Glorious Army on 17 July'. Nevertheless unification had come, not from negotiation with the party leaders but as an imposition from above. Since the parties could come to no agreement 'from below', Franco, as he put it in his wireless speech 'assuming in myself the national will' to unity, imposed it *'por vía de superación'* – in other words, over the heads of the parties. The Decree meant the end of independent political life in Spain. The phrasing was simple. 'All other organizations and political parties are hereby dissolved.'

The Unified party bore the cumbrous name of *Falange Española Tradicionalista y de las Juntas de Ofensiva Nacional-Sindicalistas*. The Carlists got the vaguest of indications that the monarchy might be restored when it suited Franco; from the Falangists the new party adopted the first twenty-six points of the Falange programme (it would not adopt the twenty-seventh since this forbade union with other parties). The Falangists were to wear the red beret of the Carlists, the Carlists the blue shirts of the Falange in the new single militia under Franco's command. Hedilla had not been consulted – he read the names of the new party's junta in the papers – and refused to accept the subordinate post of Secretary General. Rumours of a conspiracy of Hedilla against the virtual dissolution of the old Falange led to his arrest and life imprisonment. Hedilla had acted out of outraged dignity; he was a proud man, not a conspirator. His fate was a warning to others; he became the forgotten man of the right. Falangists in the radical tradition might consider the Decree of Unification as unconstitutional and a sell-out to clericalism; but with their jobs secure as long as they kept their mouths shut, most of them remained silent.

The militant Carlists were the greater losers in this process of unification *por vía de superación*; they had, an embittered Fal Conde remarked, 'lost the lot'. The programme of the new party was basically that of the Falange. Franco and Serrano Suñer believed that the main problem of the Nationalist movement was to gain, or regain, the allegiance of the 'great unaffiliated neutral mass that has never wished to join any party'. The Traditionalist creed lacked 'a certain modernity' necessary for this task. The Carlists' leader was in exile and their prince received no formal recognition; they felt that they had been beaten in the race for official posts by their rivals the Falangists, whom they could never bring themselves to think of as other than a mafia of Andalusian adventurers. Clandestine attacks on the Falange circulated, bitter jokes were common, but open opposition was impossible; critical voices were drowned in the orchestrated praise of the new leader and the new unity. Pradera's daughter praised the unity of hearts that would have delighted her martyred father.* The fundamental divergencies in visions and hopes of the Falange and the Carlist-Traditionalists remained below the surface, appearing only in minor manifestations. Falangists wore their blue shirts without the red beret; Carlists the red beret without the blue shirt. But even such symbolic opposition was ended by Decree in 1938.

Franco now, as chief of the single party as well as generalissimo and chief of state, controlled directly all important appointments in the government, the party and the army. It could be asserted that the only organism he did not command directly was the Church.

* Victor Pradera (b. 1873) was the ideological renovator of Carlism. His book *El Estado Nuevo* (The New State) influenced Franco's political thinking. Pradera was shot in San Sebastian in the early days of the war.

'Such a concentration of power in time of war,' observed the French General Duval, 'had been realized nowhere since Napoleon.' The Movement, as the new amalgamation came to be termed, embraced the totality of Spanish official life. No one could get an official job without joining. It became the basis for uncontested one-man rule rather than the expression of 'the thought and style of our Revolution'.

Apart from Franco, the victors were the old rightists who had slipped into the administration (as the Falange historian bitterly remarked, while the Falangists were fighting at the front) and the army. 'In the last resort,' wrote Serrano Suñer, architect of the unification, 'the centre of gravity of the régime, its true support, was and continues to be, the army.'

* Additional note to p. 179. In his conversations with his cousin, published in 1976, Franco gave a different version of events. 'There was no Academy, nor was Fal Conde exiled, nor did anyone attempt a coup d'état.' (Francisco Franco Salgado-Aravjo, *Mis conversaciones privadas con Franco*, p. 483.)

11
The Tip of the Balance

In March 1937 the Nationalists switched their efforts from Madrid to the northern front; the conquest of the industrial and coal-mining areas would strengthen the Nationalist resource base. The conquest was completed by October.

The Republican army sought to mount operations on other fronts aimed, in part, to force Franco to reduce the scale of his northern operations. These later summer offensives were unsuccessful, and the most important, the Brunete offensive, was a costly battle for both sides.

I

By the spring of 1937 General Franco's closest military advisers reached the conclusion that Madrid could be taken only at great cost. They persuaded him to abandon the 'obsession' with Madrid and to concentrate all available forces on the conquest of the north. A northern triumph would shorten his lines, cut off the Republicans from one of their sea avenues of supply and, above all, place the great industrial power of the Cantabrian coast in Nationalist hands. It would alter the resource balance decisively.

The northern campaign exposed once more the military weaknesses of political coalitions. The front comprised the Basque Province of Vizcaya, Santander and Asturias. The two strongest sectors were controlled by competing political creeds. In the Basque state of Euzkadi, the festivals of the Church were public holidays and private property protected; in Asturias (where the Council of Asturias manned by the CNT and the UGT was outside the control of the central government) priests were persecuted and private property collectivized.

In the military sphere the independence of the autonomous region of Euzkadi (recognized by the Republican Cortes in October 1936) inhibited proper coordination and the establishment of a unified command in the north. Aguirre, the immensely popular President of Euzkadi, like the Catalans, engaged in 'robbing' the central government and the central army command of their powers. His aim was a Basque'army, and he rejected the whole concept of a northern army which could operate on the whole front and be controlled by the Republican general staff and War Ministry. When General Llano de Encomienda was appointed in November to command the northern front, Aguirre set about reducing Llano's command to a nullity and his army to a paper force even to the point of denying its existence; the President claimed the power to make promotions and to put 'all the units . . . which operate in the country under the superior authority of the Councillor [i.e. Minister] of Defence of Euzkadi'. In desperation Llano telegraphed Largo Caballero: 'Request your Excellency to inform me whether the army to which I had the honour to be appointed to command exists or not.'

Aguirre was unanimously backed by his government which included Communists, those protagonists of rigid centralization, and Valencia had to give in. There was no alternative. The Catholic Basques, respectable bourgeois far removed from the 'reds' of Catalonia and Valencia, were a showpiece in Europe of the democratic spirit of the Republic. Aguirre has been accused of excessive 'cantonalism', of constantly putting the interests of the part against the survival of the whole. But we must remember that the central government, cut off by the Nationalist occupation to the south, could do little to help him. He wanted tanks and aeroplanes, not an interfering general. Euzkadi was the most orderly region in the Republic and Aguirre's control more effective than that of any other political leader. Why should he take orders from Largo Caballero and model his militia on those of the Popular Army? In the end the government gave in: it created a Basque army under General Gamir and pushed Llano to the command of Santander and Asturias.

Mola attacked (30 March) with forty thousand men of the Navarrese division supported by the mixed Spanish and Italian Black Arrows with two hundred guns and 140 aeroplanes. Every attack was preceded by heavy artillery and aerial bombardment.

Franco had built a new aerodrome at Vitoria and it was overwhelming air superiority that was the decisive factor. Resistance was uneven; superb Basque and UGT militia units were let down by sudden collapses on their flanks. These collapses were occasioned by the heavy artillery fire and inaccurate but psychologically effective aerial bombing, its effects enhanced by press reports and by the contagious fears of the civilian population. The commissar of the army of the north reported that aerial bombardments 'produced a vertical fall in the morale of our forces'; they were 'paralysed by nerves'. Air cover became 'an obsession'. Hence the agonized demands for more aeroplanes which Valencia could not risk flying across Nationalist territory. Aguirre sent daily telegrams, even threatening a separate peace if left unsuccoured.

By 25 April the first defensive line had gone. On Monday 26 April came the most notorious event in the whole war: the bombing of Guernica, a small market town where grew the tree that was the symbol of Basque nationalism. It was carried out by the Condor Legion of the German air force command. Heinkel 111s and later the lumbering JU 52s bombed at intervals through the late afternoon. High explosive bombs were followed up by incendiaries. A fire, fanned by the wind and with no fire engines to control it, destroyed the town. The Republican air force, demoralized by defeat and the death of its 'ace', del Río, made no attempt to interfere.

That the bombing was the idea in the first place of the German Air Command – above all of von Richthofen – there can be now no doubt; it regarded the episode as a legitimate operation of war, a saturation bombardment of an important communications centre six miles behind the front which would accelerate what was becoming a painfully slow advance. (Given the use of incendiaries it is hard to maintain that the *sole* target was the Rentería bridge and the roads.) What was at the time the burning issue still remains: 'Did the Nationalist GHQ order or tolerate the German action?' There is little evidence; but at least someone on Mola's staff must have been consulted. Since the Jarama battle, relations between the German pilots and the Spanish air command had been strained, and during the northern campaign the Germans complained loudly of the slowness of the Spanish ground forces in exploiting opportunities opened up by the Condor Legion's bombardments. This may explain their independent attitude.

The horrified world reaction wiped out any conceivable military advantage. Compared to the destruction of Dresden or Hiroshima, Guernica may appear a minor act of vandalism and the Nationalists could argue that the Republicans themselves had made bombing raids on towns like Saragossa and Cordoba. But, at the time, this was irrelevant; the destruction of Guernica was complete. It is a measure of European emotional involvement that Guernica gave rise to more column inches of bitter controversy than Hiroshima; it inspired poetry and Picasso's most famous painting; it outraged not merely the standard supporters of the left, but French liberal Catholics. Guernica made such an impression on the European imagination because it was the first example of the horrors of modern war. To those who felt a great war in Europe was inevitable this gave Spain its tremendous significance; to those who felt the aggressor might be Hitler's Germany, Guernica, as a Foreign Office official scribbled in the margin of a dispatch, 'told us what to expect from the Germans'.

Once the news of a bombardment by Germans was splashed across the English press on 28 April – the most important cable was sent by *The Times* correspondent George Steer, a passionate supporter of the Basques – the Nationalist press agency in Salamanca panicked; it blamed the whole destruction on the retreating army – the CNT had, after all, they argued, burnt Irun in September 1936. When the Republican news agencies told of the bombing, the Nationalist radio countered with 'Lies, Lies, Lies'; the destruction was the work of 'red separatist incendiaries'.* Once the 'official' Nationalist version was out, it could not be disowned. Franco could scarcely reveal to the world that he could not control his German friends or, indeed, that the Germans were there in force at all; nor could he attribute to his own air force a bombardment that had shocked the world.

The committed press, above all the Catholic press in England, accepted the Salamanca version which had to be defended at all costs in order to conceal from the world the degree of German intervention. Geoffrey Dawson, editor of *The Times* of London could not understand the sharp German reaction when he printed the reports of Steer, who was one of the first journalists to visit the

---

* Almost all defenders of the Nationalist version concentrated on the fact that there were relatively few traces of high explosive bombs. The town was destroyed not by explosive bombs but by incendiary bombs.

town. German pilots kept their mouths shut. 'We did not like,' wrote Galland, the Second World War ace, 'discussing Guernica.' Official Germany accepted the 'red incendiarism' version and spoke at great length about Republican atrocities on the Non-Intervention Committee. Eden knew that von Ribbentrop was lying; blatant lies were something else one might expect from the Germans. The Republican propaganda machine exaggerated the casualties. But it held the trump card of essential truth: the town had been destroyed by German bombers, not by 'red incendiaries'.*

It is curious to reflect that without Picasso's *Guernica* the raid might have become just one more episode in the list of 'fascist' atrocities.† Its power continued to stamp Guernica on the mind of the world, and Picasso was now presented as the greatest example of the committed artist in the struggle against fascism. As a recent commentator has cynically remarked, had Picasso's picture been called 'The Death of Durango' – another Basque town bombed but, since no incendiaries were used, not totally destroyed – then Durango rather than Guernica would have become the great symbol, resurrected to condemn the US bombings in Vietnam.

Once the front had broken, the Republican general staff put all its faith in the 'iron ring' of Bilbao. A system of forts and trenches built by civilian engineers with no defence in depth, it was militarily vulnerable. To make matters worse, the plans of the iron ring had been handed over in February to the Nationalists by Goicoechea, inventor of the Talgo train. It was now that artillery, and above all air, superiority counted and that unevenness of resistance proved fatal. Two divisions held, but the division between vanished; another division fled in a 'rout', 'shameless and concerted'.

Bilbao had been starved, its port blockaded. There was no water and bombing and fears of bombing had reduced the population to apathy. Prieto's orders to resist and destroy all industrial

---

* The Basque government gave the 'official' figure as 1,645 dead and 889 wounded. The Nationalists, though they must have known the truth, insisted on maintaining their original version – Franco publicly supported it in 1948– till it could be maintained no longer. They then changed their line of defence. The bombardment of Guernica was carried out without the knowledge of the Nationalist Command. It was a purely German venture. No blame could attach to Franco.

† In a lesser degree English left-wing intellectuals were influenced by Steer's *Tree of Gernika*. Steer was a fine journalist and a powerful descriptive writer, whose judgments were sometimes skewed by his sympathies for the Basques, whom he considered vastly superior to 'Spaniards'.

installations were not carried out, and the Basque government rejected the Soviet adviser's demand for 'another Madrid', a house-to-house defence. After the government had withdrawn and the militia had escaped, the Nationalists entered unopposed on 19 June. Leizaola, the Basque Minister of Justice, saw to it that there were no last-minute murders of Nationalist prisoners.

The Basques had fought bravely, less for the social and political ideals of the Popular Front than, as Azaña put it, for 'their autonomy and semi-independence'.* Once this prospect vanished with defeat, they lost heart. They were Catholics on the wrong side in a crusade against the murderers of priests and monks. Hence the virulent hatred they inspired in those Basques – the Navarrese above all – who were not 'separatists'; hence the executions of Basque priests who had put Basque nationalism above Catholic unity.

The rest of the northern campaign was relatively easy for the Nationalists. The Basque militia were losing their fighting spirit and attempted to organize a separate surrender with the Italian local commander – a surrender disowned by his superior. Santander fell on 26 August after a model manoeuvre. Next day Mussolini claimed an Italian triumph in his newspapers; Ciano wanted captured Basque flags for an Italian Invalides – 'A flag taken from the enemy is worth more than any picture.' Even Franco expressed emotion. He came out of his office crying, 'We've taken Santander! Santander is ours!' In the Asturias, core of the Socialist resistance in 1934, the regular formations were outflanked on side roads by motorized columns as they attempted to hold the passes: an initially tough resistance suddenly collapsed 'like a meringue dipped in water'. On 21 October, much helped by the activity of the local fifth column, Aranda entered Gijón unopposed and the whole northern front disappeared. The collapse of 'red Asturias' was a great moral blow. The Madrid government believed that the miners would hold out and the Socialist leader Belarmino Tomás had talked of a 'Numantian Resistance'. (The garrison of Numantia had committed mass suicide rather than surrender to the Romans.)

---

* Some Basques, among them the surviving brother of Sabina Arana, the founder of Basque Nationalism, argued that the Basques should remain neutral in the Civil War. There were many approaches by Catholics (including Cardinal Gomá in January 1937) to negotiate a separate peace. Rumours of such negotiations, rejected by Aguirre and by one of his closest advisers Father Onaindia, did not improve relations with Valencia.

President Azaña remarked in his bitter pessimism that 'no one in this war tells the truth'. There were tragic, heroic resistances both before and after the fall of Gijón; but on one day the local commander shot three brigade and six battalion commanders for cowardice.

The northern victories were decisive. The iron ore and industry of the north were in Nationalist hands; the retreating Basques had refused to blow up the foundations of the economic strength of their *patria*, the iron foundries and metal works around Bilbao. Franco now controlled 62% of Spanish territory and over half the population; 25% of the Republican armed forces had vanished in defeat. Moreover, this slow, methodical campaign revealed that the Nationalist army was a formidable fighting force. It could carry out manoeuvres which obeyed Franco's dictum that no attack should be made unless its momentum could be maintained. 'To follow through' was all-important, and it was precisely the incapacity to 'follow through' which was the great weakness of the Republican army.

II

This was the lesson to be learned from the relative failures of the attacks mounted on other fronts in the summer of 1936. Well conceived strategically by Rojo, they came to pieces tactically. The initial days' advance lost its momentum; the punctured front was held by inferior forces until Franco could bring up reserves. It was then that the initiative of the offensive passed to the Nationalists.

The Republican summer offensives have usually been considered as conceived to relieve the pressure on the all-important northern front by forcing Franco to switch his reserves elsewhere. That 'decongestion' of the north was in part the aim is true; but we must remember that the Nationalist concentrations in the north weakened their lines in the centre and opened up the possibilities of a successful Republican offensive. This was quickly realized by Largo Caballero's planning staff. They suggested an all-out offensive in Extremadura which would cut Andalusia off from the rest of Nationalist Spain, dividing the zone in two. This was resisted by Miaja, always reluctant to surrender any of his troops for an operation that might add to the laurels of a rival commander. In his obstinate delaying tactics, of which he was a consummate practitioner, he was backed by the Communists who refused air support for the projected offensive, perhaps because they feared the political leverage Largo Caballero would earn from a successful operation. After the fall of Largo Caballero, Rojo was appointed chief of staff; this meant the end of the Extremadura offensive. Rojo was loyal to Miaja and had long been obsessed by the idea of an operation against Brunete.

The first of the diversionary attacks came in May on Segovia – a failure. An episode in this attack is the central episode in Hemingway's *For Whom the Bell Tolls*. One of the unexpected results of the offensive was the death in a plane crash of General Mola (3 June) who had come to consult with General Varela.

Then came a typical attempt to break through the weak Aragon front which a visiting French general had described as '*une position de surveillance plutôt que de résistance*'. Huesca was a tempting target, a few kilometres from the front, connected with Jaca by a road within range of Republican batteries. But the attack failed. So did the strategical intent behind Prieto's plan. Not a single aeroplane or brigade had been taken away from the Nationalist northern offensive.

The major Republican offensive became the battle of Brunete: Rojo's plan was to break through the Nationalist front at its weakest point fifteen miles west of Madrid. Like most 'fronts' it was not a continuously held line, but a series of strongpoints in the dreary, nondescript villages of the Castilian *meseta*, a featureless, arid landscape where troops easily lost their bearings. Rojo's instrument for the planned breakthrough and a subsequent pincer movement to get behind the Nationalist troops facing Madrid was the two corps of the newly formed Army of Manoeuvre to be supported by four corps of Miaja's Army of the Centre; in all 80,000 men with two hundred tanks against 2,400 troops.

Complete surprise was achieved. At dawn on 6 July, after limited penetration during the night, Republican armour smashed through towards Brunete. Unutterable confusion followed as newly brigaded troops poured through the gap and were held up by stiff resistance in villages which should have been by-passed. Reserves were not brought up rapidly enough to relieve exhausted troops or to exploit the initial breakthrough. Political jealousies had created trouble even in the planning stages; the attack was a pure Communist affair pushed through against the wishes of staff officers who had supported Largo Caballero's *idée fixe* of an offensive in

Battle of Brunete, July 1937

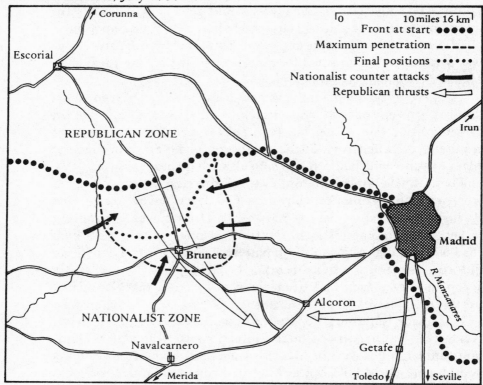

Extremadura. Confusion was intensified by the contingencies of battle – in the appalling heat, field telephone lines were burnt on the ground – and by Nationalist air supremacy which was achieved by 13 July. Brunete saw the first appearance of the new Messerschmidt 109s, the first fighters that could deal with the Russian Chatas and Moscas. Franco rapidly brought up reserves from the north and the battle ended, after three weeks of heavy and costly fighting, not in Rojo's grand sweep, but in the occupation of an awkward salient.

Was the battle worth the fighting? All it achieved was a temporary halt in the operations against Santander. Losses had been heavy – particularly in the International Brigades. George Nathan, the British brigader and ex-Guards officer who had resigned his commission over privates' pay, capable of rallying a battalion with his swagger stick, was killed. So, too, was Julian Bell, son of Vanessa and Clive Bell. He was an ambulance driver. His last words are memorable. 'Well, I always wanted a mistress and a chance to go to war, and now I've had both.' He then indistinctly recited what appeared to be verses of Baudelaire's poetry. Perhaps more important than the 25,000 casualties (the Nationalist casualties were seventeen thousand) was the loss of nearly a hundred aeroplanes.

Even so, Franco's counter-offensive was a costly and unnecessary operation and his chief of staff, Vigón, was appalled lest the Generalissimo's 'obsession' with Madrid should lead him to abandon the critical offensive in the north. The battle had stalemated before the Navarrese troops from the north arrived on the battlefield. Just as Rojo had badly miscalculated the resistance of the Nationalist strongpoints – his whole plan was based on a resistance of two or three hours when Quijorna, a key position, held out for two days – so Franco underestimated the defensive strength of the Republican Mixed Brigades. There had been some disgraceful episodes – on 23 July three hundred men of the XIII International Brigade deserted *en masse* and fled to Madrid – but on the whole the Republican army behaved well on the defensive.

The next Republican offensive began on 24 August; again it was planned as an ambitious pincer movement towards Saragossa by Rojo and was fought in equally appalling heat with the ever-present stench of rotting bodies around the Aragonese town of Belchite. It came to nothing. A surprisingly modern, concentrated, massed tank attack (one of the weaknesses of the use of tanks at Brunete had been their 'fanning out') came to grief through a communications breakdown – the Russian tank commander apparently insisted on giving orders in Russian – and the failure of the infantry to follow through. At Brunete – an attack on a narrow front – flank counter-attacks flung commanders off balance and led to panic withdrawals; at Belchite, a battle of manoeuvre on a wide front, commanders displayed what General Rojo called 'fear of space'. Both reflected the imperfections of the Popular Army where highly trained units fought beside weak units. And as at Brunete, the resistance of local units surprised the Republican command; this resistance was so fierce that Franco did not, as at Brunete, weaken his forces in the north.

The Communists had always held that the Republican failure to break through to Saragossa must be laid at the door of the indiscipline of the CNT militias and the treason of the POUM. The CNT replied that they could do little because their political enemies starved them of weapons. Now the well-trained, most disciplined and best-equipped Communist units had failed. Segovia, Huesca, Brunete and Belchite all told one lesson: the Popular Army, valiant in defence, had developed no capacity for a sustained offensive even where it enjoyed a crushing local superiority.

It is arguable that this local superiority could have been even greater, i.e. Prieto should have concentrated all his forces, say, on Brunete instead of wasting them on the relatively minor actions of Segovia and Huesca; in this sense the Extremadura offensive of Largo Caballero was better conceived. Rojo, likewise, tended to disperse his forces through his obsessive fear of an enemy breakthrough on a distant front; in July he was concerned with a possible Nationalist offensive in Teruel and was later criticized by Lister on this count. Rojo's strategy, which I discussed with him in the 1950s, now seems to me a curious combination of excessive

Republican Aragon Offensive, August 1937

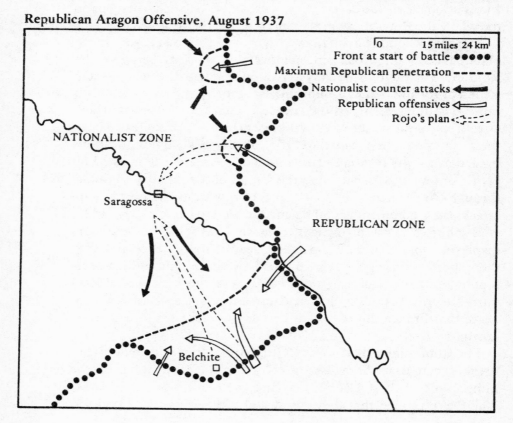

0   15 miles 24 km

Front at start of battle ●●●●●
Maximum Republican penetration ------
Nationalist counter attacks ◀━
Republican offensives ⬅=
Rojo's plan ◁----

NATIONALIST ZONE

Saragossa

REPUBLICAN ZONE

Belchite

optimism and excessive pessimism. It is possible to argue that his ambitious plans to cut off Nationalist forces by a sweep through to their rear hid a fear that few of his directives would be carried out on the ground. None of my arm-chair criticisms of the general diminish my admiration for the man and for the noble way he bore adversity. His generosity to me was as unbounded as it is unforgettable.

12

The Government of Victory: Teruel and the Aragon breakthrough

The events of May 1937 constituted the most serious political crisis on the Republican side in the Civil War. Largo's resignation as Prime Minister and Minister of War represented a triumph for the Communist insistence on the primacy of the war effort over the revolution; it entailed the withdrawal of the CNT and the Caballeristas from the new ministry of Dr Negrín and a 'concentration' of government.

In December 1937 the Republican government mounted the most ambitious offensive of the war, taking Teruel after a costly winter battle. Designed to stop an offensive against Madrid planned by Franco, it had the effect of bringing the Nationalist armies into a position from which they could break through the Aragon front and cut the Republican zone in two. After the loss of Teruel the Popular Army failed to hold the Nationalist offensive and on 15 April Nationalist troops reached the Mediterranean at Vinaroz.

This defeat enabled the Communists to get rid of their main enemy in the government: Indalecio Prieto, Minister of Defence, whose prestige suffered from military failure. He was forced to resign and on 5 April Dr Negrín reconstituted his government.

I

The summer battles of 1937 were the work of Negrín's government of victory, pledged to end the July revolution. His ministry represented a return to the initial purpose and conception of the Popular Front: the formation and maintenance of a broad democratic political coalition to defeat fascism. It included Prieto as Minister of Defence, his friend Zugazagoita at the Ministry of the

Interior, Giral for the Left Republicans as Foreign Minister, the Basque Irujo, a Catalan, and two Communists.

Much has been made of the 'counter-revolutionary' nature of Negrín's government and its subservience to Communist directives. Its declared purpose was to create a strong war government 'to unify the command of military operations as well as the control of economic life'. 'Concentration' was the slogan. This was first attempted in the military sphere. Prieto as Minister of Defence (before there had been a Ministry of War and a separate Ministry for the navy and air force) immediately created a central general staff for all arms: he now became the central figure in the Republican war effort and the great proponent of governmental centralization in a campaign against the remnants of 'cantonalism' in Catalonia and Aragon. His initial allies were the Communists in the cabinet. Zugazagoita appointed a Communist as Director General of Public Security – the key post in his ministry which gave the Communists effective control of all police forces.

Negrín was a man of considerable charm and enormous animal energy – his appetite for food and drink was huge and he was reputed to be a sexual athlete. Erratic in his working habits, he could work for twenty-four hours at a stretch and then do nothing for days. His qualities came as a relief to his fellow intellectual President Azaña, who found himself 'no longer speaking to a corpse' (Largo Caballero). He has been violently attacked, especially by anti-Communists and ex-Communists, as at best a bourgeois politician, cut off by his sybaritic instincts and his failures as a crowd orator from the popular enthusiasms, at worst a mere tool of the Soviet Union via the Spanish party; in the words of Jesús Hernández (then a Communist Minister who subsequently left the party) as 'the confidence man of Moscow'. All the new government's measures – strict censorship, the tightening-up measures against spies and political dissidents, the prohibition of criticism of the only foreign ally – can be regarded as either the normal measures of a war-time government or as support for a ruthless Communist campaign against political opponents. Efficient police are necessary to enforce black-out regulations as much as to rough up the opposition.

Negrín's policies rested on two axioms: firstly that sooner or later France and Great Britain would have to come out against the dictators and help Spain, at least by ending non-intervention and restoring the government's right to purchase arms; secondly that, until this happened, nothing could be done that would offend the Soviet Union to the point at which it would refuse arms supplies. This implied a working alliance with the Communist party, without sacrificing every democratic principle to the demands of the party machine. It was a delicate and dangerous balancing act.

Negrín's dilemma emerges most painfully over the question of political trials. Irujo and Zugazagoita in particular made every effort to regularize trials, to the extent of restoring judges' birettas; this would rid the Republic of accusations of terror which did so much harm in the West. But in this vital sphere the Communists' determination to eliminate their political enemies took priority over their projection of an image of a regular respectable government. When they could not pervert the new judicial apparatus they used their own parallel organizations. Thus the cabinet insisted on a regular trial of the POUM leaders; and it would not consent to the execution of the POUM leader Andrés Nin. He was clumsily murdered by Communist agents, and Negrín accepted the *fait accompli* rather than provoke an open breach with the Communists. His moral stature has never recovered from this act of weakness. Yet Prieto had already tasted the consequences of resisting party pressure; the Russians retaliated by holding up an arms shipment. 'Thus I was punished.' Negrín was determined that the Republic should not be punished.

Accusations of supine acquiescence verging on fellow-travelling spring from Negrín's failure to arrest Communist control of the army and the police. Communists never sought direct political preponderance; it would brand the Republic, to Stalin's British and French friends, as 'red'; indeed, on one occasion Soviet advisers tried to get the Communists to withdraw from the Ministry. They sought to control the army: 'He who controls the army controls the state.' They sought, largely in order to pursue their own political feuds, the control of the police. They sought, in order to influence western opinion, complete control of press agencies.

The new secret police, the SIM, organized by Soviet specialists, soon came to reflect the Russian advisers' propensity to find spies and traitors everywhere – a mania which Gustav Regler called the 'Russian syphilis'. The tap of the SIM agent at the door replaced the pistol of the anarchist uncontrollables as the image of Republican justice. George Orwell and his wife suffered the beginnings of this new atmosphere of terror. 'It was as though some huge evil intelligence were brooding over the town [Barcelona]. . . . I had an overwhelming desire to get away from it all; away from the horrible atmosphere of suspicion and hatred.' Even the chief Russian military adviser, Berzin, dared to criticize the ruthlessness of Soviet police, who treated the Spaniards as 'colonials'. The methods by which the party controlled the image in the foreign press of the issues at stake in the war were more effective than those employed at Burgos and Salamanca where the rudeness of Nationalist press officials made the press department universally detested by foreign reporters. Experienced Communist censors dealt with unsympathetic journalists more subtly: their cables were mysteriously delayed, 'exclusives' were given to less critical rivals.

Hence they could foist their version of the May events on left-wing Europe without much trouble. Journalists resented this partisan censorship and sometimes sent embittered cables from Paris. 'All democratic forms and usage of government,' wrote an American journalist, 'have disappeared in Spain. There is no freedom whatever allowed journalistic investigation and the strictest censorship imaginable is imposed on all news dispatches sent out from Madrid.' It was, perhaps, a little naive to expect that a government at war would allow journalists a peace-time freedom or that democracy ever functions normally in war time.

The main political target of the Communists was Largo Caballero. Since his fall he was a dangerous nuisance through his continued hold over the UGT. The Communists and Socialists, after splitting the Union, forced him out of the leadership and reduced him and his followers to impotence.

One way to regard the last stage of the Civil War is to see it as the final triumph of the political parties over the trades unions in a struggle that had started with the Civil War itself. The defeated of May 1937 were Largo Caballero and the CNT. The victors were Prieto and the Executive Committee of the Socialist Party, the Communists and the Republicans. After May, Largo Caballero returned to his old dream of a trades union embracing all Spanish workers; but even in the bitterness of defeat the CNT and UGT could not unite.

The new government's desire for order involved a domestic offensive, limited but precisely organized, against those whom the Communists and Republicans had long castigated as proponents of the permanent revolution and opponents of centralization.

In Aragon the CNT Council of Aragon was an *imperium in imperio*. Negrín and Prieto agreed with the Communist party that it must be dissolved, though their reasons were distinct; for them efficient centralization meant more than party revenge. And it was as a political offensive, rather than an administrative reform, that the proposed dissolution appeared to the CNT; it was part of 'an infamous Communist plot' and according to its Secretary General boded 'the systematic elimination of the CNT' and the 'dictatorship' of the Communist party. Cordón, the new Communist chief of staff to the Army of the East, anticipating resistance, moved up loyal brigades. It was Lister, a reliable Communist commander, who dissolved the Council *manu militari*. The CNT leaders were gaoled, its newspapers closed down and Durruti's portraits removed from offices. This was going far beyond the instructions and intentions of the Valencia government as set out in the Decree of Dissolution (11 August 1937): 'The moral and material necessities of the war demand the concentration of the authority of the State so that it can be exercised in a unified and purposeful manner.' They did not demand 'a brutal repression' in which the CNT 'should receive all the blows'. The dissolution of the Council was followed by forcible de-collectivization restrained only by a desire to keep labour for the harvest. Communist fears of the effect on the harvest would seem to prove that at least to the labourers collectivization did represent a real gain, an end to the subjection of the underemployed to the employer.

Nor did the government merely tackle the agricultural collectives. After May, government control extended rapidly over collectivized industry in Catalonia. It was the end of the spontaneous revolution. The Italian anarchist Louis Bertoni wrote from the Huesca front: 'There remains a terrible question of life or death, but no longer a war to build a new society.' Nor were the CNT the only victims. By 1938 the last vestiges of Catalan autonomy in the economic sphere disappeared.

In August the Catalan minister resigned from the government in protest against the steady erosion of the powers of the Generalidad, with its competence reduced to the level of 'folklore'. The vision of a pluralistic Spain had finally vanished in a Communist-dominated centralized state, as obnoxious to Catalanists as any of its predecessors. With the central government installed in Barcelona,

President Companys was now, as President Azaña had long been, in a backwater. Companys consoled himself by reading Catalan poetry; Azaña by writing a bitter political commentary.

II

With the defeats in the north the war had gone on for over a year without a victory for the Popular Front. Prieto and Negrín believed that the reformed Republican army must attack if it was to avoid creeping defeat. General Rojo convinced them he could mount a successful offensive on a weakly held section of the front. Apart from restoring Republican confidence in its army, the Republican offensive against Teruel – a provincial capital – was aimed at turning Franco away from Madrid, against which his armies were once more concentrating after his victorious northern campaign. Franco was still obsessed by Madrid and his plans were known to the Republican command, partly through the extraordinary feat of Cipriano Mera, the best of the CNT commanders. A man of grizzled and weatherbeaten appearance, it is alleged that he disguised himself as a shepherd and penetrated the Nationalist lines.

The offensive against the awkward salient of Teruel was to be the work of the now well-organized Popular Army – three corps of the Army of Manoeuvre – with no help from the International Brigades, now resting and enjoying visits from Major Attlee and Mrs J.B.S.Haldane. Teruel, perched on a rocky eminence, was already almost surrounded by the Republican lines and dominated by the surrounding heights.

As at Brunete, Rojo achieved complete surprise and broke through the Nationalist line near Teruel with 77,000 men (15 December 1937). Franco, after some delay, sent Varela and Aranda to plug the gap. If the weather had held the Republican army would have been in a difficult position; but a temperature of − 5° and four inches of snow immobilized fighting outside the city where Nationalist and Republican troops suffered terribly from frostbite. Sentinels had to be relieved every quarter of an hour; the aeroplanes at Burgos were grounded by ice; lorries slipped off icy roads into the ravines below. Thus the Nationalist counter-attack was held. This allowed the Republicans to capture the town house by house in bitter street fighting. On 8 January the garrison surrendered. It was now that the International Brigades were brought up into the line.

The effect of this capture of a provincial capital – except for

Albacete the only capital to fall to the Republicans – on the Nationalists' Italian and German allies was appalling. They never understood Franco's concept of 'liberation'; rather than fighting a costly battle in order to 'redeem' Teruel from the reds, he should, they believed, have pushed on to Madrid – correct strategy in terms of 'ordinary' war. Stohrer, the German Ambassador, sent a strong dispatch urging more supplies and more technicians. Ciano panicked: he foresaw 'a Republican offensive to push back the whole Nationalist front'. If there were no victory, the Italian legions might have to be withdrawn, and there was a rumble of discontent in the Condor Legion.

Franco was as unmoved by reverses as he was by victory. There was no significant progress in January. But north of Teruel the Republican front was weak; its collapse in the battle of Alfambra (5–9 February 1938) directed on the spot by Franco, was sudden and complete; it saw one of the last cavalry charges of modern warfare and the heaviest aerial attack of the war. In a few days the Republic lost a thousand square kilometres and possibly six thousand prisoners. On 22 February Teruel was once more in Nationalist hands.

The battle for Teruel laid bare the strength and weaknesses of Rojo's strategy – it was his battle – and of the Popular Army. Rojo was faced time and time again with units which simply refused to obey orders. Three brigades of the 84th Mixed Brigade – a CNT unit – mutinied when ordered into the line; it was dissolved and 46 mutineers shot. But it was not only the CNT; Lister and 'El Campesino' both disobeyed orders, but their units were protected by 'friends' in high places.

Teruel proved that the Popular Army could mount a surprise attack on a limited sector with a large army. The Alfambra battle proved that it could not match the Nationalists, with the air and artillery superiority they enjoyed after the Republican losses in the north, in a battle of manoeuvre in the open country. The optimism of early January dissolved into pessimism and a collapse of morale. On 22 February the XIX Corps gave way; 'all was due,' wrote Rojo, 'to a wave of panic.' On 23 February his Order of the Day pointed 'the contrast between those who fought heroically and those who abandoned their positions without the least resistance'. Prieto was worried that Franco would break through an army that had lost any fighting spirit. 'My doubts arise from the combination of the enemy's strength with the enormous weakness produced in our forces by demoralization.'

It was now, with his troops concentrated in the east and Republican morale in tatters, that General Franco mounted the most ambitious operation of the war: the six weeks' spring offensive of 1938 which would bring him to the river Ebro and the sea, cutting the Republican territories into two zones without direct communication. Next to the capture of the north, the general breakthrough to the sea was to be the decisive battle of the war. The attacks were preceded by heavy artillery bombardments – twenty-one batteries on a four-mile front – and aerial attacks. So complete was Nationalist command of the air that the ace Morato complained of meeting no opposition: 'the sky was ours.'

The offensive was aided by a collapse of morale and consequent operational confusion even more serious than the collapse on the Alfambra. There was little close fighting; Republican units retreated after punishing air and artillery bombardment. 'Positions are lost with little or no resistance . . . the result of aerial bombardment is overwhelming and most units, including fresh reserves, retreat without fighting.' Whole divisions gave way in panic as the Nationalists fanned out in the rear; the advance was held up by shortage of petrol rather than by organized resistance.

Units which resisted bravely were let down by failures on their flanks. The XII Corps 'dissolved' while the XXI held. On 13 April Rojo reported 'total moral crisis'; to replace the sixty thousand men who had disappeared in confusion he flung in his reserves all over the place. When the International Brigades were rushed up, Hans Kahle could not find out where the front was except by listening to a captured Italian wireless set which picked up announcements of the fall of towns. The Brigades suffered appalling casualties; Marty, the French chief of the Brigades, lost his head, beating worn-out troops over the head with his pistol butt. The Brigades, now only a shadow of a great enterprise, never recovered.

Resistance stiffened, but by 4 April Aranda had reached, across very difficult country, the old Carlist capital of Morella; on 15 April the Navarrese brigades reached the sea at Vinaroz. The Republican zone had been cut in two. Valencia could only communicate with Barcelona by air or by sea – the post was carried for a time by submarine.

At least some of the causes of the failure at Teruel and the collapse

Nationalist advances, April to October 1937

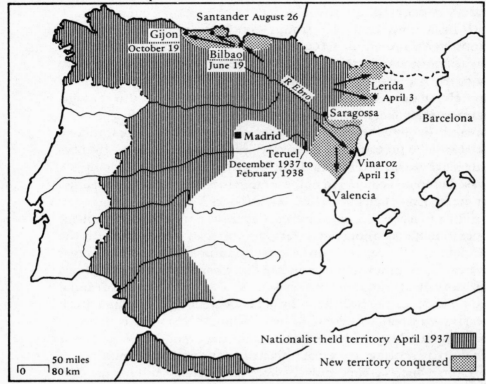

Santander August 26

Gijon
October 19

Bilbao
June 19

R. Ebro

Lerida
April 3

Saragossa

Barcelona

Madrid

Teruel
December 1937 to
February 1938

Vinaroz
April 15

Valencia

Nationalist held territory April 1937

New territory conquered

50 miles
0   80 km

in Aragon were due to the failure of the government to end the faction fights and to accomplish the tasks of concentration and unification that it had set itself. Rojo, for instance, could not bring General Miaja to sacrifice troops from his Army of the Centre, whereas Franco could switch all his available reserves to the new front. Rojo was deeply troubled by the state of the rearguard and the inveterate political infighting, the atmosphere of accusation and counter-accusation.

The oddest accusation of all was that later brought against the Communist party's Russian and Italian advisers by 'El Campesino', the commander of the division that held Teruel for the Republic after its capture. The politician whose reputation had grown with Teruel was Prieto, now Minister of Defence and increasingly hostile to the Communists. According to El Campesino, to ruin Prieto and force his resignation the Communists wanted to turn Prieto's operation – Teruel – into a disaster. The method they chose was to sacrifice El Campesino's division by failing to send Lister and Modesto, reliable party men in the plot with the Soviet advisers and the Kremlin, to relieve him. His division would have been captured *in toto* had not El Campesino – according to his own story – with heavy losses, broken out of Teruel on his own initiative and unaided. If true, this is the most damning of all the accusations brought against the party; but El Campesino wrote when he had become a violent, professional anti-Stalinist. Lister's account, needless to say, rejects El Campesino's story and accuses him of 'miserable' cowardice, of deserting his troops and running to a village fifty kilometres behind the lines.

Defeat forced a final attempt to remedy disorganization by a new 'government of concentration': Negrín's Government of National Union replaced his Government of Victory on 5 April. Prieto was sacrificed to his political enemies (see below, p. 218), and the CNT brought into the government. But it was essentially a reinforcement of the bourgeois nature of the régime; 'respectable' Republicans outweighed the CNT and the UGT. The battle between politicians and the unions had ended with the victory of the former. The last vestiges of the revolutionary experiment vanished with the Aragon débâcle.

One of the new government's first acts was a cautious step towards re-establishing Catholic worship; but the Vicar-General of Barcelona refused to reopen churches. After the Aragon break-through Franco's victory was only a matter of time. The Vatican now formally recognized Franco (17 April) and Spanish priests preferred to be liberated from the catacombs by Franco rather than negotiate a doubtful freedom from their former persecutors. In a victorious Nationalist Spain the Church would not be merely tolerated. It would be privileged. For Franco's Spain appeared to realize the vision of Maeztu, the most intelligent of the pro-pagandists of the monarchist right, killed in the massacre of the Madrid Model Prison: it was 'a religious, military monarchy', except that there was no monarch in place.

13
The New State

Franco formed his first regular ministry in January 1938. While what came to be known as the 'principles of the Movement' were the official ideology, the ministry represented rather conservative right-wing forces. The only concession to the Falange programme was the Labour Charter which set up 'vertical' syndicates, an arrangement which ended trades unionism as an independent force in wage settlements.

The economy of the Nationalist state was, compared with that of the Republic, relatively strong – especially after the conquest of the north. Its intellectual atmosphere was stifling.

I

On 30 January 1938, during a lull in the battle of Teruel, Franco's first ministry took its oath of allegiance in the historic monastery of Las Huelgas. The ceremony was 'fervent and devout, like an armed vigil'.

It was characteristic of Franco that this political decision was delayed. It also revealed what was to be the simple secret of his statecraft: the balance of the forces. Members of the Falange got two posts and its Secretary General, Serrano Suñer, brother-in-law of the *caudillo*, became Minister of the Interior; there were three generals; the Carlist Rodezno; and two technocrats, a naval friend of Franco's and a civil engineer. Two ministers came from Renovación Española.

It was less easy to balance political programmes than it was to balance politicians. Inevitably the programme of the new government appeared a compromise between the residual social radicalism of the Falange, the Catholic conservatism of the Carlists, and the monarchist right in general. But the tone of the new government was set less by the two publicly permitted, formally

united parties of the régime than by conservative monarchists –
like Vice-Premier Jordana whom Serrano Suñer called 'a man of a
past epoch'; men like Saínz Rodriguez, Minister of Education and
Andrés Amado, Minister of Finance, both of them Alfonsine
monarchists. The whole of their weight was flung against any
radical remodelling of the society which survived the shock of 1931
and which regarded the generals as its guardians. The group of
intellectuals and politicians who had found their centre of attraction
in Acción Española which had attempted to transpose the
programme of the authoritarian French Catholic right – Charles
Maurras above all – into a Spanish key, provided much of the new
régime's ideology and its general tone, more than has been thought
by those who have been impressed by the apparently important rôle
of the Falange as the party of the régime. Indeed, it can be argued
that the founding fathers of the new state were Calvo Sotelo, the
murdered leader of the National Bloc, and Victor Pradera, the
representative of the Carlist tradition in Acción Española. José
Antonio Primo de Rivera, the 'absent one', was commemorated on
every church wall in Spain, but his ideas were less influential than
his image. It was to the collected works of Victor Pradera, the
Carlist ideologue of Renovación Española, not to those of José
Antonio, that the *caudillo* wrote a preface in 1945.

The ideal of Acción Española was order and a rejuvenated,
dynamic capitalism aided by the state and informed by a
paternalistic social conscience. Like the later defenders of a
dynamic neo-capitalism, the Opus Dei technocrats of the 1950s,
these monarchical capitalists lacked any mass following and worked
by personal influence in high quarters. It was the subtle pressures of
this group that constituted some limitation on Franco's power. He
did not need to accept their political programme – the restoration of
the monarchy – but he could not reject their model of society.
For Hitler, Franco's Spain with its priests, landowners and
businessmen was a disillusionment; he prophesied that Falangists
and 'reds' might make a common cause 'to rid themselves of the
clerico-monarchical scum that had floated to the top'.

II

In this conservative state the Falangists were offered a compensation prize that was to give them a vast field of patronage and a
continuing rôle: the control of the labour movement. It was

Falangist ideals of a radically transformed Spain in which liberal *laissez-faire* capitalism would be replaced by the cooperation of capitalist and worker under the paternal direction of the state that provided the ideological basis of the Labour Charter issued in March 1938.

The Labour Charter attempted to satisfy all with 'an energetic revision, truly revolutionary, of the whole social structure *without upsetting the respective situations of the different classes*'; in other words, the paternalistic regulation of a disciplined labour force. It granted workers holidays with pay, security of employment – the one real concession of the régime to labour – minimum wages and family allowances. It assured employers that private enterprise was the 'foundation of the economic life of the country'. The competing claims of both were to be reconciled in the vertical syndicates which would embrace all economic activities: unions that would include workers and employers – the class struggle was held to be a Marxist exploitation of the liberal state – and would be controlled by the Falange. One of Franco's biographers has praised the Charter as 'a law worthy of any enlightened British Labour leader'.

On paper, yes. Few of the promises went into action in the war. Nationalist Spain emphasized war austerity (there was a 'one-course meal' campaign); while hours of work were reduced in Republican Spain they were raised in Nationalist Spain. The vertical syndicates were to prove a not altogether ineffective instrument for the protection of labour in post-war Spain; indeed, employers complained that they safeguarded job security to such an extent that modernization was impossible. Nevertheless, the autonomy of the labour movement had been completely destroyed. 'The Vertical Syndicate is an instrument at the service of the state through which it realizes its economic policy'; it was an 'ordered hierarchy under the direction of the state'. Security of employment was, in these conditions, the minimum concession to labour denied the right to organize or to strike for better conditions.

Within this rigid authoritarian framework the war economy of the Nationalist zone was tolerably organized: wages were fixed, inflation was controlled. It was an economy based on confidence in victory: banks in the Nationalist zone gave loans on properties in territory still held by the Popular Front. Nor was this confidence confined to Spain: foreign exchange rates held well above those of the Republic.

As we have seen, the Nationalist zone held much of Spain's traditional agriculture and with the fall of the northern front it possessed by 1938 almost *in toto* the country's mineral wealth and its export earnings. With the unions destroyed and the workers cowed, there can be little doubt that the Nationalists made better use of their assets than the Republicans: iron ore production in Vizcaya rose from 25,000 tons a month to 138,000 tons after a bare six months of Nationalist rule. With the foreign exchange (in addition to German and Italian loans) the Nationalists could buy from the sterling-dollar area; a third of Nationalist Spain's imports paid for in cash came from Great Britain; a half of its free foreign exchange was spent on petrol without which the war could not have been fought at all.

Republican Spain contained the manufacturing zones whose export capacity was dependent on the import of raw materials. Hence unemployment rose as factories ran short of supplies, while there was a labour shortage in the Nationalist zone. Moreover, the great cities had to be fed and the great wheat-lands were in Nationalist Spain. There was no serious shortage, except for rice, in Nationalist Spain and the main black market commodities were tobacco, spirits and warm winter clothes and the only noticeable domestic shortage that of hotel rooms (unobtainable in Burgos and Salamanca), cigarettes and electric light bulbs. The first action of the Nationalists on taking over a Republican town was to rush in lorry loads of 'the white bread of Franco'.

III

In outward appearance and political language Franco's new state seemed a re-creation of the reign of the Catholic kings with Italian fascist trimmings. It fulfilled the prophetic vision of Victor Pradera: 'We have discovered that the new state is nothing more than the old state of Ferdinand and Isabella.' The repellent early rhetoric of the régime was diffuse, indeed incomprehensible to the rational mind, in its attempts by 'renovating' tradition to reconcile the sixteenth century with the modern authoritarian reaction against 'the inorganic democracy of parties'. 'The new state must be founded on all the principles of traditionalism to be genuinely national,' wrote José María Pemán, an early ideologue of the régime in 1939. 'The Falange must be in Spain the technique of traditionalism. . . . Our fascism, our juridic-Hegelian absolutism, must necessarily sustain itself, as form, in the substance of historic-Catholic tradition. Spanish fascism will be the religion of Religion. . . . German and Italian fascism have invented nothing as far as we are concerned, Spain was fascist four centuries before them. It was one, great and free, and truly Spain in the sixteenth century when state and nation were identified with the eternal Catholic idea, when Spain was the model nation and alma mater of western Christian civilization.'

Serrano Suñer was an admirer of Mussolini; yet he felt a mystical affinity with the Spain of the Catholic Kings. The return of the Jesuits, the reappearance of the crucifix in schools, half-holidays for Aquinas, were symbols of this return to the past. The real conquest of the Church was its total recapture of the educational system. Republican teachers were purged, those who remained subjected to intensive retooling courses in Catholic thought. Though it was the Falange that was given control of the Students' Union, religious conformity was the test for students and professors alike.

From Navarre, the focal point of mass religious commitment, there radiated the brand of fierce orthodoxy and Catholic puritanism that was to mark, for many years to come, the tone of life in Navarre. It was Navarre that first legislated against shirt sleeves in cafés and 'immodest' dress in women, campaigned against make-up and instituted (unsuccessfully) 'smokeless days'. It was in Navarre that the orthodoxy of Tridentine Catholicism, fierce in its resistance to all modernizing trends in the Church, first extended its grip over intellectual and social life in an attempt to wipe out the ravages of nineteenth-century liberalism from Spanish life. It was in Navarre that cinema shows were first censored. In Pamplona there were public burnings of the books of Jews (the Civil Governor pilloried Jews as black-marketeers who weighted sugar with sand) and Masons (Martínez Barrio's masonic regalia were on public display). A private club was denounced for possessing the works of an obscure nineteenth-century anti-clerical.

To Carlists, their historian remarks, the battle of books in the rearguard was as important as the battle on the war fronts. Nationalist puritanism even extended to an assault on modernisms in linguistic usage: *ragoût* on menus was criticized as a decadent word. Russian salad, more understandably, became 'National salad'. By December the rest of the Nationalist state was following the lead of Navarre: cinema censorship which suppressed an excerpt from Lincoln's Gettysburg speech in a Charles Laughton film; no advertisements for bathing-dresses 'with women inside'; newspaper articles to be written 'in the language of Don Quixote'; libraries to be cleared of 'pornographic, Marxist or dissolvent works'. 'Imperialism' – though its programme remained rather obscure – became the slogan. Catalan refugees, apt to talk their native tongue in exile, were enjoined to 'speak the tongue of the Empire'; it was 'spiritually inelegant' to use Catalan.

These innovations were embodied in a heady rhetoric and a mystique of selfless devotion to the cause. Thus to object to the *plato único* (a single-course meal charged at 50% extra) was to be tainted with 'liberalism which discusses all and rebels against all'. The Falange in Navarre adapted their propaganda to a local audience: the Falange militia were the 'soldiers of Christ'. On St James's Day 1936 the Falange published *A Salute to the Requetés*: 'You are the same as yesteryear, with the same eternal blood of knights, of soldiers of heroes, blood that ran in the veins of your fathers, the invincible warriors of God, Country and King. And now, when we are escaping from the wretched, dirty and materialist history of the twentieth century, in these days anointed religiously with Tradition and knightly valour, you return to the fight with the firm gaze, the generous hearts, the strong arms under the elegance and exquisite rose tint of your red berets.' (Red berets were worn by the *requetés*.) This was hardly the language of Cervantes.

Plastered over with this propaganda, Nationalist Spain had thus an old-world flavour in spite of propaganda about a future just deal between capital and labour. The Generalissimo's war-time headquarters were a reflection of the court of the monarchy. He received the Italian ambassador in the splendid palace of the Salamanca municipality, 'surrounded by a large number of officials and officers, all in uniform – in a room decorated with superb sixteenth-century tapestries and eighteenth-century porcelain brought specially for the occasion from Vitoria.' No such ceremony surrounded Azaña – though he would have liked it – nor would it have been to the taste of Largo Caballero. Refugees from the Republican zone arriving in Nationalist Spain were immensely relieved to find waiters ready to take orders. A few miles from the front the hotels of Saragossa had hot baths and there were restaurants 'with bright lights and *animación*'; the officers' mess struck a visiting French general as up to French cavalry standards.

The Duke of Lerma, fighter pilot, found Valladolid replete with 'mountains of pretty girls'. San Sebastian was *'muy animado'*; he and a brother officer collected all the shoes put outside the doors of the best hotel, took them to another floor and filled them with soda-water. Such goings-on are difficult to imagine in Barcelona or Madrid, where the furnishings of upper-class life had been either consciously destroyed – palaces converted into offices or barracks – or had fallen into decay with war shortages. Nothing appalled the Nationalists more than this seemingly deliberate run-down of the garniture of upper-class life. 'The stench was awful,' wrote Captain Bolín, head of Censorship and Tourism, on entering Barcelona, 'part of the accumulated filth the reds bequeathed to every town. . . . The dust at the Ritz was inches thick.'

So was the dust on Spanish intellectual life. While to liberals modern Spain had recovered, by her achievements in the realm of arts and sciences, an international repute unknown since the sixteenth century, to the average Nationalist the 'true' Spain of history had been betrayed by cosmopolitan professors. They had fallen via liberalism into the Marxist trap; the universities of the country had been perverted by the familiar demonic triad: Masons, Jews and Marxists. Free-thinking intellectuals gathered together in the Institute of Free Education of Madrid had perverted a generation of the élite. To their exposure Father Tusquets devoted his limited talents and persistent efforts. Azaña was the incarnation of degenerate intellectualism: a monster, whom Mola described as a Frankenstein not born of love of woman.

Unamuno had criticized the Republic for its 'low' tone. Yet he soon became disgusted with what he saw and heard in Salamanca where his protests earned him dismissal. No one could class him as typical of anything, yet he does represent the dilemma of the middle-class intellectual. The 'style' of the Republic repelled him; but he found militarism and the heroics of General Millán Astray even more distressing. Spain, the Nationalist press bureau declared, needed mystics, not intellectuals; mystics who would teach Spaniards that there was no 'true liberty except in submission'. The rantings of one of the founding fathers of Falangism, Giménez Caballero, who had seen Mussolini as the saviour of 'Catholicity' and Cervantes as an anti-Spaniard betraying the true values embodied in Don Juan and the bullfight, were characteristically not merely of an atmosphere that classed intellectuals as pessimists, 'eunuchs unworthy of a place in virile Spain', but of a relapse into verbal barbarism. The linguistic excesses of the Falange and of 'the ethical missionary state' were to debase political and literary language for a generation. Its counterpart in 'red' Spain was the slogan-soaked world of Marxist propaganda.

The new state not only distrusted intellectuals; it purged them from the civil service and the teaching profession. Identity cards became necessary for every step in life; and they classed Spaniards as 'disaffected', 'indifferent' or 'addicted' to the Nationalist cause. For every official position an applicant had to be vouched for by the local Civil Guard, the Falange and the priest. This degree of regimented control – it extended to postmen and attendants at thermal establishments – is used in all wars; in civil wars with refugees pouring in it became a necessity, employing a large bureaucracy. When a town was captured the political *bona fides* of every self-proclaimed Nationalist 'addicted one' had to be verified.

In spite of Falangist rhetoric which infected the public pronouncements of the government, the fundamental values of the new state were military order and Catholic orthodoxy,* the values of Castile, creator of Spanish unity, hammer of heretics; the Spain of the Catholic apologist Menéndez y Pelayo. The Crusade was the Nationalist counterpart to 'Unite Proletarian Brothers'; the greatness of Spain the reply to the glorification of the Soviet Union. 'I understood,' wrote Captain Reparaz, 'the *conquistadores*.' He compares the humiliation of the Civil Guards he commanded by the Popular Front to the '*Via Crucis*: the passion of Our Lord which was converted into passion for Spain'. He was only echoing the priests of the Crusade. 'Our generals and our soldiers are worthy of the golden age. . . . Love Spain and you will love God.' It was not until the late 1960s that these tones vanished from Franco's Spain.

They represented an interpretation of the history of Spain profoundly different from that of the best minds of the Republic. The two interpretations started from a common premise; what the

---

* The Falangist National Council was responsible for the wording of the Labour Charter. Its preamble presents the régime's rhetoric at its worst: 'Renewing the Catholic tradition of social justice and humanitarian sentiment which informed the legislation of the Empire, the National staté, totalitarian in so far as it is at the service of national integrity, and syndicalist in so far as it represents a reaction against liberal capitalism and Marxist materialism, takes up the task of realizing – with a military air, constructive and gravely religious – the revolution that is coming over Spain, which will return to Spaniards for all time the *Patria*, Bread and Justice.'

Spanish historian Americo Castro has called 'the state of progressive despair' at the disappointing performance of Spain, once the greatest imperial power in Europe, in a modern, technical, pragmatic world. The Republicans sought to raise Spain – for they were patriots too – by imitating the 'progressive' nations. For the more vocal Nationalist ideologists of 1936 only a return to the vision of a universal empire and the inward looking values of Philip II could save Spain from the continuing ravages of a decadent materialism.

Foreign correspondents found the patriotic rhetoric of the régime disconcerting. The secretiveness of a press bureau that had to deny the existence of the Germans and Italians whose presence in the hotels of Salamanca was obvious, when combined with inefficiency and delays, infuriated them. Even the *Daily Mail* correspondent was 'treated like a dog' and Bolín, as press chief, was 'hated like poison by the English and American correspondents'. Another aristocratic press official boasted that he had shot six of his own labourers *'pour encourager les autres'*.

Like the Spaniards themselves, correspondents found some relief from the pressures of official rhetoric and the more bloodthirsty outbursts of the Nationalist *enragés* in jokes: summoning a taxi with the cry, 'One, big and free' – a take-off of the official slogan 'Spain One, Great and Free'; or calling the walk of an attractive woman 'the Glorious Movement'.

IV

It was these institutions and these ideologies which were offered to 'liberated' Spain. The war was to Nationalists a war of liberation. Republican Spain was in slavery to a régime, absolutely evil in itself and dependent on a foreign power – the Soviet Union. The purpose of the war was to end this bondage: liberated Spain would be *independent*. The implications of this concept, central to Franco's whole thought, was never understood by his allies.

After the failure to end the war by the capture of Madrid which Franco came to realize meant the 'end of a glorious and immediate liberation', the Germans and Italians were always advocating *Schrechlichkeit* or a *Blitzkrieg*. They could not understand why Franco did not bomb and shell enemy cities out of existence, how he could remain so imperturbably calm. His 'slowness' became an obsession with German staff officers and drove Ciano and

Mussolini to fury. 'Are there no men in Spain?' 'Give me aeroplanes, artillery, tanks and ammunition, give me diplomatic support and I shall be grateful,' Franco told the Italian Ambassador in April 1937, 'but above all *don't make me hurry*, do not force me to win at top speed, for this would mean killing more Spaniards, destroying a greater part of the wealth of the country.' Strategically this committed Franco to a war of attrition, of *desgaste* or 'wearing out'.

But if liberation could not be achieved by *Schrechlichkeit*, neither could it be brought about by a compromise peace. Necessarily Republican peace feelers included the right for Spaniards to choose their own régime and amnesty for those who had supported the Republic. Free elections, Franco told Faupel, when Eden was making one of his many efforts to secure peace, would mean a 'leftist government . . . all Nationalist Spaniards would rather die than place Spain in the hands of a "red" *or a democratic* government'. Such a government was, in Serrano Suñer's phrase 'the absolute enemy'.

Just as Communists cannot allow a member of the Socialist camp to defect, so Franco could not allow an inch of liberated territory to fall back into the hands of the 'reds'; this again irritated the Germans and again it had an important effect on the conduct of the war. Militarily there was a strong argument for leaving the Alcazar and Teruel to their fate and pushing ahead against Madrid. To have done so would have betrayed Franco's central politico-military concept.

Liberated, Spain must be 'great'; and to be great she must be independent. Franco quickly saw that the most immediate threat to the independence of his new state lay in the economic demands and political pressures of his own allies: Germany and Italy. Yet he desperately needed arms. To balance his necessities and his allies' importunities against the defence of his own freedom of action was a difficult exercise in brinkmanship. By 1939 Franco had proved himself the most successfully obstinate statesman ever produced by a secondary power.

The contest with Germany, rearming fast and importing sixty per cent of its iron ore, concerned the mineral resources of Spain. 'Germany,' Hitler admitted, 'needs iron ore. That is why we want a Nationalist government – to be able to buy Spanish ore.' Franco was determined to keep his economic options open against German pressures to corner all Spain's minerals for the Reich – an operation called the 'Montana' scheme. To get his 'war booty' Goering was 'willing to hold a pistol to General Franco's breast'. 'In fact the damned fellow,' complained the German Ambassador, 'habitually does exactly the opposite of what we suggest, just to demonstrate his independence.' Every demand of the Germans was fought every inch of the way; but Franco's need for German military aid was so compelling that by July 1937 Nationalist Spain was on the way to becoming an economic colony of the Reich. The Nationalist government had to allow part of the huge debt to Germany to be paid off by the purchase of Spanish mines. The Montana scheme was, at last, home and dry. Franco was forced back on German support. In April 1938 he had been talking of a withdrawal of volunteers; in May he was begging that the Condor Legion be brought up to strength.

14
The Last Lap: the Battle of the Ebro

I

By 7 April 1938 the Nationalists were within eighty miles of Barcelona. García Valiño and Aranda were pressing forward through Aragon to the sea and the Nationalist army reached the fishing town of Vinaroz on Good Friday. The Republic was cut in two. It had been, as Ciano noted with relief, a case of 'full speed ahead'. Franco told his armies that they were now engaged on the last stage of the reconquest. Few now could believe in the survival of the Republic. 'The Civil War,' *The Times* reported in March, 'has entered upon its last lap. Nothing now can save the cause of the government in Spain unless foreign intervention comes to their rescue in terms approximately equal to the help Italy and Germany are giving to General Franco.'

The military disaster in Aragon had appalled Negrín. 'The front was broken,' he wrote later, 'it scarcely existed; a large part of our army was being routed; panic was widespread; the morale of our rear was collapsing.' Military and political recovery seemed impossible. Yet 1938 saw the Indian summer of the Popular Front. It was patched up sufficiently to support the greatest battle of the war; the final Republican offensive on the Ebro.

II

The revival of the Popular Front was based on the consolidation of the power of Negrín and his Communist supporters. This consolidation was brought about at the cost of a further narrowing of working-class support. Largo Caballero's supporters in the UGT retired to their tents; the CNT fell asunder, riven between collaborators and militants. The great domestic struggle of the Civil

217

War had ended. The politicians and the parties had ended the revolutionary rôle of the syndicates. The unions had been domesticated and were at the service of the government for boosting war production, a government in which the unions were thinly represented. For all its collaborationism the CNT was rewarded with one minor cabinet post.

In the last full meeting of the libertarian movement in Spain – the long and disputatious *Pleno* of October 1938 – the movement fell apart. The FAI abused the Communists and denounced the 'false optimistic collaborationism' of the leadership. The CNT leadership abandoned every shred of anarchist doctrine which might impede a united war effort. 'What is the use of dignity and principle if we are defeated?' argued Horacio Prieto, the apostle of collaboration and exponent of abandoning the 'literary and philosophic baggage' of 'Don Quixotism'. The division between collaborationists and 'purists' was not to be healed, even in exile after defeat.

The FAI saw the Republic as the victim of one vast Communist plot; so did Indalecio Prieto, whose relations with the party and its Soviet advisers steadily degenerated. In April 1938 Communist pressure, ruthlessly exerted, secured his dismissal. He regarded himself as a propitiatory victim of Negrín's determination not to be 'punished' by the Soviet Union. The Prime Minister and his Minister of Defence had come to the end of a long political friendship: Negrín believed (or professed in public to believe) that the war could be won if France would allow arms supplies; Prieto, after Teruel, believed that defeat was inevitable (as Azaña had always held, keeping his governments in perpetual fear that he would suddenly resign) and that the best that could be done was to secure a compromise peace via British mediation. Negrín still believed that French policy might change; at the height of the disasters in Aragon he had flown to Paris. He arrived within days of the formation of Blum's second Popular Front government which reacted strongly to Hitler's march into Austria. In French government circles non-intervention was temporarily discredited and there was even talk of 'avenging Austria in Spain' by sending troops to Catalonia. This was going too far for the French army, French opinion and the British Ambassador. But at least France opened the border on 17 March and arms began to flow into Spain: two hundred lorries a day were bringing supplies to Barcelona.

The tragedy is that both Negrín and Prieto were operating with illusions. The West would never, as Negrín continued to believe, change its policy; nor would the Nationalists, as Prieto hoped, consent to a mediated peace. Of necessity Negrín was hypnotized by his own slogan 'To resist is to conquer'. Prieto now knew that conquest was out of the question. He could not believe the decision was Negrín's own; he had 'yielded to the demands of the Communist party'.

To Negrín, Prieto's 'pessimism' was revealed by his concern over morale. He had always maintained that the side with the healthy rearguard would win the war. Now there could be no doubt that as Nationalist morale stiffened with hope of victory, Republican morale was disintegrating into recrimination with the prospect of defeat.

This steady process in the Republican zone was partly political and partly the reflection of war shortages. The economy of the Republican zone was running down.

Shortages of raw materials paralysed a war industry shaken by the collectivist revolution and its reversal: after 1937 and the loss of the north, high-grade steel was in short supply; textile production declined rapidly. But it was chronic food shortage that undermined morale. There were long food queues in Madrid and all the major towns; coffee, meat and eggs almost disappeared; electricity was rationed; consumer goods like electric stoves had long vanished; Ernest Hemingway's dwindling store of whisky seemed, to thirsty journalists, a unique remnant of the pre-war world of plenty. In December 1936 Orwell found Barcelona already a gaunt, untidy town, with shabby, half-empty shops. By mid-1937 he found the situation worse: bread scarce ('dreadful stuff like putty'), no tobacco, a flourishing black market and long queues for the poor. By 1939 resistance could not be maintained by 'Dr Negrín's resistance pills' – lentils.

In the midst of all these growing difficulties the continuation of two of the activities of the days before the war provided some light relief. The cinemas and theatres were crowded in Madrid and Barcelona. In the big cities audiences could watch Shirley Temple and the Marx brothers as well as the heavy diet of Soviet films; in the provinces the old Spanish films were shown over and over again because audiences who could read only with difficulty, if at all, could not catch the sub-titles of foreign films. In Madrid there was even a theatrical revival that lasted into 1938. In Barcelona the equal pay for actors and staff imposed by the CNT syndicate caused difficulties. 'I'll look after the lavatories,' said a celebrated Mexican light comedy actress, 'and let the lavatory woman do the striptease act.' One amusement did not flourish – bullfighting. The *aficionados*, managers and ranch owners were in the Nationalist zone. Bullfighters were apt to give a charity performance for the militia in return for a safe conduct and then slip to Salamanca. Fighting bulls were slaughtered for meat and bull-rings used as vehicle parks. The *fiesta brava* did not fit easily into the ethics of the Popular Front.

III

We can best study the effect of shortages and political infighting on morale at the local level. If, in the summer of 1937, the party leaderships came to a compromise peace behind a revival of the Popular Anti-Fascist Front, the memory of the May struggle and the destruction of Largo Caballero and his allies remained, working like a poison in municipal councils and food committees.

The Levante was one of the worst areas; it was divided, and the feud between *Caballeristas* and the CNT on one side and the orthodox Socialists and their Communist allies on the other was particularly bitter. Elche, famous for its palm-trees, was a solid Socialist town where, according to the CNT, the revolution had passed unnoticed and where 'all was as it was in 1936'. Elda, with its leather industry, and Alcoy, a textile and metallurgical centre, were CNT fiefs. Towns like Denia and Alicante were divided. Party and union meetings degenerated into slanging matches. To the CNT the Communists were 'fascists in disguise', 'Judases ready to sell themselves for a shirt'; no peace was possible with them until they dropped their foul campaigns of calumny; the Communist 'Shock Brigades' sent out to help peasant farmers on Sundays were 'a farce', a propaganda device and an insult to peasant dignity. The Communists replied in kind: the leather workers of Elda were getting a week's salary for a day's work; Alcoy was a CNT dictatorship supported by a now (April 1937) illegal militia. A Communist poetaster printed a poem against the CNT militias' 'fatuous' gun-toting. The CNT of Alcoy were 'identical with the Rome-Berlin Axis'. At Elda the CNT were putting 'fascist' nurses in the hospitals. In Alicante the Libertarian Youth rejected the

Popular Front: it did not want to work for 'a rotting social democracy'. The Aragon breakthrough set off a new campaign of mutual recrimination. CNT militia units claimed that Communist doctors neglected non-party patients.

All these squabbles tended to concentrate on the Committees of Supply (*Comisiones de Abastos*) responsible for food supplies. By late 1937 the food situation in the Levante was desperate, and malnutrition caused a minor outbreak of malaria. All staple foods were rationed, but, as in every war, there was a flourishing trade in false ration cards and a prosperous black market. Profiteers formed a new class to which all parties referred as 'the new rich'. Barter was replacing cash transactions (even between municipalities), and cigarettes – twelve packets for a pig – and soap became almost recognized legal tender. Peasants refused to sell to the large towns; a hidden war between town and country developed, with raids on crops and minor military foraging expeditions. All parties held their enemies on the committees of supply or on the municipal council as responsible for shortages through their corruption and inefficiency. In Alcoy the CNT accused the Communists of organizing a demonstration of housewives; in Altea the Communists maintained that the CNT fishermen's collective doled out fish to those with CNT cards while others got nothing.

The persistent and dour, often high-minded and always pro-Soviet, propaganda drives of the Communist party (it set up a rival paper to the CNT in Alicante and spent some effort getting it on the early bus to Denia before its CNT competitor) combined with CNT puritanism to make life drab. The CNT – at Elche – came out against alcoholism ('Every alcoholic is unsociable, a nullity, human rubbish unfit to live among civilized men'). Hence all bars should be closed. In brothels 'the mind atrophies'; they should be closed too. But above all the 'vice of vices' – smoking – must be stamped out. All this was happening while municipalities were running out of money to build air-raid shelters against a succession of air attacks, while basic services were neglected (the lepers escaped from the provincial leper colony) and schools were closing down (juvenile delinquency became a problem in 1938). By the end of the war the civilian hospital at Alicante had run out of cotton wool and bandages.

Those committed to the Popular Front – and Alicante had a long liberal, radical Republican tradition – stuck it out nobly. But to the 'ordinary citizen' the war meant a colourless, difficult life. He might have refugees from Madrid and Malaga – the latter came to be particularly resented – billeted on him. His diet was almost exclusively vegetable and a vegetarian cookery book written by a local gourmet was a best seller. His light and heating were strictly rationed; the trams a skeleton service. He could still go to the theatre and the cinema, where he could buy only dried sunflower seeds in the interval. If he was a Catholic he could go to mass only in a private chapel run by a Civil Guard captain. All around him he could sense the growing strength of a well-organized Fifth Column, ready to take over when the final collapse came. The authorities confiscated his radio set, or fixed it with adhesive tape to the Republican stations. But the tape melted in the heat and he could tune in to the Nationalist stations and hear news of food lorries entering conquered towns. The end of the war would mean the end of a foodless, run-down existence.

Thus the general greyness of life gradually overwhelmed the simple enthusiasms of the summer of 1936. That morale weakened in an atmosphere of steady military defeat – Guadalajara was the last uncontaminated triumph – and when the Republican zone was cut in two is scarcely surprising; indeed it is a tribute to the propaganda services of the Republic that there was not a complete collapse, and if the Nationalists had held out prospects of reconciliation rather than the dire threats of the radio general Queipo de Llano the decline might have been more dramatic. The Republican zone lived in a simplified world of slogans drummed in at mass meetings and on the wireless, and from omnipresent wall posters. Slogans like 'to resist is to win' seem to have kept a hold over the mind.

In spite of these terrible simplifications imposed by war and politics, the faith of the Republicans in education, even if the faith could seldom be implemented, provides a moving contrast to the anti-intellectualism of National Spain: the literacy campaign in the armies; the Militias of Culture; the Workers' Institute and the declared intention to open the University to all classes. 'Trench newspapers' multiplied, with their tips on how to avoid venereal disease and stray bullets; their campaigns against bad language and rusty rifles; their amateur poetry and comic short stories. All this was more than political indoctrination and a crude form of basic training. It was a declaration of belief in the open society of equal opportunity.

IV

In the summer of 1938 the costs of Negrín's policies and general war-weariness were not apparent. By 30 May, with the French frontier open, *The Times* changed its tune: it now prophesied 'a long death struggle'. In early August it seemed to the world as if the Republic were on its feet again and fighting. Mussolini succumbed to one of his waves of Spanish pessimism. 'Put on record in your diary,' he told Ciano, 'that today, 29 August, I prophesy the defeat of Franco. . . . The reds are fighters, Franco is not.' Stohrer thought, once more, that the war might have to end in a compromise peace. Franco was to call 1938 his most difficult year.

To his critics these difficulties sprang from a strategical blunder. Instead of committing his armies, now concentrated on Aragon, to a difficult drive through mountainous country for the doubtful moral advantage to be gained by the capture of Valencia, he should have smashed through Catalonia, the heart of the remaining war industry. This was the attack the Republican general staff feared; with the Ebro defences in a bad way, they were greatly relieved when Franco swung his armies in the opposite direction towards Valencia. General Kindelán had tried hard to dissuade Franco 'from an operation which seemed pointless to me'.

The drive along the coast through Castellón was of necessity on a narrow front, hemmed in by mountains. General Aranda, its executant, described his task to me as 'trying to force a mass of resistant material down a narrow tube'. The flank operation through the mountains was even worse, dogged by heavy rain in difficult tank country and awkward relationships between commanders. García Valiño's troops arrived at the coast, as he himself confessed, 'worn out by fatigue . . . with an appreciable loss in efficiency . . . 2,528 casualities among which were irreparable losses in regimental and battalion commanders'. When the Nationalist armies, after months of fighting, reached the edge of the Valencian *huerta,* tank attacks were impeded by irrigation canals and a carefully constructed trench system.

Again the campaign of the Levante proved the recuperative powers of the Republican army on the defensive, once reorganized and re-equipped after the Aragon disaster. The hard-fought battle had lasted three months and it must be considered as the mos remarkable and least recognized achievement of the Popular Army

Nevertheless, on 23 July the Nationalists were only twenty mile from Valencia. To save Valencia and the Republic, Negrín mounted a surprise attack on the Ebro front along the river from Mequinenza to the sea. It unleashed the bloodiest battle of the Civil War; beginning in the blistering heat of late July, it ended in the snows of November.

Rojo's planning and the careful training of Modesto's forces for the river crossing achieved a brilliant initial success. Concentrating 100,000 men and all available supplies, the Nationalist front was broken along the Ebro from the Mequinenza–Fayon pocket to Cherta. The Nationalist front was thinly held – in places the river bank was unguarded – and the Republican command had concentrated its forces by night in lorries without headlights, and carefully hidden its boats and pontoon bridges. Yagüe, in command of the Nationalist forces along the Ebro, suspected an attack but could form no clear idea of its direction or seriousness.

The attack, therefore, achieved tactical surprise. Commandos

Battle of the Ebro

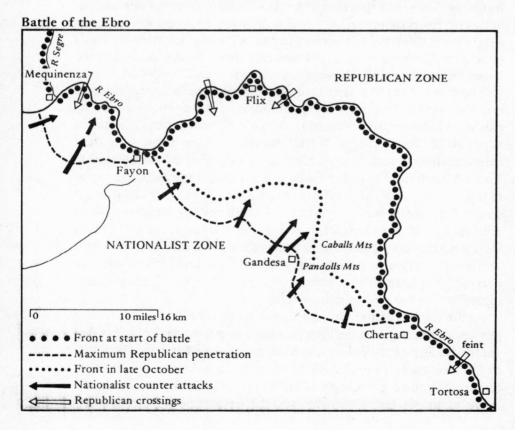

• • • •	Front at start of battle
- - - - -	Maximum Republican penetration
• • • • •	Front in late October
◀━━	Nationalist counter attacks
⇦	Republican crossings

crossed with muffled oars on the night of 24–25 July; next day pontoon bridges carried the main advance. Between Gandesa and the starting point all the important hill positions were captured at little cost, in spite of delays in bringing up tanks and artillery and a breakdown in the telephonic communications. Franco delayed reinforcements, but by 1 August the Republican attack had stuck at Gandesa after a heavy attack of the XV International Brigade. In this, one of its last actions, died the man whom English opinion chose to regard as a 'typical' brigader: the South Kensington Socialist borough councillor, Lewis Clive (Eton and Christ Church). By now the Brigades were filling with Spanish conscripts; their withdrawal at the end of September, a gesture in Negrín's desperate search for European approbation, was not a serious military blow.

The Ebro had turned out to be another Brunete. As at Brunete, Rojo had planned not a mere breakthrough of a weakly held front but a great sweep through to the rear. At Gandesa these plans came to nothing. On 22 July Rojo's operational orders to Modesto called for a strong bridgehead near Gandesa 'to serve as a basis for future operations'; on 24 July he was ordered to 'dig in and hold at all costs'. As at Brunete, the gains were made in the first days in a vacuum and then the offensive bogged down when the Nationalists organized defensive positions and proceeded to counter-attack. Moreover the Republicans were now confronted with a crushing superiority in the air. The air ace. Morato complained, 'red aeroplanes appeared now and then but generally flew off when they saw our fighters.' Even more telling was the Nationalist superiority in artillery.

The Nationalist counter-attack came in waves, spaced between 6 August and 16 October. Franco watched and directed operations much as a divisional commander would have done.

Franco had become the Haig of the Civil War, committing himself, as General Duval pointed out, to 'the most costly operation in war' – frontal attacks on a twenty-kilometre front. Why did he accept fearful casualties, on a terrible terrain chosen by an enemy who had shown himself weak in manoeuvre but stubborn in defence? The commander of his air force put it mildly: the time expended on the battle 'might have yielded more results in another theatre'. General Aranda put it to me more bluntly: it was a mistake to accept a battle of attrition to recover a strategically meaningless zone where all attacks were tactically difficult.

After ninety days the Nationalists had advanced five miles from their starting point; then, at last, the Nationalists began to operate at the flanks and the final attack, with five hundred guns, drove the exhausted Republican army over the Ebro.

Franco's Clausewitzian convictions that to destroy the enemy's army is the aim of all war found their defender in General García Valiño. Known by his troops as the 'gravedigger', García Valiño was the toughest of Franco's generals to whom he had already entrusted the difficult drive across the Maestrazgo and whom he now flung into the Ebro offensive in early September. The Republicans resisted and only after fourteen days' very hard fighting did García Valiño reconquer twenty-one square miles of hills. To García Valiño the battle was worth it. The Generalissimo took advantage of the enemy's obstinacy to destroy his army, 'the principal object of any war. . . . For this reason we believe that the fight to the finish, with all its consequences, was the great stroke of the *caudillo* and the true key to his rapid and definitive victory.' But even García Valiño found the attacks on narrow fronts exhausting. The Republicans fought well, obeying Modesto's orders to resist to the end, digging in and defending each hill position.

On both sides the casualties in the 115 days' slogging match were appalling: perhaps 110,000 in all. The victors lost six thousand men killed – the heaviest loss of the whole war. The Republican losses in casualties, prisoners and desertions were heavier; only thirty-five thousand men retreated back over the Ebro.

Was the battle worth the fighting? For the Republicans it achieved one of its aims. On the Valencian front the Nationalists had reached the XYZ line – the last defence. They were forced to switch troops to the Ebro and the city was saved. Nevertheless, it is just conceivable that the Republicans with their armies intact and without the losses on the Ebro – a hundred vital aeroplanes as well as guns and men – could have fought a defensive war until the outbreak of the Second World War. But even that could not have saved them; they could not have held out till the tide of war turned in Europe and Africa and Negrín's ideal realignment of the balance of power became a possibility.

One result was as unfortunate for the Republicans as it was unforeseen. Since June, Franco's chief of staff had argued that the attack on Valencia was a mistake; it should be halted and the armies brought to attack the weak Army of the West in Catalonia and to destroy the last great industrial zone remaining to the Republic. The Ebro offensive perforce cured Franco of his obsession with Valencia. The Nationalist armies were now concentrated on the confines of Catalonia.

Just as the hopes raised by the early victories on the Ebro were dashed by November, so the optimistic predictions of friends of the Republic in the summer that the international situation would, at last, favour the Republic turned sour by the autumn.

The attention of Hitler was centring on eastern Europe. Would the democracies risk war to save Czechoslovakia from Hitler? 'We Spaniards,' wrote the government press chief, 'sat by our radios [through the Czech crisis] sick with suspense.' If war came, France and Britain would need a Republican Spain as an ally, and crush Hitler's Spanish friends. While Negrín prayed for a European war, Franco feared one.

These hopes came to nothing. By the culmination of the Ebro battle the international tide had turned remorselessly against Negrín. Rather than risk the war, which would have made Republican Spain a coveted ally, the western democracies sacrificed Czechoslovakia at Munich on 29 September. With Blum out of power, the French frontier was closed once again. German arms once more were providing Franco with the means of total victory. Europe, as Prieto had prophesied, betrayed Spain.

15
The International Commitment

It was the deliberate policy of both sides, pressing for aid from their allies, to present the Civil War as involving issues beyond the frontiers of Spain. No doubt both sincerely believed in its universal significance. But for foreign consumption the press agencies of Nationalists and Republicans alike emphasized the war as part of a larger, European struggle. The generals came to present a military rising that had drifted into a civil war as a crusade in the defence of Catholic, conservative values against international Communism, social dissolution and the bolshevization of Europe. 'For this reason,' General Franco told a reporter, 'our enterprise goes beyond national issues and is converted into a crusade in which the fate of Europe is at stake.'

From the beginning the left saw the Civil War as part of a wider struggle against fascism triumphant in Europe. As the course of the war became, through the politics of non-intervention, part of the power conflicts of Europe, so this involvement gave Spanish issues an international significance. As in the 1830s the battlefields of Spain presented a contest between the ideologies that divided the continent – this time between democracy and fascism. To Hans Beimler, a German Communist, killed fighting with the International Brigade on the Madrid front, it seemed that 'the only way we can get back to Germany is through Madrid'. Lloyd George hoped that the resistance of Republican Spain would 'save European democracy' from the designs of its enemies and the cowardice of its friends. In Latin America the left-wing supporters of President Cárdenas saw the struggle of the Republic against 'old Spain' as part of their own struggle against old Mexico. 'General Cárdenas,' ran the posters, 'defeated at Teruel.' A process of identification with one or other of the two combatants transformed the war into a dividing line in domestic politics and intellectual discourse.

II

Given the passions generated by the Civil War in Europe – and they have lingered to this day – it is easy to overestimate the interest of the Great Powers in Spain. The wrangles of the Non-Intervention Committee, the coverage in the press of the West, concealed the fact that Spain was a sideshow. To Neville Chamberlain, anxious to avoid a general war and to bring about reconciliation with Italy, Spain was an embarrassment; Ciano sensed that Chamberlain's foreign secretary 'would be glad if Franco's victory were to settle the [Spanish] question'. Non-intervention therefore was a useful fiction that must be supported because it sealed off this inconvenient Spanish question. In 1938 Stalin eased off the arms supply; to him, too, Spain was an expendable as his mind concentrated on Soviet weakness in the East. Hitler wanted to defeat 'bolshevism'; but his main interests were economic and the hope that the Spanish war would create difficulties for his diplomatic opponents, divide them and distract their attention from his more threatening moves. 'A 100% victory for Franco is not desirable from the German point of view.' At the time, propaganda obliterated these hesitations: Russia was aiding 'the reds', Germany the Spanish 'fascists', to the limits of their capacity.

Italy proved in the end to be Franco's best political friend. Mussolini may have expected a quick victory and an ally gained on the cheap, but as Cantelupo, his first ambassador to Nationalist Spain, pointed out, Mussolini was 'deluded'. The war was long and expensive. Franco had never asked for Italian ground troops and seemed singularly cool as Italian blood was shed for his cause. 'Here,' wrote Cantelupo, 'the coinage of gratitude has a restricted circulation.' He did his best to bring the Italian venture to an end, only to be sacked for his pains. Italy, in the end, gained the glory Mussolini sought. He saw the fall of Barcelona as an Italian triumph.

Germany, after September 1936, left the burden of sacrifice to Italy and reaped the diplomatic rewards. Italy had no alternative but to abandon herself to the German embrace. 'The Axis,' wrote Cantelupo, 'was made in Spain.' If Mussolini was much moved when Franco reported to him (as he thought) as a subordinate, he himself had become the subordinate of Hitler.

It is true that over Spain the Soviet Union recognized the weakness of any system of collective security based on the resolution of France and Great Britain, and that the Axis powers sensed the weakness of the 'degenerate' democracies when faced by virile nationalisms. But the destiny of Europe was being settled, not in the Iberian peninsula, but in Austria and Czechoslovakia. The European war of 1939 overshadowed Spain and the passions Spain had aroused were swallowed up by other issues. It was widely believed at the time that Spain was the 'Aldershot' where the Axis powers and the Soviet Union tested their weapons for this greater conflict and that, by their support of Franco, the Axis powers had secured a valuable ally. In fact the Soviet Union seems to have drawn few lessons from the small-scale tank battles of the Civil War. Germany gained her mineral concessions, combat training for Goering's air force and, strangely enough, valuable practice for her new fleet in non-intervention naval patrols.* She did not gain an effective ally against the democracies in the war. Franco's sense of Spain's exhaustion overcame his gratitude to the Axis. He kept Spain out of the war; Ribbentrop complained bitterly about 'that ungrateful coward Franco who owes us everything and now won't join us'.

III

As far as France and Britain were concerned, the Civil War not merely demonstrated their diplomatic impotence, but weakened their position by the domestic divisions it inspired and symbolized. The hesitations of Blum, the backpedalling of his successors and the indifference of Britain were a source of despair and anger to the politically conscious left. Traditional rôles were reversed: the British Labour party had been strongly pacifist and now demanded action in support of the Popular Front – 'the pacifists from the English universities', reported a British newspaper's special correspondent from Spain, 'make excellent machine-gunners.' It was the Conservatives who preached the dangers of any step that might bring on a general war.

In a Europe that, to the left, appeared doomed to go down before fascism, the resistance of the Spanish Republic was a 'beacon of

---

* According to the air ace Galland, the Civil War experience 'only yielded knowledge in the technical and tactical fields' – above all the use of air support in infantry operations.

hope', and aid to the Spanish workers a moral imperative. The effect of 'aid to Spain' on domestic political debate in France, Great Britain and the United States was of great consequence. Inevitably, this debate and concern for Spain were reflected in the work of a generation of politically conscious writers: it provoked, in Arthur Koestler's words, the last twitch of Europe's dying conscience.

In Britain, most Conservatives instinctively supported Franco against the 'reds'. Nonetheless, Conservatives were divided: Churchill (who had earlier remarked that his relations would have been shot in Republican Spain), came to believe that Britain was sacrificing its interests as a Great Power in the Mediterranean by aiding the creation of a pro-Axis Spain; Eden, who at first believed that the Soviet Union was the main culprit in supplying arms to the belligerents, came to distrust concessions to Italy when it openly flouted non-intervention by sending its divisions to Spain. The Italians had signed a gentlemen's agreement (2 January 1937) to respect the status quo in the Mediterranean; now Eden no longer considered them gentlemen whose word could be trusted. But the majority of Conservatives shared Chamberlain's subordination of the fate of the Spanish Republic to the necessities of appeasement; a significant minority, which was to come to the fore in the world war, opposed him.

The Labour party was likewise divided over Spain and the policy of the leadership – Ernest Bevin above all – was so cautious that in 1939 the left could accuse the Labour leaders of 'failing to use the great resources of the Labour movement' to help Spain. Why?

First the leaders, above all the trades unionists, were bitterly hostile to the Communists, who for years had abused them as 'social fascists', i.e. a more dangerous brand of being than honest-to-goodness reactionaries. It was now the Communist party and their allies on the left of the Parliamentary Labour party – Stafford Cripps and Aneurin Bevan – who pressed for active aid to Spain via a United Front in Britain. To the Labour leaders this appeared a 'Trojan horse' policy by which their old enemies, the Communists, would control the United Front. More fundamentally, Bevin was a realist and as a trades unionist he was in closer touch with working-class feelings than Cripps: he believed that the British working class *as a whole* did not want to go to war over Spain, and that an unprepared and unarmed Britain was in no position to risk a policy that might result in general war. The leftists, who were demanding action to save Spain, were at the same time the pacifists who opposed rearmament; Bevin rammed home this inconsistency. The trades union bloc vote defeated the left's attempt to commit the party, at the Edinburgh Conference of 1936, to support for the Republic. It was their sense of outrage and bitterness at this defeat that led Bevan and Cripps to found *Tribune* in order to campaign for the United Front in Britain as the best way to help Spain and contribute to the defeat of Fascism – while still campaigning against rearmament. It was not that the leaders had no sense of responsibility for the Republic; they denounced the 'farce of non-intervention' as a denial of a legal, democratic government to buy arms to defend itself (Attlee's speeches are some of the bitterest in British parliamentary history); but there was little they could do beyond this verbal violence and expression of sympathy with the Republic.

Britain, then, was deeply divided by the Spanish question. Until these divisions were healed, Britain could have no coherent policy.

IV

Important as the Spanish war was in revealing the impotence and divisions of Britain – and France – its impact on writers and intellectuals of the left was tremendous. With few exceptions (Catholics like Evelyn Waugh, the poet Roy Campbell, the inhabitants of ivory towers like T.S.Eliot) most writers were broadly liberal. They saw in the support of the Republic at war the 'last cause'. That their commitment was ruthlessly organized and exploited by Communists or that it was often emotionally and psychologically self-regarding, should not blind us to its genuine nature.

All over the world men responded to this call precisely because they were liberals of one sort or another, shocked at the overthrow of a 'progressive' government. John Kennedy, in spite of his family Catholicism, recognized that the Republican government was 'right morally speaking'; that 'its program was similar to the New Deal'. To capitalize on this liberal sentiment, in the United States the Communist party turned to the heroes of American democracy. When Earl Browder, the Communist leader, wished to criticize the Roosevelt administration for its neutrality policy which denied Spain arms, he demanded, 'Let us ask Jefferson where he stands on this issue.'

To help the Spanish resistance gave a generation of intellectuals in Britain – beaten down by the depression, unemployment and the National Government – the sensation of effective action. A sense of personal liberation can be felt in most of the writing on the Civil War. Before the inexorable end came in sight, intellectuals felt on the side of history for once; they identified with Spaniards 'fighting for freedom'. It is an uncomfortable phenomenon of identification in some ways. Gustav Regler, who joined the International Brigades, observed, 'Only on this occasion have *I* known that sense of freedom and feeling of unconditional escape, of readiness for absolute change. . . . We don't write history now, we make it.' The time when the Republic looked like winning was to Hemingway and his friends 'the happiest period of our lives'. 'You are all bad,' growled Ezra Pound, more concerned about the ravages of usury than the issues at stake in Spain, 'Spain is an emotional luxury to a gang of dilettantes.' Put less brutally, there was a sense in which Spain had become what antiquity was to the classicists and the middle ages to the Romantics: a symbolic land of the mind to which the conflicts of the writer's own society were transported and transposed.

Almost every writer of significance sympathized with the Republic. Hemingway wrote his longest novel on the war; James Baldwin his first short story at the age of twelve. In Spanish-speaking Latin America the effect of the war as a struggle against Fascism altered the vision of its two greatest poets. The Peruvian César Vallejo saw in the emotions aroused by the Civil War only the possibility of escape from his neurotic loneliness, the hope of 'communion'; but in the younger Chilean poet Pablo Neruda (b. 1904) it completed a more dramatic change. Having deserted personal for political poetry, he joined the Communist party.

The war posed, indeed, in an acute form the social and political responsibility of the author: 'Picasso's stand for freedom and democracy should deal the death blow to the unsound argument . . . that the artist has no concern with public affairs.' Whether the total commitment of authors produced great literature is another matter. It was Tolstoy's maxim that the tension necessary for a great work of art comes from understanding the motives of both sides. To Cecil Day Lewis, the English poet, the war was simply a 'battle between light and darkness'. There was no place for the tender liberal conscience. When a journalist complained to Modesto, fighting the battle of the Ebro, that terror was counter-productive, the colonel slapped his revolver on the table and shouted 'Then you are a fascist – My God, do I have to shoot you to put some sense in your head?' Similar scruples would have evoked a similar response in Burgos or Salamanca. War is a terrible simplifier.

At the Communist-organized writers' conference of 1937 in Madrid a defence of social realism became an unscrupulous attack, manipulated by the Communists, on the French novelist André Gide as a Trotskyite because he had written a book criticizing the Soviet Union. 'You must say yes or no to Fascism,' said Koltsov, the Soviet journalist, at the conference – and this meant accepting his condemnation of left-wing dissidents as Trotskyites.

The effect on Communists was curious. Both Gustav Regler and Arthur Koestler were on the verge of leaving the party: the mystique of the Popular Front brought them back for a 'second honeymoon', only to make ultimate disillusionment more complete. Koltsov is an even stranger and tragic case. One can feel in his *Diary* that he came to believe in the Popular Front that he preached: Spain was for him a truly liberating experience. Like so many other Russians who had been exposed to Spain, he vanished mysteriously on his return to the Soviet Union.

It was in France that the intellectual and political repercussions of the war were most intensely felt. The Communist party was powerful and its connections with French intellectuals much more intimate than in Britain where the party was miniscule and its intellectuals were suspect. Paris was the centre of Willi Muenzenberg's exertions in organizing front organizations and propaganda drives. Hence the French party's onslaught on non-intervention – the policy of a Socialist, Blum – was bitter. The French Popular Front, weakened, now dissolved in recrimination. The Socialist Van der Velde left the Belgian government over non-intervention and wrote a bitter open letter to Blum on 1 May 1937 accusing him of 'derisory impartiality'. As in France, Spain divided the Socialist party.

The defence of the Republic in arms united the French intellectual left, already alarmed at the strength of the right, and aligned it behind the Communist party and the Soviet Union which had proved itself as the only saviour of democracy. La Pasionaria became the heroine of Louis Aragon, the party line poet. Support was uncritical, French intellectuals swallowed the party line on the

May events in Barcelona. La Pasionaria's view that Trotskyists must be 'exterminated like beasts of prey' became the orthodoxy of the fellow-travelling left. There was no George Orwell to trouble consciences with the truth about the May troubles in Barcelona; the denunciations of Victor Serge went unheeded. (Victor Serge organized a protest movement among left Socialists with little result; the French left-wing press printed the Communist version of the May events and the murder of Andrés Nin. 'Only in a minority and among isolated individuals did conscience still burn.') Aragon, as late as 1946, was defending André Marty against the 'lies' of Hemingway in *For Whom the Bell Tolls*. Marty was 'the glorious organizer of the Brigades who . . . saved French honour'. Seven years later Aragon, ever a dutiful follower of the party line, denounced Marty as an agent of Tito out to liquidate the French party.

Apart from those who gave their lives, like the English poet Cornford, the fate of those who committed themselves to the Republic was often tragic. In the Soviet Union contact with the West was always dangerous. In the army purge of 1937 and the struggle between the military intelligence agencies and the NKVD, Berzin, Kléber and Gorev were shot – only Malinovsky escaped of the major military advisers in Spain. It was not until the 1956 Twentieth Congress that Soviet citizens were told by Khruschev that between 1937 and 1941 the 'cadre of leaders who had gained military experience in the Far East and Spain was almost completely liquidated', victims of Stalin's 'suspiciousness' and 'slanderous accusations'. Antonov Osveenko, consul in Barcelona, veteran of the 1905 Revolution and the hero of the attack on the Winter Palace in 1917, and Rosenberg, first Soviet Ambassador to Spain, vanished without trace.

To have been in Spain proved fatal to some Czech Communists after 1951. 'Service in the Brigades' became synonymous with 'Trotskyite activities' or service in the American intelligence network. 'Later,' wrote Arthur London, 'the word "volunteer" alone became the equivalent of the most pejorative terms. . . . There was the same prejudice against volunteers as there had been against Jews. . . . The International Brigades were simply put on the same level as the units which had fought against the Red Army from 1918 to 1922.' Such dangerous 'cosmopolitans' were tried and most of them executed. 'Your whole group is in the bag. Now we know what veterans from Spain really are.'

The experience of the Lincoln Brigaders and their sympathizers in the United States forms an interesting parallel. During the war, once the Soviet Union had become an ally in the struggle against Fascism, Lincoln Brigaders and Spanish Republican refugees were on the right side; indeed the US Ambassador to Spain, Professor Carlton Hayes, believed that they were much listened to when they sought to destroy Franco by a press campaign and by Allied pressure at a time when US strategic interests demanded careful cultivation of the dictator. In the Macarthy period they became suspect and were harassed. Just as in the Hiss trial, actions which, in the thirties, had reflected the 'progressive' atmosphere of the New Deal and the struggle against Fascism, these same actions were, in the late forties, judged in the context of the Cold War. Those who had praised the Soviet Union's support of Spain or joined Communist front organizations were now accused, in the words of the prosecutor in the Hiss trial, of being involved in 'these foreign philosophies', i.e. Communism. It is ironical that Lincoln Brigaders who stuck to their ideals and memories fell into the same category as Czech communist volunteers. 'The only way of proving your loyalty towards the Party,' as a Czech interrogator put it in the Slansky trial, 'is to adapt yourself to its *present* means of judging *past* events.' But there were Czechs like London and obscure Lincoln Brigaders who could and would not deny their pasts.

The response of the right can be dealt with more briefly. Franco found conservative apologists; the most extreme were prepared to call him 'perhaps a saint' and to swallow the 'red plot' as an explanation of the immediate origins of the war. British and French financial interests, with their large investment in mining and public utilities, thought the Nationalists would win, and that Franco's need of foreign capital would free him from any exclusive dependence on Germany and Italy who could not provide the foreign exchange needed to rebuild the Spanish post-war economy. American companies provided Franco with oil on credit, without which his operations would have been paralysed. Nevertheless the American financial press became, on the whole, hostile to Franco: the American workers were less concerned with the fate of the Republic than Wall Street.

It was the observed ruthlessness of the Nationalists in victory, particularly the persecution of Basque priests in 1937 (sixteen shot and three hundred in prison for sympathy with the 'poisons' of Basque nationalism and Marxism) that drove liberal Catholics to oppose the enthusiastic support of the hierarchy for the crusade. This was most evident in France, where the 'red Catholics' like Maritain and Bernanos supported the Republic. Originally a supporter of Franco, Bernanos reacted as any sensitive man must to the shedding of blood; his book on the 'butchery' of the Falange and the Italian Rossi in Majorca created a scandal in Catholic circles. Like all engaged in the war, he accepted propaganda at its face value. Just as British conservatives believed the 'red plot', so Bernanos swallowed the Nazi plot invented by a Comintern propagandist agency in Paris. In his view the generals were so bereft of any widespread support that only the *previous* firm assurance of German and Italian aid could explain their rebellion. This promise of aid, as we now know, was never given.

In the United States a considerable proportion of the American Catholic laity did not follow their bishops – an indication of the strength of the American progressive tradition. What hardened the resistance of American catholicism was the nature of the attacks on Franco supporters made by American Protestants. The Black Legend of Spain was also part of American progressive tradition; it delighted in the sound of broken images and readily believed that, as in the 1830s, priests acted as snipers from their own steeples.

For many in America and Britain the Spanish problem posed dilemmas that were real enough. How could pacifist Socialists, who were fighting rearmament, advocate a degree of support for the Spanish Republic which might entail a general war? How could Roosevelt, who came to regard his arms ban on Republican Spain as a moral error, attack non-intervention when his whole policy depended on friendship with France and Great Britain, the creators and proponents of non-intervention? How could American Jewish liberals – Goebbels had said all Jews supported the Republic – and Negroes demand from the administration a stand against Franco when it was the Catholic vote which had helped to bring their standard-bearer, Roosevelt, to the White House? How could liberal Catholics support the conquerors of Ethiopia and those who had brought about the decline and fall of the League of Nations? Moreover, those in the literary and political establishment were uneasily conscious that their own passionate obsession was not shared by the majority. Bevin sensed the shallowness of the general reaction of the British working class which, as George Orwell was to observe, 'saw their Spanish comrades slowly strangled and never aided them by a single strike'. True they raised money for Spain; but their contributions 'would not equal five per cent of the turnover of the football pools'.

The consequence of their involvement on the intellectuals of the left is reflected, in many cases, in the apoliticism and disillusionment of the writers of the forties. Some, like Orwell, were nauseated by propaganda – 'the screaming lies and hatred'. Koestler had helped Willi Muenzenberg concoct atrocity stories in Paris. 'He would pick up a few sheets of typescript, scan them through, and shout at me: "Too weak. Too objective. Hit them! Hit them hard! Tell the world how they [the Nationalists] run over their prisoners with tanks, how they pour petrol over them and burn them alive. Make the world gasp with horror."' Claud Cockburn excelled in invention – his masterpiece was an account of an anti-Franco rising in Tetuan with street names culled from a guide book. His description of this non-event Cockburn later called 'one of the most factual, inspiring and at the same time sober pieces of war reporting I ever saw.'

Intellectuals became increasingly uncomfortable and it can be said that those who were killed in the early days were fortunate in their deaths for they died when enthusiasm was genuine and unsullied by 'double-think'. Auden never spoke of his experiences in Spain. Koestler, an undercover party member, was released from Franco's jail on the grounds that he was a liberal rather than a Communist, and as liberal he had to address meetings on his return. Stephen Spender, who attended the Madrid Workers' Congress of 1937, was uneasy at the vicious Communist-led campaign against Gide; nor did Spender relish the posturings of committed intellectuals (the French delegate left Madrid lest, as he believed, his death in the shelling of the city might precipitate a world war). But he did not reveal his doubts till later. To serve a cause one must deceive. 'A certain degree of untruthfulness in supporting it,' writes Julian Symons, 'was perfectly justifiable.' But deception, however well meant, corrodes and enervates all but the most committed. 'After Spain . . . there was little left of the thirties movement but a feeling of resignation and a sense of guilt.'

It was the activists rather than the writers who carried on the revolutionary tradition. They fought in the French Resistance;

Tito, who had organized the flow of Yugoslav volunteers to Spain, later used them to staff his National Liberation Army. It was a Spanish veteran who gave Fidel Castro the elements of his military training.

16
The End: Catalonia and the last days of Madrid

I

With the retreat of the armies over the Ebro, Europe knew that the Republic was doomed. The last months are a depressing chronicle of military collapse, of political squabbles, of declining morale and, finally, of domestic civil war. Negrín's personal ascendancy was uncontested – to his opponents he was a dictator – but the processes of government had lost all coherence. Thus the Republican army in Catalonia, wrote Rojo, faced the greatest offensive of the war 'with a government machine vitiated at its very roots, a low morale in the rearguard; lack of desire to cooperate in the war effort on the part of subordinate authorities – so evident that mayors were 'covered' if they encouraged desertion; finally an exhausted army with few material resources and no reserves.' The armies were short even of food: Ludwig Renn's company was supplementing its diet with hazelnuts. Civilian morale was lowered by unopposed aerial bombardment when the Nationalist advance had cut Barcelona from its food supplies and its electric power in the Pyrenees.

It was on the *disjecta membra* of the Popular Army – Modesto's Army of the Ebro and the Army of the East – that the final offensive fell. On 23 December the Nationalist armies attacked on the Ebro–Segre front at the moment that the ever-optimistic Rojo was planning to execute his long-cherished 'Plan P' – a Republican offensive in Extremadura. The Catalan campaign repeated the Aragon disaster. The Republican armies were a match in numbers, but not in artillery and air support; just as at Teruel and on the Ebro, while they could resist well in strong positions, they could not fight a battle of movement. No amount of strategical imagination, none of the successive 'regroupments' so characteristic of Rojo's staff work, could overcome basic tactical deficiencies. Units were outflanked; brave resistance by improvised groupings of seasoned troops wasted through the unreliability of new regiments of conscripts. It was this collapse of cohesion which gave Franco a victory he had not expected to win so easily or so soon. On the first day of the offensive a panic-stricken company of carabineers, deserted by their officers, opened the whole Segre front. 'It was a rout,' wrote Rojo, 'one of the many which it has been my lot to witness during these operations.'

With the collapse of the XII Corps the army of the Ebro disintegrated and Rojo's ambitious plans of a counter-attack with fresh reserves were ruined when he was forced to fling them in haphazardly to stop the gaps. Mass desertions followed. Fresh arms supplies could not be distributed to an army in dissolution. By January the relentless Nationalist advance was held up only by shortage of petrol. At noon on 25 January Yagüe's troops entered Barcelona, its citizens' morale broken by hunger and air raids. Women were pillaging food-shops and insulting Republican officers; out of a population of a million, only a thousand had volunteered for a last ditch resistance. 'Barcelona,' wrote Rojo, 'fell without glory.' Perhaps it came as some relief to a grey city that the cinemas reopened to show the Marx brothers' *Night at the Opera*.

With the Republican armies in complete disorder, the politicians struggled towards the Pyrenees. The truncated Cortes of the Republic met for the last time on Spanish soil on 1 February in the clammy cellars of the castle of San Fernando, twenty-four kilometres from the border. Negrín told the deputies of his determination to fight on with the only army remaining to the Republic – Miaja's Army of the Centre. The 'government' was transferred for a few days to the squalid hamlet of La Bajol. On 8 February the Prime Minister was bombed out and crossed the Pyrenees just ahead of the Nationalists.

II

The final and confused agony of the Republic lasted from February to March. General Franco had consistently rejected the idea of mediated peace. On 13 February Burgos published the Law of Responsibilities: this made it clear that those who 'had contributed to create or aggravate subversion' before July 1936 and even those who had opposed the National Movement after that date by 'grave passivity' would be guilty of a crime. Given Franco's evident insistence on unconditional surrender and his rejection of the mediation of France and Great Britain, when and how could Negrín surrender in such a manner as to save the lives of those who had fought for the 'other Spain'? 'The only thing to do was to resist.'

Negrín, with even his vast energy exhausted, flew back to Alicante from France on 9 February. What hopes were there for the policy of resistance? The Army of the Centre was intact and had just staged an offensive in Extremadura that had captured more territory than any other government offensive. The international situation might, even now, set in the Republic's favour. Might not France and Great Britain force Franco's hand over peace? In an atmosphere of wishful thinking and the illusions of desperation, Munich was re-interpreted: France and Britain might at last make a stand, and if the Republic could hang on for a couple of months then a European war might save Spain – a war that Serrano Suñer recognized would be 'a catastrophe' for Burgos. Whether Negrín really believed these fantasies, or whether they influenced his actions, must remain in doubt. In the last resort, the Prime Minister and the Communist leaders could see no alternative to a resistance that would at least give time for those whom Franco would never forgive to pack their bags and get out.

Reduced to two secretaries in his migrant office, Negrín attempted to force resistance on reluctant commanders by telephone. But when he summoned them to meet him at the aerodrome of Los Llanos (16 February) it became clear that, apart from General Miaja, only the Communists and his 'unconditionals' supported him. The most outspoken of the advocates of peace was Admiral Buiza; if the Prime Minister did not open negotiations within four days he threatened to put to sea with his fleet.

The situation looked hopeless. France and Britain recognized General Franco's government; all hope of a mediated peace vanished. Azaña, bitterly opposed to Negrín's policies resigned (27 February) and for the partisans of resistance he became 'a man on whom a worm spits'. Martínez Barrio gathered together the permanent deputation of the Republican Cortes in the La Perouse restaurant in Paris; he was prepared to succeed Azaña if Negrín would give him powers to end the war. Negrín did not answer. The very legitimacy of his government, in strict constitutional law, was now in doubt.

The opponents of Negrín's resistance grouped themselves round Colonel Segismundo Casado of the central army. Casado was on bad terms with the Communists and their Soviet advisers, jealous of their commands in the army; he told the commander of the air force 'on his word of honour' that he could secure better terms from the Nationalists than Negrín, and he seems to have believed he had some kind of 'pull' in Burgos. If the Prime Minister insisted on resistance and rejected peace then he must be overthrown; to resist was 'to be blind to all reason'. Already early in February he was in touch with Franco's agent in Madrid – a colonel who, when in charge of the Republic's factory of precision instruments, had sabotaged production. He failed, however, to convince Negrín who, sensing his insecurity, appeared to rely more and more on his Communist commanders; with defeatist generals in charge, the front, he said, could be broken with bicycles. Fearful of a growing strength of Communists in the Army of the Centre, Casado decided to revolt on 4 March, when he read a whole batch of Communist promotions in the gazette of the Ministry of Defence.

The form of Casado's rebellion against Negrín is of particular interest. With civilian opponents of Negrín and of the Communists (the most prestigious of whom was the respected Marxist Julian Besteiro, and the most unexpected the CNT leaders, to whom Casado was 'Segis') he formed an anti-Negrín National Council on 4 March. Negrín's government was no longer, in his view, the legal government. Casado's arguments were those of any nineteenth-century general on the eve of a successful *pronunciamiento*; the insane policies of Negrín had alienated the people; the army therefore represented their real will and the officers' revolt was 'a movement of the people to free themselves from a hated government'; the Negrín politicians were 'cowards' and 'buffoons' who had 'thrown away' the government, now 'in the gutter' – a phrase which, to a historian, appears lifted from any successful military rebel's apologia for sedition. The government was a 'putrefying corpse' kept in a semblance of life by Communists and their foreign advisers. In the final act – a telephone conversation – Casado apparently told Negrín he had rebelled against him 'as an officer and a Spaniard'. Azaña, bitterly opposed to Negrín and his policies as he was, saw the terrible irony of a military revolt, a *pronunciamiento* which, like the revolt of 18 July, claimed to be saving Spain from Communism. How could a civilian politician like

Besteiro appeal to Spaniards to obey 'the legitimate power of the Republic which temporarily (*transitoriamente*) is in the hands of the military'? The wheel had come full circle.

The second centre of the dramatic dissolution and confused conspiracy that so often mark the end of civil wars was the great naval base of Cartagena. To secure against a naval mutiny Negrín sent a reliable Communist commander, Galán, to take over command. Galán arrived at 9 pm on 4 March. His arrival set off a complex coup at 11 pm.

The core of the conspiracy was a group of artillery officers. Some of these officers wished to force Negrín's resignation and to eliminate the Communists in order to prepare for a negotiated peace. Others wanted to hand over the base to Franco and were in contact with civilian Nationalists and officers who had been retired as 'factious' and who now emerged from the shadows. The confusion of aim was apparent in the passwords of the conspirators: 'For Peace and for Spain' which implied loyalty to the Republic; '*Arriba España*' to be answered by '*Viva Franco*'. When local Falangists seized the wireless station, those who merely wanted to get rid of Negrín and keep Galán and his troops out of Cartagena had second thoughts. In a tangle of negotiations between Galán and his opponents and sporadic fighting to recover buildings in the control of the conspirators, the coup began to collapse on 6 March. Admiral Buiza took the fleet to sea and, after hesitating about whether or not to join Casado, sailed for Bizerta taking Galán with him. Now all depended on whether the coastal batteries would shell the ships bringing Nationalist troops; two brigades loyal to Negrín took the town and the ships were shelled. The conspiracy had failed. It had only served to highlight the war-weariness and irresolution of officers who saw no point in continuing the war and yet feared retribution in a Nationalist victory.

Elda, the temporary seat of government, was in chaos. Telephone messages did not get through, commanders could not be contacted. Negrín's staunchest allies, the Communists, were deserting Spain. General Borov told Jesús Hernández on 6 March, 'We are leaving, we are leaving.' With Alicante in the hands of Casado's allies, Negrín himself left for France by air. On 7 March Elda was deserted.

At the very moment that their leaders were deserting them the Communist corps commanders of the Army of the Centre decided to crush the 'traitors' in Madrid: Casado's National Council. Barceló, commander of the 1st Corps, occupied the centre of the capital, supported by three other Communist commanders. On 7 March there was heavy fighting and Casado's troops were hanging on by their teeth in street fighting where one side of a street would be held by Council troops and the other by Communists – in the same uniforms. So desperate was Casado that he asked Franco to attack to relieve him of Communist pressure. As in the early days of the war, the control of wireless was an important weapon – and it was in the hands of Casado and the Council. In the end the National Council was saved largely by troops from the CNT 4th Army Corps. Caught between the CNT troops and Casado's own forces, the Communists capitulated on 12 March. Perhaps 240 lives were lost in this pointless eruption of an irrelevant political feud. Barceló and his commissar were shot.

'Only we generals can get Spain out of the war,' declared Casado. Like Negrín, his aim was to protect active Republicans from reprisals though his means differed: not resistance but a negotiated peace. Casado's illusions were as overpowering as those of Negrín. The colonel talked of a successful negotiation with Franco as 'the grandest spectacle of all history'. After defeating his and Franco's common enemy – the Communists – he seems to have believed that Franco would recognize his services. But Franco was unmoved. He did not make terms, he exacted unconditional surrender. After a week's fruitless, confused negotiations and terrible uncertainties, Casado's policy was bankrupt. Whereas in early February, if he had got rid of Negrín, he might have stood an outside chance, he now had nothing to offer Franco who had planned his final offensive for 26 March. The Republic's troops were deserting *en masse* or fraternizing with the enemy; civilians were seeking out ways of ingratiating themselves with the conquerors. Franco knew there was nothing left to fight.

All that Casado had done was to waste time in which an evacuation of the compromised might have been rushed through. Now those who could get transport (including Casado) crowded to the Mediterranean ports. There the defeated waited in vain for French naval protection to cover their evacuation. Some committed suicide in desperation, as Italian troops advanced on Alicante where the Falange was already in control. The armies surrendered rather than resist the Nationalist offensive. On a brilliantly sunny day the

Nationalist armies entered Madrid; their welcome was enthusiastic.

On the evening of 31 March General Franco, down with an attack of influenza, was informed that his troops had occupied their objectives and that the Civil War had ended. 'Very good,' he replied, staring at his desk, 'many thanks.' The crusade had ended. 'Lifting our hearts to God,' wrote Pius XII to its leader, 'we give sincere thanks with Your Excellency for the victory of Catholic Spain.'

III

The Spanish Civil War is sometimes presented as a war *sui generis*, somehow exempted from the general run of wars by the intensity of ideological commitment and the importance both sides attached to voluntarism, to sacrifice for the cause.*

As the war dragged on, fought increasingly by conscripts rather than by volunteers, it became like other wars. A chasm opened between combatants at the front and the rearguard civilians in government offices and 'cushy' jobs: these latter, in cafés and clubs, cultivated a brand of hatred towards the enemy which was less palatable to fighting men. Soldiers wanted what they have wanted in every war: a let-up in the fighting; leave; a period in hospital with a slight wound. They endured what the soldier endures everywhere: endless, dismal train journeys to new postings in sweltering heat or freezing cold; lice; flies; bad rations; the general muddle of war.

The propaganda of both sides refused to treat the war as an ordinary war. In retrospect, distortions in the interest of political commitment drove George Orwell to the belief that, as he told Arthur Koestler, 'History stopped in 1936'; by this he meant that historical truth could never be disinterred from propaganda. He observed bitterly how the formerly pacifist intelligentsia of the left had swung over from 'War is hell' to 'War is glorious' with stories of wounded soldiers clamouring to get back into the line, stuff that

---

* Both sides, for instance, made appeals to women to participate in the struggle. The Nationalists were probably more successful in mobilizing women via the women's section of the Falange; however, this was far removed from any 'liberation' of women as such. The Falange emphasized the place of women in the home once the war was over. Nevertheless war work, as in the 1914-18 war, did begin a slow process by which women (particularly before marriage) took work outside the home – a rarity before 1936.

might have gone into the *Daily Mail* in 1918. The *New Statesman* 'enthused' over the Spanish war as if 'for a soldier in the Spanish Republican army [war] was somehow not degrading'. Orwell was particularly sensitive to smells and it was the smell of latrines that brought home to him the thought 'there we are, soldiers of a Revolutionary army, defending Democracy against Fascism, fighting a war which is *about* something, and the detail of our lives is just as sordid and degrading as it could be in prison, let alone in a bourgeois army'. No amount of fighting for the right side (and he believed he was fighting in a just war, a class war in which the defeat of the working classes would delight dividend holders all over the world) could dismiss from his mind 'the boredom and animal hunger of trench life, the squalid intrigues over scraps of food, the mean, nagging quarrels which people exhausted by lack of sleep engage in.'

Like all soldiers, men on both sides wished the war to end. But whereas for the Nationalists, at least after the fall of the north and the Aragon breakthrough, the end of the war meant victory and all that that implies for morale, for the Republicans it could only mean defeat and merciless persecution at the hands of the victors. There would be no forgiveness, no national reconciliation; the only course was exile.

IV

Refugees poured into France – militiamen, foreign volunteers and civilians. By July 250,000 had crossed the frontier and most were interned in camps. The camps soon became an issue that reflected and intensified the divisions of right and left in France. To the right, the refugees were an expensive nuisance and a threat to be encouraged to leave by harsh treatment; to the left, their humane treatment by France was a moral obligation. Conditions in some camps soon became a scandal: at Argelès the refugees were living on sand, with no latrines and no huts. The French authorities were overwhelmed by sheer numbers – between January and February alone more refugees arrived in southern France than had left Germany under Hitler; sometimes they were brutal and indifferent to conditions that Arthur Koestler found worse than Dachau.

Even the French left began to show signs of indifference. 'The Spanish collapse,' wrote Victor Serge, who wore himself out in his efforts to get refugees into jobs, 'provoked a moral breakdown in

France. . . . They [the left] were annoyed with the Spaniards for having been beaten.'

Sadder even than the record of French indifference was the continuation of the faction fighting that had so often marred the unity of the Popular Front. The Communists attempted to control the camps, handing over lists of 'undesirables' to the French authorities, censoring the post and running the canteens. The camp at Gurs saw a bitter faction fight between Communists and 'anarchists'; Juan Comorera sang his old refrain of 'unity' to be created by 'the cleaning up of bandits, saboteurs and traitors: anarchists and Trotskyites, old and new allies of the renegade Franco.'

The European war of 1939–45 could only worsen the conditions of the Spanish diaspora in France. At first there was well-paid employment in war industry but the fall of France made Franco's ally Hitler ruler of Occupied France with his admirer, Pétain, in Vichy. There were still 250,000 Spaniards in France. Most of the leaders – Negrín, Azaña, Prieto – escaped; a few, among them Companys and Prieto's right-hand man Zugazagoita, were handed over and shot; the less eminent were condemned to forced labour. Those who could joined either the Free French or the Maquis – a company of Catalans turns up in Evelyn Waugh's *Officers and Gentlemen*, attached to a commando unit in Egypt. To them the triumph of the Allies would mean the overthrow of Franco; their clandestine newspaper was called *Reconquest of Spain*. Those who died, died in vain. The victory of the Allies, as the post-war years were to show, did not entail the downfall of Franco.

As in the war itself, the one country committed to the Republic was Mexico, and that commitment was largely the work of President Cárdenas and his immediate circle. Fighting reaction in Mexico, Cárdenas saw the Republicans as brother revolutionaries defeated by priests, the rich and the army – the old enemies of the Mexican Revolution. Already in 1938 he had welcomed prestigious intellectuals who could not work in a war atmosphere. They were the origin of what later was to become the Colegio de Mexico, one of the foremost research and teaching institutions of Latin America. Once Cárdenas heard of the conditions in the French camps, he offered to accept an unlimited number of Republican exiles (April 1939), provided that their settlement and travel expenses were met by Republican organizations. In a country with a restrictive immigration policy it was an unparalleled act of political generosity and it was met with howls of protest by the right-wing enemies of the President; Mexico would be flooded with left-wing extremists, 'assassins, incendiaries, violators of nuns'.

Perhaps twenty thousand exiles came to Mexico. They regarded themselves as the bearers of Spanish culture – they included ninety full professors and 150 associate professors – when the Spain of Franco was paralysed by censorship and repression. From their number – together with the exiles in Europe – would be formed the government of Spain once the Allies had helped drive out Franco. They were 'the other Spain'; the alternative ruling élite.

By 1950 hopes had withered. The Allies did not help the exiles and the restoration of the Republic. Even more depressing, the exiles could not present a viable, unified alternative Republican government. They were haunted by the recriminatory hatreds which flourish in exile; by obsessions with the past. Prieto attacked the Communists and believed their participation in government had been a disaster and would continue to be; Negrín still worked with his 'unconditionals'. Both set up separate exile organizations; each brought down any government in exile on which the other was represented.

Republican unity had failed and the exile community lapsed into factions, leaving the Communists as the core of resistance to Franco in Spain itself. For the older exiles a restored Republic remained the only possible régime for a post-Franco world and an indispensable emotional anchor; but for their sons and their relations in Spain it had become, by the 1960s, a moving historical memory. The exiles wrote more and more for themselves. Paris and Mexico City were no longer, by 1960, the intellectual and political capitals of the 'other Spain'. Outmoded, the exiles continued to set up organizations which then split along the lines of obsessive, outworn party conflicts. They lost any real hope of return and settled down somewhat uneasily in nationalistic Mexico with its deep-rooted suspicion of Spain, or more comfortably in Argentina where there was a strong tradition of immigrant absorption. They watched their leaders die off as Franco lived on. 'Emigration,' wrote one of them, 'is showing our bald heads and burying each other's dead.'

EPILOGUE

Part I: *Franco's Spain: The Difficult Years 1939–50*

Franco in these years developed what was to remain his characteristic political technique: the appointment at his discretion of ministries which balanced the forces which supported him, combined with the repression or ostracism of all those who could not accept his personal dictatorship. Changes in ministries indicated both shifts in policy and the varying strengths of the components of the régime (the Falange; the Church; the army; the conservative monarchists). The main ministerial changes were

1. 1942. After a bomb attack by Radical Falangists on General Varela, a monarchist, both Serrano Suñer, supporter of the Axis and the Falange, and Varela were dismissed. This was typical of Franco's ministerial 'judgements of Solomon'.

2. 1945–1951. Entry of ACNP Catholics and relative decline of the influence of the Falange.

These were the years of a state-controlled economic autarky, poverty and international isolation. International isolation was the punishment inflicted by the democracies and the USSR on Franco for his support of the Axis until 1943: his subsequent change from 'non-belligerency' favourable to the Axis to a 'neutrality' more accommodating to the Allies did not save him from condemnation by the United Nations. Only a liberalization of his régime that Franco was willing to make only in appearance (institution of a purely consultative Cortes in July 1942, the Spanish Bill of Rights 1945) would have saved him from ostracism as a 'fascist', an ostracism which cut Spain off from the foreign credits necessary for economic recovery.

The international condemnation of Franco was platonic. The opposition hoped for active support; this was denied and the opposition

253

in a police state was impotent. By 1950 a violent overthrow of Franco (e.g. by guerrilla action) was inconceivable.

I

In January 1939, as the Nationalist armies were sweeping across Catalonia, Mussolini counselled against the restoration of the monarchy. 'He [Mussolini] prefers a united and pacified Spain under the guidance of the Caudillo, head of the country and the party. It will be easy for Franco to govern if he first achieves full military success. The prestige of a leader victorious in war is never questioned.' Yet the Spain Franco had to govern was an exhausted country, much of its population on the verge of starvation and the prospects of recovery blighted by the outbreak of war in Europe.

How did Nationalist Spain face up to the problems of recovery? It is essential to realize that it was the child of war, and its policies a legacy of that war. Not until the mid-fifties did Spain begin to slough off some of this inward-looking war mentality.

How were Spaniards to be fed and to be given jobs with wages? The difficulties were forbidding. The physical destruction of war can be exaggerated: the Republicans burnt churches rather than destroyed factories. The Spanish economy was not in ruins as was the Russian economy after the Civil War of 1919–21; rather, it was run down. Roads had degenerated – the road down which Franco's troops marched to cut the Republic in two at Vinaroz was, when I went down it in 1950, still a series of potholes connected by stretches of tar left over from the 1920s. Nearly half the railway rolling-stock had been lost in the war and transport, according to the American Ambassador, was 'indescribably bad'. Industrial equipment was worn out. Skilled labour was scarce. By the late forties electrical power was in short supply: factories and homes suffered frequent cuts. Above all, agricultural production – and in 1940 over half of the active population of Spain was still employed in agriculture – stagnated and fell dramatically in 1949; stricken by persistent drought and with no imported fertilizers, cereals, which occupied 40% of all cultivated land, stuck at a level 25% below the yields of 1931–5. Hence the massive wheat imports of the early forties. The first bumper harvest came only in 1951.

Until the 1950s Nationalist Spain pursued recovery and reconstruction with the tools of a war economy forged in the years 1937–9 under the influence of Fascist models. The two key concepts were autarky and interventionism. A self-sufficient, self-capitalizing economy protected from outside competition by high tariff barriers would be created and regulated by state intervention.

It must be emphasized that autarky was no new ideal; it was already the working philosophy of civil servants, opposed only by a few liberal economists. Industrialists and wheat farmers had clamoured for high protection. Sector after sector, pressure group after pressure group had forced protection and state subsidies for 'nationally' important economic activities on successive governments after the 1890s. Such privileges were regarded as a kind of natural right to be enjoyed by high-cost, competitively weak, national producers; as a decree of 1916 put it, 'to attain the desired end of avoiding that so important a part of the national wealth (in this case shipping) should be a tributary of foreigners.' There was the more recent model of Primo de Rivera with his pained disapprobation of the preference shown by the upper classes for French wine and by doctors for imported scalpels, and his attempts to regulate all aspects of the economy from wheat to rabbit-skins by regulatory commissions. Autarky was now clothed in the rhetoric of the new Falangist economic nationalism. As the Industrial Law of 24 October 1939 put it, Spain must be 'redeemed (the word is significant) from the importation of exotic products'. Spain must be forced to produce *everything* it needed, regardless of cost; it must be cut off from the outside world.

All the customary instruments of interventionism and of direct controls flourished in the forties. Prices and wages were controlled; foreign trade and exchange rates closely regulated; the National Wheat Service fixed the production of wheat and marketed it; the Institute of Industry (INI), based on an Italian model and run by an admiral and intimate of the Caudillo, was to direct the establishment of basic industries and supplement private investment.

The penalties of interventionism and direct controls, of the consequent 'fear of the market' as a regulator of the economy were the same in Spain as elsewhere in the capitalist economies of western Europe. Bottlenecks created by bureaucratic decisions encouraged corruption – for instance in the grant of import licences and currency permits. There was a flourishing black market – in the early years particularly in food – that supported a host of minor pedlars and enriched fewer speculators, though it might be argued that such a corrupt system offered at least an indirect approach to the flexibility of a market economy. Thus the availability of scarce industrial raw materials on the black market allowed a 'redistribution' of the official quotas.

Industrial production had begun to rise in 1949. Nevertheless, by 1950 the limitations of autarky combined, as it was, with a monetary policy – or lack of it – that encouraged inflation, were evident. Official utterances still reflected remnants of the agrarian ideology of the early forties which considered agriculture less as an economic activity than as a way of life that supported patriotic peasant families immune to the 'dissolvent' influences of the great cities, where the working-class supporters of the Republic were concentrated. But there can be no doubt that by the mid forties the régime was determined to encourage rapid industrial development. Yet this was an impossibility in an autarkic economy, surrounded by high tariff walls. Such an enclosed economy must be dependent upon a poor domestic market, enfeebled by war, with a very limited power to purchase and consume industrial products and incapable of importing capital goods to re-equip industry. To cut Spain off from the international market would mean inhibiting recovery for many years to come.

Critics attributed the administrative excesses and economic failures of autarky and interventionism to the ideological idiosyncrasies of the new state born of the Civil War. The 'official' excuse in after years was that interventionism and self-sufficiency were less the imposition of a quasi-fascist ideology than of necessity. In the scarcities of war and the post-war years most western European states were forced to use direct controls; Spain therefore does not constitute a special case. To plunge the country into a market economy – domestically and internationally – might have invited disaster, and certainly the free market was an ideal the risks of which few European economies could afford in the forties. What was unique about the Spanish economy was, not that scarce supplies were rationed and prices controlled, as they were elsewhere in post-war Europe, but the degree of control, the clumsiness of the apparatus that administered it, and the strange-sounding nationalist jargon with which economic decisions were presented to the public.* What distinguished Spanish economic policy from that of

---

* For instance, see the Decree of 20 August 1938. 'It is the function of the state to *discipline* production.' Suppose for the word 'discipline' the word 'plan' had been substituted, would any post-war economist of the left have quarrelled with the statement?

other western European states was that state *dirigisme* and autarky were seen as an ideal and *permanent* solution, not only as a response to the post-war crisis. The economists of the régime did not seek to justify autarky in economic terms, as had the protectionists in the nineteenth century. It was presented and defended as a political ideal; the recipe for a stable society, as a suitable policy for an 'imperial military state'.

If there was no alternative to autarky during the World War, the price Spain paid in economic terms for the victory of the right was heavy once the war was over. It desperately needed imports of capital goods to re-equip its industry, to import fertilizers and food; and to do this it needed foreign exchange that could not be generated by its exports. The rest of western Europe was set on its feet by the Marshall Plan; Spain could not raise loans from the democracies that ostracized it as a fascist state. Ostracism, isolation from the international money market, meant that autarky was a *political* choice: only a liberalization of the régime, which Franco was utterly determined to resist, and which the Allies would or could not impose by overthrowing him, might have widened the economic options by making Spain respectable in the eyes of potential creditors.

Throughout the 1940s Spain was poor. These were the 'years of hunger'. They were years of hardship throughout post-war Europe: the era of 'Fish and Cripps' in Britain; but it was the *absolute* level of hardship that distinguished Spain. Per capita income had been cut by nearly a third compared to 1936. In a Spain where prices were rising faster than wages, where meat and leather shoes were luxuries to the lower paid and underemployed, poverty was made more painful by the conspicuous waste of the fortunate few. Yet however much Spaniards pillaged each other, they did not exploit the then relatively few foreign visitors. Travelling in the rest of post-war Europe I was cheated and stolen from universally. That in Spain I was not, I hold as a tribute to the Spanish character rather than a result of the presence of the policeman round the corner.

II

After 1939 the policeman was round the corner in every town and *pueblo*. Repression was fierce; the forties were a period of revenge, not of reconciliation. For to attempt reconciliation, in the eyes of the victors, was to deny the legitimacy of a régime based on the rising of

18 July. To have been an officer in the Republican army, or a mayor, or a schoolteacher in a Republican school might mean death, but almost certainly imprisonment. 'At least half the nation,' wrote Churchill, 'are for the moment crushed and impotent.' Ciano visited Spain in the summer of 1939. Executions in the great towns, he wrote, 'caused a gloomy air of tragedy to hang over Spain'.* But it was not only in the great towns that repression reigned or on the politically active that punishment fell. In the *pueblos* of eastern Andalusia the 'powerful ones' of the now reinstated village *camarilla* used the procedures of the *denuncia* to clear out any elements that 'lacked respect'. When it was not the revenge of fear, it was the work of spite. 'In villages like this,' remarked ex-mayor Manuel Cortes after thirty years of hiding in his own house lest he be denounced, 'there are always personal grudges.'

The politics of revenge created and consolidated what was known as *'el pacto de la sangre'* – the covenant of blood. How could those who had supported the elimination of their political enemies expect any mercy should the enemies once recover political power? The mechanisms of self-preservation were to underwrite Franco's rule and to make any opening toward liberalism a dangerous experiment for those who held power and jobs under it.

Not merely in terms of the physical force of its police but in its political theory Franco's Spain was a Hobbesian state. Sovereignty was indivisible. All power, legislative and executive, was vested in the Caudillo. It was a personal dictatorship, an anachronistic authoritarian régime, and by 1945 nearer in spirit to the Spain of Philip II than the Italy of Mussolini. ('Given the choice of a period of Spanish history which would you choose?' the Caudillo was asked. 'Undoubtedly that of Isabella the Catholic, Cisneros, Charles I and Philip II.') Yet however much the ideological clothing of the régime was patched up from a traditionalist view of Spanish history, it resembled Mussolini's Italy in the ruthlessness of its police procedures, its flouting of the rule of law – for instance in the Penal Code of 1944. Lawyers, in these early years, did little to defend the individual against the omnicompetent state; they were rather, as civil servants, recruited from the 'respectable classes', its agents.

---

* There can be no accurate figure for the number of post-war executions. Estimates vary wildly from 10,000 to 400,000. The number of prisoners is a more accurate indication of the extent of the repression: roughly 250,000 political prisoners in 1940; 100,000 in 1942; 27,000 in 1950.

Force was all the more necessary since the new state lacked the legitimacy of the old monarchy. The political trajectory of Franco's Spain is incomprehensible unless we realize that its original legitimacy was the legitimacy of conquest. Hence the necessity to keep alive the memory of the victory of 1939. Even if legitimacy by conquest was tempered later by the achievement of 'social peace' and a prosperity which sustained the concept of legitimacy by performance, for the hard right (as its mouthpiece in the seventies put it) 'the Civil War has not ended'.

Franco's rule rested, therefore, on the powers granted by a group of generals to a supreme war-lord and on the victory he had achieved by the use of those powers. As Head of State and Head of Government, ran the Decree of 21 September 1936, 'he shall assume all the powers of the New State'. Only Franco could limit these powers, powers that sprang from successful revolt against 'the liberal institutions that have poisoned our people'; his title to rule derived 'from the crucial episode of 18 July, which is a transcendent event and cannot be subject to any conditions'.

Later the constitutional theoreticians of the régime were to talk of a 'constituent dictatorship' which would adjust political institutions to the needs of a changing society. This 'evolution', as it was called, was timid. In 1942 the Cortes was set up: but its function was merely to assist the government in its exercise of legislative powers, and its composition based on the principles of organic democracy, indirect election and nomination. It remained an obedient appendage of the administration, not an independently elected parliament to which that administration was responsible. It represented, as did every subsequent constitutional enactment, a voluntary surrender that did not limit the Caudillo's reserve powers. He remained responsible to God and History.

No government can survive by physical force alone. Where the opposition of the early years went astray was in consistently underestimating the degree of support, passive and active, which the régime enjoyed. In the early forties passive support, in no small measure, came as a result of war weariness and wartime privation, of the perils of resistance and of the sheer struggle to survive in an impoverished, stagnant economy where to get enough to eat was an enduring problem, a perpetual preoccupation for much of the population. Almost the entire population was breaking the law in some form or other. Industrialists bought supplies on the black market, neglected official selling prices and practised traditional tax evasion on a new and monumental scale. Those urban householders who could were buying on the black market and most peasants were keeping a proportion of their crops safe from state agencies and understating their production. Wholesale law-breaking in one's private life tended to encourage a supine passivity in public life.

Active support came from the groups committed to the régime: the army; the 'respectable classes' saved from the fires of the Republic; and the Church.

The army had grown prodigiously in the war; when de-mobilization started, it once more suffered from a superfluity of officers. Increasingly hermetic, increasingly self-recruiting, the army was, in Franco's words 'the backbone of the Fatherland', officered by men, often promoted sergeants, who had served under Franco, and directly under his control. More immediately the Civil Guard and Armed Police – numbering a third of the army itself – were responsible for public order. There were a few military *frondeurs*, a few generals like Aranda and Queipo de Llano who fell into disfavour; but these were exceptional cases, easily dealt with. The army with its 'sacred mission . . . to maintain order' remained the ultimate sanction, the final arbiter of the régime. The overthrow of that régime would mean the end of officers' careers. Their reward was status, privilege and a share of power rather than pay; officers eked out their salaries with jobs as accountants, as they had done in the pages of Galdós' novels. Nothing impressed me more in the late forties – given that I had expected a society in which the military would be an obvious privileged class – than the general shabbiness of the army. Starved of foreign exchange, Spain could afford neither tools for her industry nor modern weapons for her army.

The second so-called 'pillar of the régime' was the Catholic Church. No institution has changed its attitude more dramatically since the early years of Francoism. In the 1940s, with its martyrs and its burned-out churches, the Church provided, as the Cardinal Primate had prophesied that it would in February 1939, 'the sinews of the Spain that is to be'. Very soon half of the secondary schools were in its hands and there the new generation was taught that during the Republic's 'five years of frightful chaos, Freemasons were seeking to turn the people against Catholicism with sectarian laws, vile abuses and force.' All 'good Spaniards' joined with Franco to 'save Spain from Communism'. (From a school textbook, republished in 1964.) There were frictions between Church and state, jurisdictional conflicts as there had been in the reign of that most orthodox of monarchs, Philip II. As early as 1940 Franco was quarrelling with the Papacy over his power to nominate bishops, and the dying Cardinal Goma was challenging Franco's pro-Axis policy. But in the early years of the régime the moral force of the Church stood firm behind the new state; bishops held important posts in its political institutions.

Many Catholics did not like Falangists, but the Falangist corporate state chimed in with the long-held, corporative ideology of anti-liberal social Catholicism. The symbiosis of Catholicism and Francoism in 'national Catholicism' seemed complete in the early 1950s. Indifference to Catholicism was construed as political disaffection. The ACNP (National Association of Propagandists), as the lay organization of active Catholics, had always aimed to infiltrate the intellectual and political élite of the country; it now provided its quota of ministers and professors. The Concordat of 1953, the work of the ACNP, not merely gave the Church extensive privileges; it also consecrated Franco's state, giving it international respectability.

In these post-war years the Spanish Church lost one of the greatest opportunities of its history, an opportunity to recapture the ground lost in the nineteenth century to secular society. Instead it swam with the political tide, the Church of vengeance, not of reconciliation. As the only quasi-autonomous institution in the Francoist state it returned to the narrow, intolerant integrist tradition, to the hunt for heresy in every manifestation of the modern world from Italian films to the works of Unamuno and Ortega. It elevated Menéndez y Pelayo (1856–1912), to whom the historic glory of Spain was her defence of Tridentine Catholicism as the 'hammer of heretics', into the lay patron saint of Spanish intellectual life. Many Catholics were later to regret this consecration of a personal dictatorship and a moribund intellectual tradition. The result was, as we shall see, the emergence of an oppositional Church beside a conformist Church. But there were few with second thoughts in the 1940s.

Committed Catholics apart, the régime enjoyed the support of landlords and bankers and of the middle sectors in both country and town. Franco in the forties did what Salazar had done earlier in neighbouring Portugal; he re-established the threatened authority of the dominant groups of the old society. Already in early 1937 the Italian Ambassador Cantelupo had remarked that 'all the parties that support Franco have a bourgeois base', a base so solid and so resolutely conservative that any hope of a 'popular transformation' in the new state, which was the Utopian vision of radical Falangists, was ruled out from the beginning. Already on 24 September 1936 all lands occupied since February 1936 – that is under the Popular Front – were returned to their owners. Spain of the early 1940s saw what has been called an 'agrarian reaction': rural wages remained low and the black market flourished. These conditions benefited not only great landlords – who nevertheless complained of the security of tenure granted to tenants – but the more substantial peasants who were gradually increasing the size of their holdings. Throughout the war the conservative peasantry of Old Castile had been a reservoir of manpower; as sociological studies and opinion surveys have shown, their conservatism did not diminish after 1939 – only their numbers with the flight to the cities in the sixties.

Bankers saw their control of the heights of the economy reinforced. No new banks could be founded (Law of 30 December 1940) and the credit operations of the existing banks were only remotely controlled in spite of a good deal of petty bureaucratic interference. Industrialists benefited by high tariffs, subsidies and tax exemption. Nevertheless the benefits went to those *inside* the system; there was little room for a new entrepreneur and even existing industrialists – especially in Catalonia – railed against the bureaucracy of interventionism.

In all political systems the opposition tends to create scapegoats for the economic ills of society. In Spain a favourite scapegoat of critics is the private banking system, the 'financial oligarchy', that interlocking of bank and industrial directorships which, it is alleged, by providing all significant industrial and other invest-ment, gives a few rich men control of the economy. The private banks will pay for their prosperity under Franco and the favours they have enjoyed under his régime, regardless of their economic performance, simply because they are the most conspicuous feature of the economic landscape of Francoism.*

* Spanish banks are mixed banks on the German model, i.e. they market and hold a great deal of stocks. The attack on the private banks goes back to the Socialist economist-historian Ramos Oliveira; the campaign has been renewed recently by another left-wing economist, Ramón Tamames. It should be stated that radical Falangists consistently attacked the private banks and the progressive nationalization of the banks was point 14 of its original programme.

It was the grim alternative of a renewed civil war – the dangers of which were the constant theme of government propaganda – that forced the middle classes as a whole to support or, at least, to see no alternative to, the régime. They became increasingly conservative, a conversion particularly noticeable during the immediate post-war years in Catalonia, home of the progressive bourgeoisie. As always in Spain, kinship and friendship could and did protect those who had been on the losing side from the full rigours of political and social ostracism and persecution. But the price of protection was silence from the protected.

Apart from fear, the main adhesive was the prospect, in a poor economy, of government employment or government favour. It was not until the mid-fifties that wide sectors of a growing middle class tasted the benefits of a growing prosperity. There were half a million posts in the public sector. The attraction of the higher ranges of the civil service was particularly strong for academics and lawyers: an able professor could hope to head a ministry as a sub-director. Conformist ability could rise.

III

The forties were a terrible time for the poor. There was still chronic underemployment in rural Spain – the great exodus into the towns and to the factories of Germany and the farms of France had not begun to 'solve' the agrarian problem. Wages were low and the struggle for better conditions was in the hands of the official trades unions.

These syndicates were controlled by the Falange and were the vestigial remnant of José Antonio's ideal of an authoritarian labour movement which would end the 'slavery' to which liberal capitalism condemned the worker. But the forces that dominated the post-war state made the equality of worker and employer in the state-controlled syndicates a fiction. Falangist rhetoric remained radical – 'We must destroy the strength of the bourgeoisie' – and it was reflected in an ambitious programme of social security. But it remained largely a declaration of intent; the Falange was given the 'social' ministries – Labour and Housing – but denied the central ministry of Finance, manned by representatives of that financial bourgeoisie which radical Falangists castigated as a monstrous growth of liberal democracy. As Girón, an old Falangist and long Minister of Labour, confessed in 1968, 'Out of these social forces which triumphed in the Civil War only a fraction would have been willing to serve a state in which the two elements of production, labour and capital, would be equal.' Even had they been more equal, the enfeebled economy in these years would not have supported the costs of Girón's ambitions for pensions and sickness benefits; nor could it afford any dramatic increase in the wellbeing of the working class.

The official syndicates retained the paternal authoritarianism of the Falangist scheme – the Law of Syndical Organization of 1940 referred to them as 'ordered as a militia'. In the wording of the Labour Charter of 1938 the official syndicates would be inspired by 'the principles of Unity (i.e. vast, monolithic unions), Totality (the coexistence of employer and worker in the same union structure) and Hierarchy (i.e. appointments made from above). This was in complete contrast to trade unionism as it was understood in the West: election of union officials in a union independent both of the state and the employers and the right to strike. In the Spain of the forties strikes were a crime under the Penal Code. Wages were set by the Ministry of Labour. In the early forties labour remained docile and controlled; the Civil Governor of Barcelona found such docility 'miraculous', given the harshness of working-class conditions and the distrust the workers felt for unions 'in which they were not represented'. It was not until the 1950s that there were serious strikes.

IV

As every commentator has explained, the secret of Franco's political success lies in the manipulation and *partial* satisfaction of the groups *within* the régime – within in the sense that they were held together in the Nationalist state by those same shared values and fears that made them join the rising in 1936 – and the successful persecution or ostracism of those who do not accept it.

The groups that provided the régime with its ministers and administrators have been called 'families'. They could not be parties – the mere word was obscene in the political vocabulary of the régime – and since they act within the régime they cannot properly be called pressure groups which, by definition, act on a political system from outside it. Other than the army the main families were the Falangists, the monarchists, the Catholics, the authoritarian technocrats connected with high finance and business, and a residuum of colourless, 'neutral' civil servants.

Like most families they were not united among themselves and frequently jealous of and hostile to other families. There were 'conformist' Falangists and those who kept alive, at least in their strange rhetoric, the utopian ideal of a 'revolution' that would incorporate the working, class in the national state. There were authoritarian monarchists and those with a mild nostalgia for the liberal monarchy. There were intransigent Carlists and accom- modating Alfonsists. There were Catholics who remembered 'social catholicism' and the party of Gil Robles and those who might have come out of the sixteenth century. There were technocrats who were less authoritarian than their colleagues. There could be curious cross alliances: Falangists and Catholics against 'Catholic' technocrats. All this imprecision was hidden beneath the 'tri- umphalist' rhetoric of the régime: autarky and 'development' could alike be presented as unique achievements of Franco and his faithful servants.

This assemblage of disparate and divergent families constituted a highly successful ruling class. What common factors kept them together in the ministerial business for forty years? A common vision of the necessity for the rising of 1936, a distrust of political systems based on ideologies (of the left above all), an authoritarian temperament, an unswerving loyalty to Franco, Catholicism in both public and private life – all these created a shared mentality, a style that, for those who professed a profound distaste for ideologues, would seem to constitute an ideology *sui generis*. There was, ambition apart, in the end a stronger bond: a common social origin, a common intellectual apprenticeship. Once the survivors of the 'Blue Epoch' – the early years of militarism, Falangism and national Catholicism – had been thinned out, Franco's ministers came overwhelmingly from the preserves of the 'traditional' middle class: the civil service, the university and the professions, especially the law. They were above all clever examinees who had passed their professional examinations with flying colours. Before they became ministers they had often served on the boards of public and private companies and as ex-ministers, with little chance of office, they went into business to secure their new standards of living. Thus the ministers who presided over the economic miracle of neo- capitalism in the sixties were closely connected with the benefic- iaries of 'development', the development that put an end to the

Falangist dream of a national socialist state, the antithesis of liberal capitalism. For all their anti-liberal rhetoric, their scorn of 'mere' politicians, the leaders of the families of the régime came to bear a strange similarity to the politicians of Restoration Spain. They were representatives of a triumphant bourgeoisie, an amalgam of the 'traditional' bourgeoisie and the 'new' bourgeoisie of finance and industry. They were the hegemonic class of Franco Spain.

There is a sense in which Franco after the war satisfied none of the political groups or families which supported him because he denied each of them effective power. The monarchists did not get their monarch and the Alfonsists indulged in mild plots; genuine Carlists retired in disgust. The Falange did not get its mass party any more than it got its national revolution. This was the most important non-event in recent Spanish history. A mass party on Falangist lines would not merely have prevented the gradual emergence of a quasi-pluralistic society – a pluralism controlled from above, and with no political parties and no freedom of association to give it vitality. It would also have severely limited Franco's personal dictatorship and his powers of manoeuvre.

Franco controlled absolutely the composition of his ministries. Major shifts in policy were reflected in cabinet changes made by him. But in each cabinet the parallelogram of political forces balanced out to neutralize each group: no one group gets a preponderant power, no one group is left completely in the wilderness. A minister who overstepped the mark was slapped down; when policies seemed ineffectual or unpopular the ministers 'responsible' for them were relieved of office.

One consequence of this balancing act was important: cabinets contained representatives of disparate groups in competition with each other. There was no collective ministerial responsibility, no agreed policy. Each minister pursued his own policy, each group its own interests. Proponents of economic liberalism sat beside convinced believers in a controlled economy; liberal Catholics beside hard-liners to whom any concession represented a threat to a precarious social peace; radical Falangists beside conservative militarists. The pharmaceutical blending of forces within the régime combined with the suppression of those without it to remove policy from the realm of public debate. For Franco, the art of politics consisted in preventing, by astute manoeuvring or force, the clash of ideas, the polarization of opinion that is the life blood of liberalism. Franco Spain was politically anaemic. The disputes of cabinets reached the informed public only in the form of 'coded' messages, decipherable only by the initiated.

The final arbiter was Franco, who presided over cabinet meetings. 'Hour after hour the sessions roll on; and while some ministers occasionally step outside to stretch their legs, Franco himself has never been known to quit a cabinet session. This is how he rules Spain. From start to finish, he remains imperturbably in his place, attentive, seldom interrupting, unruffled even when his ministers break into angry quarrels.' One minister, elaborating on the phrase 'to stretch their legs', described cabinets to me as the domination of the continent over the incontinent.

Without political parties and public opinion to back them, ministers were in a weak position both against Franco and against their own civil servants. Without the control of a public political life, policy becomes the resultant of the action of pressure groups on ministers, or the sheer pressure of events – a drain on the foreign exchange in 1957, an outbreak of labour troubles in 1952 and 1956 – and is shaped by technocrats. The form that emerged in the 1950s was therefore a constituent dictatorship tempered by technocracy. Though Franco professed to admire the Catholic kings, his rule rather resembled that of Charles III: the absolute monarch served by *golillas* – career civil servants from the upper middle classes.

It was these civil servants (collecting around themselves when in power clientèles, faint images of the personalistic political groupings of the old monarchy) who were the strongest group in the Cortes and who came to provide the core of cabinets. Franco professed as his aim the destruction of nineteenth-century liberalism and all its works. Yet he did not destroy one of its creations, a civil service strong in the defence of its own privileges and scarcely restrained by a judiciary, itself a part of the administration. It can be argued that the civil service was the ultimate legatee of the Crusade; and it is not without significance that the cry of Spanish critics of parliamentary liberalism had always been 'Less politics; more administration'.

To grasp the nature of the Franco state we must look forward to the fifties and sixties. One thing it did not become: a totalitarian state in the sense that Nazi Germany was a totalitarian state. In the early years, before the defeat of Fascism in Europe, this was not apparent. Falangism was in the ascendant. Its emblem stood at the entry of every town and village; its enthusiasts largely controlled local government. Audiences gave its salute at the end of every cinema performance. Its youth movement trained boys in para-military formations and prepared girls for household duties. Non-participation in such activities was interpreted as disaffection. Falangism mingled the *pudeur* of Catholicism with the 'austerity' of its own movement. In Alicante the Falange held appearance in summer in shirt-sleeves as 'perpetuating one of the censurable customs of the epoch of red domination'. It was 'against our mission' to hold dances. Where the anarchists had once shocked passengers in a passing train by bathing 'according to nature', the Movement enjoined one-piece bathing dresses on the beaches of Denia.

But by 1950 the Falange emblems were beginning to rust by the Spanish roadsides as a mass party failed to emerge from these early enthusiasms. When I was in Spain in the late forties and early fifties the obtrusive force in society appeared to be not the Falange but the Church. The characteristic expression of the régime was not the mass meeting (these were rare, though they occurred as when Franco defied the United Nations) but the Catholic Mass blaring out over loudspeakers; not the building of Nuremburg stadia but the restoration of churches destroyed by 'reds' and the building of the vast basilica and graveyard of the Valle de los Caídos, an attempt on a monumental scale to keep the memory of the Civil War alive.

The Falange as a 'party' of the régime ceased to exist as an independent force. In 1956 and 1957 the Falangist minister Arrese attempted to 'institutionalize' the régime via the strengthening of the Falange; his projects were rejected in cabinet by those who preferred a personal dictatorship to a totalitarian party. Arrese's projects were the swan song of 'authentic' Falangism, leaving behind only faint echoes of the rhetoric of a national revolution. The party was absorbed within the Movement. If the Principles of the Movement, promulgated unilaterally by Franco in 1958, included Falangist principles, the state was no longer 'a national syndicalist state' but 'a social and representative Catholic kingdom'. The Movement was less a party committed to a programme than an amorphous collection of those individuals who were ready to support the régime by accepting jobs under it. A commitment of loyalty to the régime and to its Caudillo. Above all a negative commitment – at the same time emotional and rooted in the instinct of self-preservation – against those forces which would have 'destroyed Spain' but for the providential victory of 1939.

Franco's personal dictatorship was buttressed, not by a mass party but by the massive political indifference still evident in the (emasculated) opinion surveys of the 1960s. Juan Linz classes Franco's Spain as 'a stabilized authoritarian régime'. 'Such régimes are characterized by lack of extensive and intensive political mobilization. . . . Membership participation is low in political and para-political organizations. . . . Rather than enthusiasm or support, the régime often expects passive acceptance.' And this is what it successfully contrived to obtain. If the Republic had seen a process of mass politicization, the Franco régime survived on the opposite condition: mass de-politicization. The apologists for the régime saw in this political passivity the supreme tribute to Franco's rule, a consensus of prosperity based on 'social peace'. 'Political apathy,' wrote Fernández de la Mora, the apologist of technocracy, in the booming sixties, 'is not a symptom of social disease but of health. . . . The health of free states can be measured by the degree of political apathy. It is not a disturbing factor but a hopeful one.'

In spite of the use of phrases like 'authentic democracy' and 'organic democracy', which professes to replace the sterile and destructive conflict of political parties based on universal suffrage with the harmony of the 'natural' groupings of society – the family, industry, the professions and so on – in a corporate state organized from above, Franco Spain was not remotely like a free society. 'Any political organization,' ran Principle VIII of the Movement, 'whatever its character, outside the representative system (i.e. the representatives denominated by the state) shall be deemed illegal.' The one central feature of a free society was therefore lacking: the power to organize opposition based on free access to information.

There could only be two political cultures: that of acceptance of all that Franco stood for (at least in public, for few Spaniards can resist the excitement of subversive rumour) and that of alienation. Hence the cultivation of 'black' humour in cartoons. Spain, one and great, could not be criticized; but humanity in general could be lampooned.

The political premises of the régime cut Spain off from the mind of Europe. It is characteristic of intellectuals to lament the loss of intellectual freedom, and in particular of left-wing intellectuals to bemoan the fate of the critical spirit in Spain; the atrocities of Spanish fascism remained their King Charles' Head and a convenient cover for more terrible oppression to the East. Nevertheless, the loss of freedom of speech and association had severe consequences in the forties and fifties. A controlled press of appalling newspapers appeared, stuffed with the driest chronicles of official activity and the lavishly illustrated minutiae of social life, with no serious political content and an extensive coverage of sport. These were the years when football became a national mania, shared by the Caudillo, who watched the match of the week on TV. Films were mutilated into incomprehensibility by censorship. The news agencies and the wireless programmes (like television later) were tightly controlled and emitted a curious blend of commercial advertising (which in the 1960s was to encourage the appetites of a consumer society) and cultural chauvinism.

The Spain of the forties and early fifties was not known abroad by its poets and philosophers but by its bullfighters. And this was a loss, not merely to Spain but to Europe, of Spanish native intelligence and imagination. The régime attempted with some success to cut off Spain from 'liberal' culture seen as a diseased growth of political liberalism that came to full flower under the Second Republic; but it failed in its attempt to create for Great Spain some new amalgam of the Catholic culture of the sixteenth century and modern authoritarian, anti-liberal ideologies. Instead it left a cultural vacuum unique in Europe. Francoism so lowered Spanish intellectual standards that when, in the sixties, a new generation sought to recover some of the lost territories of the mind, they could only look outside Spain. Certainly this meant that the new generation rejected the wordy philosophizing formerly so characteristic of Spanish culture. But the supreme irony of the intellectual history of Francoism is that the void it created was filled largely with the products of the very culture it regarded as its greatest enemy: Marxism – and often second-rate Marxism at that. By 1960 Franco had lost the battle for the mind of Spain begun in 1936.

This battle he was bound to lose. The novelist Francisco Umbral has brilliantly described the atmosphere of early Francoism. The conformism of apathy and exhaustion in 'the long winter' of food queues, old clothes and black-marketeering; the presence of the Church in every aspect of life; the overwhelming boredom of the official culture. As in politics, so in its broader aspects the culture of the régime was 'integral', a structured whole which, if challenged at one point, threatened to disintegrate all along the line. The challenges were there – not the later challenge of Marxism and its derivatives, but the challenge of American and Italian films with their vision of a richer life. 'The cinema gave us the measure of our misery.' Odd protagonists of liberty though they were, the young Rita Hayworth and Esther Williams nibbled away at the image of the régime in the years when no overt protest was possible. The heroics of the régime propaganda films of the war, and the folkloric films glorifying 'eternal Spain' seemed tinsel stuff. The Republic could not have been such a bore; and adolescents listened with respect to fathers who still held faith in it. (This is shown by the fact that the first generation of student radicals came often from Republican families and had Republican, as opposed to Marxist, sympathies.)

The patriotic rhetoric of 'eternal Spain', 'authentic Spain' reflected the deepest convictions of the Caudillo himself. His notion of the greatness of Spain, rooted in the sixteenth century and destroyed by 'politicians' and intellectuals in modern times, is manifest in a film-script called 'Race' which he wrote in these years. But this vision was to be neither central nor permanent either for Franco or for his subjects; in the sixties the vision of a Great Spain, heir of the *conquistadores*, was replaced by that of a prosperous Spain: the slogan was 'Development', not 'Empire'. But one constant there was. Franco remained a soldier. Troops, well commanded, obey. Subjects, well ruled, obey.

v

Apart from the army and public order, the one sphere that was Franco's own was foreign policy. Here the legacy of the Civil War was alliance with the Axis powers; they expected gratitude and cooperation in their own war with the western democracies that had, albeit feebly, stood by the Republic. Franco made no attempt to hide his sympathy with Hitler's New Order and his hostility to 'decadent' democracies; though distressed by the attack on Catholic Poland, he congratulated the Führer on his conquest of France. But this did not mean that he intended to sacrifice what he conceived to be the interest of Spain to the demands of the Axis. To the intense irritation of Sir Samuel Hoare, the British Ambassador, as a 'non-belligerent' he granted refuelling and intelligence facilities to Germany and permitted Falangists to mount press campaigns against the Allies and to attack the British Embassy; but to every demand that he should join the Axis in the *immediate future* he proffered a string of difficult conditions for entering the war. Apart from excessive requests for war material and food, Franco demanded territorial concessions in Morocco. These Hitler could not grant since they would have entailed a conflict with Vichy France; he promised them only after victory. When the two dictators met at Hendaye in October 1940 the Spanish team (it is characteristic of the epoch that its train broke down) rejected the demand that Spain should enter the war at Germany's bidding, substituting a vague if polite promise. Franco likewise rejected out of hand a request that German troops be allowed to march into Spain to take Gibraltar: this denied Hitler the power to impede the Allied landings in North Africa.

The Führer was maddened at Franco's 'cowardly defection' and likened his interview with him to a particularly unpleasant visit to the dentist. It was an astonishing performance in brinkmanship. Too rigid a resistance might have brought a German invasion.

Why had Franco acted thus? Certainly not because he was persuaded by Sir Samuel Hoare. It may be that Spain would have joined the Axis war effort, *if* Hitler had granted Franco's conditions. Probably, however, three considerations of internal policy held Franco back. To have given in to Germany would have upset the balance of forces in Spain by giving power to the Falange with its dream of Empire. But Franco was well aware that the Falange imperialism was unpopular with sections of the army and the Church. Most monarchists were pro-Ally, courted by Hoare, obsessed as he was with the possibilities of an 'English-type' constitutional monarchy in Spain. In any case Franco was dependent on the tolerance of the British; only Britain could grant the navicerts which he needed to bring food to a starving country. Finally his statements to Hitler that Spain was exhausted, its army equipped with antiquated weapons, as the German Ambassador admitted, were not excuses but an exact description: the Germans at Hendaye noticed that the rifles of the guard of honour were unusable. As for Hitler himself, Franco neither trusted nor admired him: 'an affected man with nothing sincere about him . . . a stage actor'. As for Franco, Hitler never understood his reserves of patient obstinacy; the Caudillo's favourite sport, after all, was fishing.

Whatever his intentions up to 1943, once the Allies looked like winning the war he had no alternative but to seek a rapprochement with the United States and Britain. In June 1944 the autographed photograph of Pope Pius XII on the Caudillo's desk was flanked by similar tributes from Hitler and Mussolini; by July 1944 the two dictators had been removed. Jordana, who replaced Serrano Suñer in September 1942, was so pro-Ally in sentiment that he sent his son to the United States for his education. Franco thus did nothing to hinder Operation Torch – the Allied invasion of Africa – accepting Roosevelt's assurance that Spain's neutrality would be respected and that 'Spain has nothing to fear from the United Nations'. Churchill never forgot this; Roosevelt did. It was now, with his former allies on the road to defeat, that Franco returned to his leading conception of the world struggle: the notion of two wars – one against Germany and the other against Russia. He had always maintained that the Soviet Union was the real enemy of the Christian West and Germany the only bulwark of its civilization. He had sent the Blue division to fight in Russia and now he sought to separate the West from their Soviet allies. His advances were decisively rejected by Churchill and he drifted into a bitter dispute with the United States over the supply of wolfram to Germany. If he thought concessions to the now obvious victors would enable him to gain their friendship 'by presenting his bill', as he put it, for latter-day favours, he was mistaken. The war ended with Franco ostracized by the triumphant democracies as a fascist and an ally of Hitler. Without allies in the West, Spain appeared a minor power, an archaic appendage to a progressive Europe. In June 1945 it was denied a seat in the future United Nations Organization.

This ostracism continued, formally, till 1955. Why? It was not so much a consequence of Spain's *actions* in the war as of the nature of her domestic régime. The extreme charges of cooperation with Germany made in the United Nations were palpably absurd and those who made them cannot have believed them. Churchill openly acknowledged the debt the Allies owed Franco in 1942; Roosevelt and, later, Truman forgot it. France, the Soviet Union and the British Labour government condemned Franco not because he had hindered the Allied war effort, but because he was a 'fascist'; because in Franco Spain there was no freedom of the press, no independent unions; because there were political prisoners. Ostracism was the price Franco paid for his absolute refusal to attempt any reconciliation with the defeated. For him and for his enemies the Civil War was still going on.

VI

It was in this climate of universal disapprobation that the oppositions to Franco believed that there lay an opportunity to overthrow the régime. A push from outside would do the trick. Never did the régime appear so insecure. Why had these hopes turned to bitter disillusionment by the 1950s?

The miscalculations of the opposition – and in these years its leadership was perforce in exile – were tremendous. The Allies were willing to condemn Franco but not to help overthrow him other than by pious declarations of intent. 'We detest the régime,' Bevin thundered in the House of Commons; but he added that the Spanish people alone were entitled to determine their political future. How could they? The opposition hoped that Franco would be compelled to give way by a resolution of the General Assembly of the United Nations. It came on 13 December 1946, condemning Franco as a fascist and ally of Hitler and Mussolini: if within 'reasonable time' a government which derived its authority from the governed was not established then the Security Council should consider 'adequate measures to be taken to remedy the situation'. Ambassadors were withdrawn as a symbolic gesture. The opposition was plunged into despair; Franco organized a successful mass demonstration to condemn his international critics.

Above all, the opposition miscalculated the temper of the Spanish people: a proletariat in a police state concerned above all with scraping a living in difficult circumstances is unlikely to be the vanguard of a revolution. Guerrilla actions supported by the Communists had petered out, as they must without local support, by 1952.

The worst legacy of the Civil War in opposition circles was division and distrust; the external opposition of the exiles was increasingly mistrusted by the internal opposition; Communists were mistrusted by the Republicans and Socialists they had exploited and deceived. The Communists' National Union was at odds with the Republican-Socialist National Alliance which rejected its emphasis on the armed struggle of the guerrillas; when the Communists did make real efforts at a united front, the coming of the cold war made them a liability for those who still believed that, somehow or other, salvation would come from the West and the United States. Prieto classed Communists with Falangists as totalitarians, not to be touched by decent democrats; he even preferred to attempt joint action with the monarchists for a transitional régime to be backed by the democracies (August 1948). But the monarchists cast in their lot with Franco; Prieto's desertion of Republican orthodoxy brought only recriminations.

Franco had survived the worst years, helped by the divisions of his opponents. The fact that disgruntled monarchists stopped their plottings is important; they were opposed to the régime only as long as it looked an insecure protection for the interests of the upper classes, a régime at the mercy of some pressure from the democracies. But this pressure was never effective; it was an illusion of exiles. 'To overthrow him [Franco],' the head of the Republican government told his fellow exiles, 'needed only one breath from the new Europe, the slightest gesture by the victors. But, by a cruel irony of history, the longed-for triumph of the democracies served only to uphold the usurper and only tightened the fetters of our people.' The democracies were getting used to Franco; they were soon to need him.

Part II: *The Paradoxical Years: Economic Growth and Political Immobilism: 1951–75*

Economic growth began in the 1950s with the abandonment of autarky. The main proponents of a liberalization of the economy were the technocrats of Opus Dei, *but while these right-wing Catholics served the régime the progressive forces in the Church (particularly in the Basque Provinces and Catalonia) drew apart.*

Prosperity had paradoxical results; it reconciled many to the régime but raised unsatisfied expectations in others (e.g. the working class in new industries).

Opposition came in the form of strikes (in the 1960s organized by Workers' Commissions independent of the official unions), student demonstrations and finally the terrorism of the Basque nationalists of the ETA and the militants on the extreme left. The régime responded by drastic police action and suspension of the constitutional guarantees. The attempts by the proponents of an 'apertura' (which would widen the area of participation and attract some of the opposition forces by a 'liberalization' within the Principles of the Movement) failed.

Franco's political balancing act went on as before and the successive ministerial changes illustrate shifts in policy:

1. *1951–7. The beginnings of economic recovery. Falangists (Fernández Cuesta) and Catholics (Ruiz-Giménez) clash over the latter's attempts to 'free' the University. Both Ruiz-Giménez and Fernández Cuesta were dismissed. The Bases Agreement with the USA and the Concordat with the Vatican in 1953 gave Franco international respectability.*

2. *1957. After the failure of Arrese to institutionalize the Falange as the party of the régime (resisted by the Catholics and*

conservatives) the Falange programme was subsumed in the vaguer Movement (Law of the Principle of the Movement, May 1958). Influence of the Opus Dei neo-capitalist technocrats and the further 'liberalization' of the economy.

3. *1962–9. 'Liberalization' within the régime (Fraga's Press Law of 1966; proposals for the formation of political associations; the Organic Law of 1967 and the admission to the Cortes of deputies elected by heads of families) in conflict with the political conservatism of the Opus Dei technocrats. In July 1969 Franco solves the succession problem by the nomination of Prince Juan Carlos as future king of Spain and the prince accepts the Principles of the Movement.*

4. *1969. A ministry dominated by the technocrats supported by the vice-Premier Admiral Carrero Blanco (Prime Minister June 1973). Carrero Blanco seen as the representative of* continuismo *and the engineer of succession of Juan Carlos without significant political change.*

5. *Assassination by the ETA of Carrero Blanco (December 1973). Appointment of Carlos Arias Navarro, who combines re-pression and* apertura *(speech of 12 February 1974 promising a law on political associations). The* aperturista *ministers removed October 1974 and a consequent return to immobilism.*

Terrorism apart, the 'illegal' opposition, though still divided by personalism and fear of Communist ambitions and policy, grows in strength and public debate much more vigorous, though its participants are still liable to fines and imprisonment. The Communists form the Junta Democratica *together with a group of political notables; the Socialists and the left-wing Christian Democrats the* Platforma. *Both demand full democracy and full amnesty for political prisoners.*

Franco is taken seriously ill and on 12 July hands over temporarily the Headship of the State to Prince Juan Carlos; he resumes office on his apparent recovery 2 September 1974.

I

Fourteen years after the end of the Civil War General Franco seemed an irremovable feature of the international landscape. He had survived the post-war troubles by ruthlessness and political nerve. While the United Nations was debating his fate he spent the afternoon painting. 'I enjoy painting more every day.' 'Spain,' he remarked in the late sixties, 'is easy to govern.'

The 1950s were to see his power sanctioned by the recognition of the democratic West and bolstered up by the beginnings of economic recovery. Between 1950 and 1956 the index of industrial production tripled. In the sixties came the take-off of what was to be called an economic miracle: an industrial growth rate exceeded only by that of Japan, and the emergence of the lineaments of a consumer society.

The post-war years of autarky, of rationing, of a stagnant economy had found a fitting parallel in a stagnant political system. Now economic growth which brought Spain towards the levels of western Europe – say a time-lag of five years in respect to Italy – was unaccompanied by any significant political change. Economic and social movement was combined with political immobilism. After years of privations and struggles, to share in prosperity, for a relatively broad sector of the population, took precedence over the quest for what the United Nations resolution had called 'a government which derives its authority from the consent of the governed'. Yet prosperity was to bring the discontents of rising expectations, especially in the proletariat of a new industry, and a growing awareness in sections of the élite of bankers and businessmen, who were the beneficiaries of expansion, that there existed a widening political and social gap between Spain and the Europe they wished to join.

The later fifties were, therefore, the paradoxical years of Francoism. On the one side was the legitimacy of performance, a prosperity presented in the 'triumphalist' propaganda of the régime as the work of its technocrats who believed modernization of the economy was a surrogate for modernization of the political system; on the other the discontents of development and a revolution of rising expectations. All this was a prelude to the crisis of the seventies when the political structure appeared increasingly archaic, held together in its original form by the iron will of one man in spite of profound changes in the society he ruled.

One way of understanding the contradictions of this period is to examine the response to them of the Communist party which contained the most consistent, disciplined and courageous of Franco's opponents and whose recruiting drives were carried out in prisons. The party abandoned in the fifties any idea that the régime could be pushed over by guerrilla action. In the countryside pockets of guerrillas, survivors of a resistance movement in the last months of the Civil War, found little support; in the towns isolated acts of urban terrorism were counter-productive, bringing down on cadres of militants the full force of the repressive apparatus of the state. In the fifties the Secretary General of the party, Santiago Carrillo, abandoned direct action for a policy of infiltrating existing official trades union organizations and of 'national reconciliation' – the building of bridges to bourgeois opposition elements. Hence he seemed to recognize the necessity of a long march. Yet, at the same time, he prophesied the imminent collapse of a régime which he professed to see as composed of a narrow clique which exploited the rest of the nation for its own profit.

Carrillo's analysis thus both recognized, at least implicitly, the strength of the Franco state – it was not fragile enough to succumb to direct action – and at the same time overestimated the possibilities of its demise. The contradictions of his strategy were exposed by his opponent Fernando Claudín, the best brain in the party and whom Carrillo expelled in 1964. Carrillo's mind was still stuck in the model of the Popular Front of the 1930s: Spanish society was a semi-industrialized, semi-feudal society ruled by a narrow oligarchy, and therefore the first step in the overthrow of Francoism must be an alliance of workers and bourgeois to implant a bourgeois democracy. Claudín believed that this model was out of date in the burgeoning neo-capitalism of the 1960s. Neo-capitalist prosperity, he argued, strengthened the social basis of the régime, making nonsense of Carrillo's facile optimism with its hope of overthrowing Franco by, say, a national general strike. The new bourgeoisie were the beneficiaries of expansion and the workers' main interest was higher wages and better conditions. They were unlikely to join hands in an anti-Franco Popular Front in the immediate future. At the same time, the 'correct' long-term strategy was to pass directly from monopoly capitalism to socialism without any truck with an intervening period of bourgeois democracy.

Carrillo's analysis – as the repeated failure of political strikes showed – was false in the sixties. It was only in the seventies that financiers and businessmen, increasingly frustrated by an archaic political structure that could no longer protect their interests and which kept them out of Europe, began to organize round-table discussions with the historic opponents of Francoism.

II

The precondition of prosperity and the *point de départ* for neo-capitalist development was an injection of foreign capital. American aid, wrote Professor Sardá, Spain's leading economist, 'irrigated Spain like water in a parched land'.

The benevolence of the United States, which needed Spain as a base in the cold war, could be presented by Franco as a triumph of his political vision. He had always maintained that the enemy of Christendom was the Soviet Union. Now his enemies had come round to his point of view. In 1953 the United States granted economic aid in return for the use of bases in Spain. On the evening the agreement was signed Franco is said to have told his friends, 'At long last I have won the Spanish War.' He had worked his passage. President Truman retained his Baptist dislike of the general even when he recognized, in 1950, his value as an ally. President Eisenhower embraced him to the tune of 'The Yellow Rose of Texas.'

The rewards of the American embrace were momentous and timely for domestic policy. By the 1950s the consequences of autarky and interventionism and, more important, the denial of foreign credits, were painfully apparent; after fifteen years of a controlled economy Spain had by 1954 climbed back only to the per capita income of 1931. If Spain was to prosper she must become part of the international economy of the West and this meant that she must abandon fear of the market, both at home and abroad; rapid industrialization demanded massive imports of capital goods. With the prospect of US loans the economy could slough off its fear of imports and begin to open the Spanish market to international trade and to allow the free play of the market to dictate distribution of resources. It was now no longer a necessity to produce everything at any cost. The political system was flexible enough to adapt itself to new necessities; a gradual approach to economic liberalism began with the cabinet reshuffle of July 1951.

This cautious approach to a new economic policy was resisted by Falangist economic experts, old-style bureaucrats and officials of INI loth to abandon controls. But a modest liberalization of the economy, if constantly impeded by relics from the past, slowly paid off. The 'agrarian' phase of Spanish development was at last overtaken by the drive for industrial growth that had been preached since the 1940s; agricultural prices fell relative to industrial prices;

the import of machinery replaced the import of food; industrial production grew at the rate of 8% a year in the 1950s. This new growth implied, for its continuation, that inflation should be held at a reasonable level and that imports should come to be financed by exports. But exports grew slowly and inflation grew fast. With inflation and falling real wages came strikes, and soon the exhaustion of Spain's reserves of foreign exchange reached crisis point.

In February 1957 a new ministerial team took over. The two key posts of Commerce and Finance were taken over by members of the Catholic Opus Dei. The Opus Dei was a Catholic lay organization, considered by its critics a sinister secret society, a Holy Mafia. It had a strong representation in the business world and in the universities. From 1957 on, it steadily increased its influence in the cabinet and the administration, attaining its maximum influence in the so-called 'homogeneous' cabinet of 1969. Its driving force was Laureano López Rodó and its main support Admiral Carrero Blanco. The men of the Opus professed a scorn for ideology and 'politics'; conservative and authoritarian by temperament, they posed as 'neutral' technocrats. They were disciples of neo-capitalism and enthusiasts for the integration of Spain into the European community and the international economy. As orthodox financiers, under pressure from the World Bank, their remedy for the crisis in the balance of payments was the Stabilization Plan of 1959: a wage freeze, devaluation and the encouragement of foreign investment.

After teething troubles – 1959, 1960 and 1961 were years of recession – the new recipe worked. The later sixties were a period of rapid economic growth, the years of the economic miracle, presided over rather than directed by the technocrats of the Development Plans. The psychological effect of the plans exceeded their economic impact; a cynic might maintain that planning was little more than an exercise that kept the bureaucracy busy and employed while the controls they had administered were dismantled. Massive imports of capital goods combined with an abundant supply of labour from the countryside for the industrial towns did the trick. Plans or no plans, growth would have been spectacular.

Franco (whose personal habits apart from shooting and fishing were bourgeois) had created – or perhaps had allowed to be created by the ministers he had chosen – a Spain in the image of his tastes rather than of his intellectual convictions, a Spain of the romance of material progress, not of the Catholic kings. 'Produce is the cry of our time. Never as now had the greatness of the fatherland and your wellbeing been so identified with it.' This in a speech in 1948; how much more now.

He had presided over a dramatic transition. In little over a decade Spain passed from an agrarian into an industrial nation, or at least a semi-industrial nation by European standards; between 1960 and 1970 the proportion of the active population in agriculture sank from 42% to 25%, that in industry rose from 29% to 37% and in the services from 29% to 38%. Industrial exports replaced the old primacy of agricultural products and minerals; if we take the structure of the pyramid of occupations as an indicator, then Spain changed more between 1950 and 1970 than in the previous hundred years.

From a poor, provincial country Spain was beginning to look like a modern, industrialized, consumer society, a society with pollution and parking problems in its cities, television and refrigerators in its homes, a secure investment for foreign capital. The Spanish-made SEAT 600 car was the symbol of the decade for the increasing numbers of Spaniards who could afford it. The official ideology of the régime contained fewer and fewer traces of the old 'ruralism' of the forties with its exaltation of the Castilian peasant farmer – still protected by high guaranteed wheat prices – as the rock on which the Spanish race was founded; its policies were resolutely in favour of industrialization and agrarian interests felt on the defensive.

The underemployed rural population from decaying villages, the labourers replaced by mechanization on the *latifundia* (the *cortijos* which dominated the landscape of Andalusia as white castles in a yellow landscape will vanish as their rough accommodation for seasonal workers is replaced by tractor-sheds) flooded into the great cities. Madrid almost doubled its population between 1960 and 1970, draining the surrounding countryside and becoming in the process the metropolis of a desert province, a case of urbanization unique in Europe. Those who could not find jobs in the cities of Spain found them in the factories of France and Germany; in the sixties their remittances brought in twice the foreign exchange produced by a traditional export: citrus fruits. The tourist trade gave employment; in 1969, 21,441,701 tourists brought two thousand million dollars of foreign money. All this refuelled the economy and underwrote industrial development. Building booms gave employment. The aesthetic horrors of Benidorm and Torre Molinos were the symbols of a new Spain, open to everything in the western world save free association. Mini-skirts and discotheques, but no political parties. Great industrial complexes, but no independent trades unions.

To those for whom nothing good could come out of the Franco régime, the growth of the sixties which, by the seventies, had made Spain the eighth industrial nation of the western world was both lopsided and fragile.

It was lopsided because, while the great cities and their surrounding areas were becoming richer (though their social services could not cope with the new influx of workers), the depressed countryside from which the cities drained the labour force for new industries was (in spite of a rise in rural living standards) sinking into relative poverty. This consequence of rapid economic development is castigated by critics as the 'desertization' of the backward rural areas : three million Spaniards were uprooted from their homes.* As the rural underemployed leave the poorer regions the agrarian problem is being 'solved' without the social upheaval of agrarian reform ; the cry for a *reparto*, a handing out of land to the landless, is less audible. Emigration has produced a statistical improvement : per capita income rises with fewer heads. But the division between the 'two Spains' of contrasting economic development is perpetuated and intensified ; in backward provinces like Almería, Soria or Huesca real wages are lower, hospitals and schools give poorer services than in Vizcaya or Navarre.

Critics argue that the economic miracle is not only lopsided but fragile. With imports of goods at twice the value of exports and the deficit in the balance of payments made good only by foreign investment, tourist expenditure and emigrants' remittances, it can be argued that *continued* development is at the mercy of outside factors. As wages in Spain rise and the foreign demand for Spanish labour drops off, so the profits of emigration will decline. Europe in recession would export fewer tourists. Foreign investors would

* Between 1960–69, 1,425,913 Spaniards emigrated to Europe – mostly to France, Germany and Switzerland at an annual rate (1962–6) that exceeded the great late-nineteenth-century emigrations to Latin America. Whereas the 'traditional' emigrants to France had taken up low paid agricultural work in south-western France, the emigrants of the sixties went into factories in industrial regions, especially Paris.

retire from the scene when they could no longer count on a docile, cheap labour force.

A more relevant criticism is that the concentration on economic growth at all costs pushed into second place the question of the distribution of new wealth. The profits of the expansion of the sixties benefited the employers rather than the workers: the share of wage-earners in the increased national income remained stable. Income tax was derisory, corporation tax evaded. Nor was income redistributed by a high level of social services available to all. It was the workers who bore the rigours of the stabilization programme of 1959; they worked extra hours, took on 'second jobs' to survive. 'The only thing that has not developed' preached Cardinal Herrera, brain of the old CEDA, in 1968, 'is social justice.' Even so the *absolute* standard of the average worker had risen significantly. In 1975 the wife of a striker was asked what sufferings her husband's absence from work had meant for housewives. 'We have had to give up using sprays for cleaning,' she replied, 'and have gone back to soap and water.' This is a long cry from the scarcities and hardships of the 1940s.

However much Spain suffered from the customary distortions and disturbances of rapid growth, however much the new prosperity was a reflection of and dependent on the European boom, the economy was successfully refuelled and in the process profoundly modified. The ultimate product, however, was not classic free enterprise capitalism, in spite of much talk of liberalizing the economy. Traditions of bureaucratic interference, of state interventionism died hard. Spain of the sixties was a hybrid economy. Inheritances from a 'paternalistic' past such as the law of 1938 forbidding the sacking of an employee, hampered modernization and rationalization; the money market was complicated by official credits given at favourable rates to selected enterprises on the so-called 'inner circuit'. This hybrid economy bred the corruption that flourishes on the borderlands of high finance and government. It was such a scandal, the Matesa scandal of 1969, that discredited the long and, on their own terms, successful rule of the technocrats.

III

The technocrats who drew up the Development Plan of 1971 made a confident prediction. 'In 1980 Spain will have passed the barrier of $2,000 per capita income which will mean that life will be more pleasant and the degree of social cohesion greater.' This was prophesy based on false premises. False because, though prosperity induced acceptance of the régime from large sectors of a depoliticized society (and every survey of the sixties revealed a massive depoliticization) there remained a fundamental con- tradiction: economic advance had not been accompanied by political change.

The proponents of social peace through economic advance already had before them evidence that should have given them pause: the increasing radicalism of labour in the sixties, especially among skilled workers in the modern, dynamic sectors of the developing economy, for instance in the new, large metallurgical plants of Madrid. The 'paternalism' of the bureaucratized official syndicates as a means of settling labour conflicts broke down once the closed economy in which it had operated vanished. Modernizing employers wanted to negotiate productivity deals directly with the workers. Collective bargaining was recognized in 1958 as part of a 'modern, liberalized economy'; by the late sixties collective agreements affected millions of workers. But if the employers wanted to negotiate with workers' organizations which would carry weight on the shop floor, the workers of Vizcaya, Barcelona, the Asturias and Madrid wanted fully *representative* autonomous unions. They fought tenaciously for wage increases which would enable them to enjoy more of the benefits of a consumer society in an inflationary economy. But behind these conventional labour demands and their enforcement by strike action, now recognized as legitimate if not legal, was a 'political' issue: the control of unions by the workers themselves and, via their own unions, a voice in the control of the economy, demands beyond a mere defence of living standards and real wages.

These demands could not be satisfied by the state-controlled, bureaucratized official syndicates. They were therefore partially satisfied outside them by the elected Workers' Commissions declared illegal in 1967. Militant workers went to prison, many of them young workers, less docile, more politicized, than their elders. The result of combining authoritarian politics with the economics of modernization was a radicalization of the labour force that saw the state of Franco as a concern of planners and capitalists. The repressive mechanisms of authoritarianism kept that radicalism below the surface with increasing difficulty. There were serious strikes in 1952, 1953, 1956, 1958 and 1962. Even Navarre, cradle of the Crusade in 1936, became the scene of bitter labour struggles.

The increasing inadequacy of the official unions reflects the failure of the post-war state to create institutions that would 'fit' Spain, institutions that would owe nothing to the liberal, social democratic tradition. It signalled the final collapse of Falangism, the incapacity of its radical tradition to evolve into some kind of nationalist left. The Falangist vertical unions had been given great prominence in the régime: but the régime was not a truly corporative concern where the class struggle was 'eliminated' and where 'official' unions could function. It was a modified capitalist régime where unions confronted employers. The class struggle became a reality and with it the 'official' character of the unions deprived them of most of their value for the workers.

The radicalization of the workers might have been expected. What no one could have predicted in 1939 was the defection of sectors of the Catholic Church. By the 1960s not merely young priests who sheltered illegal workers' organizations in vestries, but the hierarchy itself, as the older generation of bishops died off, showed less confidence in the alliance with Francoism forged in the Civil War. Increasing numbers of Catholics felt uneasy about the powers granted to the state by the Concordat of 1953 – the government's rôle in the nomination of bishops, for instance, was condemned by the Vatican itself. Bishops openly championed a freer form of trades unionism that would permit Catholic unions to operate. By 1974, die-hard Falangists were shouting insults to the Archbishop of Madrid as a traitor, worthy of the firing squad, and the Bishop of Bilbao came out in defence of Basque nationalism – long supported by his parish priests.

Just as no one could have predicted in 1939 that Spain would have to maintain a special prison for contumacious priests, so no one could have foreseen the liberalization of official Catholic attitudes that came with Vatican II, a mutation that must have seemed an incomprehensible stab in the back to Franco and his court still living in the world of the Crusade. The Catholic technocrats of Opus Dei were political conservatives or indifferent to the forms of government; not so the opposition Christian Democrats. 'We are not particularly afraid,' says the French police chief in *The Brothers Karamazov*, 'of all these socialist anarchists, atheists, and revolutionaries; we are keeping an eye on them and all their moves are known to us. But there are several peculiar men among them, though only a few: these believe in God – they are Christians and at the same time Socialists. It is these we fear most of all.' Many who call themselves Christian Democrats would fit comfortably into a discreetly modified Franquista successor state; but the left-wing Christian Democrats seek the complete disappearance of the Franquista régime and its replacement by full democracy, together with far-reaching reforms in the structure of Spanish society. Their leader Ruiz-Giménez has become one of the most outspoken critics of the régime and his magazine *Cuadernos para el Diálogo* stood for a time alone as the only periodical published in Spain open to the non-violent opposition.*

These divisions reflect the concern of Catholics to recover the ground lost in the 1940s, even to reverse the 'dechristianization' of the working classes during the nineteenth century. Some see the separation of Church and state, the formal desertion of Francoism, the recognition of religious pluralism, as enough; others, more radical, argue that unless the Church is against the régime it cannot be with the people. For them the Church must move from conformism to confrontation (*contestación*), from Aquinas to Karl Marx.

With the workers radicalized, the Church divided, where does latter-day Francoism – the army apart – find its support? This support is by no means negligible. Using opinion surveys – of necessity uncertain guides in an authoritarian régime – it would seem that committed 'historic' Francoists together with the politically indifferent constitute a majority. 'Whether we like it or not,' wrote the disillusioned Falangist Dionisio Ridruejo in the early sixties, 'there can be no doubt but that the Spanish régime has been supported by a decisive majority for many years.'

It has been argued that the new bulwark of the régime in the sixties was the 'new' middle class, the product of economic development; by the sociologist Amando de Miguel that Spanish *society* is authoritarian in its attitudes and therefore easily contained in an authoritarian state. Clearly this hitherto unorganized middle

* Joaquin Ruiz-Giménez (b. 1913) fought in the Civil War and was Franco's Ambassador to the Vatican (1948–51) and Minister of Education (1951–7). By 1965 he had rejected 'official' Spain, founding *Cuadernos* in 1963. He defined himself as 'more of a social democrat than a Christian democrat'.

class is an important stabilizing factor; it has a great deal to lose – one of the novel features of recent years is middle-class investment on the stock exchange – in a political and social upheaval. But it seems rather to be confused than either resolutely authoritarian or liberal. It wants both 'social peace' as a condition for continued development, which implies a continuation of Francoism, and a more liberal open society, which is its contradiction.

In 1971 a thesis presented in Madrid University (the examiners included a former Minister of Information, Manuel Fraga Iribarne) made clear that, if the attitude of middle-class parents was confused and ambivalent, the attitude of their children at the university was one of rejection. Between the political culture of conformism and alienation, they chose alienation. While most Spanish youth were indifferent to politics, university students now considered the state as legitimized neither by a Civil War its generation had not known nor by a bounding prosperity whose social injustices it criticized.

Student radicalism was one more proof that the processes of development bring problems that are not solved by an increase in the GNP. An industrial society demands mass education and increased higher education; increased higher education brought student radicalism and student riots to Madrid, Barcelona and other universities. The 'mass' university of the sixties and seventies could no longer be dominated by the official Falangist students' union; it could not hope to maintain the principles of the law of 1943 which proposed a university 'of the centuries of Crusades and Cathedrals'. The Faculty of Political Science and Economics, designed to produce a conformist generation, equipped to man the institutions of the régime, produced instead a generation of student rebels from middle-class homes and spawned a flourishing, naive Marxist subculture, regrettably the predominant intellectual challenge to the ideologues of the régime.

The generation gap was one of the consequences of economic development. The values of the new industrial, 'get-rich-quick', technocratic society of the new middle classes cannot be reconciled with those of 'austere' traditional Spain, values which remained embedded uneasily in the official culture and which had found their characteristic expression in the 'traditional' middle class. As in every society such shifts in values are most evident in the young. Hence the erosion of the institution of *noviazgo* – the prolonged courtship that must terminate in marriage. 'Marriage is slavery', 'To love is to endure' – such precepts still occur in popular Catholic literature; but the *noviazgo* which institutionalized such precepts is being replaced by a less rigid and binding relationship between the sexes. Women, confined to the home by the more old-fashioned Catholic apologists and by the early ideologues of the Falange, are seeking work outside it. The moral 'austerity' of the Civil War cannot be maintained in a consumer society where 70% of the population own television sets. But changes in inherited attitudes are slow; what purports to be a modern society still carries within it the values of traditional, Catholic Spain triumphant in the Civil War and maintained for nearly forty years by General Franco.

The tensions, in personal and generational terms, are often acute and painful; sometimes bizarre. I once observed a truly awful parade of leggy drum-majorettes in bright blue mini-skirts and coloured wellington boots in a small Levante town. The attitude of the older generation was a mixture of disapprobation at the sight of so much naked flesh and pride that their *pueblo* was so 'modern'.

IV

How have the régime and the opposition responded to these changes?

The rising of 18 July and the shared experience of the struggle against 'Marxists and Masons' remains the emotional content of Francoism to its hard core, the *duros*. Yet a new generation, which did not know the Civil War, is less impressed by the argument that any deviation from established norms might plunge society into chaos. There is a sense in which the very prosperity the régime created or presided over was self-defeating and a precondition for the discontents of the seventies. The political establishment could be challenged without danger to the fabric of society itself. And there were those in that establishment who believed that the 'immobilism' of the *duros* was imperilling the régime; to survive it must evolve.

If the political establishment – or some of it – had put on some new clothes, the Emperor was still there. Unlike many dictators General Franco was not afraid of delegation; but if he did not do everything, nothing could be done against him. If he occasionally mitigated the excesses of those to whom the Francoism of 1939 was an unalterable dogma, his 'constituent dictatorship' did not evolve along the road to representative and responsible government. A fifth of the 504 deputies to the Cortes are now elected by heads of families and married women; but it remains politically impotent, lacking the central power of a parliament in a parliamentary régime: ministers were responsible, not to it, but to the Head of State, who appointed and dismissed them. Its laws could be vetoed; the Head of State could 'appeal to the people' over its head by a referendum. Francoism had become a Spanish species of Bonapartism.

In 1969 Franco 'solved' the succession problem by choosing Prince Juan Carlos, son of Don Juan and grandson of Alfonso XIII, as King of Spain when he, Franco, as Head of State chose to lay down his responsibility before God and history. But Juan Carlos' claim to rule derived not from the secular rights of his predecessors as kings of Spain but from the fact that Franco had chosen him as opposed to his father who was, according to dynastic tradition, the true heir (the father supported some form of democratic monarchy, a 'neutral' monarchy above factions). The new heir-apparent swore loyalty to Franco and to the Principles of the Movement. All the paraphernalia of the Francoist constitution might turn this chosen successor into something remotely resembling a constitutional monarch. But it did not limit the discretionary powers of his creator.

The late sixties and early seventies were, therefore, dominated by a single factor: the physical condition of an ageing, sick dictator revealed in every photograph as a mummified edition of his old self. When would he surrender his powers to his successor? He did after a severe illness in July 1974, only to resume them in the following September. Paradoxically, the prospect of the dictator's early death – he has Parkinson's disease – secures the survival of his régime while he lives by inducing a paralysis in the opposition. Why take the risks of overthrowing a personal dictatorship when the dictator himself is condemned by nature?

V

As always, ministers and ministries continued to be Franco's creation; they reflected the alternatives open to the régime after the hungry forties and uncertain fifties. It could either 'evolve' and give itself a 'liberal' varnish or pride itself on its rigid authoritarianism and fidelity to the principles and men of 18 July: either *apertura* – an opening through which new forces might enter and accept the régime – or the 'philosophy of the bunker'. Both positions were recipes for political survival. The men of the bunker could argue that change, however gradual and however careful to preserve the 'essence' of the régime, once initiated, could never be stopped; *aperturistas* could maintain that only by opening up some prospect of political change (and their recipes for this 'opening' ran from a 'constitutionalization' of the régime and a respect for legal forms to a gradual advance towards representative government) could that régime survive the changes in Spanish society and appear as a respectable part of modern Europe.

This division, though only in the realm of cultural policy, can be traced back as far as the Ministry of July 1951 when Ruiz-Giménez as Minister of Education attempted a limited liberalization of university life unacceptable to rigid Falangists. Eleven years later (July 1962) Franco's seventh government included the conservative technocrats of Opus Dei and supporters of a political *apertura*. The ministry that executed the Communist leader Julian Grimau in 1963 passed a 'liberal' press law in 1966 and a law of religious freedom in 1967.

The Press Law was the work of an energetic professor, then Minister of Information, Manuel Fraga Iribarne, and it represented what he called a phase of 'progressive liberalization'. Though the law was, in Spanish terms, a significant move that was to usher in a new phase of public discussion, it illustrated the limitations of any intra-régime liberalization. It ended censorship but the government could seize newspapers before publication; editors were responsible in the courts for any article that attacked 'the spiritual, national or social unity of Spain'. This Damoclean sword replaced censorship by auto-censorship and a series of fines and suspensions that tarnished Fraga's liberal image. It was in these years that 'Political Associations' – the word 'party' was still politically unusable – were much discussed; but the 'contrast of opinion' allowed by the Organic Law of 1967 was to be 'healthy' and contained within the 'Principles of the Movement'. Even a law permitting what would have been innocuous pressure groups or political clubs was blocked. Any opening in the system was perforce narrow. Political logic was with the extreme right. The régime could not be liberalized without destroying its essence; change, the hard-liners argued, merely increases appetite for change. Governments could find no means of institutionalizing the conflicts of a rapidly changing society; protest was therefore continuous and sometimes dramatic. And protest reinforced the arguments of the right.

In the ministerial changes of October 1969 'liberalization' was dropped with the ministers who supported it. The eruption of terrorism in the Basque Provinces, where the 'military' wing of the ETA (Basque Freedom Movement) was active, and student violence strengthened the arguments of the inhabitants of the bunker. With the appointment of Admiral Carrero Blanco, an intimate friend of the Caudillo, as Prime Minister (June 1973) the continuity of the régime as a bleak authoritarian concern serviced by technocrats seemed guaranteed. The brilliantly planned assassination of Carrero Blanco by ETA terrorists (December 1973) was probably designed to push the régime even further to the right. This it did not do. It opened a prolonged crisis within the régime of quite new dimensions, exposing once more the conflict between those who hoped to survive by 'liberalization' and those who believed – as Carrero Blanco himself had once said – that to offer liberal concessions to Spain was like offering a drink to a confirmed alcoholic.

Carrero Blanco's successor as Prime Minister was Carlos Arias Navarro. The technocrats of Opus Dei were summarily dropped and a civilian government held out bright promises for a law of political associations, to be combined with a tough policy against terrorism and the illegal opposition. This mixture of the carrot and the stick has failed. The government, with terrorism in the Basque country and on the far left reinforcing the hard-liners on the far right, proved incapable, even on its own terms, of absorbing the more moderate opposition and widening the area of participation. Admittance to the system under the Law of Associations was to depend on loyalty to the 'Principles of the Movement' and the sanction of any political association by the Movement's council. This was a condition unacceptable to the régime aperturistas, let alone to the democratic opposition. Two prominent aperturistas left the cabinet in October 1974 – a triumph for the logic of the hard line.*

* The chief victim of a vicious political campaign by the right led by the old-style Falangist Girón was the Minister of Information, Pio Cabanillas. As minister he had made a genuine attempt to make the press a source of 'free and honest information'. His colleague Barrera, Minister of Finance, resigned in sympathy. Barrera's resignation is particularly significant. He was President of the Spanish branch of ITT and the sort of businessman who would have been a stalwart supporter of the régime. When he resigned the Stock Exchange fell.

No doubt those who forged the heady rhetoric of the early years believed that they were laying the foundations of a new state, that they were the architects of a political system that would be a permanent and viable alternative to liberal democracy and party politics. They have failed, less because of the strength of the opposition than because whole sectors of society believe that their interests either never were, or are no longer, protected by Francoism. Workers and bankers are therefore, for different reasons, dissatisfied with the régime: workers because it is still too strong; bankers because it appears faltering and unsure. With the future uncertain, the stock exchange boom has ended and private investment has fallen off.

The system is threatened because the one feature of liberalism that must be excluded if non-liberal values are to be rejected – free discussion – has come timidly in by the back door. The beginning of this process came with the Press Law of 1966. Books, when the paperback explosion is creating a new reading public, can and do contain savage attacks on the structure of the régime, if not on the people who man it. The periodical press in Spain has in the last years become the substitute for an open political system; periodicals like *Cambio 16*, with a circulation far beyond any British equivalent, are making criticisms of the system, in detail and in general, unthinkable in 1960. Criticism is no longer confined to the endless rumour-ridden private conversations that had no public consequences; it finds its way, often in coded and obscure language which future historians will find difficult to interpret, into the newspapers.

Public debate, limited as it still is (1975), can only logically end – as de Tocqueville saw long ago and as Primo de Rivera found after 1928 – in full democracy: an authoritarian system cannot function for long with concessions to liberalism lurking in the interstices of the body politic. The régime can still execute and imprison;* it can withdraw passports and refuse to give driving licences – and no one who has not experienced administrative repression can conceive how effective these relatively mild instruments can be. It may well, fearful of a vociferous right claiming to represent the true principles

---

* cf. the fate of Marcelino Camacho, leader of the Madrid Workers' Commissions. Imprisoned 1940–41; 1941–3 in a Labour Battalion; in exile 1943–57; 1957–64 a car worker and active organizer of the Workers' Commissions; arrested June 1966 and again in January 1967; imprisoned again March 1967 and December 1973.

of the Crusade, return to sharp repression and seek a temporary refuge in the bunker. But it cannot remain in the bunker, increasingly a refuge for the figures of the past. In the long run Spain must become like the rest of the West.

It is not merely that the crisis opened up in December 1973 was seized on by the old committed 'illegal' opposition. A wider disenchantment with the régime runs from the quasi-opposition of ministers and their clientèles out of power, from the radical chic of Madrid to the democratic opposition – tolerated but outside the system – of those like Dionisio Ridruejo or Ruiz-Giménez who have lost faith and to whom their past is a painful political miscalculation. Opposition now runs from liberal bankers to workers – and their representatives are now discussing the future of Spain together*; it runs from students to stevedores; from Communists to Christian Democrats; it takes the form of ETA terrorism in the Basque Provinces, and a massive anti-Franco, pro-Catalan movement in Catalonia; there are frequent strikes from the SEAT workers in Barcelona to the actors and civil servants of Madrid. The régime cannot resist these pressures. In the Basque Provinces police action has not ended terrorism; it has merely alienated a population with no fundamental sympathy for the ETA extremists. Nor, for that matter, can governments command the support of the ultras of the extreme right; for the Guerrilleros of Christ the King and the old men of Blas Piñar's *Fuerza Nueva* liberalization has already gone too far.

Yet *in the end* there is no other solution but democracy, complete democracy, for no quasi-democratic compromise will stick. Democracy will not come while General Franco lives; but it must come with his successor in the form of an elected Cortes to which ministers of the crown will be responsible.

VI

The process of transition to democracy and the problems which a democracy may face are daunting.

To graft democracy on to a nation that has enjoyed no democratic freedoms is a difficult task. It is not merely that democratic politics demand a democratic society and that the implantation of

---

* For instance the round table organized by a prominent lawyer and businessman J. Garrigues-Walker. The meeting included Ramón Tamames, the most prominent opposition economist and an enemy of the domination of the private banks.

democratic institutions does not create such a society. It is that the processes by which democracy will be installed are uncertain and problematical. There are those – politicians and bureaucrats – who will be in positions of power during a transition period after Franco's death who will exploit these difficulties and seek to implement some model of change that will, if not keep them *in situ*, at least save them from vengeance – for instance by controlling from above the nature and formation of political parties and access to the press and television. The various opposition coalitions may well split on the degree to which they are willing to accept an intermediate stage 'managed' from government or an electoral law, handed down by the government, which will exclude the Communists from participating in elections as a legal party.

As the constitutional arrangements stand, much will depend on the political initiative and nerve of Juan Carlos as king. An unknown figure (except for his athletic prowess, his dedication to work and his determination to keep the army behind him), he is still inevitably under the shadow of his creator. His problem will be one of timing. Too long a delay on the road to democracy, too hesitant an approach to a 'revolution from above', can only increase the dangers of a revolution from below. It is a delicate balance which must combine a refusal to become the prisoner of the fears of the right with an equal determination to maintain public order. For it is the theme of collapsing public order that has always given the voice of the right its resonance in Spain.

If the Francoist hard right is weak in the country as a whole it is still strongly entrenched in the 'institutions': the Cortes (which will have to pass the laws establishing any new democratic system); the Council of the Realm (which has the right to suggest three names as Prime Minister from which the king must choose one); the National Council of the Movement (which, under the Law of Associations can 'admit' associations to the political arena). The cry of *continuismo* is 'After Franco the Institutions' and its disciples will use those institutions to slow down the pace of reform if they cannot stymie it altogether. The king, at some stage, will have to defy them.

The one relief is that a conservative party is unlikely to emerge as a combination of outraged interest and outraged religion. The clerical question, in the form it plagued the politics of the Second Republic, is dead. The new generations are either 'progressive' Christians or indifferent to religious issues; there are few violent anti-clerical Jacobins left prepared to burn churches and persecute priests. But if the clerical question is dead conservatism is not after nearly forty years of conservative government. The representation of conservative interests, the leadership of conservative parties, is complicated by the issue of the 'contamination' of potential leaders by a 'Francoist' past. Nor does this affect merely a few conspicuous figures; it hangs over vast numbers of Spaniards. If and when the democrats come to power they must avoid the wholesale pro-scriptions of Franco in 1939. The elimination of the contaminated must be left to the ballot-box and the civil courts, however galling and painful such a decision may be to those who have suffered greatly from those now in power. The régime's determination to keep the Civil War alive as the divisive issue must not be inherited by its successors, for this is precisely what the *duros* of the right wish to do.

Will a new democratic Spain inherit the characteristic weakness of politics in Spain from the Second Republic through to the opposition to Franco, namely: the incapacity to cooperate, the penchant for factionalism? There were thirty-six separate parties in the Cortes of the Popular Front in 1936; there are now hundreds of political groups that have ambitions to become political parties when this is legally possible. Wherever three Spaniards are gathered together two parties are formed, and one of Franco's strengths has been handed to him by the division of his opponents.

It is a paradox that the Communist party has both been the cause of these splits and yet consistently, since the 1950s, preached cooperation with any group seeking 'national reconciliation' on a common front for full democracy in Spain. Catholics in opposition are no longer the allies of feudalism and the distributors of opium to the people but are the 'yeast of progress'. This 'bourgeois revisionism' of the party leadership has been challenged by the extreme left (itself tormented by Byzantine feuds) which captured the student radicals in the sixties. The party's Secretary General, Santiago Carrillo, runs the risk of being caught out between a disillusioned left which will seek to oust him and a bourgeoisie that will regard the party as, at best, a circumstantial ally and its leader's declared democratic intentions as a mere tactical device. Yet in spite of repeated internal splits and the defections of those who reject its Italian style on the one hand and those who condemn the party's resolute independence of Moscow on the other, the party remains a firmly organized opposition group with committed cadres in the working class.* The revived PSOE under energetic young leadership may not inherit the historic distrust of the PCE; but it is competing for the loyalty of the new proletariat. Competition may drive the left of both parties towards the 'maximalist' position; another Largo Caballero may emerge to capture the discontents of those who reject Santiago Carrillo's pragmatism, his reconstruction of the Popular Front of 1936. All parties which do not rely on capitalizing on a conservative reaction see that the industrial working class will play an increasingly important rôle as the catalyst of change, for they have in their hands the most effective weapon in the present political armoury: the strike.

Finally there is the regional question. The Franco régime is founded on unity, on rigid Castilian centralism, on the domination of Madrid. The suppression of the slightest manifestation of Catalan and Basque culture was, in the early post-war years, ferocious and unrelenting: a poem or sermon in Catalan was seen as the first step on the road to separatism. It was this suppression that made Francoism peculiarly unpopular in Catalonia; whereas in most of Spain Francoism repressed the defeated of 1939, in Catalonia *everybody* came to feel repressed: rich businessmen refused import licences in Madrid as well as workers fighting for a living wage; parish priests as well as students. It was repression not *in* Catalonia, but *of* Catalonia. Even the flood of migrants from other provinces absorbed the resentments of this oppressed province.†
Only in the sixties did a slight relaxation of Castilian chauvinism – a relaxation which did not extend to the mass media – allow Catalan culture to reveal its enduring vitality.

The assertion of regional cultures and languages was therefore a form of opposition to the régime which suppressed them; in the forties, to dance the *sardana* – the Catalan dance – was to exhibit one's political sympathies. The last years have seen a remarkable resurgence of nationalist sentiment in the Basque Provinces and

* The image of the Communists as the only serious opponents to the régime has been weakened by several factors: the influence of left-wing Christian Democrats; the loss of a monopoly of Marxist culture (anyone can now buy Marxist literature); finally, the emergence of ETA as the most committed and violent opponents of the régime; the revival of the PSOE.

† Clearly a time may come, if Catalanist demands are satisfied, when the immigrants may resent dominance of a non-Spanish culture and language. The insistence on the use of Catalan in schools – a concession Madrid will never make under Franco – is, for Catalanists, essential since it is the only way the immigrants' children can be assimilated and won over for Catalanism.

Catalonia and to a lesser degree in Galicia and the Levante – there is even an 'Andalusian' movement based on neglect by Madrid of its economic interests as a 'backward' region. In the Basque Provinces the national protest has found violent expression in the terrorism of the ETA which demands the creation of a separate Basque state; in Catalonia there is the powerful movement for the use of Catalan in schools and the restoration of the autonomy granted by the Republic.

How will the post-Franco régime face these problems? Will it evolve some federal structure that can successfully absorb a regional demand fostered, though not created, by the excesses of ideological centralism? Will the Catalans, like Macià in April 1931, try to 'impose' their terms on Spain? Will young Basque terrorists continue to wage war on a democratic state that cannot conceivably concede their maximum programme? Without an agreed solution 'within Spain' to the irresistible demands of peripheral nationalism there can be no civil peace. Years of silence and repression have made that solution more difficult.

The final arbiter of change in the future will be the army. Its collective public utterances repeat the classic themes: it is the guardian of order, of the true will of the Spanish nation, a neutral force above political partisanship. What this might mean in any future situation is obscure. In the past such declarations have meant that the army stands as the *ultima ratio* of the régime. 'Let no one,' said Carrero Blanco in 1968, 'entertain the slightest hope of altering any aspect of the institutional system, because even though the Spanish people would never tolerate it, the armed forces remain as the last resort.' It is clear that the army will, like the Church, do everything it can to survive *as an institution*, regardless of the past loyalties, political convictions or social prejudices of the officer corps.

Like the Church, though infinitely less dramatically, it is divided between the generation that was formed by the Civil War and a younger generation concerned that declarations of neutrality conceal the fact that the army *is* committed politically, committed to an outworn authoritarian system. Some younger officers do not relish the rôle of policeman for an unpopular government nor, as in the Burgos terrorist trials of 1970, that of a substitute for civil jurisdictions. Will the army, to save itself, stand guard and secure an orderly transition to democracy?

The *peaceful* advent of the Republic on 14 April 1931 depended on the decision of one man: General Sanjurjo. Ennobled and flattered by Alfonso XIII, he let in the Republic and refused to defend the monarchy by force in order to save the discipline of the army and to avoid the dangers to 'the harmony of the military family' by committing it to the defence of an unpopular cause. The Republic would have arrived with or without Sanjurjo, but it might well have arrived with bloodshed. Again it can be argued that the outcome of the political crisis precipitated by Carrero Blanco's assassination might have been substantially different had the Chief of Staff been a hard-line believer in the maximum use of force rather than the liberal General Diez Alegría – characteristically later relieved of his post in the see-saw of the régime.

The course of history no doubt depends, in the long run, on those great social and economic forces that mould societies. In the short run, however, the course of Spanish history may depend on the decision of one man at the moment of crisis: the Chief of the General Staff, the Captain General of Barcelona or Madrid.

Indeed all now, in 1975, depends on the decision of one almost inaccessible man, now in his eighties and sick: General Franco, living still in the world of 1936, a world threatened by Marxists and Masons and the furies of anti-Spain. The longer he clings to power, the more difficult the situation his successor will inherit, the more terrible the prospect of another civil war.

Postscript

In 1938 Franco had rejected a negotiated peace.

'Those who want mediation' he announced 'consciously or unconsciously, are the tools of the reds and the concealed enemies of Spain.

The War of Spain is not something artificial. It is the end of a historic process: the war of *la patria* against *la anti patria*, of unity with secession, of morality against crime, of the spirit against materialism. There is no solution but the triumph of eternal principles against bastard and anti Spanish principles. He who thinks of mediation is fighting for a broken Spain, materialist, divided and poor in which will be realized the chimera that criminals and their victims can live together; a peace today and war tomorrow. The blood of our glorious dead and our martyrs, will fall on those who listen to such an insidious proposition. Nationalist Spain has conquered and will not allow victory to be snatched from it or be sullied by anyone.'

Given such a cast of mind in the caudillo who was to rule Spain till 1975 there could be no reconciliation. The scars of the Civil War remained in the tissue of Spanish society. Spain remained divided between *vencedores* (the victors) and *vencidos* (the vanquished). The *vencidos* must be purged from the public life of Spain and, in the early years, shunned in private. Spain was to be the patrimony of the victors.

Brutal repression and the hunger of the 1940s inhibited resistance. Yet in the years after 1945 the exiles hoped that the allies who had defeated fascism in Europe might bring about its downfall in Spain. But it needed more than international ostracism imposed by the allies on Franco Spain as the friend of Hitler and Mussolini to bring down the regime. Beyond this token gesture the Western democracies were unwilling to go: Ernest Bevin, the Foreign Secretary of the Socialist government of Britain argued that the nature of the Spanish regime was the domestic concern of the Spaniards, as if 'Spaniards' could express that concern. With the onset of the Cold War strategic considerations swamped the undoubted distaste with which the democracies regarded Francoism. In 1953 the US accepted Franco on his own terms as 'Sentinel of the West'.

With international respectability ensured by the 1953 agreement with the US and the concordat with the Vatican, in the 1960s economic growth, fuelled by emigrants' remittances, tourist revenues and foreign loans brought relative prosperity to those who still remembered the hungry forties. The iconography of the regime reflected the acceptance world of a burgeoning consumer society. Franco was no longer the victorious general mounted on a charger but the paterfamilias surrounded by his grandchildren. No one has portrayed the new society better than the novelist Semprun describing his return in 1975 to a beach once the preserve of the few.

'You remembered the Carraspio beach as almost deserted, until you came back one morning in August of 1975 and contemplated, in despair, the hundreds and hundreds of sun umbrellas, the hundreds of families, of potato omelettes, of Pepsi-Cola and orange drink bottles, the hundreds and hundreds of plump, screaming children, of women with big asses and bare breasts, of transistor radios blaring out the hits of the day, of bathers who had frightened off the seagulls, perhaps forever.

Well, what's gotten into you anyway? What's so surprising? This is progress, you said to yourself, laughing fit to kill and immensely sad, this is the result of the irresistible and praiseworthy, and perhaps even well-deserved, rise of the middle classes, of the long-suffering, insufferable middle classes, to levels of consumption comparable to those of the rest of Europe, this is the unmistakable sign of the massive spread of economic well-being in your country.'

This new society favoured a passive acceptance of the 'Peace of Franco' and the prosperity it claimed to have made possible. It diminished the need for physical repression though it always remained the reserve instrument of the regime. There are subtler mechanisms – never appreciated by those who have not experienced them – by which an established authoritarian regime controls its subjects. Censorship, absurd in its puritanical excesses, disgusts the informed but it keeps the mass of the uninformed in ignorance. In every sphere of life – particularly in the civil service including the Universities – no promotion goes to the dissident; even minor favours – a driving licence, a telephone, a passport – are the reward of acquiescence.

Thus, in spite of the efforts of an opposition that ran from the Communists to Christian Democrats and that included the suppressed nationalities of Basques and Catalans, Franco died in his bed in November 1975.

Yet from the seventies it was evident that the regime could not survive its ailing creator. Indeed that it survived at all was perhaps because it seemed fruitless to overthrow an octogenarian whose rule nature itself would terminate. One of the paradoxes of latter day Francoism is that while prosperity induced acquiescence it also imported values and habits that were irreconcilable with a politcal regime which appeared an anomaly in democratic Europe and whose old fashioned Catholic ideology inhibited what one may call the social liberties that go with a consumer society. Francoism did not fit a society that was becoming increasingly like the open societies of Western Europe and that no longer wished to remain moulded by the memories of a Civil War which was outside the direct experience of an increasing number of Spaniards.

The need for change was recognized by the 'reformists' among the Francoist establishment; they saw that some democratization of a regime that had always lacked democratic legitimacy, in spite of the tortured semantics of 'organic democracy'; that some 'opening' must take place if Francoists were to survive as members of the political elite beyond the lifetime of their master. It was these repentant modernizers (under fierce pressure from an opposition that demanded, not some form of doctored democracy handed down from above, but 'democracy without adjectives') who were to install pluralistic democracy in Spain within three years of the Caudillo's death. Supported by a king who made it clear that he wished to reconcile the *vencedores* and the *vencidos*, democracy came through the legal apparatus of Francoism. In November 1976 the Francoist Cortes passed the Law of Political Reform; in June 1977 Spaniards voted in the first democratic elections since 1936. The opposition, including

Socialists and Communists and Conservatives co-operated with the centre-right government of Adolfo Suarez to draw up the fully democratic constitution of 1978. It represented a consensus; that Spaniards wished to escape the political legacy of the Civil War.

It is now the representatives of the *vencidos*, the heirs of Prieto, who rule Spain, determined not to fall into the errors of Largo Caballero. It is the memory of the last Civil War, the emergence of a society no longer polarized as was the society that lurched into fratricidal conflict in the 1930s, the absence of authoritarian, fascist regimes in Europe which gave sustenance, both material and ideological, to the rebels of 1936, that make impossible another Civil War. Only the minds of ageing nostalgic reactionaries and romantic revolutionaries are haunted by the division between *vencidos* and *vencedores*.

Select Bibliography

All selection involves prejudice; this applies to the present bibliography, especially given the enormous recent growth of literature, good and bad, on the Civil war. I have concentrated on works in English.

THE ANCIEN RÉGIME

Gerald Brenan's *The Spanish Labyrinth* (1943) remains to me the most stimulating introduction to modern Spain. More recent work is embodied in Javier Tusell Gómez *La España del Siglo XX* (1975), Richard Herr *Spain* (1971) and M. Martinez Cuadrado *La burguesia conservadora* (1973). Salvador de Madariaga's *Spain* (1960) contains the reflections of a liberal; for a socialist view A. Ramos Oliveira *Politics, Economics and Men of Modern Spain* (1946). Two opposing interpretations are R. de la Cierva *Historia básica de la España actual* (1974) and M. Tuñon de Lara *La España del Siglo XX* (1966). See also R. Carr *Modern Spain 1875–1980* (1980).

The nature of the 'liberal' economy has been the subject of much debate and scholarly enterprise, e.g. in Jordi Nadal *El fracaso de la revolución industrial en España 1814–1913* (1975). For the 'mistaken investment' thesis see G. Tortella Casares *Los origines del capitalismo en España* (1973). S. Roldan et al *La consolidación del capitalismo en España* (1973) is a useful account of the consolidation of Basque and Catalan economic interests 1914–20.

Three collections of essays summarize recent work: P. Martin Acena and Leandro Prados de la Escosura present the results of the 'new history' in *La nueva historia economica en España* (1985). More accessible to the general reader are J. García Delgado (editor) *La*

España de la Restauración (1985) and Nicolas Sánchez Albornoz, *La modernización económica de Espāna* (1985).

For working-class politics Gerald H. Meaker *The Revolutionary Left in Spain 1914–23* (1974) covers the early period. Two important studies are J. P. Fusi *Politica obrera en el pais vasco 1880–1923* (1975) and A. Balcells *Trabajo y organización obrera en la Cataluña contemporánea 1900–1936* (1974). For the POUM there is an 'inside' history by Victor Alba *El Marxismo en España* (1973). There is an excellent study in depth of the anarchist mind in J. Romero Maura *La Rosa de Fuego* (1974) and of 1909 in Barcelona in Joan Connelly Ullman *The Tragic Week* (1972). See also Peirats below.

For the rôle of the army see S. G. Payne *Politics and the Military in Spain* (1967) and Carolyn P. Boyd *Praetorian Politics in Liberal Spain* (1979). The attitude of the Church to political life is well illustrated in J. A. Gallego *La politica religiosa en España 1889–1913* (1975) and briefly in Stanley Payne *Spanish Catholicism* (1984). For the dictatorship of Primo de Rivera see Schlomó Ben Ami *Fascism from Above: The Dictatorship of Primo de Rivera in Spain 1923–30* (1983).

There are many books on the Catalan question. For the non-Spanish reader a strongly pro-Catalan case is presented in Jaume Rossinyols *Le problème national catalan* (1974).

THE SECOND REPUBLIC

G. Jackson *The Spanish Republic and the Civil War* (1965) provides a good introduction; S. Payne's *The Spanish Revolution* (1970) is a hard-hitting criticism of the left. Edward Malefakis *Agrarian Reform and Peasant Revolution in Spain – Origins of the Civil War* (1970) is essential reading. For opposing views on the rôle of the right see Richard Robinson *The Origins of Franco Spain* (1966) and the articles of Paul Preston: 'Alfonsist Monarchism and the Coming of the Spanish Civil War' in *Journal of Contemporary History* Vol. 7, Nos 3 & 4, July & October 1972; 'Spain's October Revolution and the Rightist Grasp for Power' *Journal of Contemporary History* Vol. 10, No. 4, October 1975; 'The "Moderate" Right and the undermining of the Spanish Republic 1931–1933' in *European Studies Review* Vol. 3, No. 4, October 1973; and 'El Accidentalismo de la CEDA: Aceptación o Sabotaje de la República?' in *Revista Internacional de Sociologia* (Madrid), Nos 3 & 4, February 1974. For the *Bloque Nacional* see R. Robinson 'Calvo Sotelo's *Bloque Nacional* and its ideology' in *Univer-*

sity of Birmingham Historical Journal (Vol. X, No. 2, 1966) pp. 160–84.

For Carlism see M. Blinkhorn 'Carlism and the Spanish Crisis of the 1930s' in *Journal of Contemporary History* (VII 1972, pp. 65–88). Other political studies are the four volumes of J. Arraras *Historia de la Segunda Republica española* (1956), hostile to the Republic, J. Becarud *La segunda República española* (1967) and Carlos Seco Serrano *Historia de España* Vol. VI (1968). Perhaps the most useful is M. Tuñon de Lara, *La II República* (1970).

There are articles on the right and the left during the Republic in *The Republic and the Civil War in Spain* R. Carr (ed.) (1971). For a new study of the Republican Left see J. Aviles Farré *La Izquierda burguesa en la II República* (1985). For the results of modern research see P. Preston (ed) *Revolution and War in Spain 1931–39* (1984).

For contemporary accounts of the revolution of October 1934: A. Ramos Oliveira *La revolución de Octubre* and M. Grossi *La insurreción de Asturias* (1935), both written in prison after the revolution; Azaña's account of his role in Barcelona in *Mi rebelión en Barcelona* (1935). A modern account is J. A. Sanchez y Garcia *La revolución de 1934 en Asturias* (1974).

For the CNT: J. Brademas *Anarco sindicalismo y revolución en España 1930–37* (1974). The Largo Caballero-Besteiro conflict is the subject of *Anti-Caballero* (1975) by G. Mario de Coca, an uncritical supporter of Besteiro. J. Maurin's *Hacia la segunda revolución* was first published in 1935 (Fr. trans. 1937); a new edition called *Revolución y contrarevolución en España* was published in Paris in 1966.

For the economic problems a useful study is A. Balcells *Crisis económica y agitación social en Cataluña 1930–36* (1971). Two important studies, one on employers' organizations and one on the labour movement in Madrid are Mercedes Cabrera, *La patronal ante la II República* (1983) and Santos Julía Díaz, Madrid, 1931–1934, *De la fiesta popular a la lucha de clases* (1984).

For a detailed study of the election of February 1936 see J. Tusell Gómez *Las eleciones del Frente Popular en España* (1971). For parties generally J. Linz 'The Party System of Spain: Past and Future' in S. Lipset and S. Rokkan *Party Systems and Voter Alignments* (1967).

General Mola's collected works (*Obras Completas* [1940]) are the best source for the attitudes of the army.

There is an enormous output of memoirs. The most useful are: Azaña's in his collected works (*Obras Completas*, 1966, 4 vols); José

Maria Gil Robles *No fue posible la paz* (1968); J. Chapaprieta *La paz fue posible* (1971); A. Lerroux *La pequeña história* (1945); M. Maura *Así cayó Alfonso XIII* (1966). A journalist's account is H. Buckley *Life and Death of the Spanish Republic* (1940).

For the church: M. Sánchez *Reform and Reaction: the politico-religious background of the Civil War* (1964) and J. Tusell Gómez *Historia de la Democracia Cristiana en España* (2 vols, 1974).

The biographical studies in Chapter III section (iv) are based on R. Fraser *In Hiding: The life of Manuel Cortes* (1972); M. García Venero *Falange en la guerra de España* (1967) corrected by Manuel Hedilla *Testimonio* (1972) and J. A. Ansaldo *Para qué* (1951).

The account of social conflicts in Aragon comes from Carmelo Lisón Tolosana *Belmonte de los Caballeros* (1966). For the peasant revolt and subsequent massacre of Casas Viejas which discredited Azaña's government see J. R. Mintz *The Anarchists of Casas Viejas* (1982).

The complexities of Catalan politics are succinctly set out in A. Balcells *Cataluña Contemporánea 1900–1936* Vol. II (1974), and those of Euzkadi in S. Payne's *Basque Nationalism* (1975).

THE CIVIL WAR
Hugh Thomas *The Spanish Civil War* (3rd edition 1977) remains the best work. P. Broué and E. Temime *The Revolution and the Civil War in Spain* (1970) is sympathetic to and illuminating on the extreme left. R. de la Cierva *Historia ilustrada de la guerra civil* (2 vols, 1970) uses Republican sources to criticize the Republicans from a point of view sympathetic to the Nationalists J. Zugazagoita *Historia de la guerra de España* (1940) was written soon after the event by a political friend of Prieto. The results of modern researches are summarized in vol. IX of M. Tunon de Lara's *Historia de España* (1981) pp. 243–626. There are excellent essays in P. Preston (ed) *Revolution and War in Spain 1931–9*.

1. *The Rising* For the Mola conspiracy see H. Lizarza Iribarren *Memorias de la Conspiración* (1952) and Felix Maïz *Alzamiento en España* (1952) and J. del Burgo *Conspiración* (see below).

The events of the first three days are described in a graphic form in L. Romero *Tres dias de Julio* (1967). For Barcelona there are some interesting sidelights in the account of a young Falangist, J. Ma Fontana, *Los catalanes en la guerra de España* (1951), as in another early sensational version F. Lacruz, *El alzamiento la revolución y el terror en Barcelona* (1943). The murder of García Lorca and the Nationalist terror in Granada are examined in detail by I. K. Gibson *The Death of Lorca* (1973). There is an account of the rising in Galicia in Carlos Fernández *El alzamiento de 1936 en Galicia* (1983). For Madrid M. García-Venero's *El General Fanjul* (1967) contains details of the rising.

2. *Military operations* For all operations of the war the best guide are the nine volumes of J. M. Martínez Bande (1968 onwards) which now cover every major campaign and replace Manuel Aznar's *Historia militar de la guerra de España* (1940). The *Historia de la Cruzada española* was published in 1940 by the Nationalists; it still contains some useful information. Ramon Salas's huge *Historia de Ejercito Popular* (4 vols, 1973), contains a mass of material and has good maps. J. Martín Blázquez *I helped to build an Army* (1939) is a useful account of the early difficulties of army organization in the Republic.

For the war in the air, J. Salas Larrazábal *Air War over Spain* (1974). F. G. Tinker *Some still live* (1936) is an account by a mercenary on the Republican side. For the bombing of Guernica see H. R. Southworth's *La destruccion de Guernica* which exposes in detail the Francoist version. Recent research is summarized in A. Viños 'Guernica: las responsabilidades' *Historia 16* no. 25 1978.

For the defence of Madrid by the Republican officer responsible for it see V. Rojo *Asi fue la defensa de Madrid* (1967) and R. G. Coldony *The Struggle for Madrid* (1958).

Two essential first-hand accounts of campaigns by those who fought them are Lt Gen. R. Garcia Valiño's *Guerra de Liberación Española* (1949) for the Aragon campaign, and Gen. V. Rojo's *Alerta los pueblos!* (1939) for the Catalan collapse, written three months after the events.

From the many memoirs of participants the following are of some use. L. Renn *Der Spanische Krieg* (1956) (orthodox Communist); E. Lister *Nuestra Guerra* (1966) (outrageously so). M. Tagüeña *Testimonio de dos guerras* (1973) and V. González (El Campesino) *Listen Comrades* (1953) are accounts by former Communist commanders. José Llordes *Al dejar el fusil* (1968) are the memoirs of a sergeant.

On the Nationalist side P. Kemp *Mine were of Trouble* (1957) and Duque de Lerma *Combate sobre España* (1961) give lively accounts of the Requetés, the Foreign Legion and the Nationalist Air Force. Most of the Nationalist military biographies err on the side of hagiography. G. de Raparaz *Diario de nuestra guerra* (1937) is a minor work that reveals the general tone of rebel Spain in 1936/7.

3. *Politics of Republican Spain* A detailed study, concentrating on the rôle of the Communists in B. Bolloten *The Grand Camouflage: the Communist Conspiracy in the Spanish Civil War* (1961). It goes up to May 1937. A Sevilla Andrès *Historia politica de la zona roja* (1963) is still interesting. A general account of the Communist party's rôle is given in D. C. Catell *Communism and the Spanish Civil War* (1955). For a bitter attack on the Communists by a POUM leader see J. Gorkin *Caníbales politicos en España* (1941), and for Prieto's attitude his early work *Cómo y por qué salí del ministerio de defensa nacional* (1940). For a defence of the 'revolutionary' interpretation of the war see the essays in P. Vilar, *Metodología histórica de la guerra y revolución española* (1980). E. H. Carr *The Comintern and the Spanish Civil War* (1984) was published posthumously.

For the rôle of the CNT, J. Peirats *Los anarquistas en la crisis politica española* (1964) and his *La CNT en la revolución española* (1955) are essential source books as is C. M. Lorenzo, *Les anarchistes espagnols et le pouvoir* (1969). See also D. Abad de Santillán *Por qué perdimos la guerra* (1940). F. Largo Caballero *Mis recuerdos* (1954) is disappointing, as is Dolores Ibarruri *They shall not pass* (1966). Jesús Hernández *Yofuiministro de Stalin* (1957) contain the 'revelations' of a repentant Communist minister. J. Alvarez del Vayo defends Negrín's policies in *Freedom's Battle* (1940) and *The Last Optimist* (1950), as does Juan Simeón Vidarte in *Todos fuimos culpables* (1973). Prieto's views are refleclted in his *Convulsiones de España* 2 vols (1908) and *Entresijos de la guerra de España* (1953).

For my treatment of local politics in Alicante and Valencia I have relied on V. Ramos *La Guerra Civil (1936–9) en la provincia de Alicante* (3 vols, 1972) on an unpublished Oxford thesis by T. Smyth *CNT Politics in the Valencian Region 1936–37* and on the local press. A revealing story of the political conflicts in Madrid in 1936 is Julio Aróstegui y Jesús A Martinez *La Junta de Defensa de Madrid* (1984) which reprints the informes of the Junta.

For the Basque Republic at war see G. L. Steer *Tree of Gernika* (1938) and A. de Lizarza (A. M. de Irujo) *Los Vascos y la República Española* (1944).

The Catalan side is discussed in most of the general histories, memoirs, etc. Manuel Benavides *Guerra y revolución en Cataluna*

(1946) is favourable to the PSUC. A biography of Companys by an admirer is A. Ossorio y Gallardo *Vida y sacrificio de Companys* (1943). Constituional issues are illustrated in J. A. González Casanova *Federalisme i autonomia a Catalunya 1868–1938* (1974). For the ill-fated Mallorcan expedition M. Cruell's *L'expedicío a Mallorca* (1971) also his *La societat catalana durant la guerra civil* (1978). Hilari Ragueri Suñer has written on Catalan Catholics in the Civil war: for a summary see 'Uns cristians per la Republica' in *Taula de Canvi* no. 3 January 1977.

The number of 'first hand' books is legion and selection arbitrary. The best are: H. E. Kaminski *Geux de Barcelona* (1937); for the May troubles in Barcelona George Orwell's classic *Homage to Catalonia* (1938); for an illuminating journalist's account F. Borkenau *The Spanish Cockpit* (1937). There is an account of his experiences in Spain by the American journalist L. Fischer *Men and Politics* (1941). Of the more naive pieces of rapportage I find T. C. Worsley's *Behind the Battle* (1939) still illuminating as is, for a different reason, M. Koltsov's *Diario de la guerra de España* (1963). For an interesting popular account of life in the rearguards see R. Abella *La vida cotidiana durarante la guerra civil: La España republicana* (1975). R. Fraser *Blood of Spain* (1979) is a reconstruction based on interviews in 1973 and 1975.

Two famous novels are Ernest Hemingway's *For whom the Bell Tolls* (1940) and André Malraux's *Days of Hope* (1938). Georges Bernanos *Les grands cimetieres sons la lune* (1938) is the work of a Catholic shocked at Nationalist atrocities in Mallorca.

4. *Collectivization* (See above Kaminski and Borkenau.) The most able (but controversial) defence of the collectives is to be found in N. Chomsky *American Power and the New Mandarins* (Pelican Books 1969) pp. 62–129: J. Bricall *Política económica de la Generalidad* Vol. I (1970) gives production figures; Albert Perez Baró *Trenta meses de colectivisme a Catalunya* (1970) considers the legislation and its reflection in reality. On workers' control see F. Mintz *L'autogestion dans l'Espagne révolutionnaire* (1970); on agrarian collectives H. Thomas in R. Carr (ed.) *The Republic and the Civil War in Spain* pp. 239–55. For an early contemporary and enthusiastic account see A. Souchy *Colectivaciones: la obra Colectiva de la Revolución Española* (1937); G. Leval's *Espagne libertaire* (1971) is a rare book. An authoritative account of the Consejo de Aragon is Julían Casanova, *Anarquismo y*

revolución social en la sociedad rural aragonesa (1985) and for Andalucia see L. Garrido *Las colectividades agrarias en Andalucia: Jaen, 1931–39* (1979).

5. *Politics of Nationalist Spain* Franco's biographies are legion. G. Hills *Franco* is illuminating on his army career; J. P. Fusi *Franco* (1985) is by far the best interpretation, concentrating however on the period after 1939. R. Serrano Suñer *Entre Hendaye y Gibraltar* (1947) gives the background to the events of April 1937; also General Kindelán's *Mis Cuadernos de Guerra* (1945) for Franco's rise to power (and also for an account of his strategy); For the creation of the Movimiento see M. García Venero *Falange en la guerra de España: la unificación y Hedilla* (1967) and Hedilla's *Testimonio* (1972) together give the Falangist version of unification; for the Carlist view see J. del Burgo (below); see also S. Payne *Falange* (1961).

E. Suñer *Los intellectuales y la tragedia española* (1938) reveals its crude anti-intellectualism.

For the general atmosphere Jaime del Burgo's *Conspiración y guerra civil* (1970) and R. Abella *La vida cotidiano durante la guerra civil* Vol. I. *La España nacional* (1973) are illuminating. A. Peña Boeuf *Memorias de un ingeniero politico* (1954) gives a lively account of the attitudes of an early ministerial technocrat; A. Bahamonde y Sánchez de Castro *Un año con Queipo de Llano* (1938) gives some insight into that general's rule in Andalusia. Cardinal Gomá's pastorals are collected in *Pastorales de la guerra de España* (1955). An account of his activities in the Civil War: Maria Luisa Rodriguez Aisa *El Cardenal Goma y la Guerra de España* (1981). The anticlerical activities of the Republicans, together with statistics of assassinations are described in A. Montero *Historia de la persecución religiosa en España, 1936–39* (1961).

Very critical are H. Southworth's *El mito de la Cruzada de Franco* and *Anti Falange, Estudio critico de 'Falange en la guerra de España' de M. García Venero* (1967).

6. *Foreign Policy* The best straightforward account is still that contained in *The Survey of International Affairs* published by the Royal Institute of International Relations, London, vol. II for 1937 and 1938. The splendidly researched book by Angel Vinas *El oro español en la guerra civil* (1976) is essential reading. S. T. Harper *German Economic Policy in Spain during the Spanish Civil War 1936–1939*

(1967) describes German efforts to control Spain's mineral resources.

For British policy see Jill Edwards *The British Government and the Spanish Civil War* (1979). For non-intervention D. Carlton 'Eden, Blum and the Origins of Non-Intervention', *Journal of Contemporary History*, July 1971. For the German decision to intervene: A Viñas *La Alemania nazi y el 18 Julio* (1974). The motives for Hitler's decision are discussed also in S. L. Winberg *The Foreign Policy of Hitler's Germany* (1970) and its course in M. Merkes *Die deutsche Politik im Spanischen Bürgerkrieg 1936–9* (1969). H. Southworth is about to publish his exhaustive examination of the bombing of Guernica of which there is an unsatisfactory account in General Galland's *The First and the Last* (1955). See also V. Talón *Arde Guernica* (1970). For the negotiations with Italy Luís Bolín's experiences are given in his *Spain: the Vital Years* (1967). R. Cantalupo's *Fu la Spagna* is the account of an ambassador who regretted intervention; there are sidelights in Count Ciano's *The Ciano Diaries* (1947). For Italian military operations see General F. Belforte *La Guerra Civile in Spagna* (4 vols, 1938–9). There is an excellent account of the Italian intervention in J. F. Coverdale *Italian Intervention in the Spanish Civil War* (1975).

For Russian intervention D. T. Catell *Soviet Diplomacy and the Spanish Civil War* (1957); W. G: Krivitsky *I was Stalin's Agent* (1940).

7. *The International Commitment*   The bibliography is huge. For the intellectuals see: R. Benson *Writers in Arms: the Literary Input of the Spanish Civil War* (1967); S. Weintraub *The Last Geat Cause: the Intellectuals and the Spanish Civil War* (1968); A. Guttman *The Wound in the Head: America and the Spanish Civil War* (1962); A. Garosci *Gli intellectuali e la guerra di Spagna* (1959). For France, D. Wingate Pike *Les français et la guerre d'Espagne* (1975). *Authors take Sides* (1957) contains a selection of pieces in defence of the Republic at war.

For the International Brigades a general account in V. Brome *The International Brigades* (1965). The latest and best study of the Brigades is A. Castells *Las Brigadas Internacionales de la Guerra de España* (1974). For a Communist view Luigi Longo *Le Brigate Internationali in Spagna* (1956). For British volunteers B. Alexander *British Volunteers for Liberty: Spain 1936–1939* (1982).

There are many accounts by Brigaders listed in the standard bibliographies (e.g. H. Thomas). I list only two – both by English volunteers: T. Wintringham *English Captain* (1939) and J. Gurney *Crusade in Spain* (1974).

Arthur London's *L'aveu* (1968) reveals the fate of some Brigaders in Czechoslovakia.

8. *The Last Days*   For the Catalan collapse see V. Rojo *Alerta los pueblos* (1939). For the Madrid rising S. Casado's own version is in his *The Last Days of Madrid* (1939) and there is a detailed account in J. M. Martinez Bande *Los cien ultimos dias de la República* (1973). The Cartagena 'mutiny' is described in detail in L. Romero *Desastre en Cartagena* (1971).

The fate of the Republican exiles in Mexico is studied in P. W. Fagen *Exiles and Citizens* (1973).

Index

accidentalism, 39

Acción Española, 61, 207

Acción Popular, background, xii; defence of the Church, 39; dissolution, 177

ACNP (Asociación Católica Nacional de Propagandistas), 39, 261, 301; background, xii

Action Française, 63

Africanistas, 80 and n.

Agrarian Law (1932), 34 and n.

agriculture, disparities between areas, 2–4; unemployment in, 33; agrarian reform, 33–4, 60; collectivization, 97, 100–1, 114, 200; post-war production, 254, 255; change to industrial nation, 280–1, 282, 283

Aguirre, José Antonio, biographical note, xv; Euzkadi becomes an independent canton under, 115; relationship with CNT, 158; and Basque army, 185, 186; rejects rumours of peace negotiations, 189n.

Alava, 87

Alba, Victor, 174

Albacete, 143, 157, 158, 202

Alberti, Rafael, 59, 78, 162n.

Alcalá la Real, 130

Alcalá Zamora, Niceto, biographical note, xv; as Prime Minister, 28, 32; resigns from Provisional Government, 33; and a centrist party, 38; mistrusts Gil Robles, 46, 48; intrigues in formation of Governments, 48; dislike of Lerroux, 48; political am-

bitions, 48n.; and 1936 election, 59

Alcazar, Toledo, 121, 153, 215

Alcora, 101

Alcoy, 95, 220, 221

Alfambra, 202, 203

Alfonsists, 55–6, 57, 265, 266

Alfonso XII, King of Spain, 1

Alfonso XIII, King of Spain, ascends throne, 1; fall of monarchy, 2, 27–8, 29; withdraws support from Primo de Rivera, 26; rejected by Carlists, 55; and Renovacion Española, 177

Alianza Popular, 303–4

Alicante, air raids on, 94; collectives in, 100; José Antonio Rivera executed at, 120; politically divided, 220–1; in Casado's hands, 244; Italian troops advance on, 245

Almería, 162, 283

Altea, 221

Alvárez del Vayo, Julio, 169; biographical note, xv

Amado, Andrés, 207

anarcho-syndicalists, 13, 111–12; *see also* CNT

Andalusia, agrarian society in, 3, 4; rural unrest, 69; insurgents gain, 87, 88; in 1970s, 310

Ansaldo, Juan, 84–6

anti-clericalism, 10–12, 37–8

Anti-Fascist Militia Committee, 111, 112

Anual, 23

AO, 138, 139

Aragon, Carlism in, 11; CNT in, 13; collectivization in, 96–7; Council of